Kassandra and the Censors

Reading
WOMEN
Writing

a series edited by
Shari Benstock and Celeste Schenck

Reading Women Writing is dedicated to furthering international feminist debate. The series publishes books on all aspects of feminist theory and textual practice. *Reading Women Writing* especially welcomes books that address cultures, histories, and experience beyond first-world academic boundaries. A complete list of titles in the series appears at the end of the book.

Kassandra and the Censors

GREEK POETRY

SINCE 1967

Karen Van Dyck

Cornell University Press

ITHACA AND LONDON

First published 1998 by Cornell University Press.
First printing, Cornell Paperbacks, 1998.

Printed in the United States of America.

Cornell University Press strives to utilize environmentally responsible suppliers
and materials to the fullest extent possible in the publishing of its books. Such
materials include vegetable-based, low-VOC inks and acid-free papers that are
also either recycled, totally chlorine-free, or partly composed of nonwood fibers.

Library of Congress Cataloging-in-Publication Data

Van Dyck, Karen.
Kassandra and the censors : Greek poetry since 1967 / Karen Van Dyck.
     p.   cm. — (Reading women writing)
Includes indexes.
ISBN 0-8014-2704-5 (alk. paper). — ISBN 0-8014-9993-3 (pbk. : alk. paper)
1. Greek poetry, Modern—20th century—History and criticism.   2. Greek poetry,
Modern—Women authors—History and criticism.   3. Women in literature.   4. Politics
and literature—Greece—History—20th century.   5. Greece—Politics and government—
1967–1974.   6. Greece—Politics and government—1974-   7. Women—Greece—
Athens—Politics and government.   I. Title.   II. Series.
PA5250.V358   1997
889'.13409355—dc21   97-18527

Cloth printing   10 9 8 7 6 5 4 3 2 1
Paperback printing   10 9 8 7 6 5 4 3 2 1

For Katherine Anne Ludlum

1961–1980

Contents

Acknowledgments

In the autumn of 1977, I spent a semester on Kalymnos, a small Greek island off the coast of Turkey, at a high-school study-abroad program where many intellectuals from Athens—writers, cartoonists, archeologists, directors—taught. At the impressionable age of sixteen I found myself caught up in the intellectual fervor that marked the years following a seven-year dictatorship (1967–74). Though my Modern Greek literature classes focused on Greek poets of the 1920s and 1930s, it was here that I also had my first course in contemporary Greek literature, here that I met the people and heard of others who much later were to make up the cast of my study on writing under and after the dictatorship. During college I spent summers as a research assistant to Edmund Keeley and learned Greek by translating the poetry of Yannis Ritsos. It was only later that I realized here too the subtext was the dictatorship. The collections I worked on were all written during that seven-year period.[1] After college, by now more familiar with the poetry of established poets such as C. P. Cavafy, George Seferis, Odysseas Elytis, and Yannis Ritsos, I returned to Greece to study what the younger generations of poets were doing. It was in the poetry of the women poets who first began publishing under the dictatorship and whose mature work had just begun to appear in the early 1980s that I found a map of the cultural period I had been immersed in and a poetics that I wanted to introduce to a broader audience. I was intrigued by the cumulative effect of the resistance to meaning in collections by Rhea Galanaki, Maria Laina, and Jenny Mastoraki, among others. I was interested in how their insistence on rehearsing misunderstanding broke

---

[1] Keeley's collection of translations came out under the title *Exile and Return: Selected Poems, 1967–1974* (Ritsos 1985).

with representational models put forward by earlier generations of Greek poets, or for that matter by many American poets. The willingness of these women to connect not only censorship under an authoritarian regime and censorship under patriarchy, but censorship and poetic form, offered an exciting alternative to the more confessional feminist poetry prevalent in America in the 1970s and 1980s.

In this book I attempt to tell the story of Greek poetry since the beginning of the dictatorship in 1967, focusing on the work of the younger generation of poets, the generation of the 1970s, in particular the women, but always discussing them in terms of wider trends. To present this story to an English-speaking audience I have at times simplified histories and critical debates. In such retellings the writers who have opened their archives to me, shared their accounts of those years, and laboriously worked with me on my translations and interpretations of their poems may not always recognize themselves. In thanking them I am also apologizing for the inevitable gaps opened up by my act of cross-cultural translation.

This book, then, owes its first debt to them, the writers, critics, and publishers who not only created the cultural text I have studied but shared their libraries and insights so generously with me over the years: Katerina Anghelaki-Rooke, John Chioles, Kay Cicellis, Andia Frantzi, Rhea Galanaki, Nick Germanacos, Margarita Karapanou, Edmund Keeley, Maria Laina, Margarita Liberaki, D. N. Maronitis, Jenny Mastoraki, Pavlina Pampoudi, Stavros Petsopoulos, Lefteris Poulios, Vasilis Steriadis, and Haris Vlavianos as well as Kevin Andrews, George Savvidis, and Phillipos Vlachos, who did not live to see the final result of their efforts and kindness. My gratitude here also extends to other scholars of Modern Greek culture whom I met in Greece in the early 1980s and who continue to be my best interlocutors on contemporary Greek issues: Jane Cowan, Janet Hart, Mark Mazower, Charles Stewart, and Fay Zika. Also to colleagues in England and the United States who have read all or parts of this manuscript at different points: Margaret Alexiou, Roderick Beaton, Peter Bien, Stathis Gourgouris, Laurie Hart, Gail Holst-Warhaft, David Holton, Gregory Jusdanis, E. D. Karampetsos, Vassilis Lambropoulos, Artemis Leontis, Maria Leontsini, Peter Mackridge, David Ricks, and Dimitris Tziovas.

Equally important to this book, however, were the discussions with colleagues in feminist and cultural and literary studies outside of Modern Greek studies who believed in the integrity of the project and its lessons for a comparative audience. Here my appreciation goes to April Alliston, Dianne Chisholm, Terry Eagleton, Helene Foley, Natalie Kampen, Siobhan Kilfeather, Michael Levine, Mark Petrini, James Porter, Yopie Prins, Martin Stone, Clair Wills, Susan Winnett, Elisabeth Young-Bruehl; to my writing group at the Institute for Research on Women and Gender—Linda Green, Zita Nunes, Maggie Sale, Priscilla Wald, Judith Weisenfeld, and Angela

Zito; to the editors of the Reading Women Writing series at Cornell, Celeste Schenck and Shari Benstock; most of all to Dorothea von Mücke, who read and commented on the entire manuscript in its penultimate form.

I would also like to acknowledge those who made this project possible in other ways. I thank Gelina Harlaftis for providing a home at a crucial point in my research; Theodora Polychrou for helping photograph illustrations at the National Library in Greece; the staff at ELIA and the American Educational Foundation in Athens for their assistance; the Columbia University Faculty Seminar for subvention funds for illustrations; the ITT International Foundation Fellowship Program, the Marshall Commission, the ACLS, and the Columbia University Council for Research in the Humanities for research and writing fellowships; Janet Mais for her copyediting; and Athena Athanasiou and Vassiliki Yiakoumaki for their proofreading.

Finally, though, my greatest appreciation goes to my family: to my children, Jacob and Benjamin, for providing comfort and distraction; to my parents and sisters for taking care of Jacob and Benjamin when comfort and distraction were no longer productive; and to Nelson for all of the above and more—the comfort, the distraction, the years of conversation, the advice on writing, and the critical muscle and faith that have made this book possible.

K.V. D.

Note on Transliteration
and Translation

"In the spelling of Greek names every writer appears to take out his own patent," begins a nineteenth-century traveler's account; I am afraid I am no exception. Although for the most part I have followed the phonetic system of the *Journal of Modern Greek Studies*, there are times when I have found it visually too reductive (for example I choose *ou* for *ου*, not *u*; *ch* for *χ*, not *h*; *y* for *υ*, not *i*). My semivisual approach facilitates a certain recognition of roots for those who know other forms of the Greek language. If a name is already known a certain way by English-speaking audiences, I resort to the known spelling so as to not cause undue confusion, for example, George Seferis, not Yiorgos Seferis; Nicolas Calas, not Nikolas Kalas. I also respect authors' own wishes, thus Margarita Liberaki, not Lymberaki. The spelling of the name Cassandra has presented me with a problem which in many ways is paradigmatic of the larger theoretical problems my project raises. To use the anglicized spelling for the classical heroine would mean inclusion in more bibliographies, yet my Kassandra is not that Cassandra. Following Nick Germanacos's translation of Karapanou's novel *Kassandra and the Wolf*, therefore, I opt in this case for the less traditional, more Greek spelling. For purposes of comprehension I have translated Greek titles into English in the text. When two references follow a title or quotation the first date refers to the Greek edition, and the second to the translation, the exception to this rule being bracketed dates, which refer to original editions not cited here. No reference after a passage means the translation is my own. I should add that in translating whole collections of poetry, such as those to which I refer in the last three chapters of the book, I have often made translation choices that work for the larger collection; individual lines, therefore, may not correspond exactly to the original.

Kassandra and the Censors

Και τώρα τι θα γένουμε χωρίς βαρβάρους.
Οι άνθρωποι αυτοί ήσαν μια κάποια λύσις.

And now without barbarians what will become of us?
Those people were a kind of solution.

—C. P. Cavafy

What are the political consequences of the fact that language is not a transparently expressive medium? What role does literature's radicalization of this fact play? How can the study of suppressed, disseminated, or marginalized messages within texts equip us to intervene against oppression and injustice in the world? Is a willingness to carry an inquiry to the point of undecidability necessarily at odds with political engagement? Is the exploration of logics other than the logic of binary opposition necessarily a way of avoiding participation in the process of change?

—Barbara Johnson

Introduction

In Margarita Karapanou's novel *Kassandra and the Wolf*, written in the final years of Greece's most recent dictatorship (1967–74), Kassandra, the protagonist, has a hard time on her first day of school. She stutters and is impertinent to Miss Ada, her teacher. She does not want to break words into syllables or do subtraction. She consistently denies that anything can be definitively cut out.

> "We have numbers, children, so as to be able to count."
> Miss Ada puts 4 pears on the table.
> "1, 2, 3, 4," she says. "Yannis, you take 1. Kassandra, how many do we have left?"
> "1, 2, 3, 4. Yannis has the 4th." . . .
> "My child, if Yannis, takes 1, we have 3 left over."
> "And that makes 4, together with the 1 Yannis has."
> "My child, we are doing subtraction."
> Tears come to my eyes. I don't understand.
> "Miss Ada, why are you so bad to me? Even if Yannis eats the pear, we'll still have 4 pears. Together with the 1 in his belly, we'll still have 4."
> (1976, 114)

In this female Bildungsroman of loosely connected vignettes, math and spelling lessons intertwine with episodes of playing doctor, masturbation, and molestation. The two fictional debts of Karapanou's title—Kassandra from ancient tragedy and the wolf from the fairy tale "Little Red Riding Hood"—confirm an intimate connection between linguistic and sexual initiations. Whether one turns to Kassandra, whose prophecies went unheeded because she refused Apollo's advances, or to Little Red Riding

Hood, whose word game was cut short by the wolf's appetite, the message is that issues of language cannot be divorced from those of sex and power. With Athens during a coup as the backdrop to these tales and frequent references to the General, the royal family, and the paraphernalia of the regime, this novel suggests the interrelatedness of growing up female and growing up under censorship.

In introducing my book with a scene of Karapanou's, I want to situate the problems of a little girl struggling with various censors and, by analogy, of contemporary Greek women's writing in the formative context of the dictatorship. My project maps out the resistance to censorship practiced by writers of different generations, political persuasions, and aesthetic ambitions under the dictatorship—from silence to outspoken disavowal to subtle parody such as Kassandra's stubborn unwillingness to accept the finality of subtraction. I then focus on the attempt by women poets since the dictatorship to write *with* censorship, to develop, that is, the methods of evasion learned under an authoritarian regime for the purposes of addressing other forms of censorship—anti-obscenity rulings, sexism, homophobia, and the self-censorship involved in writing. I argue that after the dictatorship women poets continued to deploy certain writing tactics that, although initiated in response to an authoritarian regime, proved useful in articulating domestic power struggles. By outlining the cultural conditions under the dictatorship—in particular the regime's fear of sexual and linguistic undecidability[1]—I show how the figure of woman (such as Kassandra or Lysistrata), associated with undecidability, becomes an important site of resistance. I trace a shift from the allegorical use of the subversive woman in comic strips and novels written in the early 1970s, to the linguistic attention women's poetry of the 1980s gives to mechanisms of censorship. Through the use of elliptic syntax and unorthodox punctuation (among other tactics) women's poetry continues to perform the undecidability that the figure of woman had come to represent. Their poetry's displacement of attention from a public enemy to the enemy at home led to the implication of their own writing in the power dynamics they analyzed, relating censorship to self-censorship. Recognizing, as C. P. Cavafy observes in the first epigraph to this book, that the oppressive presence of "the barbarians"—whether the regime's censor or the wolf—is always "a kind of solution," this poetry attempts to move beyond substituting one enemy for another, admitting its discursive complicity in the enemy's operations. Over the course of this book the term *censorship* therefore accrues

---

[1] My choice of the term *undecidability* will become clearer; for now let me recall Barbara Johnson's (1989) set of questions that provide an epigraph to this book and add that I use this term and the related terms *indeterminacy* and *undeliverability* because my undertaking is more indebted to a politically charged deconstructive line of inquiry than the ahistorical New Critical approach that the terms *ambiguity, paradox,* and *contradiction* signal.

new meanings, beginning with the less complicated notion of censorship under an authoritarian regime and moving to the expanded definition imagined by recent women's poetry.

Writing an introduction recalls in some ways the process of unpacking one's library, especially as Walter Benjamin has described it. There is the same anticipation, the same disorder "to which habit has accommodated itself to such an extent that it can appear as order" (1968, 60). It, too, is a process of surveying the texts that have been formative in one's life. But the extra "unpacking" involved in writing an introduction requires figuring out the questions to which the assembled books provide a shorthand. The library that an introduction represents is not for personal use but is a public space designed with various readers in mind—in this case the cultural critic, the feminist literary scholar, and the Modern Greek specialist.

Kassandra, Karapanou's modern reincarnation of the misunderstood prophetess of antiquity, provides a useful way of organizing my library and my intervention in debates on censorship, women's writing, and Modern Greek culture. With regard to censorship, she explores how Apollo's act of linguistic rape functions not only as prohibition but also as the grounds for a new poetics. She poses the possibility of an alternative writing style full of stuttering, babble, and wordplay. In terms of women's writing, her insistence on connecting language and sex suggests that this alternative writing style is also a response to patriarchy's strict codes. Kassandra writes differently because she grows up under an authoritarian regime but also because she grows up female. As far as Modern Greek studies is concerned, she marks Greek literature's local specificity, the discontinuity of contemporary Greek experience with respect to its classical past, and the ambivalent relation Greece has with Europe and the United States. Kassandra writes differently because she grows up in a culture in which literature, despite an increasingly international world, is still predominantly a national institution.[2] Karapanou's point is that Kassandra is neither a fallen version of an original "classic" nor a poor copy of a Western prototype but rather a complex translation of the mixed allegiances of her times.[3]

I would like to describe some of the ways in which my project intersects with censorship studies, women's studies, and Modern Greek studies, beginning with its relationship to recent work on censorship. Kassandra's concern on her first day of school is with what is there, rather than with

---

[2] I borrow this phrase from Vassilis Lambropoulos's title *Literature as National Institution: Studies in the Politics of Modern Greek Criticism*. Other works that analyze this phenomenon are Tziovas 1986, Jusdanis 1991, and Leontis 1995b. Michael Herzfeld's anthropological work *Ours Once More: Folklore, Ideology, and the Making of Modern Greece* ([1981] 1986) was crucial in paving the way for such analyses.

[3] For an interesting parallel to my use of Karapanou's Kassandra as emblematic of writing under and after the dictatorship, see James Faubion's anthropological use of Karapanou, the author, as paradigmatic of the postdictatorship Athenian intellectual (1993).

what is missing, and underscores an important difference between the English term *censorship* and the Greek term λογοκρισία. In Greek λογοκρίνω refers first and foremost to the act of approving a text; literally it means "I judge the word," and only secondarily does it refer to the act of cutting out, erasing, or blacking out. "Ελογοκρίθη," the word stamped on texts under preventive censorship (1967–69), meant "passed by the censor with any alterations that might be necessary" rather than "censored." The Greek term λογοκρισία focuses attention on the set of rules one has to obey in order to get a text past the censors, on the administrative process whereby something is legitimated, rather than on simple elision. Writers under the dictatorship and women writers afterward tend to treat censorship as a system that opens up alternative modes of signification at the same time as it closes down more traditional ways.[4] Whether Kassandra is pointing to Yannis's pear or stuttering her name—"Ka-Ka-Ka-Ka-s-s-s-sandra"—her point is that censorship has effects and these effects don't go away. The missing pear or the broken name is still there, just reconfigured. Censorship provides a poetics that can be deployed to other ends.[5]

This attention to the residual effects of censorship and the discursive production censorship engenders has also been at the center of psychoanalytic and Foucaultian discussions. Here, too, censorship is not something you can get outside of. It is a process that simultaneously reproduces ideological constructs and produces alternative modes of social relations.[6] It is a hermeneutic matrix active in the production of literature. Annabel

[4] The poet and critic Nasos Vayenas (1988) acknowledged the productive side of censorship in an interview with the critic Yiorgos Pilichos in the following terms: "It can motivate subtle mechanisms for channeling meaning, it can function as a filter that distills the raw, realistic excitations brought on by repression, turning them into forms more artistically wrought and in the long run more effective" (139–40).

[5] For a discussion of the term *poetics of censorship* in Greek and in English, see Van Dyck 1990b, 13–14.

[6] In writing this book I have found particularly useful Sigmund Freud's discussion of censorship in *The Interpretation of Dreams*, Anna Freud's in *The Ego and the Mechanisms of Defence*, and Michel Foucault's in *The History of Sexuality*. A wave of works on censorship indebted to such psychoanalytic and discursive analyses is well represented by two collections of articles, the *PMLA* Special Topic issue *Literature and Censorship* edited by Michael Holquist and *The Administration of Aesthetics* edited by Richard Burt. Holquist's introduction to *Literature and Censorship* points out a new perception of censorship "in which relations between censors and victims appear dynamic and multidirectional." He writes: "Despite Freud's stoic assertions that censorship is unforgoable, all too often it is still treated through a crude axiology, as an absolute choice between prohibition and freedom. This position denies the reality of interdiction and masks the necessity of choosing between the myriad specific conditions that embody censorship's fatedness. To be for or against censorship as such is to assume a freedom no one has. Censorship *is*. One can only discriminate among its more and less repressive effects" (1994, 16). Burt's introduction to his collection offers an overview of discursive approaches. Drawing on the work of Foucault, Pierre Bourdieu, and Jürgen Habermas, he outlines the "new" censorship of aesthetics from Madonna's video to Robert Mapplethorpe's photographs and also calls for an approach to censorship that is less oppositional. It is no longer satisfactory to view the Right as for censorship and the Left as against.

Patterson in her study of censorship and literature in early modern England concludes, "We owe in part our very conception of 'literature' as a kind of discourse, with rules of its own, to censorship" (1984, 4). I would add that we also owe in part our conception of censorship as a set of mechanisms that can be redeployed to literature. Censorship and literature are mutually reinforcing practices. What I am exploring here are writers' responses to censorship—whether silence; parody; or difficult, ambiguous language—for how they repeatedly turn restrictions into a poetics of sorts, how the rules of censorship are reinscribed in texts as dissimilar as George Seferis's poem "Οι γάτες τ' Αη Νικόλα" (The cats of St. Nicholas); Thanasis Valtinos's parody "Ο γύψος" (The plaster cast); Dionysis Savvopoulos's songs; Kyr's comic strip Λυσιστράτη (Lysistrata); Karapanou's novel; and the poetry of Jenny Mastoraki, Rhea Galanaki, and Maria Laina. I also examine how this body of literature rearranges our expectations of censorship and other oppressive operations by working with them as formal constructs. What, for example, does the absurd quality of Savvopoulos's songs tell us about the paralogical times under the dictatorship?[7] How does the use of American pop culture in the poetry of the generation of the 1970s reflect the expanding sense of what politics means in Greece? To what extent is the hermeticism of recent women's poetry an alternative feminism? I am concerned with how political practices and discursive styles are embedded in each other.

Reading literature through censorship and censorship through literature over the past few decades in Greece, one cannot help but notice the central role gender plays in relating social and literary texts. Misunderstandings, confusion, and other effects of censorship are always presented through the figure of woman, and this conflation is worked out in recent women's writing, particularly poetry. If one of my aims is to complicate discussions of censorship with the question of women's writing, another is to complicate discussions of women's writing with the question of censorship. What does the configuration of censorship and sexuality represented by Kassandra have to offer more general debates over the relation of gender to writing?

Writers and critics in Greece have begun to acknowledge the importance of women's writing, γυναικεία γραφή (Frangopoulos 1976, 1982; Vitti 1987b, 450; Maronitis 1987, 232; Chioles 1993). A round-table discussion "So Does Women's Poetry Exist?" held at a prestigious cultural institute in Athens in 1990 attested to the growing sense among poets and critics that the question of women's writing was worth discussing.[8] This change in perspective

---

[7] By "paralogical" I mean the lack of logical connections and the confusion created by the regime's press law and other policies. I explore this term in depth in Chapter 1.

[8] This round-table discussion was then published in Frantzi et al. 1990.

is undoubtedly related to the increasingly prominent role women writers
have assumed on the Greek literary scene. The most influential poets from
the generation that began writing under the dictatorship are women (e.g.,
Katerina Anghelaki-Rooke, Laina, and Mastoraki, among others), and
many of the best-selling novels published in the late 1970s and throughout
the 1980s have been written by women, for example, Maro Douka's Η
αρχαία σκουριά (Fool's gold), Eugenia Fakinou's Το έβδομο ρούχο (The
seventh garment), Galanaki's Ο βίος του Ισμαήλ Φερίκ Πασά (The life of
Ismail Ferik Pasha), Karapanou's Ο υπνοβάτης (The sleepwalker), and Alki
Zei's Η αρραβωνιαστικιά του Αχιλλέα (Achilles' fiancée). Nationality, political beliefs, class, region, even the health of the author are factored into
criticism in Greece, but gender, until very recently, has been left out. In the
instances when it has been discussed, it has had a derogatory, or at least
restrictive, meaning. The critic and novelist Immanuel Roidis made this
clear in his 1913 discussion of women's writing: women should write
"about needlework and cooking." When they discussed public matters,
they were mere imitators: "If the hen begins to crow like a cock, kill her immediately" (85).[9] Until the late 1970s, for the majority of readers in Greece,
the terms *women's poetry* and ποιήτρια (poetess) have brought to mind lyric
verses full of butterflies, dewy mornings, and maternal affection.[10]

The social transformations in Greece, beginning with the seven-year
dictatorship, have helped to resignify and reevaluate women's experience
and to create a cultural environment in which the question of women's
writing could be explored by critics, the poets, and their readers. As in
America, Germany, and elsewhere, *women's writing* becomes an empowering term with the rise of a new generation of the women's movement.[11] But
though some poets found this tentative openness to and redefinition of
women's experience liberating, others were still wary of its reductive and
essentializing potential. Pavlina Pampoudi denied the usefulness of this
category (in Niarchos 1980, 198)[12] as did Mastoraki, who responded face-
tiously to the question Do you write women's poetry?: "Of course. In so far

[9] For a discussion of Roidis and of the *Ladies' Journal* he is attacking here, see Varikas 1987,
16, 193–94.
[10] It would be interesting to explore how Athena Tarsoulis's oeuvre with its anthologies of
women's poetry and its illustrated collections of folk costumes, though certainly intended to
discount Roidis's views and meant as a paean to women, in ways reinforces Roidis's stereotype by aligning women's writing and needlework.
[11] Anghelaki-Rooke, probably the most influential proponent of women's writing in
Greece, wrote in 1976: "It is impossible for anyone to talk about women's poetry anymore
without referring to the women's movement" (53). For comparison, see Daniels 1991 on
American women's writing and Weigel 1984a, 1984b on German women's literature.
[12] See also her humorous return to this topic, "Ο άνδρας λογοτέχνης και τα προβλήματα της
ανδρικής γραφής ή η αντιστροφή των όρων του παιχνιδιού" (The man writer and the problems of
masculine writing or inverting the game's terms) in Katsari 1995, 56–59.

as a doctor from Volos practices Voliot medicine and a bakery from Piraeus bakes Piraean bread" (1982a, 65). There are obvious differences, of course, between Roidis's misogyny and biological determinism and the reluctance displayed by Pampoudi, Mastoraki, and others. Mastoraki's response situates gender as one of the complex set of factors (such as regional difference) that condition any cultural practice. Those women who do not espouse the idea of women's writing (Pampoudi, Laina, Mastoraki) and those who do (Anghelaki-Rooke, Galanaki, Nana Isaïa, Ioanna Zervou) unlike Roidis all seem to be struggling to reconcile the shifting role of women in Greek society with their assumptions about women's poetry.

This struggle, if not always obvious in their critical comments, is clear in the poetry collections these women wrote in the 1980s. Collections as different as Athena Papadaki's Αμνάδα των ατμών (Lamb of steam), Pampoudi's Καρτ ποστάλ (Postcard), Galanaki's Το κέικ (The cake), Mastoraki's Ιστορίες για τα βαθιά (Tales of the deep), and Laina's Δικό της (Hers) nevertheless all focus on the relation between women's experience and women's language, and all foreground the indirect and complex ways in which language is marked by experience and in which experience is linguistically constructed. What women's collections of the 1980s acknowledge is that the impossibility of saying what one means—which under the dictatorship was everyone's problem—becomes, after the dictatorship, a feminine problem, especially in the context of a rising feminist movement. Suddenly the Pythian quality of Kassandra's language has something to do with her sex. What these collections seem to accomplish, then, is a shift of terms: discussions of women's writing in the 1990s focus less on how women's writing reflects women's experience and more on the sexually charged linguistic project of writing as a woman, moving attention from the sex of the author to the style of the writing.[13] In a poem by Maria Kyrtzaki, language is actually doing the work of women's experience, "pushing the carriages" of meaning.[14] It is notable that in 1992 even Mas-

[13] Peggy Kamuf theorizes such shifts more generally in "Writing Like a Woman" (1980). Her analysis both recognizes the indeterminacy of writing "as a woman" and traces the historical specificity of it: "So where can this lead us or leave us? Writing as a woman . . . no place, but neither is it a perfect tautological circle. Rather it leads through whatever it has meant, will mean, and can mean (as well as all it has *not* meant, will *not* mean, and can *not* mean) to be 'as and like' a woman, as if a woman were something one is—or is not—purely and simply" (298).

[14] In an article commissioned by the poetry magazine *Strand*, Anghelaki-Rooke (1992) discusses the importance of language in recent Greek poetry and quotes these passages from Kyrtzaki's collection Σχιστή οδός (Split road) in her own translation: "Ariadne really existed. / First appeared this ball of words. / Nothing else pre-existed. / Poor words gathered together / they appeared wanting and abandoned / words slaves rolling and dragging behind, / their children-threads / remnants of stones that once were, / had been precious / rolling and pushing carriages of meaning" (Kyrtzaki 1992, 29–31).

toraki admitted that language was gendered, calling the more elliptic poems in *Tales of the Deep* "γυναικεία" (feminine).[15]

In many ways the shift in question is as much an issue of being read as a woman as it is of writing as a woman. Not until this poetry had been around for awhile, read by critics and by the poets themselves, could it become women's poetry in this more complex sense. In *What Does a Woman Want?* Shoshana Felman sets Simone de Beauvoir's famous dictum "One is not born, one becomes, a woman" beside a comment Beauvoir once made to Sartre about *The Second Sex:* "I *became* a feminist when the book was read and started to exist for other women." Felman then writes: "*Becoming* a feminist is undertaking to investigate what it means to *be* a woman and discovering that one *is* not a woman but rather *becomes* (somewhat interminably) a woman; discovering, through others' reading and through the way in which other women are *addressed* by one's own writing, that one is not born a woman, one has become (perhaps never quite sufficiently) a woman" (12).

By tracing, moreover, the term *women's writing* from the perjorative or limited definition of the late nineteenth and early twentieth century, to the feminization of writing under the dictatorship and the ensuing expanded definition of women's experience, to the subsequent formulation of women's experience as a linguistic construct, it becomes clear that Greek poetry by women in the past two decades offers a more complicated picture, not only of the category of women's writing but of all contemporary Greek literature. It is no accident that a critic reviewing the round-table discussion on women's poetry ended his piece by suggesting dismissively that the "thorny problem of whether or not women's poetry exists has many analogies to the problem of Greekness" (Kourtovik 1990). I have taken this analogy more seriously, examining the ways in which the attention to language in women's writing in Greece has begun to coincide with the heightened problematization of language under and after the dictatorship. No longer a ghetto of tender sentiment, women's writing has grasped, gotten hold of, taken over, the language and made women's writing central to Modern Greek literature.

Finally, if the case of women's writing under the dictatorship offers the study of censorship a gendered perspective, and if the study of women's writing in Greece underscores its complex social context, then what does this particular brand of cross-cultural analysis offer Modern Greek studies and especially Modern Greek literary studies? The poetry of the generation who began publishing under the dictatorship, the generation of the 1970s, with its wide net of references and textual strategies, suggests an

---

[15] Mastoraki (1992b) brought this up as we were working on the translation of *Tales of the Deep.*

approach that reaches beyond the national and literary focus of traditional literary histories.[16] A new cosmopolitanism characterizes the Greek intellectual climate under and after the dictatorship, and the poetry produced in this period, in particular. In 1975 the political theorist Nicos Poulantzas described the transformation that had occurred in Greek attitudes to the outside world, and noted "[the] effort to liberate ourselves from our social background, from the suffocating atmosphere of Greek bourgeois society in the post civil war period . . . by turning to foreign languages, books" (in Joachimides and Rosenthal 1975, 5). The dictatorship years only reinforced this outward-looking tendency. I am concerned, therefore, with how this poetry intersects with discursive practices that are both national and international in scope and both literary and cultural in a broader sense: social texts such as censorship, advertising, and consumer culture; social theories such as feminism, marxism, and psychoanalysis; genres such as the novel, the popular song, and the political speech; and visual art forms such as the comic strip and film.

Though this approach stems from my reading of these poets, undoubtedly it is also informed by my immersion in feminist, cultural, and literary theory. I share my critical concerns with many students of Greek culture who have done much in a few decades to read Greece from new perspectives and in an international context.[17] My book continues this trend by emphasizing the formal specificity of the Greek dialogue with cultural theory. Although I bring in other discourses and cultural practices and look at the broader social texts that inform poets' work, I also spend considerable time reading these discourses through the formal configurations of the poems themselves. In this respect I draw on the work of philologists

[16] Under traditional literary histories I would include Linos Politis 1975, C. Th. Dimaras 1972, and Roderick Beaton 1994. Though the latter differs by including a social history of the language question in Greece, it for the most part limits its discussion to canonical writers of poetry and prose. Mario Vitti 1987b is the only literary history that diverges slightly by placing a substantial amount of attention on social as well as literary texts.

[17] In literary studies, signal examples are Gregory Jusdanis, Vassilis Lambropoulos, and Dimitris Tziovas. I should add that in the United States and the United Kingdom such metacritical interventions were partly enabled by a generation of critics who had already successfully introduced Anglo-American readers to Modern Greek literature, notably Margaret Alexiou, Edmund Keeley, and Peter Bien. Anthropologists have also done much to make the Greek case relevant to cultural theory, most notably Herzfeld and, with respect to feminist theory, Jane Cowan and Nadia Seremetakis. In fact the cultural focus of my work tends to break down a rigid distinction between the humanities and the social sciences. This blurring of disciplinary boundaries is reciprocated in the work of anthropologists and other social scientists who draw on literary approaches. Faubion (1993) has a chapter on literary technology; Charles Stewart (1991, xvii) explains how he enriches his field research through philology; Janet Hart (1996) discusses social movements through an analysis of oral histories; and Herzfeld's forthcoming book (1998) is an ethnographic biography of the Cretan author Andreas Nenedakis. See in particular pp. 22–26. Eleni Varikas, though a historian teaching in a department of political science, has helped open up a field of feminist literary scholarship. See, for example, her article (1989) on Elisavet Moutzan-Martinengou's *My Story* (1989).

and more traditional literary critics.[18] This book, therefore, is as much a literary analysis of culture as it is a cultural study of literature. I am as interested in how the practice of hermeticism in women's poetry trains us to rethink censorship, consumerism, and feminism as I am with the social and cultural conditions that engender this hermeticism.

The structure of my book illustrates this particular blend of cultural studies and literary formalism. The first three chapters lay out the social texts of censorship, consumerism, and feminism through close readings of literary texts, progressively narrowing the scope, from writing generally under the dictatorship, to the poetry of the generation of the 1970s, to the women poets of this generation. The last three chapters then read the social texts of postdictatorship Greece from within three collections by women: Rhea Galanaki's *The Cake* (1980), Jenny Mastoraki's *Tales of the Deep* (1983b), and Maria Laina's *Hers* (1985a). Thus while the book progresses chronologically from under to after the dictatorship, and contextually from general to specific, framing Greek women's poetry in the poetic and political discourses of those thirty years, it also places social concerns in the context of contemporary women's poetry.

Expanding the notion of censorship over three decades of history and beyond the bounds of traditional analyses of persecution and writing enables us to read the visual, narrative, and linguistic turn poetry has taken in Greece in terms of the interrelations between categories often imagined to be discrete, such as the private and the public, the psychoanalytic and the political, the popular and the elite. It also, however, risks effacing the differences between forms of disciplining. Whereas certain techniques of censorship may be similar, the motive and impact are radically different when the censor is a stranger, a mother, a lover, or oneself. I conclude my book, therefore, with a chapter on Laina's *Hers*, a work that reveals the limits, as well as the usefulness, of juxtaposing different kinds of censorship—that of an authoritarian regime, of patriarchy, of heterosexism, of writing itself. *Hers*, with its blank stares, folded hands, and mandate of nonparticipation, creates a place where the censor's look cannot penetrate. Whether such minimalism is a simplistic conflation of censorships or a powerfully disorienting response to the complexity of censorship depends in large part on one's expectations of poetry. If one wants poetry to console and consolidate one's vision of the world, then Laina's disregard for accepted categories is infuriating. If one accepts that "she was thinking totally different words" (61), as *Hers* states, then such conflations and evasions might be greeted as an opportunity to try out other possibilities. As Laina confirms in a 1983 interview, "If it was up to poetry simply to reflect

[18] Notably, D. N. Maronitis, who though a classical scholar, consistently offers provocative interpretations of contemporary Greek literature.

reality, to show the world the way it is, and that's all, the work of art that would come of it wouldn't be worth much. . . . As far as I'm concerned, one reality is plenty."

In this book I offer the formal experimentation of contemporary Greek poetry as an alternative way of viewing Greece since 1967. Kassandra's lessons, it turns out, are to be found not only in the issues she presents but also in her insistence that seeing things differently—convincing others that the pear is still there—is an ongoing struggle. At the end of her first day of school, Kassandra is at the gate talking with the maid, Fani:

"How was school?"
"Very good. I've learned to speak, answer, and think in syllables."
"Then why are you crying?"
"It's the syllables. It hurts when I cut the words in two."
"You'll get used to it," Fani says. "You'll get used to it." (1976, 115)

But Kassandra does not get used to it. Her heuristic power lies in her insistence that writing with censorship, writing as a woman, and writing as a Greek is always an unfinished process.

1

Power, Language, and the
Discourses of the Dictatorship

Silence itself—the things one declines to say, or is forbidden to name, the discretion that is required between different speakers—is less the absolute limit of discourse, the other side from which it is separated by a strict boundary, than an element that functions alongside the things said, with them and in relation to them within over-all strategies.

—Michel Foucault

In the early part of 1967, while most of Greece prepared for elections, a group of senior generals and the new king were secretly planning a takeover if the election results were not to their liking. At the same time, and unbeknown to them, their junior colleagues colonels Stylianos Pattakos and Yeorgios Papadopoulos and brigadier Nikolaos Makarezos were also plotting a coup, and unlike their elders, this triumvirate had no interest in preserving the appearance of democracy. They intervened before the elections, taking over power in the early hours of April 21, 1967, defeating in one effort the senior officers and the electorate, and later the king. Constantine Kollias, the civilian prime minister backed by the colonels and the king, issued the regime's first formal announcement, espousing "a Greece for all Greeks" and justifying the "revolution" as an attempt to rid the country of factions and difference: no rightists, leftists, or centrists, "only Greeks who believe in Greece" (Clogg 1979, 186–87).[1] But it soon became clear that the man behind the take-over was Papadopoulos, who was already known to the public for his right-wing activity. His testimony against the communist leader Nikos Beloyannis had led to the latter's execution in 1952, and his allegation of a "communist sabotage" in the army in May 1965 helped to bring about Yiorgos Papandreou's resignation in July of the same year (183–84). Throughout his military career Papadopoulos swore, in the name of solidarity and unity, to eradicate extremism—leftist extremism. He did not, for example, take action against the rightist group IDEA,[2] the group of military officers to which he himself belonged. In the same contra-

---

[1] Richard Clogg's *A Short History* (1979) provides a good overview of Modern Greek history. For a more readable, illustrated approach, see his *Concise History* (1992).
[2] Ιερός Δεσμός Ελλήνων Αξιωματικών (Sacred society of Greek officers).

dictory vein, he rigidly enforced the "idionym" law, which prohibited any attempt to undermine the existing social order (Clogg 1979, 125; Dafnis 1955, 91–94), only months after he himself had commanded a "revolution."[3] Although his official reason for employing the secret NATO contingency plan "Prometheus" to overthrow the government was that Greece was in danger of an international communist take-over, in his speeches the chief concern seems to have been that Greece was suffering from internal disorder. He harps on the reigning confusion of pre-junta years, when as he put it, "Truth had come to be identified with falsehood and patriotism with treason" (Papadopoulos 1968, 2:172). At an ideological level, his call for order, clarity, and cleanliness had a broad appeal; only a small percentage of the population mobilized against the regime.[4] Greece's steadily rising standard of living during the first five years of the dictatorship also helped to reconcile the majority to the harsher aspects of military rule (Mouzelis 1978, 129–30). It was in fact only after the economic downturn of 1973 that growing numbers—above all students—began to express their opposition in public.[5]

There was, however, one form of resistance which had a special significance both for Greek society at large and for the colonels themselves: the resistance of writers to what could be termed *textual authoritarianism* or, more commonly, censorship. This is not to deny the importance of groups such as the Patriotic Front and the communist youth organization Rigas Pheraios or the resistance hero Alexander Panagoulis, all responsible for explicit and sometimes violent acts of resistance from the very beginning of military rule;[6] nor is it to disregard the interdependency of these forms of resistance.[7] But for writers and colonels alike, writing and language more

[3] On the difference between the terms *revolution* and *junta* in the Greek case, see Grigoriadis 1975, 1:342.

[4] George Yannopoulos (1972) discusses the factors that helped to fragment and limit the scope of the opposition forces. See also Panayote Dimitras's note on the indifference to politics in general among the populace, which helped to sustain the colonels (1987, 78 n). This view is aptly summed up by the protagonist in Marios Hakkas's short story "Το ψαράκι της γυάλας" (The fish bowl) (first published in the resistance publication Νέα κείμενα 2 [New texts 2]): "Bah, this situation won't last long. Soon they'll fall"; and later "Let the others take action, it's the young people's turn" (1988, 150–51).

[5] For an analysis of the student uprising, see Clogg 1979, 195–99.

[6] See Yannopoulos 1972, 178–84, for a survey of these and other resistance groups; for an impassioned account of Panagoulis's exploits, see Fallaci 1980.

[7] The close links between them are evident in a recent issue of the literary journal *Lexi* dedicated to "The Intellectuals and the Dictatorship." Vasilis Vasilikos, the well-known leftist author of *Z*, spoke for many writers when he acknowledged in his contribution: "During the dictatorship I wrote in the name of Panagoulis (ο λόγος μου ήταν παναγουλικός). As far as I was concerned Alexander Panagoulis chose the right target on August 13, 1968, when he undertook to assassinate the then unknown head of the junta, Y. Papadopoulos" (in Fostieris and Niarchos 1987, 282). This interdependency is also manifest in the popularity of Panagoulis's own poems (1974). Oriana Fallaci (1980) portrays him as both political activist and poet.

generally were a particularly charged site of contestation, and it is therefore no accident that censorship constituted one of the key repressive measures employed by the regime.

This emphasis on censorship, and the importance of writers' resistance
to it, are closely related to the privileged status that language has had in
Greek culture across class barriers. Ever since the War of Independence in
the 1820s, political changes have been proposed in terms of linguistic
changes.[8] The language question—which is to say the struggle between
proponents of demotic Greek, the spoken language, and *Katharevousa* or
"purist" Greek, a synthetic hybrid of Ancient and Modern Greek languages—is one example of the central role language has played in Greek
political life.[9] Though demotic Greek seems to have finally become the
official language of state and education, the debate over spelling, accents,
breathing marks, and how much Ancient Greek should be taught in school
continues. Whether in the formal terms of the language question, or more
generally with regard to how language identifies people according to region, class, gender, trade, and so forth, the question of language consumes
Greeks in their newspapers and everyday interactions.[10] From the endless
dinner conversations over usage to the popularity of poetry, the power of
the word has a claim on the Greek national imagination which provides a
striking contrast to the status of language in many other Western countries
where linguistic issues are often debated only among small groups of
intellectuals.

It is not surprising, then, that the colonels put a great deal of emphasis
on their language-related policies. The general public, less aware of the
torture and imprisonment the colonels inflicted, were immediately conscious of censorship. One of the regime's first legislative actions, for example, was to stipulate that Katharevousa, the official language of constitutions and laws since 1911, would thenceforth also be the language of state
and education.[11] Although students were used to writing Katharevousa,
tolerance of demotic in schools during the 1960s had been increasing. After

[8] On the making of the nation at the beginning of the nineteenth century as a linguistic
struggle, see Herzfeld 1986. Tziovas (1989a, 86–93) continues this line of argument and shows
how the demoticists and the purists in the 1880s equated language and nation. The recent
resistance to the Former Yugoslav Republic of Macedonia's renaming Skopje "Macedonia"
attests to the persistency of this equation.

[9] See Mackridge 1990 for a concise overview of the language question.

[10] The tradition of Greek shadow puppet theater, in which each character has his or her own
language, dialect, or idiom (Turkish, Greek, Cretan, Katharevousa, childish lisp, etc.), aptly
portrays the contestive place language holds. Here as elsewhere in Greek social life, language
is an inexhaustible source of both frustration and entertainment where no one ever has the last
word. The main character Karaghiozis is forever trying to teach his children how to speak
correctly, only to have their impudent puns and malapropisms thrown back in his face.

[11] Article 6 of the 1968 constitution (Ganoseli 1975).

April 21 this trend was abruptly halted and the use of Katharevousa rigidly enforced. The colonels' policies affected other aspects of linguistic use as well. Unquestioned freedoms—to distribute books or design newspaper lay-out, for example—could no longer be taken for granted. The Book Index banned not only those titles that openly criticized the regime but those whose authors' names sounded vaguely Russian, and even ancient texts that satirized the misuse of power, such as Aristophanes' *Birds*. For the convenience of the censors, writers and their writing were often equated: if a writer was a communist, then the entirety of his or her writing was branded as such. All the songs of the popular composer Mikis Theodorakis were banned, even though his love songs were hardly subversive (Holst 1980, 129). In one infamous case, a poet was hauled into the police station for his communist leanings when it was discovered that he had written a poem in which his lover's lips were "red" (Roufos 1972a, 149).[12]

Writers' responses to censorship ranged from silence to outright resistance to parody. As Foucault (1980, 27) has pointed out, censorship not only cuts off or blocks communication; it also acts as an incitement to discourse, with silence as an integral part of this discursive activity. An examination of the dictatorship's linguistic policies and writers' responses to them reveals the different relations between politics and poetic form established writers of the generation of the 1930s and the two postwar generations formulate and paves the way for my discussion of the poetry of the generation of the 1970s in subsequent chapters.[13] In addressing the dominant role poetry plays in Greece, especially in times of political turmoil, two models of literature become evident, a representational one, connected with the hermeneutic legacy of the generation of the 1930s and, in particular, with George Seferis's opposition of the monologic and dialogic in his famous monologue and dialogue on poetry, and a performative one invoked by Dionysis Savvopoulos, a popular songwriter and poet of the generation of the 1970s and characteristic of the younger writers' paralogical stance.

[12] The author Kay Cicellis places such repressive measures in their broader historical context: "The 7 black years of military rule acted as a sort of lens through which the picture, in retrospect became clearly focused at last. The dictatorship underlined all those elements which had for so long thwarted and shackled cultural growth in this country. It embodied, in glaring, almost caricatured form, the repression, the narrow-mindedness, the obscurantism that had for so many decades forced literature into a kind of underground or ghetto" (1977a, 9).

[13] Poetry in Greece is commonly divided into generations according to when poets begin publishing: the famous generation of the 1930s, the two postwar generations, the generation of the 1970s, and so on. On the term *generation* in Greek letters, see Kranaki 1953–54 and Garandoudis 1989. For an approach similar to mine—namely, retaining the terminology of generations, despite the obvious limitations—see Tziovas 1986, 11. I return to the subject in Chapter 2.

Greece as a Patient in a Cast

Already from the first meeting with the foreign press on April 27, 1967, it was clear that the regime would give particular attention to censorship. Papadopoulos introduced his now infamous metaphor of Greece "as a patient" in response to journalists' questions about censorship:[14]

Μη ξεχνάτε όμως, κύριοι, ότι ευρισκόμεθα προ ενός ασθενούς, τον οποίον έχομεν επί της χειρουργικής κλίνης, και τον οποίον εάν ο χειρουργός δεν προσδέση κατά την διάρκειαν της εγχειρήσεως και της ναρκώσεως επί της χειρουργικής κλίνης, υπάρχει πιθανότης αντί διά της εγχειρήσεως να του χαρίση την αποκατάστασιν της υγείας, να τον οδηγήση εις θάνατον. Αυτή είναι εκ προοιμίου η απάντησις την οποίαν πρέπει να αναμένετε εάν, ομιλούντες περί δημοκρατίας και ελευθερίας, μνημονεύσητε τους περιορισμούς. Οι περιορισμοί είναι η πρόσδεσις του ασθενούς επί της κλίνης διά να υποστή ακινδύνως την εγχείρησιν. (1967, 1:11)

Don't forget though, gentlemen, that we find ourselves in the presence of a patient, whom we have on an operating table, and for whom, if the surgeon does not strap him to the bed during the duration of the surgery and the anesthesia, there is a chance that instead of the surgery leading to the recovery of his health, it may lead to his death. This, as a preamble, is the answer which you must expect if, speaking of democracy and freedom, you mention restraints. The restraints are the straps that fasten the patient to the operating table so that he may go through the surgery devoid of any danger.

This metaphor was to become more elaborate; a year later Greece was not only a patient on an operating table but a patient in a cast:

Πάλιν θα αποτολμήσω επαφήν με τους ιατρούς. Ασθενή έχομεν. Εις τον γύψον τον εβάλαμεν. Τον δοκιμάζομεν εάν ημπορή να περπατάη χωρίς τον γύψον. Σπάζομεν τον αρχικόν γύψον και ξαναβάζομεν ενδεχομένως τον καινούργιο εκεί όπου χρειάζεται. Το Δημοψήφισμα θα είναι μια γενική θεώρησις των ικανοτήτων του ασθενούς. Ας προσευχηθώμεν να μη χρειάζεται ξανά γύψον. Εάν χρειάζεται, θα του τον βάλωμεν. Και το μόνον που ημπορώ να σας υποσχεθώ, είναι να σας καλέσω να ιδήτε και σεις το πόδι χωρίς γύψον. (1968, 2:171)

Again I shall venture contact with the doctors. We have a patient. We have put him in a plaster cast. We see if he can walk without the cast. We break

[14] Medical metaphors in political rhetoric have a long history dating back to Machiavelli (1982, 39–40) and, beyond that, the ancient Greeks (see Sontag 1990, 71–85). With respect to Nazi Germany, see Theweleit 1987. With regard to Modern Greece, Prodromas Yannas (1988) shows how the text of American foreign policy in Greece during the Second World War portrays Greece as a psychiatric patient whereas the rest of Europe is represented as a patient in need of a physical (i.e., financial) cure.

open the cast and eventually replace it with another where it is needed. The Referendum will be a general examination of the patient's capacities. Let us pray that there will be no further need of a cast. If there is, however, we shall put it back on. And the only thing I can promise you is an invitation to see for yourself the leg without the cast.

Perhaps this passage more than any other in Papadopoulos's Το πιστεύω μας (Our credo)—the five volumes of collected speeches and interviews distributed free to teachers, civil servants, and opinion makers—sums up the dictatorship's policy on censorship: on the one hand, conspicuous and much advertised tolerance—you can see for yourselves the leg without the cast—and, on the other, a sharpening of general oppressiveness to totalitarian extremes—the patient will, if necessary, be put back in a cast.[15]

During the dictatorship, a main pillar of the colonels' ideological platform seemed to rest on a populism that attempted to level differences by asserting the essential similarity of citizens, their wants and needs. The campaign to eradicate differences and confusion took many forms. Censorship was a prime example, puritanism, another. The regime's intolerance of difference is evident in such diverse practices as Papadopoulos's assumption of a wide range of ministerial positions—including the Ministry of Foreign Affairs, the Ministry of Education, and the Ministry of Defense—under one position, his own, and in the fixing of elections so that there was only one choice, himself. Again and again the possibility of difference and variety was effaced and repackaged as something familiar and the same.[16] This attention to packaging made the dictatorship look more benign than it was. Many foreigners were taken in by the regime's exterior show: tourists during the dictatorship were heard to remark that the regime must be a lenient one if it allowed the free circulation of foreign newspapers.[17] There were other gestures of false freedom such as the forms distributed in the major newspapers calling for suggestions for the constitution which then were never heeded (McDonald 1983, 34). Perhaps most telling was Λαϊκή μούσα (Popular muse), an anthology of verse in praise of the regime, supposedly gathered from all corners of Greece. Con-

[15] Rodis Roufos (1972a, 148) introduces the wording "much advertised tolerance" and "sharpening oppressiveness" to explore, more generally, the contradiction between authoritarianism and totalitarianism at the core of the colonels' policies.

[16] Such logic is familiar from authoritarian rhetoric the world over. Histories of the dictatorship often make analogies between the fascists during the German occupation and the colonels in 1967, for example. Yannis Katris pointedly quotes Hitler in an epigraph to the first chapter of his history of the dictatorship: "Our Nation is in a mess. The students are revolting and behaving violently. The communists are trying to ruin our country. We need Law and Order. . . . Yes, without Law and Order our nation will not survive" (1974, 19).

[17] Except in the first few weeks of the coup, when news about Greece in the foreign papers was carefully clipped by censors.

tributions such as this one by Sofia Kontopanoulou from Tripolis invariably concluded on a heroic note:

> Κι' έτσι, ξημέρωσε η αυγή
> 21η ΑΠΡΙΛΙΟΥ,
> ημέραν για μας ιστορικήν
> σωτηρία των Ελλήνων.
> (1969, 39)

> and that's how the dawn came
> on the 21st of April
> a historical day for us,
> a day that saved the Greeks.

The repetition and singular style of this antholoy make one wonder whether the poems in it were commissioned. The defensive tone of the prologue certainly supports this view. The regime thus represented its era as not one of repression but rather as one in which the people could finally express themselves:

> The Revolution of April 21 1967 became a source of inspiration and of new emotions for many Greeks. The abrupt end to the sufferings of the past, and the restorative breath of fresh air, undoubtedly created a sense of satisfaction and a multitude of hopes in thousands of simple folk. The Revolution became for them the excuse to express, in poetic language as well as in spontaneous letters, what for so long, consciously or subconsciously, oppressed them; it was like a volcano that erupted spewing forth whatever had been oppressed in their hearts for so long. (1969, 3)

With its unsigned prologue and unspecified publisher, this clearly propagandist volume was one in a long line of ploys designed to give the regime a better name.

Though the regime's rhetoric was premised on an intense fear of confusion, and its popular support relied on its promise to rid the country of internal disorder, its rhetoric was, nonetheless, confusing.[18] This contradiction is particularly clear in Papadopoulos's use of metaphor. The ambiguity of figural language was anathema; in the "Greece for Christian Greeks," as he called it, words and things would regain their original, unmediated

---

[18] Although not the focus here, I should add that hand in hand with the colonels' intolerance of ambiguity went their ability to inculcate just that in the populace so that solidarity was difficult to establish. For an interesting comparative instance of the use of ambivalence to instill mistrust, see the outline of the Pentagon course for Latin American military officers, "Utilization and Containment of Rumors" (in Lernoux 1980, 471–73).

relationship.[19] And yet metaphor was a necessary part of his persuasive rhetoric; he described Greece as a patient to convince journalists that the regime was curing Greece's problems. Papadopoulos's desire for a mimetic relationship between *what one said* and *what one meant* is evident in his press law, which included the ludicrous mandate that all books bear titles corresponding exactly to their contents (Andrews 1988). In a similar vein, all major newspapers were ordered to carry identical front-page stories (H. Vlachos 1972, 61). Such actions reveal his unease with semantic instability. Like some latter-day Cratylus arguing for a "fitness of signs," Papadopoulos wanted the word and the thing to be exactly the same.[20] For something to be merely *like* something else was not acceptable; metaphor's allusive potential was subversive. In the same way that Papadopoulos's fear of metaphor informed his actions and his press law, so too his use of metaphor had practical ramifications. For Papadopoulos, metaphor may have been a rhetorical device, but it also made real things happen. Not only did he continue to use medical metaphors during the course of his seven-year rule, but much of his policy actually seemed to evolve from them. His speeches testify that freedom would be administered in small doses; that the "cast" would be constantly replaced "where it [was] needed"; and that language and literature would be "cleansed." His metaphors, in effect, efface their own metaphoricity, presenting themselves as the literal truth.[21] As he quipped on one occasion, "Η δημοσιογραφία εις την χώραν μας είχε μεταβληθή από λειτούργημα εις κακούργημα. Δεν είναι λογοπαίγνιον. Περί κυριολεξίας πρόκειται" (Journalism in our country had turned from function into felony. This is no word game. This is the literal truth [2:172]). His use of metaphor and his mistrust of the opposition's use of metaphor were not contradictory but frighteningly consistent. Both were attempts to govern absolutely.[22]

Papadopoulos's ongoing attempt to drain language of its figural force did not go unnoticed by those in the opposition; it indeed led the resistance to a heightened awareness of the relation of language to political hege-

[19] "Helleno-Christian culture" was first defined by Spyridon Zambelios (1852), but a more recent precedent for reconciling ancient and Christian Greece can be found in the rhetoric of the Metaxas dictatorship (1936–41).

[20] On the implications of Plato's *Cratylus* for literary theory, see Genette 1979, 359–73.

[21] Hayden White (1978, 10) distinguishes between the unintended lapse, or regression, into a prelogical mode when a metaphor is taken literally (as in Papadopoulos's case) and poetry's conscious use of metaphor to challenge logical thinking. On the unstable opposition between the literal and figural, also see Culler 1982, 148.

[22] Michael Ryan argues: "Absolute meaning is the displacement of metaphor, is, in other words, the metaphor of metaphor." He then goes on to equate sovereignty in meaning and state and draws some interesting conclusions regarding the interdependence of rhetoric and regime: "Absolute sovereignty is itself a form of civil war in that it must be defined as the suppression of sedition. . . . The attempt to exclude division absolutely is the absolute internalization of division" (1982, 6).

mony.[23] Many set themselves the challenge of exposing the contradictions and hypocrisy that the regime was busy concealing. One of the most successful tactics was parody: writers would seem to cooperate with Papadopoulos's desire to make everything fit perfectly while actually subverting him. This was evidently one reason for titling the first resistance anthology Δεκαοχτώ κείμενα (Eighteen texts). If all books had to have titles that corresponded exactly to the contents, then the resistance would use empty titles such as *Eighteen Texts, Six Poets, New Texts,* and *New Texts 2* (Andrews 1988). Layout and typography were also effective ways of parodying censorship. Editors of certain newspapers were known for printing the regime's mandatory statements in the same type and format as obituaries. The cartoonist Bost similarly inscribed subversive messages into his comics through the use of spelling mistakes. In his famous Lochness monster cartoon, Lochness is written λοχΝΑΙ, i.e., LochYES, to protest the July 1973 referendum to create a "presidential parliamentary republic" and the enforced yes vote for Papadopoulos (Figure 1).[24] A headline in huge wood type which read "The dictatorship is rapidly receding . . ." followed by the words "in Spain" in small type performed a trenchant social commentary (McDonald 1983, 68). Placing headlines halfway down the page so that they would be hidden when the newspaper was folded and pinned up at the kiosk was another subversive tactic (44). Parody, accordingly, depended on exposing the difference between two things that sounded or seemed the same: censorship was not the same as a "cast"; a title could never adequately reflect the contents of a book; and press statements, in the guise of different, incriminating typography, no longer meant what they said. Kevin Andrews's story of how two student groups used the name Papadopoulos at a rally provides an even more explicit example of parody (1980, 23). When Papadopoulos did not show up at the rally, pro-regime students began shouting "Pa-pa-dópou-los." The students opposing the regime exploited the same word for another of its meanings, a popular brand of cookies, and shouted instead "Al-la-ti-ní," the name of a competing brand.[25] The name of the dictator

[23] Antonio Gramsci articulates the relation of language to hegemony more generally: "Every time the question of language surfaces, in one way or another, it means that a series of other problems are coming to the fore" (1985, 183–84). Gramsci's notebooks, which were first translated into Greek under the dictatorship, informed the opposition's arguments and actions. See *Anti B,* nos. 37, 38, 39 (January 24, February 7 and 21, 1976) and Cammett 1995, 21, for bibliographies of translations of Gramsci into Greek. Anna Frangoudaki's discussion of the language question in a resistance publication, for example, echoes Gramsci's: "In every difficult period, at every historical turn of the country, this problem reappears at the forefront of the social stage" (1973, 277).

[24] See also Bost's 18 Αντι-κείμενα (18 anti-texts) (Bostantzoglou 1975), his parody of Papadopoulos's *Our Credo.*

[25] Tzvetan Todorov, drawing on Russian formalism, has a useful definition of parody: he opposes parody to stylization, the latter being when a word is used as it is most often used, and the former when the same word is used in a new context (Ducrot and Todorov, 1983, 256).

himself is thus shown to have an unstable signification. Homophony calls attention to the fact that the one-to-one correspondence of signifier to signified cannot be easily regulated. Bearing in mind the regime's attempt to suppress such linguistic confusion and the efforts of those in the opposition to expose that attempt in their typography, spelling, and jokes, let us now turn to the particular ways writers responded to censorship.

Censorship and the Question of Silence

In the first few years of the dictatorship when the regime enforced preventive censorship, there was among most established writers an unspoken agreement not to publish.[26] Some circulated manuscripts to friends, but few actually went through the degrading process of taking their work to the censor's office for approval.[27] The three best-known poets when the colonels took over were all from the generation of the 1930s, the two Nobel Laureate poets, George Seferis and Odysseas Elytis, and the winner of the Lenin Prize, Yannis Ritsos. For the younger generation of writers who began writing under the dictatorship and were still unknown, these men provided important models. Ritsos, like the composer Mikis Theodorakis and the politician Andreas Papandreou, was on the list of "dangerous" people who were rounded up and taken to jail the first night of the coup. Although he was an important source of inspiration for resistance writers and his books were circulated secretly, his absence behind bars or under house arrest meant it was difficult for him to sign letters of protest or counsel young writers on how to proceed.[28] Elytis was absent from the resistance scene for different reasons. He had always made it clear that poetry and politics were distinct and that collective protest was not his mode. When asked to sign a letter of protest, he refused, saying that perhaps he would do something on his own. Seferis, a politically moderate man, was less dangerous to the authorities than Ritsos, yet more threatening than Elytis. His decision not to publish under the colonels was understood as a

---

[26] Cf. both this section and my later discussions of how different writers responded to censorship with Natalie Zemon Davis's overview (1990, 3–4) of writers' varying responses to censorship during the German occupation in France.

[27] An example of a censored text is an unpublished collection of poetry Ανακάλυμα: Ποιήματα (Recollection: Poems) by the then unknown critic and writer Yiorgis Yatromanolakis (1969). In the typescript the stamped pages were those that were approved. The unstamped pages have corrections written in. The word "ελευθερία" (freedom), for example, was inadmissable and the word "φόνος" (murder) was changed to "πόνος" (pain). For a list of writers who circulated their work in manuscripts or mimeograph form, see Frangopoulos 1974, 173.

[28] Nonetheless the profound influence Ritsos had on the younger generation of writers is suggested in Jenny Mastoraki's memorial speech (1992a), in which she connects her own poetic awakening to finding a poem by Ritsos which described the claustrophobic climate of the dictatorship.

Ὁ θαυμαστός κόσμος τῶν ζώων

ΤΟ ΤΕΡΑΣ ΤΟΥ ΛΟΧΝΑΙ

(τηλεοπτικόν σκέτς)

ΘΗΡΕΙΟΝ:

Είμε τό τέρας τοῦ Λοχναι, ἀθῶον λαγουδάκι
κέ φιλικήν επιζήτισιν ἄς κάνομεν λιγάκι:
"Ἄν ἔχης σήζυγον, παιδιά, κέ σεβαστήν μητέρα,
βασιλοφρόνους συγγενεῖς κέ γέροντα πατέρα
διάταξε νά ρίψουν ΝΑΙ κι' ὅλοι διαταγμένοι
θά ζούν ὑπό τό πέλμα μου, πολή εὐτυχισμένοι.
Μήν μέ κυτάζης ἀπορῶν εἰς τούς κοφτερούς ὀδόντας
πού ἡ φύσις μας ἐποίκισεν ἐμᾶς τούς μαστοδόντας
κέ ἄν εἰς τήν εμφάνισιν λαγός δέν ὁμοιάζω
μετά τό δημοψήφισμα ἀμέσως θά ἀλλάζω.
Ἔχομαι ρεύμα τρομερόν, τά ΝΑΙ εἶνε δικά μας
χωρίς σημέας, ἔξοδα κέ φοβινᾶς ρεκλάμας,
κι' αὐτό τό ρεῦμα φένεται ἔκλισεν ὁ λεμός μου
δι' αὐτό βραχνός νά σοῦ φανῆ ἴσος ὁ βρυχιθμός μου.

Μέ τρέφουν ψήφοι πολιτῶν κέ οἱ λεμοί φάκελοι,
μίαν παράτασιν ζωῆς μου δίδουν εἰς τά ἔλη.

Ψήφος μέ φάκελον φαιόν, εἴν βέλος εἰς τήν καρδιάν μου,
σφαδάζω κέ κηλιέμαι κέ χάνω τήν ἡγεμονίαν μου.

Ρίψατε ὅτι θέλετε· φαιόν πρίν ὅμως ρίψης
σκέψου προλέγω σοβαρά μέ τί θά μέ συντρίψης.

Ἐάν μοῦ ρίψης τό φαιόν, τότε ἀλοίμονόν σου
θέσης τήν ἐργασίαν σου, τό μέλον τῶν παιδιῶν σου.

Ὁρίζομε ἐγώ ὄνομα τῆς Ἐβαγγελιστρίας,
νά γίνω τάνυς εἰς τόν κορμόν, νά βγάλω ἐρπυστρία

Μέ φιλικήν διάθεσιν κάνο τάς εὐπητήσεις
ὅπε μέ πλήρη ἄνεσιν νά τό ἀποφασίσης.

Τόρα ἐπείσης κέ ἐσύ ἐπείσθης πῶς συνφέρει
νά ρίψης ΝΑΙ ἀσυζητεί μέ τό λεφκόν στό χέρι.

ΚΗΝΗΓΟΣ:

Ὅλοι γνορίζομε καλός πῶς ἄγρειον θηρίον
ἐπταετῶς βρηχόμενον δέν γίνετε ἀρνίον,
οὔτε εὔκολος ἤμπορη εἰς τάς σημαίας του πλέον
ἕνας φριχτός δηνόσαυρος νά γίνη χαμελαίων.

Ἄν εἶχες τάσεις φιλικάς, ἀντί νά μᾶς φρομάζης
μιλῶν διά τανκς κέ ἀπειλάς, θᾶπρεπε νά θελάξης.

Μά σύ ἄφησας βρηχιθμούς, μᾶς ὅδηξες προόρως
εἰς βάθος αἱ βρογχόσαυρος, ἔμεινες αἱμοβῶρος.
Βυλιοφόρον Ἐδηψοῦ, γιγάντειον θηρεῖον

Figure 1. Bost's "LochYES Monster."

...λάβης μέγα ἔγκαυμα νά φύγης μέ φορεῖον.

ΘΗΡΕΙΟΝ:
...σου μέ μήν ὀργίζεσε. Μάθε καὶ ἀκόμα
...ἡ τρίχα μου ἐπιώθικε εἰς ὅλο μου τό σῶμα
...χωρίζει μέ διάφοροι πού ἔξω ζοῦνε τώρα
...τραῖνα ἐσλαμάλισεν εἰς μίαν ξένη χώρα
...ἐζήλωσαν ὁ Βασιλεῦς ἐδῶ νά τά ὁδηγήσῃ
...κάνη μίαν κυβέρνισιν κέ νά μᾶς κυβερνήσῃ.

Ὄπισθεν ὅλων δέ αὐτῶν πῆγαν οἱ Βασιλεῦς,
...κ᾽ ἐνθεύσεως ενενθελόμενοι κέ ὁ καραμανλῆς.
...ἐν εἶνε πράμμαλα σοβλά αὐτοῦ τοῦ Βασιλεῶς
...σου εἰς τάς κάλπας φθάνομεν ἐσίως κέ ταχέως.
...κ᾽ ἀφλά ποῦ κάνη ὁ Βασιλεῦς κ᾽ ἄλα ποῦ ὑποθάλπη
...κόσμος ὅλος ἕνα ΝΑΙ θά ρίπτη εἰς τήν κάλπη.

ΚΥΝΗΓΟΣ:
Πάψε θηρίον τοῦ Λοχναΐ, ἐγώ δέν σέ ψηφίζω
...κραδένω τήν ἀσπίδα μου, τό ξίφος ἀνεμίζω
...διότι ἄν ρίξης σίδλιχος κέ τραβμάτα δέν λάβης
...τήν δήναμιν σοῦ ἔχομαι δέν δά τήν καλαλάβης.
...εἶσε θανούργον, γλιστερῶν, κέ ἔχης ἐτιαμψίας
...κέ μᾶς κυπιλοφορῖον παντοῦ μέ ὄνυχοῦς γαμψίας:

Τώρα ποῦ ἀναγκάσδικες νά βγῆς ἀπό τήν κρύπτη
ὀφήλει κάθε κυνηγός φριαλῶς νά σέ συντρίβη.

Μόνον ἄν λάβης μίαν πληγήν θανάσιμον εἰς τό στῆθος
ὑπάρχη ἐλαφρά ἐλπίς νά ζῇ καλά τό πλῆθος.
Ἀλοιῶ κινᾶλε ἕν θεριό σαραντασθένδε πήχων
ἀργιμελές εἰς τόν κορμόν μέ ἀπεσίων τρίχων,
κ᾽ ἀλοιῶ μέ ποδάς μόνον δύο ἐκ τεσάρων ποῦ ἔχη
κέ κολοβόν χωρίς οὐράν εἰς τήν ξηράν νά τρέχη.

ΘΟΥΡΙΟΝ: (μέ ὡρέαν μουσικήν)
Ἐμπρός πεδία κέ κινιγοί, χλωπῆλε τό θηρίον
νά λάβη τράβμα σοβαρόν νά φύγη μέ φορεῖον.
Ἄν ρίση πανλοδήναμον, χωρίς πληγάς μεγάλας
μήν ἀπορόμεν αὔριον ἄν γίνη Μαθουσάλας.

Καλή εἶνε ἡ τίλωσις, καλή κ᾽ ἡ εὐμαρεία
ἀλ᾽ ἴσος πιά δέν μᾶς δοθῆ μία τέλια ἐφημερία.
Τώρα ποῦ βγῆκεν τό λοχναΐ κι᾽ ἐξῆλθε διά τήν μάχη
περισθλωσις ὅσαν ἀφλή δ᾽ ἀργήση νά μᾶς λάχη.

ρεφρέν { Μ᾽ ἐξορκισκοῦς κέ μέ φοναί
{ δέν ἀποθνήσκει τό λοχναΐ.)δίς
ΟΛΕ.

political act. This gesture, repeated by others of his influential generation (both E. P. Papanoutsos and C. Th. Dimaras stopped publishing their essays in the Sunday newspaper *To Vima* [P. Vlachos 1987]), was viewed by younger writers as a signal and had a great deal to do with their decision not to publish.[29]

But Seferis was ambivalent about the political role he found himself obliged to take. His desires, on the one hand, to stay out of politics and, on the other hand, to serve his country are both clear in the statement he issued on March 28, 1969, after two years of silence:

> My decision to keep out of politics was taken a long time ago. I have tried on past occasions to explain why. This in no way means that I am indifferent to the political life of Greece. Thus, from that time onwards until now I have generally refrained from becoming involved in such matters. Moreover, everything I wrote up to the beginning of 1967 and my subsequent attitude (I have published nothing in Greece since freedom was gagged) showed, quite plainly I think, what my ideas were. In spite of all that, for many months now I have felt growing within me and around me an increasing imperative duty to say something about our present situation in the fewest possible words. (in H. Vlachos 1971, 137)

This less than heroic preface was quickly forgotten, and all that was remembered was that he had broken his silence and that his speech had concluded with this warning: "I see before me the abyss towards which we are being led by the oppression which has spread over the land. This situation must be brought to an end. It is imperative for the good of the Nation. I return now to my silence and I pray to God that he will not again oblige me to speak" (137).

The poets of the postwar generations for the most part viewed Seferis's silence as a necessary measure, though they were known to be more politically outspoken. Many, such as Manolis Anagnostakis, Aris Alexandrou, and Titos Patrikios, were active on the Left.[30] The challenge they address during this period is how to communicate subversive messages within the horizon of this silence. In Alexandrou's novel Το κιβώτιο (The mission box), the narrator mentions a play called "Silence" in which a totalitarian government bugs houses so that people are obliged to communicate in gestures ([1974] 1984, 207–9; 1996, 238–40). Alexandrou's hypothetical play about totalitarianism during the German occupation, within a novel

---

[29] For a parallel account of writers' activity under the dictatorship which focuses on prose instead of poetry, see Alexandros Argiriou's comprehensive introduction to the anthology Η μεταπολεμική πεζογραφία (Postwar prose) (Karvelis et al. 1992, 287–360).

[30] The critic D. N. Maronitis in his book on the first postwar generation writes, "The most important postwar poets, explicitly or implicitly, are political poets . . . and the majority are on the Left" (1984d, 15).

about totalitarianism during the civil war, written under the dictatorship, suggests that in the present situation, too, gestures may be writers' only recourse. A newspaper article by Rodis Roufos, another writer of the post-war generation, though breaking the "silence," in the end supported it as a valid alternative. He criticized other writers who had published discussions of Greece's cultural life without mentioning censorship and the general oppression of the times. His point was that one should either remain silent or make one's disagreement explicit; nothing in between was acceptable: "I am surprised that distinguished personalities have discussed the level of our cultural life without relating it to cultural freedom. Perhaps they see the connection, but pass over it in silence for reasons of expediency? That in itself shows to what depths our cultural life has sunk. Total silence would have been preferable to such self-censorship" (in H. Vlachos 1971, 135). In this context it is important to note that whereas writers known to be on the Left were for the most part either in jail or abroad in self-imposed exile, writers on the Right, such as Roufos, a respectable diplomat, were obliged to speak out if they wanted to separate themselves from the regime.[31] Insofar as he lost his job and his passport for publishing this piece, it is clear that he succeeded in making his dissension heard.

Taking an opposite view, Phillipos Vlachos, the founder and director of the press Keimena, which began publishing under the dictatorship, did not think silence was an appropriate response, even for a leftist, and actually criticized writers for following Seferis's example. He explained: "Silence was also convenient . . . an escape, not resistance" (1987). His publishing house, as well as a few others, most notably Kalvos, insisted that silence was not as honorable as Seferis made it seem and that it was not fair to leave readers with the drivel and propaganda the regime's press office published. In 1968 they began publishing translations and republishing classic Greek works, their position being that the high quality of the works themselves would be a critique of the kitsch the regime promoted. According to Colonel Yannis Ladas, the secretary general for the Ministry of the Interior and the regime's main ideologue, good art was art that served the motherland (Roufos 1972a, 153). If the regime was going to promote a functional aesthetics, then the resistance would opt for aesthetic autonomy and quality. As Vlachos put it, "Instead of bringing out the Communist Manifesto, we'll bring out Solomos's *The Woman of Zakynthos* [Η γυναίκα της Ζάκυνθος]. That is, there is another way to do resistance: by putting

---

[31] Roufos's response calls to mind the poet, in Bertolt Brecht's poem "The Burning of the Books," who "discovered with fury, when he studies the list / Of the burned, that his books / Had been forgotten. He rushed to his writing table / On wings of anger and wrote a letter to those in power. / Burn me, he wrote with hurrying pen, burn me! / Do not treat me in this fashion. Don't leave me out. Have I not / Always spoken the truth in my books? And now / You treat me like a liar! I order you: / Burn me!" (1947, 125).

next to vulgarity something of good taste or of quality, next to kitsch ... a beautifully made book" (1987).[32] Kalvos was the first of this group of publishing houses to scrape together enough money to produce books. Its heterogeneous list of publications from *The Woman of Zakynthos* to Ελληνική νομαρχία (The Greek rule of law) to a translation of Yevgenny Schwartz's play *The Dragon* was thus conceived as a more indirect form of resistance.[33]

It soon became clear however that silence was no longer an effective tool of resistance for anyone. Its premise of exposing the sterile state of the arts in Greece by withholding publications was undermined when the regime began publishing writers' work without their permission. Whereas the anthology of poetry *Popular Muse* (1969) was a fairly benign piece of propaganda, the "official anthology" of prose issued in weekly installments in all the newspapers in March of the same year was a much more serious affair. Carrying Greece's *best* short stories culled from Iraklis and Renos Apostolidis's Ανθολογία (Anthology), it gave the appearance that artistic freedom had been restored. Apostolidis, though, had not consulted any of the writers.[34] Silence was only a resistance strategy if the writers were in control of it. Some whose work was being circulated against their will decided to express their dissatisfaction. Kay Cicellis drafted a letter and collected signatures, first from those whose work had been included and then, because too few agreed to sign, from other sympathetic writers. The letter began:

We the undersigned 18 Athenian writers of the postwar generation fully share the indignation of those among us whose names are being used, without their consent, for the compulsory publication of their work in the press, in order to create the impression, both here and abroad, that our country enjoys intellectual freedom. (in H. Vlachos 1971, 197)

and concluded:

We finally wish to honour George Seferis, because he was the first to point out the ever-growing dangers inherent in the perpetuation of this state of

[32] Such an opposition bears closer scrutiny. It would be interesting in the wake of discussions of kitsch and taste such as Milan Kundera's in *The Unbearable Lightness of Being* and Bourdieu's in *Distinction: A Social Critique of the Judgement of Taste* to study the question of taste in Greece. The book Κάτι το ωραίον: Μια περιήγηση στη νεοελληνική κακογουστιά (Something beautiful: A tour of Modern Greek kitsch) provides a good starting place (Friends of *Anti* 1984).

[33] Of course the content was also important. *The Greek Rule of Law*, for example, published anonymously in 1806, is the first Greek text to openly call for insurrection against the Turks.

[34] The uproar this caused among writers is well documented in the archives of Tatiana and Roger Milliex, Etaireia Ellinikou Logotechnikou kai Istorikou Archeiou (ELIA), in particular in Apostolidis's letters to Milliex (1973-3-2 and 1977-5-22) and in Mando Aravandinou's letter to Milliex (1969-5-4), in which she includes an earlier letter she wrote to Apostolidis (1969-4-5).

affairs. Let us hope that the poet's voice will not prove to be the voice of another Cassandra. (197)

Here again it is Seferis who is invoked as the champion of resistance. Soon after the letter was published on April 18, 1969, the "official anthology" ceased. The thaw had begun. Seferis's support of the resistance, even if predominantly tacit, had had a great impact. In November of 1969, preventive censorship was lifted. At around the same time, Phillipos Vlachos's press Keimena, which had been publishing continuously though without much success, issued a selection of Brecht's poetry. In a week the edition of three thousand copies had sold out. Readers were ready for a change. Perhaps encouraged by the response the Brecht translation received, a group of established writers, many of whom had signed the "Letter of Eighteen," decided it was time to publish their own work again. In July 1970 their anthology *Eighteen Texts* was published.

This act of opposition, like the "Letter of Eighteen" and the silence that had come before, was validated by Seferis. His name was set off from the rest of the participants by a space on the cover and his poem "The Cats of St. Nicholas" introduced the whole collection. By repeatedly invoking the name of Seferis, the poets of the postwar generations located their poetics in a particular tradition. Anagnostakis's and Takis Sinopoulos's poems in *Eighteen Texts,* when compared with Seferis's, reveal a poetics that, though employed for an alternative effect, is deeply indebted to his. Seferis's position as symbolic leader of the resistance culminated with his funeral in 1971 (Andrews 1980, 41–58). Like the funeral of the national poet Kostis Palamas in 1943 under the German occupation, Seferis's funeral was attended by thousands who came to protest and mourn the death of a country as well as that of a man who had fought for its survival. The use of Seferis's person and poetry as a symbol of the struggle for democracy under a dictatorship is clearly important, but I am also concerned with some of the ways his actions and poems support a more disinterested position.[35] The need for such a reading is clear if we consider the contradictory ends to which his name was deployed in the "Letter of Eighteen" already cited. On the one hand, Seferis's voice is likened to that of Cassandra, the misunderstood prophetess who stands outside the symbolic order; on the other hand, his voice is invoked for the opposite reason: because, as that of a national poet with an international reputation, it has little chance of "falling on deaf ears" in the manner of Cassandra's. Before I analyze the political implications of his and other texts that appeared in

[35] In this respect I follow recent scholarship, though none of the material on Seferis's privileged status in Greek letters and life (Lambropoulos 1988, 44–65; Gourgouris 1989; as well as Jusdanis 1991, 82, with respect to the generation of the 1930s' attempt to defend the autonomy of literature), focuses on his person or production during this final period of his life.

Eighteen Texts, however, I want to pose some questions about discursive styles and political practices and look more carefully at the expectations of poetry which Seferis and his generation held.

Discursive Styles and Political Practices

Since the creation of the Greek state in the 1820s and 1830s, poetry has enjoyed greater esteem than prose or drama. By integrating oral and written texts into one tradition, poetry presented itself as a popular art form celebrated by shepherds and school teachers alike. Traditionally written in demotic, poetry was interpreted as the voice of the nation. Prose, often employing Katharevousa, was in contrast marginalized.[36] Even after poetry turned its back on nationalism in the 1910s with the rise of "postsymbolism" in the poetry of Kostas Ouranis, Tellos Agras, Napoleon Lapathiotis, and Kostas Karyotakis, a national calling remained in evidence. Many surrealist poems of the generation of the 1930s, for example, during the Second World War—Nikos Engonopoulos's "Μπολιβάρ" (Bolivar) (with the subtitle "a Greek poem"), Nikos Gatsos's "Αμοργός" (Amorgos), and Elytis's " 'Ασμα ηρωικό και πένθιμο για τον χαμένο ανθυπολοχαγό της Αλβανίας" (Heroic and mournful hymn for the lost second lieutenant of Albania), inspired by his experience on the Albanian front—display a nationalist fervor rarely found, say, in French surrealist poetry (C. Robinson 1981). Poetry's privileged position in Greece as national institution raises some important questions: What model of language is activated by poetry's national vocation? What is poetry being opposed to? Is it possible to motivate poetry to other ends? Drawing on Russian formalist Mikhail Bakhtin's discussion of the *monologic* and the *dialogic* as well as Seferis's, and on the French philosopher Jean-François Lyotard's discussion of the *paralogical* as well as that of the generation of the 1970s, I address these questions by mapping out connections between discursive styles and political practices in writers' responses to censorship under the dictatorship.

For Bakhtin, literary genre is closely tied up with the limits and possibilities of social interaction.[37] Certain forms seem related to certain politics: poetry is authoritarian; the novel is more democratic. This is in large part owing to poetry's monologic style, that is, its singular point of view, versus

---

[36] In Greece prose is often criticized for not having attained the same level of sophistication as poetry. Greek novelists point out that the social conditions are still not ripe for the bourgeois novel. Both Kostas Tachtsis (1984) and Vasilis Vasilikos (1989) stress that there has never been a "great" Greek novel, and this opinion prevails among writers and critics in Greece despite a recent boom in prose that suggests things may well be changing. For a historical perspective on the primacy of poetry in Greece and its relation to nationalism, see Tziovas 1986, 53–54.

[37] For an overview of Bakhtin's impact in Greece and an extensive application of his thought to Modern Greek literature, see Tziovas 1993, esp. 150–221.

the novel's dialogic style, which like ordinary discourse, encompasses different sociolinguistic registers.[38] For Bakhtin the important difference between these two types of discourse is that the dialogic, unlike the monologic, is *self-consciously* conflictual—it makes us aware that its truth claims are partial. Of course the monologic also exists in relation to the discourses it suppresses, but it tends not to represent these different discourses. Though for Lyotard literary genre is not the issue, his concept of the paralogical, like Bakhtin's of the dialogic and the monologic, suggests the interdependence of poetics and politics.[39] But whereas Bakhtin relies on a model of language in which the mimetic presumptions of representation are crucial, Lyotard understands both the discourse of politics and the politics of discourse as linguistic performances. Discursive styles and political practices are related not as mirrors of each other but inextricably.

Lyotard proposes his theory of paralogy as a critique of Jürgen Habermas's (1968) more dialogic legitimation of consensus and his recourse to a master narrative, the marxist narrative of emancipation. Lyotard is suspicious of consensus, even in the name of liberation, because he feels it ultimately stabilizes meaning by institutionalizing a new set of language games and thus is capable of the same "terror" it criticizes. By "terror," Lyotard means "the efficiency gained by eliminating, or threatening to eliminate a player from the language game one shares with him. 'Adapt your aspirations to our ends—or else' " (1984, 63–64). Fredric Jameson, in his introduction to Lyotard's *Postmodern Condition,* describes the latter's project as a search for "instabilities" and suggests that practicing paralogy implies never reaching agreement but always undermining from within the very framework in which the previous investigation had been conducted. Instead of enforcing one truth over another as monologism does, or offering divergent opinions that always presuppose a social context in which such heteroglossia exists, as dialogism does, paralogism involves different discourses without demanding that they interact coherently; it is

---

[38] For a brief definition of monologic and dialogic, see Bakhtin 1981, 426–27 and 430; for a longer analysis, see Hirschkop 1989, 6–35. For the relation of these terms to the differences between the novel and poetry, see Bakhtin 1981, 41–51, 275–300, 327–31, and de Man 1989, 111–12. Although in Bakhtin's work these discursive styles at times seem to have a transhistorical character, their different ways of structuring social interactions make it possible to establish analogies with particular political practices. Ken Hirschkop distinguishes between poetry's monologic abstraction from social relations and prose's dialogic involvement. He explains how for Bakhtin monologism proposes that history and social relations are objects of representation, not discourses in themselves, whereas dialogism, by enabling all discourses to be "simultaneously representing and represented," keeps history and social relations inside the text and insists that "meaning is contingent on both the object of discourse and the social gesture which it now visibly enacts" (1986, 102).

[39] Lyotard's theory of *paralogy,* like most philosophical discussions that use this term, or any of its cognates, draws on Kant's distinction between logical and transcendental *paralogisms* (1965, 328).

less bound by social contracts, blatantly flaunting its absurd and imaginary origins.

Bakhtin's framework is useful in explaining why in Modern Greece, a country often under authoritarian rule and rarely successful in its democratic struggles, poetry has flourished and prose has suffered. The dialogism of prose with its decentered and, therefore, less forceful authority is difficult to sustain under pressure: the short stories written before the dictatorship and published in Apostolidis's *Anthology* were appropriated by the regime. Poetry, in contrast, is more likely to fight oppression on oppression's own terms, namely monologically. The sweeping generalization implicit in Bakhtin's celebration of the novel, however, needs challenging. Surely not all poetry is monologic.[40] The poetry of the generation of the 1970s could at times be characterized as dialogic. The following chapters show how the poets of that generation, particularly the women in their sustained poetic sequences in the 1980s, unsettle poetry's monologism by taking on many of the mandates Bakhtin reserves for the novelist. They have no qualms juxtaposing all sorts of different linguistic registers and no desire to empty these registers of their sociohistorical specificity. Not only are different linguistic registers freely admitted into their poetry, but tropes function to foster ambiguity, something Bakhtin denies is possible in poetry.[41] But under the dictatorship, for the most part, their poetry is probably most aptly distinguished along the lines of Lyotard's concept of the paralogical. Whereas the older generation's literary production falls into generic categories of poetry and prose, and discursive styles such as monologic and dialogic, the younger poets' "nonsense" is more difficult to label; it avoids appropriation by its very "unproductiveness."[42] Like Kassandra's own kind of counting in the scene from Karapanou's novel, this poetry deploys alternative logics to destabilize those of the official culture.

Employing the terms *monologic, dialogic,* and *paralogical,* then, allows me to show some of the similarities between authoritarian discourse and resistance poetry (first and foremost their monologism) and to distinguish

[40] Bakhtin himself in fact seems worried about how neatly he divides poetry and prose, for he almost always qualifies his discussion of poetic speech by adding "in the narrow sense" (1981, 43, 277, 284, 285, 295, 327, 331), and in a footnote he admits that particularly in times of instability, poetic language is more hybrid than his model might suggest (287 n. 12).

[41] "It is impossible under any conditions or at any time to imagine a trope (say, a metaphor) being unfolded into the two exchanges of a dialogue, that is, two meanings parceled out between two separate voices. . . . On the contrary, one voice, a single-accent system, is fully sufficient to express poetic ambiguity" (Bakhtin 1981, 327).

[42] Cicellis mentions the generation of the 1970s' shift away from direct attacks: "There are writers, especially among the younger generation, who have emerged from the direct and violent encounter with history which was the dictatorship, with a more balanced and lucid understanding of the past. There is in them a kind of wariness, a suspicion of clichés, a refusal to be fooled. . . . There is disillusion and pessimism as before . . . [but] there is far more understatement, more irony too; the frontal attack is less frequent" (1977a, 10).

between different poetic projects: on the one hand the monologic, both the disinterested and the resistance sort, and on the other the paralogical. In this way I can suggest that the regime and writing were not diametrically opposed and that the resistance was not a unified affair. Such an approach helps to unsettle the tendency to think about the dictatorship in terms of binary oppositions—those who were silent versus those who were not, those who wrote engaged poetry versus those who did not. It is important, though, not to turn such analogies between discursive styles and political practices into new fixed categories. I introduce them solely as heuristic tools, as a way of thinking about the different responses to censorship in the particular context of the dictatorship. My appeal to Lyotard's concept of paralogy, for example, should be understood in this context. Though Lyotard provides a seductive theory of evasion, the question of how this might translate into anything but political quietism is left unelaborated. After censorship was lifted, paralogy's doctrinal tentativeness and unproductiveness were no longer as necessary. The rise of the novel in Greece in the 1980s, for example, suggests that under democracy one might turn the tables and use Habermas's dialogic concept of consensus as a critique of Lyotard's paralogy and as a way of making Bakhtin's dialogism relevant again.

Another reason I have chosen to juxtapose monologic, dialogic, and paralogical is that all three terms have a certain local specificity in Greece during the years of the dictatorship, not to mention in the Greek popular imagination more generally. The adjectives μονολογικός and διαλογικός retain the rhetorical sense of "monologue" and "dialogue" in their common usage, but the adjective παράλογος does not have an explicit rhetorical equivalent. The terms παράλογος, το παράλογο, and παραλογισμός have traditionally meant "absurd"; "the absurd," as in the theater of the absurd; and "absurdity." In this chapter, although the denotative sense of the word παράλογος is always "absurd," a particularly popular concept during this period, I introduce the connotative sense "paralogical," along the lines of the monologic and dialogic. This second sense emphasizes the discursive process of undoing logic, rather than the absurd effect itself.[43] Such a reading of this term is supported by its recurrent use by critics to describe the writing of the younger generation of poets as well as by the frequent association of this kind of writing with the absurd conditions under the dictatorship. One of the most quoted references is that of Takis Sinopoulos in his review of a new book of poetry by Veroniki Dalakoura: "This woman poet has been baptized for good in the font of the paralogical, as it prevailed after the war in the West. Kafka, Camus, Sartre, Ionesco, Beckett,

---

[43] Hereafter I translate παράλογος as "paralogical," not "absurd," in order to draw out this connotative sense.

Pinter, etc., etc. It doesn't matter if those mentioned above wrote essays, prose, or theater. The paralogical is everywhere" (1973, 236). Kimon Friar echoes a similar sentiment in his introduction to a collection of poetry by the younger generation, Ἐξη ποιητές (Six poets) (1971, 7), although he is more specific about the geography of the paralogical. Whereas Sinopoulos referred to "everywhere," Friar refers to the specific difficult conditions under which this poetry was written, namely the dictatorship. He connects the paralogical style of the poetry of Vasilis Steriadis, another poet of this younger generation, to the paralogical times.

The libelous magazine *Panderma* also wove together the discursive style and the specific political experience of the paralogical under the dictatorship, revealing their interconnectedness. Its collage format not only appealed to the paralogical as a literary style and as a means of expressing the paralogism of the times but formally incorporated its disjointedness. Excerpts of articles, advertisements, conversation, and anything else that came to the editor's attention were included. Begun in 1974 near the end of the regime, much of its purpose was to point a finger at those who had collaborated with the junta. Leonidas Christakis, its editor, includes an interesting exposé of the intellectuals who published in the pro-regime journal Θέσεις και ιδέαι (Positions and ideas). Among other excerpts and comments he reprints parts of a review by the esteemed philologist Andreas Karandonis from this journal. Karandonis has gone to great lengths to prove that the paralogical is only a theatrical phenomenon, not an actuality: "Thus we consider the paralogical, for the time being, as a phenomenon localized in art even if the analogous existentialist philosophy with its own arguments wants to see it displayed and rooted wherever there is life and existence" (Christakis 1974). Although Christakis only comments on this passage indirectly, the point of reprinting it seems to be to show that Karandonis "doth protest too much." The paralogical is not merely a literary style but can also, like the monologic and the dialogic in Bakhtin's formulations, be understood to be discursively implicated in particular political and social practices.[44]

Though the term *paralogical* appears for the most part in articles about the poets of the generation of the 1970s, it could be argued that the poetry of the postwar poet Miltos Sachtouris in many ways foreshadows this paralogical writing style. Yannis Dallas (1979) has a section titled "The Origins of the Paralogical" in his work on Sachtouris's poetics (1979). Mario Vitti writes that Sachtouris "reorganizes words in a paralogical manner"

---

[44] Margarita Liberaki's prose piece Το μυστήριο (The mystery), first published in 1976, is the kind of writing Karandonis would have been attacking. Although from the older postwar generation, Liberaki, like the younger generation of poets, blends the literary and political sense of the paralogical by setting theater of the absurd at the scene of the fall of the Polytechnic in November of 1973.

(1987b, 429). He suggests, for example, that Sachtouris's choice of the title
Παραλογαίς (Paralogues) for his 1948 collection of poetry explicitly draws
on both the word παραλογές (paralogues) (for which he deliberately uses
the archaic spelling παραλογαίς), a category of Greek folksongs, and το
παράλογο (the paralogical) (429–30). Vitti later significantly mentions Sachtouris as one of the poets most appreciated by the younger generation
(448). Yannis Ritsos, from the generation of the 1930s, is another important
precursor.[45] But these are exceptions. Most of the poetry written by the
poets of the generation of the 1930s and of the two postwar generations
was either aestheticizing ("disinterested") or politically engaged, and in
both cases the monologic prevailed; very rarely did the poetry of these
generations complicate this division, connecting for example the aesthetic
practice of ellipticism with the political conditions of the day, in the manner of the poetry of the generation of the 1970s.

Before turning to my readings of that generation's texts, though, I want
to look at how these terms are used in Seferis and Konstantinos Tsatsos's
famous exchange found in "Διάλογος πάνω στην ποίηση" (Dialogue on
poetry) (Seferis and Tsatsos [1938] 1975), and Seferis's subsequent "Μονό-
λογος πάνω στην ποίηση" (Monologue on poetry) (in Seferis and Tsatsos
[1939] 1975) because these two pieces lay down many of the fundamental
discursive rules and interpretive strategies that dominate literary criticism
in Greece from the 1930s on. Examining how monologism asserted itself,
despite these two intellectuals' willingness to address the issue of paralogism and the dialogic form of their debate, prepares the way for an analysis
of their hermeneutic legacy in the resistance collection *Eighteen Texts*.

One of the central pretexts for the dialogue between Seferis and Tsatsos
was a disagreement over the extent to which poetry should make sense.[46]
Referring to the incomprehensible element in poetry interchangeably as
the illogical, the surreal, and the paralogical, they argue over the future of
poetry in Greece. Seferis disagrees with Tsatsos's distinction between logical and illogical elements in poetry and dismisses Tsatsos's fear that soon
there would be no logical element whatsoever (Seferis and Tsatsos 1975, 6).
Tsatsos complains that recent poetry is at odds with the "Greek spirit" and
the "Greek ideal of beauty" because it uncritically mixes logical and illogical images. Seferis, in contrast, argues that illogical elements in poetry do
not by definition undermine "Greekness." There is no doubt in his mind
that poetry's authority is inextricably connected with its ability to tell the
truth and be received as the truth, but he thinks there is still room for

[45] The similarity is particularly evident in the short poems that appear intermittently
throughout Ritsos's poetic career, many of which have been collected by Edmund Keeley in
his translations (Ritsos 1979, 1985, 1991).

[46] A related concern which has received more attention was the extent to which modernist
practices were "Greek" (Dimiroulis 1985; Leontis 1995b, 121–39).

illogical elements.[47] In support of this opinion he quotes a traditional Greek folk song in which the most illogical connections are made:

> Κόκκιν' αχείλι εφίλησα κι έβαψε το δικό μου,
> και στο μαντίλι το 'συρα κι έβαψε το μαντίλι,
> και στο ποτάμι το 'πλυνα κι έβαψε το ποτάμι,
> κι' έβαψε η άκρη του γιαλού κι η μέση του πελάγου.
> Κατέβη ο αϊτός να πιεί νερό κι έβαψαν τα φτερά του,
> κι έβαψε ο ήλιος ο μισός και το φεγγάρι ακέριο.
>
> (18)

> I kissed red lips which dyed my own,
> and touched them to a handkerchief dyeing it too,
> and washed it in the stream dyeing it,
> the seashore and the depths of the sea.
> The eagle swoops down to drink water dyeing his wings,
> and then dyeing half the sun and the whole moon.

Although this song might be mistaken for a surrealist poem, Seferis writes, it is in no way "at odds with the 'deeper law of the Greek Spirit' " (18); it still makes sense and gives meaning to our experiences. He then turns to "Μήτηρ Θεού" (God's mother), a long poem by Angelos Sikelianos, one of the poets Tsatsos is criticizing, and shows that even in this difficult, mysterious verse there is a logical connection between the poetic inspiration and the poetic result (19). According to Seferis, as long as a logical connection exists, it does not matter if the inspiration is illogical. He concludes by warning that paralogism would set in if this connection were missing (19).

Reading back in time from the vantage point of the dictatorship, the crucial question is why paralogism was inadmissible for Seferis and Tsatsos. Both intellectuals imagined that poetry was the monologic voice of the Greek spirit and that the expression of this voice was poetry's "natural" function.[48] Instead of questioning Tsatsos's naturalizing of the logical, Seferis subordinates the illogical to the logical and naturalizes both in the name of Greekness. This camouflaging of culture as nature dissipates any political power the illogical, or paralogical, might have. The whole exchange between Seferis and Tsatsos can be read as an attempt to fend off paralogism to keep poetry and criticism away from politics. Yet even

[47] Seferis's desire for poetry that speaks the truth is elaborated in various poems where he emphasizes "speaking simply." See "Ο δικός μας ήλιος" (Our sun) (1981, 216–17) and "Ένας γέροντας στην ακροποταμια" (An old man on the river bank) (288–93).

[48] This position has a long history in Greece. Respected literary historians of this century such as Dimaras, Linos Politis, Karandonis, and Apostolos Sachinis all too often view authors as spiritual reincarnations of the Greek nation rather than as complex translations of history. For critiques of this tendency, see Tziovas 1985, 253–77 and Lambropoulos 1988.

though they were both fighting paralogism, their common enemy did not unite them. In the end, Seferis turned to the monologue format because he found dialogue impossible; his and Tsatsos's discourses were incompatible: "The thing that surprised me, though, was how two people, old acquaintances and friends, conversing on subjects that interest them both intensely and that they have conversed on countless times, after so many pages, such good intentions and such effort to express themselves with precision, managed to chalk up so many misunderstandings" (67). He blamed Tsatsos for imposing his own philosophical rules on their dialogue: "I resist when either Philosophy or Sociology or Theology, seated in its own throne, judges me with laws that are not at all constructed for my problems" (71). Seferis was intent on keeping things straight: philosophy and poetry were incompatible discourses. It is not that he wanted to do away with the throne; it was simply that he did not want Tsatsos's philosophy sitting up there. He would have preferred his own poetry.[49] Each in his own particular sphere relies on what Lyotard calls "terrorism"—" 'Adapt your aspirations to our ends—or else' " (63–64). The dialogue reached an impasse because each wanted the other to adapt and neither could imagine an exchange in which there was not a single master discourse in control.

The desire not to be contaminated by another discourse, not to be judged by laws constructed for other purposes, which Seferis articulates, is very likely connected to his attempt—however conscious or unconscious—to put some distance between himself and Yannis Metaxas's authoritarian regime (1936–41). Though not as severe with regard to Greece's cultural life as Papadopoulos's regime, Metaxas's nonetheless raised many similar issues for intellectuals. Seferis's struggle to distinguish his project from Tsatsos's, that is, to admit some illogical elements into poetry without undermining its logical force, may not be unrelated to the difficulties he faced talking about Greekness at a time when a dictator was also professing Greekness. Monologism evidently often sets in when one feels that one's project is being taken over by someone else, when the terms one has been using, though perhaps to different ends, seem too similar to one's enemy's.

In his "Monologue on Poetry" written in the months after his aborted dialogue with Tsatsos, Seferis turned explicitly to the question of censorship. He begins by describing how the Inquisition forced El Greco to trim the wings of his angels to a standard size: "Legend has it that the Inquisition ordered the wings of El Greco's angles to be cut; for their size was irregular. That is to say, it ordered all those who happened to find angels

---

[49] It is perhaps necessary to add that Seferis wants his views on poetry to rule only when the subject of conversation is poetry—he is not saying he wants his poetics to dominate all discourses, as Tsatsos, it could be argued, would want his philosophy to do.

with large wings beautiful, to sacrifice something they liked and to accept in its place something they did not like, for the sake of Christian dogma" (in Seferis and Tsatsos 1975, 77). Seferis uses El Greco's angels to illustrate how the pressure of political, sociological, and religious dogma can lead a critic to condemn a poem even if he or she personally likes it. For Seferis, art is at odds with censorship and the dogma that informs it, and it is the obligation of the critic to be fully conscious of how the latter affects his or her opinion of the former. He continues: "It is not that our poetical judgments should not be influenced by our opinions or our faith . . . , but it is a matter of critical consciousness to know what motives drive us to make our judgments and to warn our readers accordingly" (78). The monologue format at first seems liberating—there is the sense that he can finally speak his mind, that he can make clear the way one discourse imposes itself on another and can call for a more vigilant separation of poetry and criticism from politics, without having to contend with someone else's misunderstandings. On closer examination, however, the same conflicts are evident, just disguised. His point, as far as he develops it, is well taken: critical biases must be made explicit. But what happens if the cutting and trimming is more pervasive than he admits? What happens if "dogma" is not simply "out there" in the guise of Inquisitions and authoritarian regimes but a part of the creative act? What happens if taste, such as the "original" impulse to like angels with large wings, is also socially constructed, if the poet and the critic are always already implicated in the political contingencies of the moment?[50]

Seferis, tellingly, wrote these passages about censorship in 1938 after returning from diplomatic service abroad to work in the Press Office in Athens under the Metaxas dictatorship (Vitti 1989, 278). In 1935, after a decade of keeping a single journal for all his thoughts, Seferis had begun keeping a separate notebook for political matters. The first long entry appears in 1938. As Alexandros Xydis points out, these political journals were a part of Seferis's endeavor to separate the diplomat Yeorgios Seferiadis from the poet George Seferis (Seferis 1979, 7). Xydis does not mention, however, that this new passion for dividing his two selves may have been related to the fact that during this period Seferis could not reconcile his work in the Press Office, that is, ostensibly the censor's office, with his struggle for freedom of expression in his own poetry and criticism. The

---

[50] In a footnote Seferis clarifies how he views the relation between art and politics. He admits that "dogma" is sometimes not simply "out there" but integrated into the artistic process. But here he specifies that if it is "outside," as in the case of El Greco, or "inside," "if the dogma has become second nature," as in the case of Alexandros Papadiamantis's Orthodoxy, then it is acceptable, but if it is in between, not thoroughly integrated—the "confusion that muddies the water"—then "we are giving ourselves headaches with futile discussions" (78). The two realms must be kept distinct.

effect such an artificial division created can be traced in his guilt-ridden poem "Ο γυρισμός του ξενιτεμένου" (The return of the exile) written in 1938 (Vitti 1989, 138–39) and also in his adamant plea to critics to admit their motives in his "Monologue." The effort to separate spheres ultimately impeded his analysis of the way one discourse forces itself on another, serving to mystify rather than clarify the relation between politics and poetry.

Seferis's response to censorship changed over the years—his disapproving silence under Papadopoulos was a long way from his repressed complicity during the Metaxas regime—but he was still set on keeping poetry and politics apart. His comments at a poetry discussion just before his death in 1971 suggest that three decades, a civil war, and two dictatorships had only strengthened his belief that art should transcend politics. In place of El Greco's oversized wings, he invokes a ship's figurehead unaffected by its environment: "An important . . . element for me . . . is that balance between a calm and a rough sea. I love the figurehead on the ship's prow because, regardless of the weather, good or stormy, it never changes its expression" (*Seferis Evening* 1972, 9). This image of a figurehead, whose expression never changes, symbolizes Seferis's view of poetry as impervious to history and of criticism as trying to attain such a status by making its motives explicit. Such an outlook could not accommodate discursive styles in which clarity was secondary. For Seferis the paralogical was a threat because it explicitly admitted contamination between political and poetic spheres. The dialogic was also problematic because it too often succumbed to such contamination in the process of trying to resolve differences. He was left with only the monologic, which, because it was uninterested in its own internal contradictions, offered the illusion of a more stable and authoritative position from which to speak or, as the case may be, from which to remain silent.

Telling the Truth in *Eighteen Texts*

Seferis's poetics were still the dominant poetics when the colonels took over in 1967, and the postwar poets were very much in his debt. Whereas the postwar poets move away from Seferis's aestheticizing view of poetry toward a more engaged one—poetry in the service of real politics, not some metaphysical nation—their plea for clarity is intimately related to Seferis's. In contrast to Seferis, the postwar poets profess to shun metaphors and allegory and appeal to literal language, yet their abhorrence of indecision and incoherency recalls his. Rhetorical figures, whether rejected or tolerated, were emptied of their ambivalent meanings and used to put forth a single truth. Seferis's "Monologue," not unlike Papadopoulos's speeches, internalized rather than eradicated confusion. A similar dynamic is evident in the poetry of the postwar poets. Monologism, not dialogism, is the primary discursive model for these writers too. The fact that writers of such different ideological persuasions rely on a similar discursive style, no matter how varied its forms, raises some pertinent questions: What do authoritarian, disinterested, and engaged writing have in common? And, even more problematic, how is writing in the name of resistance sometimes collusive with the discourses it challenges?[51]

Eighteen Texts (ET), the first collection of new texts to appear after preventive censorship was lifted, was a testing ground for writers and therefore provides an interesting place to examine such questions of resistance and complicity. Writing and censorship are explicitly connected, as the prologue claimed: "In presenting original literary works for the first time in three years, we are contributing to an attempt to focus again on the problem of the Greek writer under present-day conditions" (*ET* 1972, vii). The critic D. N. Maronitis provides an excellent grounding for such a project by focusing on the discursive styles employed by writers in this collection of poetry, short stories, and critical essays: "All the texts, to different degrees and in their own way, fluctuate . . . between the literal and the allegorical, even when they attempt to get around this asphyxiating dilemma. By literal, I mean here the open (partial or complete) reference to the then hegemonic conditions; by allegory, I mean any metaphorical way of revealing these conditions. In some texts the literal prevails; in others, allegory; in others, language stares disbelievingly in both directions; but everywhere the mixture is recognizable" (1984e, 37). As examples of the literal, he mentions direct references to the dictatorship: Manolis Anagnostakis's "Ο στόχος" (The target) and Takis Sinopoulos's "Νύχτες" (Nights). As examples of allegory he singles out those stories that are set under authoritarian regimes in Latin American countries, such as Rodis Roufos's "Ο υποψήφιος" (The candidate) and T. D. Frangopoulos's "Ελ προκουρα-δόρ" (El procurador), and those stories that take place in anonymous but oppressive conditions, such as Thanasis Valtinos's "The Plaster Cast" and Seferis's poem "The Cats of St. Nicholas," which tells the story of a promontory on Cyprus infested with poisonous snakes.

But to think about the relation between Seferis's use of allegory, Anagnostakis's preference for the literal, and the monologism of authoritarianism more generally, it is necessary to complicate our understanding of figurative language. What has been left out of Maronitis's schema is the figurativeness of the literal, something I have already mentioned with

[51] The work of the Frankfurt school critic Theodor Adorno raises a similar set of questions with regard to the oppositional art of Sartre and Brecht (Eagleton 1990, 350; Jameson 1990, 187–88).

reference to Papadopoulos's rhetoric. The allegorical and the literal are not opposites but implicated in each other. As Gérard Genette once wrote, the literal is the "zero figure" because its existence "shows that the language of rhetoric is sufficiently saturated with figures for an empty square to designate a full meaning" (1982, 47). It is this reliance of the figural on the literal, and vice versa, that is unacceptable to Papadopoulos, Seferis, and Anagnostakis—for vastly different reasons, of course. Each writer in *Eighteen Texts* undoes the figurativeness of the figure so that a literal statement about the role of the writer under an authoritarian regime surfaces. In my readings of Seferis's and Anagnostakis's poems in this collection I explore why one would want to believe in the literal, why this is not possible, and what results this impossibility produces. The emptying of allegory of its other world in Seferis's "Cats of St. Nicholas" suggests that change is not possible and that neither the poet nor the poem can do anything about it; the explicit rejection of rhetoric in Anagnostakis's "Target" attempts to make words into revolutionary acts and give the poet political power. In each text the exclusionary tactics of telling the truth are reminiscent of the impasse Seferis and Tsatsos reached: to be a writer means to take a stand, and to take a stand means to exclude other positions in favor of one's own.

Seferis's poem is an eloquent meditation on the role of the poet in troubled times. It begins with a quotation from Aeschylus's *Agamemnon* in which the chorus foreshadows the fall of the house of Atreus. Nothing has happened yet,[52] but the air is pregnant with inevitable murder:

> Τον δ' άνευ λύρας όμως υμνωδεί
> θρήνον Ερινύος
> αυτοδίδακτος έσωθεν
> θυμός, ου το παν έχων
> ελπίδος φίλον θράσος.
> (*ET* 1970, 13)

> But deep inside me sings
> the fury's lyreless threnody:
> my heart, self-taught, has lost
> the precious confidence of hope.
> (1972, 1)

This introduction of despair in terms of the loss of hope is reiterated in the images of a deserted beach on Christmas, a day usually associated with hope and celebration, and of Cyprus, now threatened by extinction. The

[52] Although as Katerina Krikos-Davis points out, "The hero has already been persuaded by Clytaemnestra to tread on the sacred carpets—an act of hubris which will justify his downfall" (1984, 235).

poet and the captain, who, according to the author's note, are one and the
same, navigate between these two extreme states of mind. The question
that haunts this poem, a recurrent one for Seferis, is whether extremes—
despair and hope, ancient and modern, domestic and public, poetry and
politics—can interpenetrate or whether they are destined to remain apart.
His monologic answer is consistently the latter. Here, as in an earlier poem
in which hands reach into the past and return mutilated—"τα χέρια μου
χάνονται και με πλησιάζουν ακρωτηριασμένα" (My hands disappear and
come toward me mutilated) (1981, 6–7)—ancient and modern worlds are
cut off from each other. We moderns are merely the poor relatives of the
ancients, scrambling for "alms from another time":

Χτύπησε η καμπάνα του καραβιού
σαν τη μονέδα πολιτείας που χάθηκε
κι ήρθε να ζωντανέψει πέφτοντας
αλλοτινές ελεημοσύνες.

(14)

The ship's bell struck
like a coin from some city that disappeared
coming to revive in the mind, as it falls,
alms from another time.

(2)

In an allegory we might expect worlds, domains, and disciplines to
remain distinct. An allegory traditionally is a self-contained world. But in
this case, the self-contained nature of allegory is challenged. The literal
world, which usually remains outside the bounds of the poem, is brought
in and compared with the allegorical world. At first the allegorical world
and the present world in which the poem is being written are given equal
weight: while the captain recalls the heroic cats that gave their name to the
Cape of Cats, the poet remembers his own domestic cats. The poet / captain
at sea and the poet / captain at home both keep their course. But then it
becomes apparent that the allegory does not teach us anything; an impo-
tent domesticity begins to take over. The tolling bell only brings the poem's
protagonist back, as Keats would have it, to his "sole self";[53] the "άλλος,"
the otherness, implicit in the etymology of the word *allegory*, is effaced. The
present apathy of the cats on the poet's hearth, who in the face of death do
nothing, occludes the older, active resistance of the cats who fight in the
captain's story:

[53] "Forlorn! the very word is like a bell / to toll me back from thee to my sole self! / Adieu!
the fancy cannot cheat so well / As she is fam'd to do" (Keats 1959, 207).

'Ήτανε θαύμα να τις βλέπεις, λένε,
άλλη κουτσή, κι άλλη στραβή, την άλλη
χωρίς μύτη, χωρίς αυτί, προβιά κουρέλι.
'Έτσι με τέσσερεις καμπάνες την ημέρα
πέρασαν μήνες, χρόνια, καιροί κι άλλοι καιροί.
'Αγρια πεισματικές και πάντα λαβωμένες
ξολόθρεψαν τα φίδια μα στο τέλος
χαθήκανε· δεν άντεξαν τόσο φαρμάκι.
Ωσάν καράβι καταποντισμένο
τίποτε δεν άφησαν στον αφρό
μήτε νιαούρισμα, μήτε καμπάνα.
Γραμμή!
    (15)

They say it was a wonderful thing to see them,
some lame, some twisted, others missing
a nose, an ear, their hides in shreds.
So too the sound of four bells a day
months went by, years, season after season.
Wildly obstinate, always wounded,
they annihilated the snakes; but in the end they disappeared:
they just couldn't take in that much poison.
Like a sunken ship
they didn't leave a thing behind them on the surface:
no meow, no bell even.
Steady as you go!
    (2–3)

The mixture of hope and despair with which the poem began gives way to the latter: Aphrodite, the memory of Cyprus's glorious past, disappears—the Greek word for foam or froth, αφρός, in the phrase δεν άφησαν τίποτε στον αφρό (in Edmund Keeley's translation for *ET* "they didn't leave a thing behind them on the surface," but literally, "they left nothing in the froth") refers to Aphrodite, whose name means the one sprung from froth. Cyprus without the cats is doomed to die of the poison; there is not even a bell that might have reminded us of those other worlds in other times. The captain interrupts his story to keep the boat on course, "Γραμμή!" (Steady as you go!), and this abrupt return to the present closes the story and the poem:

. . . Τι να σου κάνουν οι ταλαίπωρες
παλεύοντας και πίνοντας μέρα και νύχτα
το αίμα το φαρμακερό των ερπετών.

Αιώνες φαρμάκι· γενιές φαρμάκι."
"Γραμμή!" αντιλάλησε αδιάφορος ο τιμονιέρης.

(15)

. . . What could the poor devils do,
fighting like that day and night, drinking in
the poisonous blood of those reptiles?
Centuries of poison; generations of poison."
"Steady as you go," echoed the indifferent helmsman.

(3)

Seferis's final question is both What is the use of fighting? and What good
does it do to invoke fighting; where does such an allegory get us? And his
answer is—surprisingly, if we are still remembering the way his name is
identified with the resistance—"nowhere." We are where we began with
the domestic cat watching death, doing nothing: "Φαίνεται ο κάβο-Γάτο . . ."
(There's the Cape of Cats . . .).

Although the standard reading of this poem is that the tale of the cats of
St. Nicholas is an allegory referring to the Greek people, who stoically
suffer the poison of authoritarian rule (Maronitis 1984e; Krikos-Davis
1984), it can also be read as the failure of that very allegory. The other
world the allegory relies on, the cats on the promontory, is gone. In fact the
title, which recalls this world, "The Cats of St. Nicholas," is oddly out of
place, a relic from a bygone era when allegory functioned properly. The
poem's conclusion suggests that the fighting cats have been subsumed by
the passive vigilance of the poet's own domestic cat, Ramazan. The poet,
the captain, the helmsman, and the passenger stand by and watch. There is
no alternative, no choice, no dialogue, just indifferent echoes. The poem
suggests the failure of allegory, of writing, to do anything, and that failure
seems to be underscored by the date "5 February 1969" at the end, referring to a time when writers chose to keep silent. Though the poem is
usually read as an epitaph for the cats, it is also possible to read the title as
an epitaph for the poem itself, for the possibility of an allegory that would
offer us other alternatives. Like an epitaph, the title stands for that which is
no longer there, prompting us to step back and wonder whether *Eighteen
Texts*, in the name of Seferis, might also be read under the sign of Ramazan,
the cat who stayed at home.

If in Seferis's poem the undoing of allegory led to despair, in Nora Anagnostaki's essay, Takis Sinopoulos's and Manolis Anagnostakis's poems,
and Thanasis Valtinos's short story in *Eighteen Texts* the rejection of rhetoric
is meant to empower the writer. Rhetoric, which for Seferis ideally would
offer an escape, is, for the writers of the postwar generations, the root of the

problem. But just as Seferis's poem about the failure of allegory relied on allegory, so the postwar poets' rejection of rhetoric is not pure. In their writing the literal, or the zero figure as Genette called it, relies on the figurative for its force. Anagnostakis's series of poems "The Target" (is a particularly subtle exploration of this dynamic. Although his and Seferis's poems have different goals, it is interesting to chart some of the similar techniques they have for achieving them. Both espouse a monologic mode of telling the truth.

To address the rejection of figurative language in the work of this poet from the first postwar generation I need, however, to go back to the attempt on the part of these "engaged" writers to communicate subversive messages within the horizon of "silence." During the three-year silence there was much reference to a mute language among these writers, but *Eighteen Texts* marks a different stage in this debate; for as Nora Anagnostaki's essay "Μια μαρτυρία" (A testimony) shows, with preventive censorship lifted, it was possible to talk about not talking. Drawing on her three years' worth of notebooks, she outlines her search for a sparser language "stripped of allegory, symbol, satire, myth" (*ET* 1970, 80; 1972, 64) and insists that the only poetry that can survive under repressive conditions is the poetry of gestures. She constantly chastises herself for having to use words: "I paid dearly for these false loans" (64). In her "language of gestures," as in Ritsos's Χειρονομίες (Gestures) (1972), a volume of poems he wrote during the same time, real acts such as Panagoulis's attempted assassination of Papadopoulos, are posed as the alternative to figurative language.[54] This rejection of metaphor is related both to Papadopoulos's flagrant use of it and to a Barthian sense that a truly revolutionary language would "act the things."[55] Anagnostaki stresses that poetic devices that once enriched, now smother, expression (*ET* 1970, 80; 1972, 64), as with

[54] Many of Ritsos's poems of this period read like lists of real acts:

> ... Μια γυναίκα βγήκε απ' το 'να σπίτι. Μπήκε στ' άλλο.
> Ο τοίχος κίτρινος, νωπός, με πεσμένους σοβάδες.
> 'Ενα κλουβί με καναρίνι στο παράθυρο του πεθαμένου.

(1972, 60)

> ... A woman got out of one house to enter another.
> The wall yellow and wet, its paint peeling off.
> A cage with a canary in the dead man's window.

(1974, 145)

[55] In Roland Barthes's formulation, inasmuch as acting the things is impossible, a second-order language is constructed which "acts the names." This second-order language is to the primary language what a gesture is to an act (1973, 146). Though Barthes's *Mythologies*, in which he discusses this, was not translated into Greek until 1979, it was read by many in French under the dictatorship. *Writing Degree Zero* and *Criticism and Truth* did however come out in Greek in 1971 and 1972 respectively. See the special issue of *Diavazo* on Barthes (Petridou 1984, 44) for a bibliography of his works in Greek.

one's own papers after the censors had read them: "You take them back, and suddenly you loathe them."[56] But also, using metaphor, allegory, and other such devices, even sparingly, would distance their texts from the primary language, from the acts themselves.[57] Sinopoulos's Το χρονικό (Chronicle), written during the dictatorship, highlights his desire for language to get as close to an actual act as possible. If his poem cannot level the prison as he hoped in Πέτρες (Stones) (1972, 15), then it can at least record events faithfully: "Words, one at a time, as naked and unbiased as you can make them" (1975, 15).[58] This is the context in which Anagnostakis in his series "The Target" in *Eighteen Texts* rails on metaphor.

His "Στο παιδί μου" (To my child) explains his generation's "target," namely that poetry finally come clean and say what it means without the aid of allegory and metaphor:

Στο παιδί μου δεν άρεσαν ποτέ τα παραμύθια

Και του μιλούσανε για Δράκους και για το πιστό σκυλί
Για τα ταξίδια της Πεντάμορφης και για τον άγριο λύκο

Μα στο παιδί δεν άρεσαν ποτέ τα παραμύθια

Τώρα, τα βράδυα, κάθομαι και του μιλώ
Λέω το σκύλο σκύλο, το λύκο λύκο, το σκοτάδι σκοτάδι,
Του δείχνω με το χέρι τους κακούς, του μαθαίνω
Ονόματα σαν προσευχές, του τραγουδώ τους νεκρούς μας.

Α, φτάνει πια! Πρέπει να λέμε την αλήθεια στα παιδιά.

(*ET* 1970, 122)

[56] This is the comment the lawyer George Mangakis made when he explained how in prison he grew to hate his own writing that had been tarnished by the censors (1984, 33).

[57] The reasons for their rejection of metaphor seem similar to those underlying the lack of metaphor in the poetry of the Cuban resistance poet Nicolás Guillén. Keith Ellis analyses Guillén's poetry in the wake of its dismissal by other critics as "propaganda." Ellis argues that poetry by definition does not have to employ metaphor; for this is merely one local definition posited more than two thousand years ago by Aristotle. "In fact," Ellis writes, "metaphor has achieved so much prestige among certain groups in our century as to prompt a tendency among those groups to regard as 'anti-poetry' manifestations of poetry in which its suzerainty is not apparent" (Ellis 1983, 48; cited in B. Harlow 1987, 50).

[58] Kimon Friar in his introduction to a collection of poems by Sinopoulos (1979), which contained poems from the same period as *Eighteen Texts*, discusses more generally the trend away from lyricism in the 1960s and 1970s, singling out Eleni Vakalo's book Πριν από το λυρισμό (Before lyricism) and Mando Aravandinou's collections entitled simply Γραφή Α, Β, Γ (Writing 1, 2, 3), but instead of relating this shift to the dictatorship, he connects it to trends in contemporary French poetry and, I think, misses a crucial point: the poets of the first postwar generation, in the tradition of Ritsos and Kostas Varnalis, were consciously trying to fashion a revolutionary language (xlii).

My child never liked fairy tales

yet they told him about Dragons and the faithful dog,
about Sleeping Beauty's travels and about the wild wolf,

but the child never did like fairy tales.

Now, in the evenings, I sit and talk to him,
I call the dog dog, the wolf wolf, the darkness darkness,
I point out the bad people with my hand, I teach him
names like prayers, I sing to him about our dead.

Oh, enough of this! We have to tell children the truth.
                                    (1972, 105)

But both his and his generation's sparse, more direct language often relies on the figures it rejects. It is the rhetorical repetition of the phrase "My child never liked fairy tales" that, for example, gives this poem much of its force.[59] It is this tension that is in many ways the topic of Anagnostakis's whole series, and it therefore bears looking at in more depth.

"The Target" begins by addressing what I shall call the "Seferis" position. Though Anagnostakis's speaker may be explicitly attacking those writers of the generation of the 1930s such as Karandonis who published their work in pro-regime publications, there is room for another reading, one that includes Seferis as an interlocutor. Rather than view poetry as helpless and inefficient in the face of the tanks, or too pure or sacred, Anagnostakis's speaker enlists poetry for his cause, as a "means," a "pack mule." Aware that he is taking an unpopular stance, he anticipates his interlocutor's response:

> Προδίδετε πάλι την Ποίηση, θα μου πεις,
> Την ιερότερη εκδήλωση του Ανθρώπου
> Την χρησιμοποιείτε πάλι ως μέσον, υποζύγιον
> Των σκοτεινών επιδιώξεών σας
> Εν πλήρει γνώσει της ζημιάς που προκαλείτε
> Με το παράδειγμά σας στους νεωτέρους.
>   (ET 1970, 121)

> You're betraying Poetry again, you'll say,
> the most sacred expression Man has,
> using it again as a means,
> pack mule to your dark pursuits,

---

[59] For a discussion of Anagnostakis's use of repetition, see Frantzi 1993.

knowing full well the damage your example
will inflict on the young.
(1972, 104)

He then defends his position by stating that poetry always has a cause,
so one might as well make it explicit. His reference to international markets and silence makes it all the more possible that he is also addressing
Seferis:

Το τι *δεν* πρόδωσες *εσύ* να μου πεις
Εσύ κι οι όμοιοί σου, χρόνια και χρόνια,
Ένα προς ένα τα υπάρχοντά σας ξεπουλώντας
Στις διεθνείς αγορές και τα λαϊκά παζάρια
Και μείνατε χωρίς μάτια για να βλέπετε, χωρίς αυτιά
Ν' ακούτε, με σφραγισμένα στόματα και δε μιλάτε.
Για ποια ανθρώπινα ιερά μάς εγκαλείτε;
(121)

Just tell me what *you* have not betrayed,
you and those like you, years on end,
selling off your belongings one by one
in international markets and common bazaars,
left now without eyes to see, ears to hear,
and lips sealed so you can't talk.
What sacred human expression are you preaching about?
(104)

Again anticipating the criticism he will receive, he admits "Ξέρω: κηρύγματα και ρητορείες πάλι, θα πεις" (I know: sermons and speeches again,
you'll say) only to turn around and use this statement to his own ends, "'Ε
ναι λοιπόν! Κηρύγματα και ρητορείες" (All right, yes then! Sermons and
speeches) (104). If the rhetoric of sermons and speeches is unavoidable, he
will enlist it for his own purposes. He, for example, will use metaphor to
get rid of metaphor:

Σαν *πρόκες* πρέπει να καρφώνονται οι λέξεις.
Να μην τις παίρνει ο άνεμος.
(121)

Words ought to be hammered in like *nails*.
So the wind won't take them away.
(104)

This metaphor "like nails" does not distance language from acts but tries to turn words into acts. As the epilogue of the series admits, even if poetry rarely succeeds in its revolutionary aims, it should not give up trying:

"Γιατί" όπως πολύ σωστά είπε κάποτε κι ο φίλος μου ο Τίτος,
"Κανένας στίχος σήμερα δεν κινητοποιεί τις μάζες
Κανένας στίχος σήμερα δεν ανατρέπει καθεστώτα"

'Εστω.
Ανάπηρος, δείξε τα χέρια σου. Κρίνε για να κριθείς.
(133)

"Because," as my friend Titos rightly said once,[60]
"No verse today will mobilize the masses,
No verse today will overthrow regimes."

So be it.
Disabled, show your hands. Judge so that you may be judged.
(116)

The word στίχος here, meaning a verse or line of poetry, echoes the title of the series Στόχος, meaning the target. Each line of the poem is in the service of resistance.

Anagnostakis's ploy of using a rhetorical figure to undo a figure, a metaphorical nail to fasten his words, is similar to Valtinos's parodic attack in his short story in which he reads Papadopoulos's famous metaphor of Greece "as a patient in a cast" literally. Both enlist metaphors ironically to reveal the literal state of affairs. Narrated as a monologue from the position of the patient in the cast,[61] Valtinos's story uses Papadopoulos's metaphor to draw opposite conclusions: the cast is not for healing but for killing Greece. And yet his scathing critique of Papadopoulos's metaphor relies on the trope of irony. This undoing of metaphor is compounded throughout the story by puns. The same term χειριστής refers to the doctor who is examining the patient and the man who wielded the pneumatic drill that originally crushed him. The word πλάκες refers both to the X rays meant to

[60] This is a reference to Titos Patrikios, an important poet of the first postwar generation who did not participate in *Eighteen Texts* because, like many Greek intellectuals, he had left the country. The line Anagnostakis cites is from Patrikios's "Στίχοι, 2" (Verses, 2) in Μαθητεία (Apprenticeship) (1963). Patrikios himself revisits this line in a later poem "Στίχοι, 3" (Verses, 3) in Αντικριστοί καθρέφτες (Facing mirrors) (1988). See also his collection written under the dictatorship Προαιρετική στάση (Voluntary stance) (1974).

[61] Symptomatically the short stories in *Eighteen Texts* are almost all monologues; they have few of the dialogic components that Bakhtin attributes to the novel.

help the doctor determine the problem and to the cement paving stones churned up by the drill, causing the patient to fall and break his bones in the first place. And the word λεκάνη stands for the basin full of plaster and the patient's broken pelvis. The destructive meaning of each pun wins out: it is ultimately from this basin that the doctor takes the final handful of plaster and fills the patient's mouth, suffocating him and ending the story abruptly:

'Ενοιωσα το στόμα μου να γεμίζει από την πηχτή υδαρή μάζα του γύψου. Η γεύση του δεν ήταν εντελώς δυσάρεστη, αλλά είχα κιόλας αρχίσει να ασφυκτιώ. (*ET* 1970, 180)

I felt my mouth fill with the thick wet mass of plaster. The taste was not completely unpleasant, but I had already begun to suffocate. (*ET* 1972, 159)

The erasure of the figurative in the name of the literal can only be achieved with the assistance of rhetoric.

In his introduction to the English translation of *Eighteen Texts*, Stratis Haviaras admits that for all their desire to get rid of rhetoric, the writers of the first postwar generation were obliged, in the end, to use allegory, symbols, and myths. He insists, however, that their emphasis on gestures as literal alters the impact of figures in their writing (1972, xviii). I would add that this emphasis even seems to determine to a certain extent which figures they use. Irony and parody, not allegory, are the dominant tropes of the postwar generation. Although, at one level, Valtinos's story, like Seferis's poem, offers a pessimistic view of what the private citizen can achieve under repressive conditions, his use of parody changes the significance of this conclusion. The writer is actively criticizing the regime, rather than passively standing by. Valtinos's parody is more akin to Anagnostakis's ironic use of metaphor than to Seferis's allegory. There seems, roughly, to be a shift of emphasis in the writing of the first postwar generation, from allegory to parody, that is, from a concern with similarity to a concern with difference.[62] Whereas allegory begins with something different and shows how it is the same—the situation in Cyprus in the sixteenth century is *like* the present situation in Greece—parody relies on

---

[62] The historian Hayden White, in his *Tropics of Discourse*, analyzes such a shift in more complex terms. He traces a progression from metaphor to metonymy to synecdoche to irony in theoretical works as diverse as Marx's *Capital*, Freud's *Interpretation of Dreams*, and Piaget's *The Child and Reality*. His point is that in the Western tradition, "the archetypal plot of discursive formations appears to require that the narrative 'I' of the discourse move from an original metaphorical characterization of a domain of experience, through metonymic deconstructions of its elements, to synecdochic representations of the relations between its superficial attributes and its presumed essence, to, finally, a representation of whatever contrasts or oppositions can legitimately be discerned in the totalities identified in the third phase of discursive representation" (1978, 5).

showing how something that is presented as the same could be understood as different: the rhetoric "Seferis" accuses the poet of using in Anagnostakis's poem is used to very different ends, the cast in Valtinos's story too has a different function, or if we go back to my earlier example of parody, the name "Papadopoulos" is given a different meaning, cookie brand rather than dictator.

The parodic undoing of metaphor in the name of a different political reality has a different impact than Seferis's emptying of allegory which signals defeat. But ultimately, although the postwar writers expect their writing, unlike Seferis's, to affect politics, their fear of contamination in the other direction—that is, that their poetry might be sullied by the regime's use of metaphor—is in keeping with Seferis's desire to keep different discourses separate. I am not arguing that *Eighteen Texts* is monologic; seen in the wider context of the resistance criticism and other writing that followed such as *New Texts* and the journal Συνέχεια (Continuity), it also employed certain dialogic tactics. The first issue of *Continuity* stated outright that it intended to be a forum for polycriticism, that is, the publication of critiques by different people about the same text. This term *polycriticism* was then used as the name of a section in each ensuing issue. "Polycriticism has the ambitions of counterpoint and polyphony, implicit and explicit dialogue . . ." (Argiriou, Kotzias, and Maronitis 1973, 1:2). But still this emphasis on dialogue was in the service of truth and clarity: "*Continuity* will attempt to avoid rampant incoherence." The postwar writers took on the hermeneutic legacy of the 1930s. Though disagreeing with Seferis that there was nothing to do, the despondency of not being able to express themselves clearly in times of confusion prevails.

The more vexing problem, though, is that a revolutionary discourse may have the same pretensions to clarity as the dominant discourse it attacks. Established writers' desire to avoid confusion is uncomfortably close to the dictator's own agenda. Both tout clarity as their goal. Like Papadopoulos's speeches, the prologue to *New Texts*, a resistance collection that followed *Eighteen Texts*, takes confusion as its primary enemy: "With all the unprecedented maltreatment words have suffered these past few years, with all the attempts to confuse and obscure meanings, our reading public still has not ceased to thirst for truth" (1971a, 9). Although writers were very aware of how the dictator was disguising a metaphor for the literal truth, they were not always so self-conscious about the implications of their own plea for clarity. What is the difference between Papadopoulos saying that book titles and contents must fit perfectly and the authors of *Eighteen Texts* persistently calling for literal language? Both, in compliance with Barthes's definition of myth, masquerade a second-order language as a primary one, gestures as acts, names as things. Is it simply that Papadopoulos's desire for the perfect matching of signifiers and signifieds, for getting past word play to the real act, is enforced by law and backed up by tanks, whereas that of the oppositional authors of *Eighteen Texts* is not? Perhaps, as Barthes aptly suggests, myth on the left and myth on the right differ more in intention and effectiveness than in strategy (1973, 148).[63]

My point in raising such questions is not to dismiss Seferis's or Anagnostakis's resistance poetics; for their statements and texts ultimately did have a profound effect. It is rather to illustrate the limits of the representational model of language they rely on and to help bring into focus the nature of an alternative resistance poetics that works on radically different assumptions about the truthfulness or clarity of poetry. By focusing on the monologic tendency of Modern Greek poetry, I can ask whether there might be another response to censorship, one that does not view language as one-way street, in which one either effaces difference in the name of truth as Papadopoulos did or uncovers difference in the name of another truth as Seferis, Anagnostakis, Sinopoulos, and Valtinos did. Might there be a mode that actually managed to sustain ambivalence? It is this more performative paradigm of language with its Lyotardian negotiation of alternative truths which I now want to introduce through a reading of the songs of Dionysis Savvopoulos.

Dionysis Savvopoulos's Plastic Flag

The poets of the generation of the 1970s were not as directly affected by Seferis's legacy as those I have just discussed. They were not sure that the signifier corresponded to a signified, that the book and its contents, the word *dog* and the dog itself, were invariably bound to each other. As a generation they had not known these real words their elders seem to remember nostalgically; the only words they knew were the "loaned words" Anagnostaki deplored. Their poems are more at home with uncertainty and incoherency; their flag was Savvopoulos's plastic flag, which meant both everything and nothing. Whereas the poetry of Seferis and Anagnostakis was quite explicit about their different positions on the role of the writer under the dictatorship, the poetry of the younger generation was challenging the possibility of taking a stand, any stand at all. If what one wanted to say and what one said were severed from one another by censorship, neither Seferis's solution to step back and wait nor Anagnostakis's decision to fight to keep words attached to their meanings seemed suffi-

---

[63] For another example of how oppositional positions employ similar rhetoric, recall my discussion of paralogy as subversive of national interests under the Metaxas dictatorship; Tsatsos, Seferis, and other poets of the generation of the 1930s as well as the regime all espoused "Greekness."

cient. These modes of retreat and resistance seemed to rest on an older aesthetic. The younger poets were not interested in opposing poetry to the paralogism of the times but rather in allowing poetry to participate in it. The ramifications will become clearer, but here I merely want to introduce this response as a valid form of resistance to censorship not to be immediately dismissed as apolitical.

The difference between this generation of poets and the older, more established poets is paralleled in the relation between a younger popular composer and songwriter, Savvopoulos, and his elder, Mikis Theodorakis. Theodorakis's compositions exhibit their commitment to a cause; his younger colleague's work challenges clear-cut distinctions. It is a well-known fact that Theodorakis brought Greek poetry to the Greek people. His popular settings of poems by Seferis, Ritsos, and Elytis, among others, made these poets known to a much larger audience than before, and whatever their authors had intended, these poets' works were politicized. To sing Seferis's poem " Ἄρνηση" (Denial) was suddenly a subversive act. Theodorakis's reworkings of poetry put poetry on the side of the resistance. Savvopoulos took a much less direct approach to undermining authoritarianism. His songs take parody beyond Anagnostakis's and Valtinos's inversions. Rather than attempting to right the wrong, they participate in the confusion. Instead of parodying the mixed messages of the times in order to dispel confusion, his songs suggest that, at least temporarily, one should absorb confusion into one's compositions. As in the alternative medical practice of homeopathy, the guiding principle is that that which is threatening can be used to strengthen the immune system. The very rhetorical figures dismissed in the name of clarity in *Eighteen Texts* are used by Savvopoulos in the service of the paralogical.

In his songs written between 1965 and 1975 he advocates a philosophy in which nothing is essentially true or real and anything can be appropriated to someone else's ends.[64] As he puts it in one popular song,

> Πολλά ήταν τα ψέματα που είπαμε ως εδώ
> ας πούμε και μι' αλήθεια κι ας πέσει στο γιαλό
> ο κόσμος είναι ζόρικος κι εμείς ασθενικοί
> και ό,τι πούμε το παίρνει η βουή
>
> σημαία από νάυλον υψώνουμε
> σημαία πλαστική
> ο κόσμος δεν έχει τίποτε να χάσει
> και τίποτε να βρει.
> (1983, 37)

---

[64] These songs are collected in Τα λόγια από τα τραγούδια (The words to the songs) (1983).

> We've told a lot of lies up until now
> let's try telling the truth, for what it's worth
> people are difficult and we're just weaklings
> everything we say gets caught up in the clamor
>
> we're raising a nylon flag
> a plastic flag
> People have nothing to lose
> and nothing to win.

Even if we cannot draw any direct connection between Savvopoulos's "weaklings" (ασθενικοί) and Papadopoulos's patronizing address to the foreign press ("Do not forget however, gentlemen, that we find ourselves in front of a patient [ασθενούς])," we can still see that here Savvopoulos is referring to Greece's infirmity, which is one of the dictator's favorite themes. But whereas Valtinos's story is explicitly from the point of view of the patient/weakling caught in the cast of Papadopoulos's metaphor, Savvopoulos's song is less clear about its origins. On the one hand, it seems to be written from a similar position. On the other hand, the military drums and march beat accompanying the song suggest another interpretation, that these are the words of Papadopoulos in defeat. Like the nylon flag, which unlike its cloth predecessor, is plastic and disposable, words no longer can sustain their meaning or stand for one thing. Everything gets caught up in the clamor and tossed about. Savvopoulos's insistence on the plasticness of the flag, with its connotations of commodification and alienation, provides a striking contrast with the usual equation of the flag and authenticity. In this one turn of phrase he manages to undo all sorts of assumptions about language, poetry, and the nation.

In his song "Ολαρία" (Olaria), Savvopoulos parodies the idea that anything is clear-cut. He offers a carnivalesque utopia that celebrates confusion:

> ολαρία ολαρά
> γύρω γύρω τα παιδιά
> ο μαρκήσιος ντε σαντ μ' ένα χίπυ
> ο φονιάς με το θύμα αγκαλιά . . .
>
> (1983, 53)

> olaria olara
> the kids in a circle
> the Marquis de Sade and a hippy
> the murderer and the victim embrace . . .

Here, parody does not invert power relations once and for all, as it did in
Valtinos's story, but keeps them in constant motion. Victim and victor are
irrevocably confused. Our role is neither to passively watch like Seferis nor
to fight on the front line like Anagnostakis but rather to play both positions
simultaneously: the "patient" and the "doctor," the victim and the victor.
In his song "Το θηρίο" (The beast), which ends abruptly, cut off midsen-
tence by censorship, the speaker is both the beast and master of the beast.
The song begins with the speaker as beast:

> Στο χωριό στην επαρχία
> βγήκα για περιοδεία
> και χορεύω σα θηρίο
> που του πρέπει παραθείο
> (1983, 23)

> In the village on the outskirts
> I went for a walk
> and I am dancing like a beast
> which should be put away.

But then the speaker abruptly addresses the beast:

> Τι θα γίνει βρε θηρίο
> του διαόλου συνεργείο
> σκουριασμένο μου γρανάζι
> λεωφορείο που νυστάζει

> What's going to happen, beast
> machination of the devil
> my rusty cogwheel
> a bus which is sleepy

And finally concludes by suggesting that everyone is implicated in everything; it is impossible to be pure:

> τέτοιο κτήνος που σε βρήκα
> σου πληρώνω και το ΙΚΑ

> έγραψα μιαν ιστορία
> να την πω στη γαλαρία
> πριν τελειώσει η ιστορία
> ήρθε η λογοκρισί - - -
> (23)

> Such a beast that's you
> I even pay your state health insurance.
>
> I wrote a story
> to tell the crowds
> but before I was done
> censorship had c - - -

Whereas in Valtinos's parody censorship was forced on the patient from outside, here it is unclear who is responsible. The "I" is both the master and the slave. There is no clear sense that censorship comes from the outside. The power of the state and the power of the subject are inextricably implicated in each other. Nothing is essentially good or evil.

In another song, when Savvopoulos invokes the mascot of the paralogical, the national hero Karaghiozis,[65] who can dream himself out of any tight spot, it is not as some transcendental sign of emancipation but again as a sign of indecision, that which simultaneously saves and destroys us:

> κείνο που με τρώει κείνο που με σώζει
> είναι που ονειρεύομαι σαν τον Καραγκιόζη
> ό,τι και να πω κάτι περισσεύει
> τρύπια ειν' η αγάπη μας και δεν μας προστατεύει . . .[66]
>
> that which bothers me is that which saves me
> is that I can dream like Karaghiozis
> whatever I say something is left over
> our love is full of holes and cannot protect us . . .

Whatever one sets out to say is inevitably undermined. Nothing is complete or monologic, something is always left over, and the fact that this something is never defined makes it all the more powerful.

Savvopoulos is useful in mapping out the cultural landscape of the late 1960s and early 1970s. Not only does a contrast between him and Theodorakis provide an analogy for the difference between the poetry of the younger generation and the older poets, but Savvopoulos himself was included in various anthologies as one of the poets of the generation of the 1970s, and his homeopathic use of the paralogical was a trademark of the poetry of many of his peers.[67] I have already discussed how Sinopoulos

[65] See Gourgouris 1988.
[66] This is the version sung on Savvopoulos's greatest hits record; a modified version can be found in the printed collection (1983, 80).
[67] On Savvopoulos as poet, see Steriadis 1977.

described Dalakoura as "baptized in the paralogical" and how Friar similarly describes Steriadis, another poet of this generation. Returning to Friar's description, it is clear that the paralogical is the absence of any logical connections, exactly what Seferis and Tsatsos resisted in their "Dialogue": "Vasilis Steriadis, who writes in a disjointed style much like our times are disjointed, sometimes using the technique of automatic writing, but more often with complete faith letting the stream of associations pull him so that one picture or thought brings the next without the intermediate logical connection ever being clear" (*Six Poets* 1971, 7). Such lack of logical connections is described in Yannis Kondos's poem "Μαγική εικόνα" (Magic picture), which is often quoted as a credo of this generation:[68]

> Άνοιξες την πόρτα και μετά
> άλλη και άλλη βρέθηκες
> στη μέση του μεγάλου τσίρκου
> στο κλουβί με τα λιοντάρια.
>
> Είπες· Θε μου, τι γυρεύω εδώ
> Εγώ πήγαινα στην τουαλέτα.
>   (in Anagnostaki 1977, 36)

> You opened the door and then
> another and another and found yourself
> in the middle of a great circus
> in the lion cage
>
> You said, oh my god, what am I doing here
> I was on my way to the loo.

Savvopoulos along with this whole generation of younger poets took advantage of the missing links that had threatened their elders. Their poetry metonymically replaces one image with another, setting up chains of signifiers whose relation to one another may be one of contiguity but which have no obvious connection to any particular signified. This idea of language as plastic, with signifiers that stand for many different things, is very different from, for example, the way the imaginary South American country "Boliguay" stands for Greece in *Eighteen Texts*. In the first case, meaning is indefinitely deferred; in the latter, it is fixed.

My point has been to move discussion of poetry under the dictatorship beyond the question of silence. I have tried to show how it was not simply a

[68] For a retrospective analysis of Kondos as paradigmatic and important poet of the generation of the 1970s, see Vayenas 1988, 165–72.

matter of whether or not one spoke out or published but, as Foucault suggests, of determining the different ways of not saying things, how those who can and cannot speak are distributed, which types of discourse are authorized and why (1980, 27). It is to the poets of the generation of the 1970s that I now turn.

2

Poetry, Politics, and the
Generation of the 1970s

Αντισταθείτε . . .
σ' όλους τους αδιάφορους και τους σοφούς
στους άλλους που κάνουνε το φίλο σας
ως και σε μένα, σε μένα ακόμα που σας ιστορώ αντισταθείτε.

Resist against . . .
everyone, the indifferent and the wise
the others who pretend to be your friend
even me, even me who is telling you to resist.
—Michalis Katsaros

The poets of the generation of the 1970s offered an alternative response
to censorship. Instead of trying to tell the truth in either the "disinterested"
manner of Seferis or the "engaged" manner of Anagnostakis, they introduced the confusion and misunderstandings of the times into the language
of their poetry. They did not reject the paralogical or the absurd as unnatural, as humanists like Seferis and Tsatsos did, or as inexpedient, as the
postwar poets and the regime did; nor did they begin from the nihilist
position that all language is paralogical and all meaning impossibly deferred. Instead these younger poets, who published their first collections
during the dictatorship (1967–74), engaged in new forms of textual resistance, strategically employing the paralogical to foreground the incon-
sistent behavior and mixed messages of the authoritarian regime.

The poetry of these younger poets demanded an expanded view of
politics. Informed by the breakdown between public and private spheres,
which was heralded both by the feminist movement, with its slogan The
Personal Is Political, and by the mass media,[1] the poetry of the generation
of the 1970s occupies a realm in which anything is potentially political. For
the most part aligned with the Left, these poets radically challenged what
they perceived to be the narrow conception of politics in the work of their
elders. For them, sexual oppression or the rift between high and low culture became as valid a topic for resistance poetry as class conflict or over-
throwing an authoritarian regime. To appropriate Stuart Hall's analysis of

[1] News, for example, could enter the private sphere of the family living room with one flick
of the television switch. See Peponis 1971 and 1974 on the impact of mass media from the
Greek perspective.

the new forms of politics that have emerged in Britain in recent decades, in Greek society since the 1960s, "there has been a proliferation of new points of antagonism, new social movements of resistance organised around them and, consequently, a generalisation of 'politics' to spheres which hitherto the Left assumed to be apolitical; a politics of the family, of health, of food, of sexuality, of the body" (1988, 28). Savvopoulos's songs illustrate this expanded definition of politics in which the questioning of traditional class hierarchies appears next to topsy-turvy sexual or religious relations. At one point in the song "Olaria," Hitler is found caressing Oliver Twist while the Virgin and Satan embrace each other (1983, 53).

Such scramblings, which implicate the political in the personal and vice versa, are a trademark of the poetry of this younger generation. The speaker, for example, in Lefteris Poulios's poem "Αμέρικαν μπαρ στην Αθήνα" (American bar in Athens) turns his own anxiety of influence into a much more general statement of disrespect. At the end of the poem he blithely invites his "grandfather," the revered Greek poet Kostis Palamas (1859–1943), on a late-night prowl to desecrate Greece's national monuments:

> Πάμε να κατουρήσουμε όλα τ' αγάλματα
> της Αθήνας· προσκυνώντας μονάχα του
> Ρήγα. Και να χωρίσουμε ο καθένας στο
> δρόμο του σαν παππούς κι εγγονός που
> βριστήκανε . . .
>
> (Poulios [1973] 1982, 22)

> Let's go piss on all the statues
> in Athens; paying homage only to
> Rigas.[2] And then each go
> our own way like a grandfather and grandson
> who have quarreled . . .

Poulios first politicizes Palamas by dragging him out of the realm of aesthetics into the streets of Athens, then personalizes him by describing their relationship as one of grandson to grandfather and their parting as a family quarrel. But the appearance of Palamas in this poem may, in one respect, be misleading. In their search for new modes of figuring the political, these younger poets, though deeply indebted to the use of the Greek language by Cavafy, Seferis, Anagnostakis, Sachtouris, and other Greek poets, usually look elsewhere for intellectual and spiritual mentors. In

[2] Rigas Pheraios is an important revolutionary hero from the War of Independence. The youth organization of the Communist Party of the Interior, with which many of these poets were involved, was founded in 1968 and named after him.

interviews, articles, and poems they frequently cite Jung, Lao-tzu, the American Beat Generation, and other foreign writers as sources for their perspectives on politics (Niarchos 1980; Belezinis 1975, 205–6). This poem by Poulios, for example (which I come back to later), is a rewriting of quintessentially American poems—tributes by Allen Ginsberg and Ezra Pound to the "grandfather" of the Beat poets, Walt Whitman—and has no formal connection to Palamas's poetry.

The poetry of the generation of the 1970s reflects the identity crisis in which Greece was embroiled at a time in which nationalist chauvinism and foreign dependency went hand in hand: ruled by a dictatorship that called itself a "Greece for Christian Greeks," the country continued to integrate itself into the networks of international capitalism with a steady flow of foreign imports and a regime supported by American politicians and the CIA.[3] The mixed messages, the articulation of these conflicting allegiances, were not limited to the colonels' speeches. Caught between two worlds, the poetry of the younger generation drew equally on the Greek literary tradition and American popular culture. But though the web of possible poetic references had expanded and cultural life was in many ways increasingly more international, the range of expression in writing was more circumscribed than it had been since the 1940s, the decade of the Metaxas dictatorship, the occupation, and the civil war. Poets who began writing under the dictatorship were faced with the strange predicament of having both more and less at hand than previous generations. The dictatorship, at least until 1973, was a time of relative prosperity, and more Greeks had access to more things. But it was also true that certain rights, especially the freedom of the press and the freedom to hold public meetings, had been drastically curtailed. The poetry of Veroniki Dalakoura, Natasa Hatzidaki, Jenny Mastoraki, Pavlina Pampoudi, Lefteris Poulios, Vasilis Steriadis, as well as others, exposes the peculiar interdependence of censorship—the discourse of deprivation—and consumerism and foreign influence—the discourse of abundance. Their poetry mimics and undermines the authority of the censors' scissors and rubber stamps while simultaneously criticizing and incorporating the abundance of commodity culture.

A poem "Θαλασσογραφία" (Seascape) by Natasa Hatzidaki illustrates some of the contradictions involved. First we are given a description that sounds like that of a quiz show announcer promising the allurements of the new consumer culture:

[3] The tension between the "Greek" and the foreign is a constituent element of Greek national identity in the modern era. On Greece and Europe, see Herzfeld 1987. The tension, though, was particularly acute—and acutely experienced—under the junta. As a cultural phenomenon, the junta in fact needs to be understood as an exasperation of this tension, a contradictory attempt to safeguard a Greek national identity more than ever before threatened by the internationalization of European and American life styles.

κι᾽ εδώ μπροστά
έχω ένα πυρίμαχο σπιτφάιαρ της τράιομφ
(in Panayiotou 1979, 270)

and here up front
I have a fiery Spitfire by Triumph

But the poem concludes accentuating the more sinister side of the times:

κι᾽ όλα λάμπουν σαν κατσαρόλες
μέσα στην αργή βράση των προβολέων.

all shining like cooking pots
in the slow boil of searchlights.

The last two lines counteract the effect of the earlier ones by first likening the car to an ordinary domestic image and then confusing both the external world of foreign imports and the domestic world of the kitchen "in the slow boil of searchlights." In Greek, moreover, the word προβολέας carries a double meaning, both "headlights" and "searchlights," suggesting that it is impossible to address the abundance of commodity culture without referring to the restrictions of being under the colonels' surveillance. This poem admits not only that the discourses of more and less are intimately related but that they are related through the domestic realm. While this chapter concentrates on the interrelations of the discourses of consumerism and censorship, it is impossible not to feel as well the pressure of a third discourse, feminism, the language that developed in Greece under and after the dictatorship for speaking about the political implications of sexual difference. This poem, as well as many others I discuss in the last two sections of this chapter, raise the issues of consumerism and censorship in terms of feminine sexuality. Although this triangle of concerns—consumerism, censorship, and feminism—is strictly linked, my discussion here focuses on the first two while providing the background for discussing in Chapter 3 the more complicated question of how all three are related.

My overarching concern in this chapter is with the subversion and transformation of the Modern Greek myth of poetry under the dictatorship, both as a national institution and as a lyric tradition. I turn first to the problematic construction of this group of poets as a generation, introducing the key concerns of their poetry (urban alienation, cosmopolitanism, consumerism, and censorship) through a discussion of its critical reception. My main interest, however, is in the various writing strategies these poets deploy for relating these discourses of urban life to one another, in particular consumerism and censorship. Critical discussions of poetry of the generation of the 1970s have placed much emphasis on the different *themes* these poets choose to write about—the city, Marilyn Monroe, the pinball machine, the gas station—but have said very little about their actual poetics, or *how* they write. What were the ways American culture, especially the Beat version, was incorporated into the Greek idiom in their poetry in a politicized fashion? and how did the visual and narrative preoccupation of pop culture, especially of comics and cinema, enable Greek poetry to move beyond its privileging of the oral tradition?[4]

The So-Called Generation of the 1970s

Poets who began writing under the dictatorship were marked by the peculiar fate of being inserted into literary history by critics before much of their work had been published. The two-and-a-half years of preventive censorship from April 1967 to November 1969 had blocked the publication of most of these young poets' work and set up great expectations for anything they might produce. By 1970 this new generation had already been christened and their style characterized. Their premature canonization led to many years of debate among poets and critics—a debate that continues to this day—over which poets belong in this generation and which styles, if any, distinguish their work from previous poetry. Four terms have been used to describe the poets born in the 1940s and early 1950s, and these four terms roughly correspond to three different views of poetry. The majority of critics who choose to describe these poets chronologically call them "η γενιά του '70" (the generation of the 1970s); those who group them thematically refer to them either as "η γενιά της αμφισβήτησης"

4 This focus leaves out poets who purposefully ignore urban landscapes and the claustrophobic internal spaces that occupy most of this generation's attention. Michalis Ghanas and Yiorgos Markopoulos of this generation, like Dinos Christianopoulos and Markos Meskos of the second postwar generation, describe life in the provincial towns and cities of Greece's periphery and draw heavily on natural imagery. Ghanas's poem "Η Ελλάδα που λες" (Greece, you say) is an excellent example of this other style (in Ziras 1979, 54). Ghanas's poem undoes Seferian poetics by working within them rather than by looking elsewhere for conceptual mentors as the more urban poets do. If, for Seferis, the memory of Greece's great history inflicts pain and existential angst—" 'Οπου και να ταξιδέψω η Ελλάδα με πληγώνει" (Wherever I travel Greece wounds me) (1981, 106–7)—for Ghanas, Greece in all her provincial poverty also has a healing power. As he writes in this poem, "She is not only a wound." Greece's salvation is found not in the statues and scattered relics of the ancient past but in the more mundane details of everyday life, the lazy coffee hour, the sheepfolds, the bitter wine. His poetic project is set on including details that Seferis leaves out, but rather than dismissing the Seferian pool of references altogether, he mixes them with images of life in the provincial towns and cities of Greece.

(the generation of protest)[5] or "η γενιά των γερανών και των φλίπερς" (the pinball generation);[6] and those who see them in relation to their immediate precursors refer to "η τρίτη μεταπολεμική γενιά" (the third postwar generation). A brief look at the origin of each term tells part of the story of how the poetry of this generation has been received by critics.

The generation of the 1970s is by far the most popular term, and its history reveals a welcome reciprocity: literary evaluation in this case is not a one-sided affair in which critics pronounce their judgments from on high and poets gratefully accept them from below. Vasilis Steriadis, an important poet of this generation, first invoked this term in 1970 in a review of the poetry of Lefteris Poulios, another key figure (Steriadis 1970a, 48).[7] He was referring specifically to a group who officially became the "six poets" when, in March of 1971, he, Katerina Anghelaki-Rooke, Dimitris Potamitis, Nana Isaïa, Lefteris Poulios, and Tasos Denegris published a collection of new works under the bland but, as far as the censors were concerned, unproblematic title *Six Poets*. Despite quibbles—the two women are now often considered to belong to the second postwar generation, and other poets such as Mastoraki, Kondos, Laina, and Pampoudi not included would later be considered accomplished members of the generation—this anthology signaled a new kind of poetry and introduced a new group of younger poets.

Around the same time there came out two other anthologies also edited by the poets themselves, Dimitris Iatropoulos's Αντι-ανθολογία (Anti-anthology) (1971) and Stefanos Bekatoros and Alekos Florakis's Η νέα γενιά (The new generation) (1971). All these anthologies were interesting not only for the quality and novelty of the verse but for their collective identity. The drawing on the front cover of *Six Poets* was telling: six heads floating and fading into one another. It suggested, in the spirit of Jung's collective unconscious, that these six imaginations were writing under the same cultural conditions and that one poem fed into and commented on the others. Many critics and poets were explicit about the collective nature of this new poetry. Iatropoulos, for example, in his *Anti-Anthology*, began with a collage of new poets' work entitled "Lernaian Hydra" in which he did not identify poems by author. In his prologue he explained how the

[5] This term αμφισβήτηση seems to be a translation from the French *contestation*. "Protest" is the closest one can get in English, though the reader should keep in mind that another connotation of the Greek term is that of doubt and questioning.

[6] Literally this phrase refers to the two types of coin-operated, mechanized games that first appeared in Greece in the 1960s: those imported from Italy in which one could pick up things with cranes (γερανοί) and those from America in which one hit balls with flippers (φλίπερς).

[7] In this book review Steriadis referred to Poulios as "a pretty good example of the poets of the as-yet-unformed generations of the 1960s and 70s." Critics immediately abbreviated Steriadis's formulation to the "generation of the 1970s."

new poetic forms demanded a new kind of anthology, one "which would connect the individual with the collective and make poetry a group testimony" (1971, 1).[8]

Lefteris Poulios, also involved in both *Six Poets* and the *Anti-Anthology*, was equally instrumental in baptizing the generation of the 1970s and in differentiating it from previous generations. In one poem he directed the whole generation to model their poetics on his:

> Γενιά μου ανάπηρη κοίτα σε μένα
> την κατάντια σου σα σε καθρέφτη· και
> χειρονόμα όπως εγώ· με δίχως χέρια
> δίχως ασπίδα δίχως αύριο.
>   (Poulios 1973, 19–20)

> My crippled generation look to me,
> your adverse plight reflected in a mirror; and
> gesture as I do; without hands
> without defense, without tomorrow.

His use of the word *crippled* to describe his generation recalls the action Katsaros took when the poem, cited in the epigraph at the beginning of this chapter, was censored by the newspaper in which it appeared. Katsaros published a postscript that concluded with the now famous line "Ελευθερία ανάπηρη πάλι σου τάζουν" (Again they promise you crippled freedom) (Katsaros 1971, 52–55). Both the poem and the postscript were reprinted in a 1971 collection of his poems published by Phillipos Vlachos's press Keimena and were extremely influential. By using the adjective *crippled* to describe his generation Poulios internalizes the conditions in which he and his peers are writing, naming his generation for the crippled freedom they endure. It is clear even at this early stage that everyone who used the term *generation of the 1970s* put great emphasis on the way in which the times shaped the poetry.

Six Poets and the *Anti-Anthology* were also the catalyst for the other most commonly used term, *generation of protest*. The word *Anti* clearly announces the oppositional component of the poetry. Vasos Varikas, a well-known liberal-left critic, was the first to offer a systematic discussion of this group of poets. In May 1971 he wrote an influential review of these two anthologies entitled "Η νέα γενιά μπροστά στο σήμερα" (Poetic anticon-

---

[8] Though critic and translator Kimon Friar denies these poets a collective status "because the times in which we live can have no ambitions of inspiring new forms of expression" (*Six Poets* 1971, 6), his position seems more motivated by a recognition of the dire political situation than by a critical evaluation of the work.

formism) in his column in the newspaper *Vima*. Here he continued an argument he had begun in an earlier article "Ποιητικός αντικομφορμισμός" (What the new generation faces today), in which he distinguished recent poets from those of earlier generations: "This recent stroll through the verses of the young allowed us to confirm a series of similarities, common elements, analogies, which compose a more or less common outlook on life. . . . An outlook that seems, at least as a tendency, to differ on basic issues when compared with previous generations" (1970). The common elements he stressed were their "rejection of the present" and their nihilism. In his second piece on the subject, however, he was more specific and placed these new poets in the context of poetry since the war, giving them a name, "the generation of protest." This label elicited mixed responses from the poets themselves, not so much for the specific sociological way Varikas had introduced it but for the way it was then more generally bandied about as a password for nihilism. Poulios explained in one of his poems, "Η Αμφισβήτηση είναι ευάλωτη" (Protest is easily corrupted), how the term *protest* was too often drained of its political content.[9] Varikas (1971) had, however, stressed that their doubt was not bred of a generalized cynicism but was rather a highly political response to contemporary events: "An 'engaged' poetry . . . with universal negation as its flag." Thus, whereas the term *generation of the 1970s* at least began as purely chronological, the term *generation of protest* had, in itself, an ideological weight and implied a particular relation to power.

The term, *pinball generation*, which similarly appealed to the content rather than the chronology of the poetry, actually predated the dictatorship but was nonetheless applied to the same generation. Vasilis Vasilikos originally coined this term in the popular weekly magazine *Tachydromos* (collected in Vasilikos 1976, 93). He very likely had in mind Menis Koumandareas's novella Τα μηχανάκια (The pinball machines) (1962) and borrowed the phrase to draw attention to the new consumerism and urban alienation of life in Athens in the 1960s.[10] Later, other critics applied the phrase to the generation of poets coming of age at that time (Karampetsos, 1987).[11]

The last term to consider before discussing how poets and critics rework these terms is *third postwar generation*,[12] which also marks the distinction

[9] When Poulios repeated the title in the poem he capitalized the word *Protest* (Αμφισβήτηση), suggesting that he had in mind the name of his generation, not just protest in general.

[10] On youth organizations and the shift to consumer culture in the 1960s, see also Liakos 1988.

[11] Instead of distinguishing this generation by its active suspicion as Varikas did, E. D. Karampetsos, focusing more on the generation as a whole, not its poets, singles it out for its indifference and ennui, quoting the last line of a poem by Yannis Yfantis, "So What?" as paradigmatic (Karampetsos 1987, 88; Siotis and Chioles 1979, 120).

[12] However limited, this term's diffusion may be partly indebted to the periodization employed by Argiriou in his popular anthology of Greek poetry, whose last published volume

chronologically but with reference to a war none of these younger poets had lived through. It makes sense to refer to poets born in the 1920s and 1930s as the first two postwar generations because most of these poets respond in some way to the experience of war and its deprivations, but poets born in the 1940s and 1950s have less personal experience of these events and are much more likely to count the dictatorship as their formative experience.[13] Galanaki summed up her generation's attitude when she qualified her answer to a questionnaire: "I am not speaking about the pre-dictatorship situation which I do not know" (1989b, 1).

Let us now look more carefully at what the critics said after the poets' own self-proclamations and Varikas's astute premonitions. When the initial excitement caused by their first publications in 1970 and 1971 died down, there were scattered reviews and presentations by the critics and poets of the postwar generations[14] and a steady flow of collective publications: Κατάθεση 73 (Deposition), Κατάθεση 74 (Deposition), and an annual volume of Ποίηση (Poetry) (1975–81) edited by Andonis Fostieris and Thanasis Niarchos. But it was not until 1979, when a spate of new anthologies came out, that critics made any systematic attempt to evaluate this new poetry. Alexis Ziras, a poet of this generation himself, became its self-appointed critic early on, and the anthology he introduced in 1979, Νεώτερη ελληνική ποίηση 1965–1980 (Contemporary Greek poetry), is the most widely respected. It included thirty-nine poets born between 1940 and 1954. Ziras explained his preference for the term *generation of protest* over *generation of the 1970s* even though, as he admitted, "it has suffered all sorts of distortions" (1979, 13). His main reason for choosing Varikas's term was that it most succinctly conveyed what was new about this poetry. But he never fully abandoned the other term, inasmuch as he constantly justified the inclusion or exclusion of a poet on the basis of age.[15] Another anthology, called Γενιά του 70 (The generation of the 1970s), compiled by the poet G. A. Panayiotou and consisting of two volumes, one of prose and one of poetry, also came out in 1979. As its title made clear, Panayiotou was in favor of the poets' own self-assigned name, and he stressed in his prefatory note that it was time to assess this generation's work carefully (7). Yet his introduction was itself superficial, and this anthology's only real contri-

---

(1983) covers the first postwar generation and whose projected next volumes include the second and third postwar generations.

[13] Vitti is adamant on this point: "They cannot for any reason be called a postwar generation since the war did not manage to leave any mark on their art" (1987b, 446).

[14] See Nora Anagnostaki's talk on humor and satire (collected in Anagnostaki 1977, 41–67) and Sinopoulos's review (1973) of Dalakoura's poetry, which both appeared in *Continuity*.

[15] Ziras excluded, for example, both of the women poets in *Six Poets* (Anghelaki-Rooke and Isaïa), who were older. He only later added that this decision was also based on the different content and form of their poetry (1979, 14).

butions are the page of excerpted critical comments that prefaces each poet's work and the index of critics at the end of the anthology.

As if in response to critics' views, the early 1980s witnessed a plethora of publications in which the poets spoke for themselves, evaluating their own situation.[16] An interview conducted by Elisavet Kotzia (1981) with Yannis Kondos, Jenny Mastoraki, and Vasilis Steriadis, introduced by the subheading "Three Representatives of the So-called Generation of the 1970s . . . ," summed up the new tone these younger poets adopted toward their name. It was no longer possible to refer to the *generation of the 1970s* without adding "so-called" and thus admitting the problematic history of the term. In his response to Kotzia's questions, Steriadis pointed out that although the term *generation of the 1970s* was initiated by the poets themselves, it was not at all satisfactory: many of its own representatives rejected it, and the term was so broad and vague that everyone used it to their own ends.[17] In the same interview, Kondos and Mastoraki also agreed that poets and critics were too eager to sum things up. Mastoraki outlined the main reservation that critics had with this new generation—that many of the collections probably did not deserve critical attention—and then explained the problem of trying to determine common characteristics among diverse work, concluding "There is no way we can say that they comprise some kind of 'identity.'" Mastoraki stressed that the cultural conditions of poetry had changed since the fall of the dictatorship and were bound to change more. Her plea contains the suggestion that criticism pay less attention to common themes and more attention to the linguistic playfulness of this poetry. She added, "The 'rockman and rockwoman' (ο βράχος και η βράχα) of Poulios, as well as the 'riddled lever' (τρυπητή μανιβέλα) and the 'tele-radios' (τελεοράδια) of Steriadis claim perhaps a similar starting point. It still remains to be seen how such a distinctive linguistic signal connects to the total code of a much larger generation, not just literary, and how those first sounds are systematized on a personal level" (in Kotzia 1981). This is the critical direction Steriadis then takes in defining what he calls "the linguistic idiom of the generation of the 1970s" (1986).

[16] In 1980, Niarchos published Κιβωτός (Ark), an anthology containing interviews with twenty-four poets; the literary magazine *Diavazo* for three years in a row published interviews with young writers (1982–84, issues 50, 69, and 87); similarly *Grammata kai Technes* devoted two issues to interviews with and unpublished poems of many of the same writers (1984, issues 35–36). For two months in 1983 the newspaper *Ta Nea* offered a full-page weekly spread titled "Our Poets," in which the critic Yiorgos Pilichos interviewed poets from the second postwar generation and the generation of the 1970s.

[17] As Steriadis explained, "The only problem that exists now is the disagreements and the different opinions among us about who should be the exponents . . . of our generation. For example, people with a stature that I never recognized become pioneers because of their dedication to becoming pioneers" (in Kotzia 1981).

Around 1983 this exchange between critics and poets over the name and nature of this generation took an odd turn. Sinopoulos, Ziras, and other critics who up until this point had been quite supportive became more skeptical of this term's merits (Ziras 1983, 2; Kotzia 1981). In his 1983 article Ziras replaces the terms *generation of protest* and *generation of the 1970s*, which he had used alternately up until this point, with the term *third postwar generation*. For Ziras, the last was less affirmative, and his switch underscores the fact that, on the whole, those critics who sought to exalt these younger poets called them "the generation of the 1970s," thereby creating an association between them and the famous generation of the 1930s, whereas those critics who called it "the third postwar generation" established a link with the less recognized poets of the first and second postwar generations. In a review of Poulios's second collection of poetry, the critic George Savvidis (1973a) made this distinction explicit, calling the generation of the 1930s "the rich generation" and the first postwar generation "deprived." It thus becomes clear why Steriadis chose to introduce his discussion of his generation's self-baptism in relation to that of Seferis's generation (Kotzia 1981) and why some of the younger poets insisted that they were carrying on that generation's poetics (Vayenas in Niarchos 1980, 38). No matter whether the poets of the generation of the 1970s were in fact more indebted to the poets of the postwar generations; their name would signal that they too were a "rich generation."[18]

The challenge three decades after these poets first appeared on the scene is to understand their poetics in the context of the dictatorship. It is no longer possible to ignore how their alternative poetics differ from previous generations nor to be content with insightful, but unelaborated, comments made at the time or in the decade afterward. It is not convincing to reduce the significance of the dictatorship, as Ziras does, to a subordinate clause: "Those who did not have the chance of being consciously present at any of the crucial historical events of contemporary Greece, except for the seven-year dictatorship when the majority [of these poets] first appeared" (1983, 2). It is necessary instead to analyze *how* this poetry, born of particular cultural conditions, differs or does not differ from that of previous poets. Following Mastoraki's suggestion that different social contexts engender different poetics, it is important not only to note that the themes were different but also to examine how the language was new.

In his essay on the generation of the 1970s, Maronitis explores how their poetry assimilated not just literary influences but their social and political

---

[18] See the interviews in *Diavazo* (see n. 16 above) in which the interviewer invariably asks who has influenced the poet most, in particular Steriadis's response in issue 87 (1984, 41), where he outlines his relation to the postwar poets.

world.[19] Whereas he is interested in determining which poets are more attentive to American, European, or Greek influences (Maronitis 1987, 242), I focus on their willingness to mix and match all sorts of incongruous traditions, as in the Greek, politicized version of the American Beat which emerges in their poetry, especially in the early work of Lefteris Poulios. What distinguishes this generation of poets is a very peculiar assimilation of both the national discourse of censorship and the international discourse of consumerism. The other crucial innovation of this generation is the shift to a more visual and narrative poetry. Maronitis, taking off from Sinopoulos's terms *dream-poem* and *hallucination-poem*, discusses what he calls the "cinematographic poem." I develop such a line of inquiry further, illustrating in Steriadis's poetry the necessity of analyzing long series of poems—what I call "poetry strips"—rather than single poems. Again my particular concern is to ask how the general turn to a more visual culture in Europe and North America is related to the local experience of censorship in Greece and whether the poetic strategies of the political beat and the poetry strip are sustained and developed after the fall of the regime.

Lefteris Poulios's Political Beat

One of the most striking aspects of this new poetry is that it mentions many things heretofore considered unpoetic: advertisements, television and other machines, comic strips, and sex. In "Ωδή στην Μαίρυλιν Μονρόε" (Ode to Marilyn Monroe), Yiorgos Chronas writes:

> Χαράξτε πάνω στο σώμα μου εκείνη την κυρία
> στην τηλεόραση να λέει: τα μανιτάρια του Θιβέτ προτιμώνται
> για το γεύμα της Τετάρτης
> Χαράξτε πάνω στο σώμα μου τη φωνή μου σε δίσκο 78 στροφών
> να τραγουδά τον Εθνικό Ύμνο των Ηνωμένων Πολιτείων.
>
> (in Ziras 1979, 169)

> Carve on my body that lady
> on television saying: mushrooms from Tibet are preferred
> for Wednesday's dinner
> Carve on my body my voice on a 78
> singing the American National Anthem.

[19] Maronitis is to my knowledge the only critic who has taken this next step and moved toward a discussion of the poetics of the generation of the 1970s. Two books on the generation, Ziras 1989 and K. Papayeorgiou 1989, are, for the most part, collections of old reviews and articles.

Yiorgos Daniil incorporates the sound of the typewriter into one of his
poems:

> Τάκου τάκου η γραφομηχανή μου
> τάκου κι έρχεται η καλή μου.
>> (1984, 31)

> Tap, tap my typewriter
> tap and my dear one comes.

Yannis Kakoulidis combines the staples of the Greek diet—bread, toma-
toes, and cheese—with the most foreign—Coca-cola—in his poem "Το
μονοπώλιον της βίας" (The monopoly of violence):

> Ήθελα μια σκέτη φέτα ψωμί
> ντομάτα κρέας τυρί και κόκα κόλα
> μουσική από γουέστερν
> κι αφίσσες διαστημικές
> με τον Φλας Γκόρντον
>> (in Ziras 1979, 62)

> I wanted a plain slice of bread
> tomato, meat, cheese, and Coca-cola
> music from westerns
> and space posters
> with Flash Gordon

The poetry of Andia Frantzi also invokes an expanded web of references,
but rather than concentrating on commodity culture her poetry is more apt
to transgress the realm of poetic propriety by explicit reference to sex. In
one poem she shocks readers by sexualizing one of Greece's most sacred
women, Penelope, who is usually portrayed patiently waiting for her
husband:[20]

> Ανάμεσα απ' τα ποιήματα
> Το αιδοίο της Πηνελόπης χάσκει
>> (in Ziras 1979, 158)

> In between the poems
> Penelope's private parts gape

[20] See also Anghelaki-Rooke's well-known poem "Η Πηνελόπη λέει" (Penelope says) (1977,
7). But whereas Anghelaki-Rooke reworks myth to empower women, Frantzi rejects myth
altogether. On myth and Greek women's poetry, see Van Dyck 1996 and C. Robinson 1996.

These younger poets did not shun references to brand names and sex because they were lifted from American popular culture; instead they welcomed them as an opportunity to expand their range of expression. To their minds, everything was borrowed and recycled; nothing could be considered purely Greek or purely American. And as Steriadis bluntly put it, if their elders did not recognize this new poetry as poetry, it was their loss:

> Μη ρωτάς σα χαζή
> αυτό είναι ποίημα
> δεν είναι ο πάτος του πάτου σου.
>   (in Ziras 1979, 153)

> Don't ask like a fool
> this *is* a poem
> it's not the bottom of your bottom.

In many ways this expanded repertoire of references had already been foreshadowed in the poetry of Andreas Embirikos, a surrealist poet of the generation of the 1930s. Many of his later poems incorporate the lessons of the American Beat into his particular Greek brand of surrealism (see in particular "Beati" in Οκτάνα [Oktana] 1980c) and certainly his poetry is the most sexually explicit of its generation, and of both the postwar generations, for that matter.[21] In the same way that some of Ritsos's paralogical short poems made him an honorary member of the generation of the 1970s, Embirikos too is often more at home stylistically among the younger poets than among those of his own generation. His poetry did not become widely read until these younger poets adopted him, and it is significant that the bulk of his work was reissued in the 1974–79 publishing boom after the fall of the dictatorship. It was, then, only with the poets of the generation of the 1970s that a more widespread engagement with American culture took place. But what happened when the American Beat generation and their philosophy of disrespect was "translated" into Greek? What exactly was the nature of this "American loan"?[22] How did the generation of the 1970s challenge the imperialist overtones of American popular culture without dismissing its poetic force?

The questioning of authority expressed by the American Beat culture in the 1950s and early 1960s was to a great degree a matter of life style, a

---

[21] I refer only to the poetry these poets published during their lifetimes; Seferis's posthumously published Εντεψίζικα (Rude things) (in Seferis 1995) also contains extremely explicit sexual references.

[22] I borrow this phrase from Maronitis, who states that "the ideological model of 'questioning established opinions' both as a form of expression and as content, first and foremost constitutes an American loan" (1987, 241–42).

general antiestablishment attitude rather than a focused response to specific political events.[23] Beatness was a weariness with forms and conven-
tions. For the majority of the Beats' heirs in the hippie movement, at least
until 1968, the Vietnam War was far away, something to watch on television, and the struggle for freedom of the press in America after the McCar-
thy era consisted for the most part of a fight against obscenity rulings.[24]
The aesthetic stance of the American Beat is evident in a documentary
directed by Richard Lerner and Lewis MacAdams, *What Happened to Kerouac?* (1985), which pieces together old film clips and more recent interviews with the leading figures of the movement. Jack Kerouac implies that
Beat had more in common with the Beatles' *Let It Be* than with any engaged
resistance. Gregory Corso is perhaps the most dismissive, denying that
Beat was even a generation: "We couldn't be a generation . . . whoever
heard of a generation that was only four people?" Even Ginsberg, who
later was politically active in protesting the Vietnam War, defined Beat as a
spiritual attitude, not a social movement.[25]

In Greece, on the contrary, the Beat attitude emerged in opposition to an
authoritarian regime. While Kerouac, Corso, and Ginsberg, among others,
were writing in the wake of McCarthyism in a society that imposed certain
limitations on the sexual explicitness of their self-expression, Greek poets
were writing under censorship with limitations on every aspect of their
writing. For them the struggle to say or write what they wanted was not
only a matter of challenging obscenity rulings but of condemning the colonels' regime. To use crude, vulgar language, for example, constituted an
explicit attack on the colonels' Greece for Christian Greeks. Popular magazines from that time such as *Tachydromos* offer endless discussions of obscenity rulings, in particular the practice of blackening out provocative
body parts (Figure 2). Articles with titles such as "The Ethics of the Magic
Marker" and "Mores Change, but Never Laws" focused readers' attention
on the specific case of pornography, in effect displacing their fears regarding the more fundamental issues of censorship. In the cultural context of a
regime and a popular press that conflated obscenities and subversive politics, sexuality became a site of political resistance. The overt sexual lan-

[23] On the 1960s in the United States and the role the Beat writers played, see McNally 1979
and Gitlin 1993, esp. 45–56, 193–221.
[24] I am thinking in particular of the obscenity case surrounding Allen Ginsberg's poem
"Howl," in which Lawrence Ferlinghetti, the publisher of City Lights, was tried, and of the
censorship case surrounding the *Chicago Review*, which was to have published William Burroughs's *The Naked Lunch,* among other Beat productions (Ginsberg 1989). For the larger
context, see Moon 1969.
[25] Ginsberg (1989, 28) states that Beat had a profound effect on society but that that was
secondary. First came the personal spiritual liberation; only then did the social liberation
follow. Without glossing over spiritualism as a major form of political protest in the United
States (one has only to think of Martin Luther King and the civil rights movement) I simply
mean to establish that Beat writers tended to downplay political implications.

Figure 2. "The ethics of the magic marker."

guage of Beat thus had a more marked political impact in Greece than it had in America.[26]

Poulios's first two collections provide a good example of how this younger generation internalized the discourses of censorship and consumerism to create a Greek, politicized version of Beat under the dictatorship.[27] Interestingly enough, the reviews written at the time did not emphasize the political critique inherent in his use of sexually explicit language or in his references to advertising and commodity culture. Even after the dictatorship there is no attempt to analyze his use of obscenity and his reliance more generally on a much wider net of references with respect to the dictatorship (Belezinis 1975). It is as if the dictatorship were so present to the critics' and Poulios's readers that it did not need to be mentioned. When Poulios wrote, in the early 1970s,

> 'Ασχημοι καιροί
> καιροί του χαμένου θάρρους
> κι η ποίηση στη μέση του
> γονατισμένου λαού
> (Poulios [1975] 1982, 29)

> Difficult times
> times of lost courage
> and poetry in the midst
> of a people on their knees

everyone knew that he was alluding to the oppressive circumstances of the dictatorship. Now it is important to reconnect the literary texts and cultural conditions, analyzing in greater depth what was then only gestured at. In a review of Poulios's first two collections, for example, Belezinis (1975) mentions how Poulios was obliged to substitute "f . . ." (γ . . .) for "fuck" (γαμώ το) in one poem. This substitution is not linked to the specific conditions of writing under the dictatorship, and the political dimension of Poulios's act is lost (218): Poulios turns the "high art" of poetry into a place for "low brow" obscenities in order to reconnect the censorship of por-

---

[26] For an interesting parallel case, see Andreas Huyssen's discussion of how American pop art was interpreted as protest art in West Germany (1986, 141–43).

[27] Poulios is adamant about his debt: "If the beatniks hadn't existed I might not have managed to write a single worthwhile verse. With their distant influence I managed to set out my own literary demands" (1993a, n.p.). Although I mainly discuss Poulios, it should already be clear that other poets of the generation of the 1970s were also extremely influenced by Beat. Mastoraki, for example, translated and introduced a selection of Allen Ginsberg's poetry (Ginsberg 1974). I should add that the exchange was not in one direction only. In 1972 the Beat poet Lawrence Ferlinghetti organized an evening of poetry in support of the Greek resistance to the dictatorship, with many famous American writers as well as the Greek poets Dinos Siotis and Nanos Valaoritis (Ferlinghetti 1995, 13).

nography to censorship more generally. His use of ellipses in a poem published just after preventive censorship was lifted in 1969 makes visible his
inability to say what he meant. As in Savvopoulos's song about censorship,
typographic games—the points of omission in "γ . . ." and the dashes in
λογοκρισί --- —redeploy the effects of censorship parodically.[28] They acknowledge censorship by purposefully leaving the signs of what has been
left out in.

If censorship of obscenities had a substantially different significance in
Greece than in the United States, so did the effect of consumerism and
advertising. As far as the Beat Generation was concerned, consumerism
was the work of the "Establishment" and its alienating effects bore the
brunt of their attack. Ginsberg's poem "Howl" rages against commodification and concrete cities, and Kerouac's On the Road explicitly referred to the
road leading out of the city and cross-country, away from America's capitalist center, New York City. By contrast, for most Greek poets "the road"
meant the road into the city, to Athens, where opportunity beckoned. Savvopoulos's first record was called Truck and charts his trip from the northern city of Thessaloníki to Athens, the capital. The idea of a city was still
novel and beguiling to these young people. The huge revival of rembetika,
the songs from the 1930s describing urban life and the underworld, also
testified to this fascination with the city. Mass production of standardized
goods and high-tech communication such as TV were relatively new, and
no one was ready to dispense with them. In the same pages of Tachydromos
which discuss obscenity rulings there are also numerous articles and advertisements introducing American commodity culture to Greek readers.
Boldface titles such as "Self-Service Supermarket: An Institution of the
Times Becomes an Everyday Necessity" and "Traditional Cornershop
Gives Way to Colorful, Well-stocked Shelves" celebrate modernization. In
contrast to the American Beat culture's rejection of the new metropolitan
world and tendency to take shelter in personal and spiritual transformation, the poets of the generation of the 1970s integrated commodity culture
into their critique of the authoritarian regime. Poulios's first two collections were exercises not only in how to incorporate commodity culture but
in how to criticize its imperialist tendencies. Belezinis's review refers to the
different consumer cultures of Greece and America,[29] ultimately suggest-

[28] As I discussed in Chapter 1, Savvopoulos's song concludes: "έγραψα μιαν ιστορία / να την
πω στη γαλαρία / πριν τελειώσει η ιστορία / ήρθε η λογοκρισί --- " (I wrote a story / to tell the
crowds / but before I was done / censorship had c ---) (1983, 23).
[29] Belezinis contrasts the American Beat poets and Poulios's generation like this: "It is not of
course the same when the verses 'I can't stand your machines any more. / You've made me
want to become a saint' come out of the typewriter of Allen Ginsberg and refer to America
with its nightmarish automatic production and life, and when they are written . . . with a bic
(or even with a typewriter) by our poets, many of whom grew up with a longing for machines
and life in the city" (1975, 210).

ing that Poulios's Beat is "Greek" because it juxtaposes pop images and quotes from Herodotus in the same poem. To move beyond such a thematic approach, let us turn to how Poulios's Beat is "Greek" and what "Greek" had come to mean in the 1970s.

Poulios's poetry includes the abundance of commodity culture without losing the specific Greek component of his poetry in various ways. One example can be found in his poem "Οι δρόμοι" (The roads), where he transposes and substantially alters the unambiguous Beat symbol of freedom, the road. For Poulios it becomes both the place of hope, "Δρόμοι παιάνες. Δρόμοι γιορτής" (Roads-paeans. Roads of celebration) and the place of oppression, "Δρόμοι-αγωνία. Δρόμοι-φονιάδες. / Ποια κατάρα πάνω σας έχει πέσει;" (Roads-struggle. Roads-murderers. What curse has fallen on you?) (Poulios [1973] 1982, 19). Poulios structures this poem as an invocation to both kinds of roads, to roads with possibility: "Δρόμοι—στιλπνά σκούρα χταπόδια τούτης της χώρας μου, / που πάνω σας δίχως μορφή και δίχως βάρος / πορεύεται το μέλλον" (Roads—smooth dark octopuses of my country, / upon you the future travels without shape and without weight) and to the single national road of authoritarian repression on which tanks move in single file: "Δρόμε έξω απ' το πανεπιστήμιο. / Έξω από το κτίριο της Βουλής. Δρόμε εθνικέ" (Road outside the University. / Outside the Parliament building. National road). The fact that the road is both plural and singular suggests the contradiction of the times: the abundance of things, on the one hand, and the restrictions, on the other. Greeks are simultaneously alienated from one another by commodification and drawn together by their shared struggle. "The Roads" concludes with a line emphasizing the complex overlap of alienation and collectivity: "Περιμένουμε ο καθένας στη στάση του. / περιμένουμε όλοι μαζί στο τσίγκινο υπόστεγο" (We are *each* waiting at our stop. / we are *all* waiting together under the metal roof) (19, emphasis mine). Not only does his use of the image of the road draw on the specific political situation in Greece at this time, but the tone of the poem recalls the famous collection of poetry by Embirikos, even to the point of word choice, borrowing the adjective "στιλπνά" (smooth) from Embirikos's text (1974). Poulios's road is a long way from Kerouac's.

Another example of his political Beat can be found in one of his earliest poems, where he seems to conflate two Dylans, the American singer Bob Dylan with the Welsh poet Dylan Thomas. On the one hand, the poem can be read as a reprimand of Bob Dylan for giving in to the commercialization of his career by his managers and as a meditation on how to avoid the same:

ο Ντύλαν μπροστά στο χωνί μασούσε χαλίκια
σαν υποταχτικό σκυλί.
γύρω του έσπαγε η κραυγή η πρωινή του

πάνω σε τζάμια σε γρανάζια σε μάνατζερς
όχι σαν κραυγή που αδυνατεί να τρυπήσει ένα τύμπανο
ή ένα τζάμι στο νερό,
                    ήρεμα
                         οργισμένα
και γίνεται ψάρι.

                              (Poulios [1969] 1982, 9)

Dylan in front of a mike was chewing on pebbles
like an obedient dog.
all around him his morning cry broke
on window panes on gears on managers
not like a cry which is unable to pierce an eardrum
or a window pane under water,
                              peacefully
                                   with rage
becoming a fish.

The poem criticizes Dylan for conforming, for adapting to his managers'
terms, the way a fish adapts to water, but it also wonders whether giving in
is not unavoidably human; perhaps resisting such conformism would
make one as inanimate and as predictable as a machine:

ω να 'ξερα να σου μίλαγα χρόνε
με διφορούμενα πέδιλα αγώνων σκοτώνοντας νόμους
συμβιβασμούς παραδόσεις ακολουθώντας τον δικό μου νόμο
μα τότε δεν θ' άξιζα όσο μια μηχανή;

                              (10)

If only I knew how to speak to you, time
with ambivalent sandals of struggles killing laws
compromises traditions following my own law
but then wouldn't I be worth as much as a machine?

The tension that structures Poulios's early poetry is how to accept consumerism and benefit from its anonymity without succumbing to its alienating
effects, how to embrace mechanization without being in the grasp of those
who own it—"the managers."[30] On the other hand, his choice of the word
οργισμένα (angrily, with rage) opens up another debt, referring as it does to
a poem by Sachtouris "Στον Ντύλαν Τόμας" (To Dylan Thomas) (1984a,
243), and his use of Thomas's famous line "Rage, rage against the dying of

---

[30] It is no minor detail that "managers" is left in English in the original, suggesting that
some aspects of the American loan, of her "superpower," are untranslatable.

the light. . . ." Poulios, by invoking this paean to the Welsh bard of nonconformism, by way of Sachtouris, the most paralogical of postwar Greek
poets, mixes and blends his own Greek version of nonconformism.

Poulios's poetry is full of images such as supermarkets, hot pants, and
brand-name items, but his involvement in the discourse of consumerism is
even more far-reaching. The pastiche of American, Greek, and other
poems owes its very structure to mechanical reproduction, consumer
fetishism, and the anonymity of the market. In "Το εμπόρευμα" (The merchandise), Poulios succinctly describes how the market levels out differences and deflates the importance of the creator:[31]

>   . . . Κάθε πράμα
> έχει την αξία του στην αγορά. Τα βρώμικα
> εσώρουχα της Μπαρντό αξίζουν όσο ένας Ρέμπραντ. . . .
>   (Poulios [1977] 1982, 75)

>   . . . Each thing
> has its value on the market. The dirty
> underwear of Bardot are worth as much as a Rembrandt. . . .

The market is a realm in which things no longer have any inherent value.
Consumer fetishism ensures that Bardot's underwear and a Rembrandt
are valued for the price they fetch, not because they are someone's handiwork. Consumerism bestows a certain anonymity on production.

Poulios's turn to the discourse of consumerism and, in particular, the
anonymity of the commodity is in response not to some postmodern celebration of the death of the author but rather to the local problem of censorship: anonymity was a well-tested and accepted tactic for circumventing
censorship. Poets of this time put great emphasis on the group—as
Iatropoulos's *Anti-Anthology* announced, it would "connect the individual
with the collective and make poetry a group testimony" (1971, 1)—and this
attention to the collective was intimately linked to the need for anonymity
under an authoritarian regime. According to the press law, each book had
to include the name of the person legally in charge of its production. The
resistance anthology *Eighteen Texts* diffused responsibility by printing
seven names and addresses of editors at the front instead of the usual one,
on the grounds that it would be more difficult for authorities to arrest
seven people than one. But Poulios's poetry, by drawing on the particular
deployment of anonymity by the market and its severing of the product
from the producer, takes the shelter of anonymity further than his elders.
He asks, in effect, what if a poet was as responsible for a poem as Rem-

---

[31] On how the aura of the original is replaced by the spell of the market, see Walter Benjamin's famous essay "Art in the Age of Mechanical Reproduction" (1968, 231).

brandt was for the millions of postcards of his work in circulation? A comparison of two pieces by the Thessalonikian poet and critic Dinos Christianopoulos, one an essay on the anonymity of songs (1975a) and the other a review of Poulios's poetry (1975b) shows how Poulios's appropriation of other poets' work is a way of drawing on this anonymity of the market to evade censorship. It is clear that Poulios's pastiche of other people's poems did not mean that censors literally could not attribute his work to him—they could, of course; his name was on the cover—but rather that poetry that aspired to the anonymity of a mass-produced product eluded censorship by parodying traditional notions of authorship and setting itself off paralogically from accepted systems of meaning.

The importance of anonymity as evasion at this time is clear in Christianopoulos's essay "Γιατί το τραγούδι δεν σοκάρει εκεί που σοκάρει το ποίημα;" (Why doesn't the song shock the way the poem does?). Though published in 1975, this article, significantly, has as its date of composition 1971, soon after the lifting of preventive censorship. Christianopoulos's point in this short article is that the composer Manos Hatzidakis can write about his "unorthodox" homosexual love without shocking his listeners, whereas the poet Cavafy cannot; a song is anonymous and circulates more freely, whereas a poem is signed. He goes on to explain that when Nana Mouschouri sings one of Hatzidakis's songs, her sex camouflages the intended homoerotics of Hatzidakis's verse, but in Cavafy's poem, the "shocking" truth of his sexual preference is clear from his signature. Christianopoulos concludes his piece lauding certain nineteenth-century poetry anthologies that left out poets' names (1975a, 138). His discussion of anonymity as a way of avoiding shock, at a time when censorship was on everyone's mind, is revealing. Taking Christianopoulos's gay politics of camouflage as a model for evading other forms of oppression, we might replace Christianopoulos's query Why doesn't the song shock the way a poem does? with the question What happens when a poem is more like a song or, for that matter, a commodity and can no longer be clearly attributed to its author?

Needless to say, this was not the direction Christianopoulos had in mind. In his review of Poulios's poetry, some pages later in the same issue of his magazine, anonymity is not the problem. By "metapoetry" in the title of his review "Ποίηση ή μεταποίηση;" (Poetry or metapoetry?), Christianopoulos means not a poststructural concept of a poetry which critically comments on Poetry but, rather, the question that often consumes Christianopoulos in his critical writing and conversations—the authenticity and originality of a work, in this case Poulios's. He criticizes Poulios's poem "American Bar in Athens," as nearly a line-for-line splicing together of Ginsberg's "A Supermarket in California" and Ezra Pound's "A Pact" (see above, in this chapter) and concludes by suggesting that Poulios is nothing but a patch-writer:

"If we like salads, then we are salad makers and not poets. The bottom line
is that if we have something to say, let's say it; otherwise, it's better that we
keep our mouths shut" (1975b, 173). Although in his other essay he lauded
the appeal of anonymous writing, Christianopoulos here ignores the radical implications of a poem that tries to accomplish this anonymity through
collage, only relating Poulios's "salad" to the general confusion of mixed
affiliations.[32] Poulios is not making "a pact" with his predecessor as Ginsberg and Pound are; he is threatening to kill him off. Like Abbie Hoffman's
famous *Steal This Book,* Poulios's "stolen" poetry can be read both as a
parody of the capitalist system and as a way of exploiting it to his own
advantage. He turns the fragments of American poems into commodities
that belong to everyone. Although, on the one hand, "The Merchandise"
can be read as a criticism of capitalism (the fact that a Rembrandt and a
Bardot have the same value can have a certain alienating effect), on the
other hand, it can also be viewed as introducing a new set of images and
ploys with which to circumvent the censors. The anonymity of the market
becomes a mode of evading and parodying the strict one-to-one correspondences of poems and poets which his elders promoted.[33]

Poulios integrates the bad and the good, the foreign and the familiar,
censorship and consumerism, creating a textual site where the contradictions of being Greek in the 1970s—as expressed in the phrases "Σουπερ-
μάρκετ και φουστανέλλες" (Supermarkets and national folk costumes)
(1982, 23) and "σε σκίζουν μπόιγκ και άγγελοι" (Boeings and angels tear
you apart) (32)—make sense. The commodified American world of Boeing
airplanes and supermarkets and the Helleno-Christian world of angels
and nationalism are no longer unimaginably incongruous. "Καυτό σορτς"
(Hot pants) and "Πλέϊμπακ" (Playback), and the statement "Εγώ ένας
Έλλην βρίσκω τον εαυτό μου στην Ελλάδα" (I, a Greek, find myself in
Greece) (1973, 27) sum up in a single poem the mixed affiliations of the

---

[32] Christianopoulos's adamancy that the confusion is mainly in Athens is a part of a long
rivalry between Athens and his city, Greece's second largest, Thessaloníki. Although my
discussion thus far has focused on Athens as *the* Greek urban center, it is perhaps necessary to
clarify that some very active poets of the generation of the 1970s also lived in and worked out
of Thessaloníki. Important journals such as *Tram,* begun by this generation of poets, were
published there.

[33] It is important to add that though this strategy of stealing is everywhere in Poulios's
poetry, I am not arguing that it is a conscious act. In contradistinction to Seferis, who borrows
very carefully and takes pains to acknowledge his debts, Poulios is known for claiming that
the material he borrows *is* his, not Bob Dylan's, Dylan Thomas's, Ezra Pound's, or Allen
Ginsberg's; hence, of course, one explanation for Christianopoulos's attack. Savvopoulos is
perhaps more self-conscious about his generation's less scrupulous relation to intellectual
property. In the notes to his collection of songs he playfully writes: "I express my indebtedness
to these people only because the lines and the ideas I took from them reminded me of them
directly and not because the rest of this book is 'mine,' though of course that's what I told the
publisher" (1983, 87).

younger generation. The redeploying of certain attributes of commodities such as anonymity had a particular political meaning under the colonels, and it is necessary to see Poulios's integration of less and more in terms of the specific discourses of censorship and consumerism under the dictatorship. Greece's dictatorship and economic underdevelopment meant that the American "loan" of the Beat and hippie ethos had a very different value in Greece.

After the dictatorship ended in 1974, and the obvious enemy, the colonels, had been overthrown, the political impact on Poulios's work faded. His poetry became more personal and confessional. This inward turn has as much to do with his mental state in the last years of the junta as it does with the changing political climate. In 1971 he shocked the literary world by chopping the fingers off his left hand and was diagnosed with schizophrenia. He slowly abandoned the project of exposing the complicated interdependence of more and less, of theirs and ours, a shift evident in his next and third book, Ο γυμνός ομιλητής (The naked speaker) (1977), as well as in the ensuing collections Το αλληγορικό σχολείο (The allegorical school), Ενάντια (Against), Τα επουσιώδη (Things of slight importance), and Αντί της σιωπής (Instead of silence). This poetry seems unable to sustain the alternative politics of his earlier poetry, either resorting to the old engaged style of Anagnostakis or losing its political impact altogether.

The former inclination is clear in "Αθήνα" (Athens), for example, in *The Naked Speaker*, a poem that relies on references to Greek place names and incidents for its Greek specificity rather than on the internalization of the American "loan" into a Greek idiom. The poem addresses the reader:

> Άκου το ουρλιαχτό του περιπολικού και κοίτα
> αυτούς που τους βάζουν στ᾽ αυτοκίνητο και
> βιαστικά τους οδηγούν στο τμήμα.
> Με προβολείς στο μάτι τούς ρίχνουν κάτω
> τούς ψάχνουν κι η μέση τούς σπάει στο τραπέζι
>
> . . . .
>
> Κι αυτοί που πολτοποιήθηκαν απ᾽ τα τανκς
> μέσα στο Πολυτεχνείο . . .
>   (1977, 10–11)

> Listen to the howl of police sirens and watch
> those they put in cars and
> take to the station.
> With headlights in their eyes they throw them down
> they search them and their backs break on the table
>
> . . . .

> And those who were reduced to pulp
> in the Polytechnic . . .[34]

Poulios seems to revert to an older model of engaged poetry which attempts to "tell the truth." Even the American loan of Ginsberg's title "Howl" in the line "Listen to the howl" loses its jarring effect in the context of the catalog of horrors that ensues—the cars that take people off to the station, the headlights/searchlights that blind them. The shift in the choices of title from, say, "American Bar in Athens" (1973) to "Athens" in this collection is revealing.[35]

Other poems in this same volume take an opposite approach and strike a completely apolitical tone. Instead of an explicit political message that drowns out the complications of borrowing from Beat, the generality of the Beat's anticonformism is adopted as it was, with no alterations. These poems sound like bad imitations of Ginsberg's rather than Greek reinventions. "Επίλογος" (Epilogue), the last poem in this collection, is a good example of imitation rather than reinvention. The poem's speaker takes on Ginsberg's prophetic tone and, first in the voice of Tiresias, and then Isaiah, instructs his reader:

> Πάρε τα όπλα ενάντια στη συμβατικότητα
> Εναντιώσου σε όλα
> Ευλογημένοι, υμνημένοι, δοξασμένοι οι δρόμοι του ονείρου
> και του αγώνα.
> (56)

> Take arms against conventionality
> Go against everything
> Let the roads of dream and struggle
> be eulogized, praised, glorified.

Either too specific and directed at an enemy no longer there, or too general and derivative of Ginsberg's apocalyptic tone, Poulios's poems after the dictatorship lose their alternative political angle. His antiestablishment attack is no longer accompanied by a homeopathic integration of "the other."

Tellingly, the further removed from the dictatorship years and the greater the threat of his poetry's ineffectiveness, the more often the revolu-

[34] Poulios is referring to the student demonstration at the Polytechnic in November 1973, when the colonels' tanks tore down the gates, killing thirty-four students and wounding many others (Clogg 1979, 197).

[35] This reversion is also clear in *The Allegorical School*; see, e.g., Poulios's poem on Cyprus ([1978] 1982, 99).

tionary password of protest and anticonformism, "ενάντια" (against), appears in his poems. Beginning with "Epilogue" in *The Naked Speaker,* his cries of resistance , "ενάντια" (against) and "εναντιώσου" (go against), seem confined to the level of content; his fifth book is even entitled *Against* (1983). Like the empty insistence of the specificity of Athens signaled by the title of his poem "Athens," the title *Against* displays a similar failure to incorporate its message formally. This volume refers to resistance instead of enacting it; the realm of politics seems to have shrunk, and much of the work to incorporate the significance of commodities and sex in his early poems seems to be forgotten. The poems continue to talk explicitly about commodities and sex, but there is little attempt to rework these references into an exploration of how censorship works. The sense of urgency is gone; these poems simply report.

Things of Slight Importance (1988) rejects the American loan of commodification and changing mores. Taking off from the more personal spirituality of Ginsberg, Poulios retreats inside himself, perhaps in acceptance of an inability to reconcile inside and outside, personal and collective, Greece and America, as he had under the dictatorship. He returns instead to the Greek literary tradition he formerly rejected and concentrates on expressing what he has known best since 1971: mental breakdown and his own struggle with schizophrenia. The speaker in "Ο Αλεξανδρινός στ' όνειρό μου" (The Alexandrian in my dream), for example, sees Cavafy in his sleep:

> —Χάνεις την εμμονή σου ιδέα, μου είπε,
> "ψάξε να εξηγήσεις την τρέλα του κορμιού,
> τη δίψα της ψυχής. Τούτο προσπάθησε
> τουλάχιστον όσο μπορείς. Βάλε τον ηδονισμό
> και το μήνυμα αντανακλώμενα στον καλό μας στίχο."
>
> (1988, 29)

> —You are losing your obsession, he told me,
> "try to explain the madness of your body,
> the thirst of the soul. Try to do that
> at least as much as you can. Reflect the sensual pleasure
> and the message in our good verse."

Here the speaker succeeds in using the literary tradition to his own ends, but elsewhere in this collection he seems to be used by the tradition. In one poem, "Ο κόσμος κολυμπάει μπρος τα μάτια μου" (The world is swimming before my eyes), the speaker is caught desiring the canonization that Poulios's early poetry explicitly fought against:

Οι λέξεις μου εκρήγνυνται γραμμένες με χρυσό
και διατηρούνται σε βιβλιοθήκες
πλάι στον Καβάφη και στον Οράτιο.

(41)

My words explode written in gold
and are preserved in libraries
next to Cavafy and Horace.

In an interview published together with *Instead of Silence,* Poulios openly admits: "I gave my second to last collection the title *Things of Slight Importance* because compared to my earlier books I think it is less significant. . . . As for the poems in this collection, I want to show how I have arrived at a place of limbo: [all I can do] is 'replace' my silence with these twelve poems" (1993a, n.p.). Although he initiated an important dynamic, a poetics of censorship that added and left things out, he was unable to sustain, or uninterested in sustaining, this internalization of the mixed messages. His most recent work answers negatively a question that other poetry, in particular women's, was not willing to relinquish: Can poetry sustain an alternative and expanded sense of resistance when, as Cavafy suggests, the barbarians are no longer a solution?

Vasilis Steriadis's Poetry Strip

The project of these younger poets entailed more than just calling attention to the specific political nuances that obscenities and references to American pop culture conveyed in poetry under the colonels. It also exploited the new visual and narrative aspects of this expanded range of references. Just as for Poulios it was a matter not simply of describing the arbitrariness and anonymity of the commodity but of actually constructing poems in which the aura of originality was undone, so poets such as Steriadis, Mastoraki, Galanaki, Pampoudi, and Hatzidaki did not merely reproduce the pop image of Superman in a poem but also modeled their poems on the visual narratives of comic strips, advertisements, television, and film. Their poetry explores the possibilities of a kind of writing that is less like an individual speaking or singing, where one word follows the next and no two things can be said simultaneously, and more like a series of pictures which offers an abundance of images and obliges the reader to do the organizing. By structuring their collections to reflect the seriality of images in comics and in film, these poets disconnect the signifier from the signified, metonymically stringing together one signifier after another, scrambling the conditions of intelligibility necessary for censorship.[36]

We can trace the turn to a more visual and narrative poetry in the 1970s and 1980s through a reading of what I call Steriadis's "poetry strips," that is, his long series of poems which rely on the visual techniques of comic strips and film. Although the internalization of the processes of visual reproduction is not fully developed until later, Steriadis's first three books, Ο κ. 'Ιβο (Mr. Ivo), Το ιδιωτικό αεροπλάνο (The private airplane), and Ντικ ο χλομός (Pale Dick), written under and just after the dictatorship, initiate an important trend. Critics have mentioned the generation of the 1970s' move to a more narrative form of poetry (Vitti 1987b, Tziovas 1987a) and called attention to its visual and cinematographic preoccupation (Ziras 1979, Maronitis 1987). Maronitis (1987) addresses both in his term "εικαστική αφήγηση" (painterly narrative).[37] My contribution is to put poetry strips and painterly narratives in the more general category of visual narratives, showing the ways in which the shift to a more visual and narrative poetry is related to an emerging visual culture in Greece and the formative experience of censorship under the dictatorship.

The steadily rising importance of visual culture globally—of film, television, comics, advertising, and computer graphics—has played a decisive role in Greece as well. In a country whose fastest growing industry is tourism, visual appearance has come to matter more and more. Under the dictatorship, however, visual culture gained significance for another reason as well: it was deemed particularly resistant to censorship. Filmmakers, cartoonists, and other visual artists suddenly found themselves at the forefront of a cultural battle. One of the first organized acts of resistance, for example, was an art exhibit by the sculptor Vlasis Kaniaris in May 1969.[38] His visual medium allowed him to criticize the regime without breaking the silence Seferis and other writers held. Kaniaris's parody of the regime was obvious to viewers who examined the chunks of plaster,

[36] For an interesting comparison, see Peter Bien's discussion (1990–91) of how Ritsos develops a painterly technique under the Metaxas dictatorship. In light of the younger poets' work, though, I would answer quite differently the question Bien then sets himself: "But how can painterly techniques be utilized in a poem that stretches over many pages and therefore cannot be comprehended all at once?" Bien replies: "The answer is that such a technique cannot be utilized to the same degree. Nonetheless long poems can acquire certain painterly qualities—which means that they can be given characteristics equatable with space rather than time" (8). The visual narratives of Steriadis and others instead suggest that by appealing to comic strips and cinema, which reintroduce the element of time spatially, one can truly sustain a visual impact in longer poems.

[37] Maronitis used this term in a review of Mastoraki's *Tales of the Deep* and Laina's *Hers*, two collections that, like Steriadis's early collections, employ long series of poems. I come back to painterly narrative in Chapter 3.

[38] See Andrews 1980, 14–25. On the relation of Greek artists to the junta, see Joachimides and Rosenthal 1975.

the ghostly figures in casts, the empty shoes strewn on the floor. As visitors left they were each given a small piece of plaster with a carnation stuck in it. This pocket sculpture summed up the whole exhibition in one image: it connected Papadopoulos's attempts to suppress the opposition before he came into power with his regime's present policy on censorship. The carnation recalled the one the communist Beloyannis had worn in his lapel throughout his trial in defiance of those, like Papadopoulos, who were testifying against him, and the plaster recalled Papadopoulos's metaphor of Greece as a patient in a cast.

Greek cinema, with its long history of being crippled by censorship (from the Metaxas dictatorship through the 1950s and early 1960s), finally began to gain the critical tools to fight back in the mid-1960s (Soldatos 1991, 8–17). The journal *Greek Cinema,* begun in 1966, managed to publish five influential issues of theory and criticism before the colonels came to power in April 1967. Among its important contributions were the translations of articles such as one by the critic André Bazin on how film as a medium was difficult to read for clear-cut messages (1967, 29–31).[39] In the face of even stricter censorship rulings under the Papadopoulos regime, many film-makers and critics took a different approach. Rather than hold censorship accountable for the shape of the Greek film industry, they began to see in film the possibility of a cryptic visual language that could elude censorship.[40] In an article published in the resistance anthology *Deposition,* the critic Vasilis Rafaelidis (1974) explicitly linked the visual world of cinema to the evasion of censorship: "Visual language is indecipherable . . . the meanings which the pictures present can be understood on many levels, of which the film censors . . . are in a position to understand only the first and simplest, that of myth" (353).

The visual language of comic strips was also recognized for its ability to undermine censorship.[41] Comics such as Bost's, with their indicting misspellings, or Kyr's, with their allegorical rewriting of the Trojan War and of Lysistrata,[42] used their visual medium to confuse the uninitiated. Tellingly, the most popular comics not only were full of hidden references to the

[39] Theodoros Angelopoulos is perhaps the best-known Greek director whose work expresses this attitude. Another example of how film censorship was finally being fought can be found in the statement of protest which Stratis Tsirkas and other intellectuals signed regarding the censorship surrounding Alain Resnais's *La guerre est finis* (The war is over).

[40] Angelopoulos's film *The Acting Troup,* with its disruptive cuts in time and wide range of incongruous visual references, is a good example. For a discussion of Angelopoulos in the context of the dictatorship, see Soldatos 1991, 246–58.

[41] On comics as cultural productions in contemporary Greece, see Loukatos 1985–86, who writes, for example, "In recent years with the technical developments of picture typography, but also with the organically integrated journalistic style of our illustrators, comics almost became 'articles,' suggestively hinting about the events, words, and personalities of the day" (144). See also Martinidis 1980.

[42] In Chapter 3, I analyze Kyr's *Lysistrata* in detail.

political situation but also came in installments and sustained their critique over many weeks. As with film, the ability to keep one's audience visually stimulated over time was crucial.

The prominence of the visual under the dictatorship had an interesting impact on Greek literary culture. Poetry, the dominant literary form in Greece, has historically been associated with an oral tradition. Ever since the nineteenth-century demoticists rejected classical models and embraced the folk song as their inspiration for Modern Greek poetry, there has been a tendency among critics to view the song, not the written page, as poetry's ideal medium.[43] In this century the collaboration of Greek composers and poets has strengthened this connection. The poetry of the Nobel laureates Seferis and Elytis has been made popular by the songs of such composers as Theodorakis and Hatzidakis. In journals, newspapers, and tourist brochures, Greek poetry is described as inextricably bound up with music.[44] But in the 1970s, the visual arts sensitized readers and writers to the visual aspects of poetry. The art of typography, for example, having proved a useful tool with which newspapers could outwit censors, was being rehabilitated. After preventive censorship was lifted, there was not only a dramatic increase in the number of books published but a greater attention to the quality of book production.[45] Older publishers such as Phillipos Vlachos and also those of a younger generation such as Stavros Petsopoulos, who would later open the press Agra, were beginning to collect old fonts and use them to distinguish their new typography. The avant-garde magazine *Pali*, started in Athens in 1964, published a manifesto many publishers and poets of the generation of the 1970s referred to as for-

[43] My attention to the privileging of voice over writing is indebted most obviously to contemporary Greek poets but also, I should add, to Jacques Derrida's relentless inquiry into this dynamic in Western metaphysics. See esp. his introduction to this problematic in *Speech and Phenomena and Other Essays on Husserl's Theory of Signs* (1973) (usefully excerpted in Derrida 1991, 6–30). Rather than simply redressing this imbalance, his more far-reaching lesson is that the written and the spoken are never discrete categories. I find Derrida's critique more compelling than Walter Ong's, in which the opposition between orality and literacy is so schematically fixed. Ong, for example, dismisses Greece as a culture that has never thoroughly internalized writing (1982, 26).

[44] By way of example one could cite from an article published in a French literary supplement: "La poésie entre la lyre et le bouzouki" (Poetry between the lyre and the bouzouki): "Essentiellement orale, la poésie grecque a traversé les ages comme le plus précieux, et peut-être l'unique instrument de communication entre les générations, les classes sociales, le peuple et ses idéaux, le sacré et le profane" (Essentially oral, Greek poetry has traversed the ages as the most precious, and perhaps most unique, instrument of communication between generations, social classes, people and their ideals, the sacred and the profane) (Analis 1979, 20).

[45] On the publishing industry during and after the dictatorship, see L. Axelos (1984a, 1984b). See also "Συζήτηση για το βιβλίο" (Discussion about the book) (Angelou et al. 1972), in which it was proclaimed that "the book has found its way into the supermarket" (30). The journal *Epitheorisi Technis* ran a series on the crisis in publishing in the early 1960s before the dictatorship; see esp. "Το βιβλίο περνάει κρίση!" (Book trade in crisis!) (1961). See also Thanasis Valtinos's comments (1988, 18–19); and D. Harvey 1987.

mative: "It will innovate in shape and in typography—it will pay particular attention to the issue of appearance—it will give a great deal of importance to the straight visual presentation" (Valaoritis 1985, 9), and this outlook spread among literary publications.

In the context of such shifts it is interesting to consider certain assumptions about the relative oral or visual impact of writing embedded in the writers' responses to censorship. Whereas the more established writers of the generation of the 1930s and the two postwar generations seemed less willing to relinquish the primacy of the oral,[46] the poets of the generation of the 1970s, who began publishing in this climate, were more willing to align poetry with the visual arts as well as with speech and music. Their poems are full of references to films and comic strips—Marilyn Monroe, Flash Gordon, and westerns. By drawing on the visual and narrative techniques of film and comics, these younger poets expand the terms of poetry to take advantage of the whole range of ways visual media were evading censorship.[47]

To set the stage for my reading of Steriadis's poetry, let me first distinguish the visual narrative that emerges in the 1970s from the surrealist tradition in Greek poetry that had consistently privileged visual and narrative techniques since the 1930s. What are the differences, for example, between the visual and narrative preoccupation of the poetry of Embirikos in the 1930s and of that of Steriadis in the 1970s? And what do these differences have to do with the conditions of writing and reading before, under, and after the dictatorship? Andreas Embirikos, Nikos Engonopoulos, Nicolas Calas, even Odysseas Elytis and Yannis Ritsos, all invoke the predominantly visual world of dreams in their poetry.[48] Many draw

[46] This is even apparent in the proclamations we looked at in Chapter 1. In his March 28, 1969 statement, Seferis very reluctantly broke the silence, referring to censorship by using the phrase "freedom was gagged" and concluding with the hope that he could return to "silence" and not have to "speak again" (in H. Vlachos 1971, 137). When the work of postwar writers started appearing without their permission in newspapers, their letter of indignation concluded with an appeal to Seferis's voice: "Let us hope that the poet's voice will not prove to be the voice of another Cassandra" (in H. Vlachos 1971, 197). Though writers of the postwar generations seemed to wish their writing could be more like the visual arts, they were still bound to this traditional sense of poetry as predominantly oral. For them, the mute language of gestures they fashioned, so close in tone to the work of a Kaniaris, say, was an impoverished language, a language that could not speak as it wished.

[47] Of course oral and visual aspects of writing are never mutually exclusive. In a conference on orality and literacy, David Ricks (1989) illustrated this by showing how even the most textual and visually attentive of twentieth century poetry, that of Cavafy and of Embirikos as well as that of the more lyric Seferis and Sikelianos, relied on the oral fifteen-syllable verse. In one example he read Embirikos's "Ο δρόμος" (The road) both for the way it employs the rhythms of the πολιτικός στίχος, the fifteen-syllable line, and for how it breaks with orality by visually rearranging the line on the page.

[48] It is interesting that in their professional lives these poets bridged the poetry and art worlds: Engonopoulos considered himself first and foremost an artist; see his note to his book

on the same narratives that inform the poetry of the generation of the 1970s: the prose of the 1880s (Alexandros Papadiamantis and Georgios Vizyenos); the adventure tales of Jules Verne (Chryssanthopoulos 1979, 120). The postwar poet Miltos Sachtouris, closer to the younger poets in age and outlook, even combines the visual and narrative preoccupations of his precursors, referring to paintings and films which, like dreams, present plot as a spatial project, such as the visual metamorphosis of man into animal in a Hieronymous Bosch painting.[49] But the poets of the generation of the 1970s take this combined preoccupation with the visual and the narrative one step further. Instead of trying to recreate the personal mythology of the dreamworld, they address the dreamwork itself, focusing on the activity of visual transformation by which one image becomes another, looking to dream and film, but also to advertising and comics.[50] Less interested in the actual image or plot and more interested in the activity of making pictures and stories, their poetry does not refer to coherent other worlds but aims at catching the photograph in the act of developing, the comic strip in between frames, the film in the process of replacing one image with another. Their poetry combines the visual and narrative preoccupation of their predecessors into visual narratives that seek not merely to reproduce the new images of mass production but to replicate their processes of reproduction.

One way to think about the different ways the surrealists and the generation of the 1970s incorporate the visual is to recall Fredric Jameson's distinction between visually representable machines and machines of visual reproduction. Jameson charts a shift from machines in the first quarter of the twentieth century which look like what they do (Charles Sheeler's smokestacks, grain elevators) to machines of visual reproduction of the last quarter (television, computers, video cassettes) whose appearance has no emblematic power but whose purpose *is* visual reproduction. Because this newer technology does not look like what it does, it is not sufficient to represent it in art and architecture; one must refer to its processes. Jameson suggests that a Japanese architect's thematic appropriation of this shift, a building in the shape of a stack of cassettes, is amusing but misses the point: if the technology that shapes our daily lives has slipped from production to the more self-referential reproduction, then so must art and

---

of poems Μην ομιλείτε εις τον οδηγόν (Do not converse with the driver) in which he admits: "I am a painter by profession, and, for that matter, consider poetry as a completely personal thing" (now in 1977, 145). Calas too was best known abroad as an art critic; and Elytis, though a Nobel laureate poet, also made sought-after collages. Ritsos was famous for his ink drawings on stones and roots.

[49] See Dallas 1979, 61–64, for a discussion of image and montage in Sachtouris's poetry and Maronitis 1980, 67–68, for a comparison of the visual worlds of Sachtouris and Bosch.

[50] On the Freudian term *dreamwork* as a poetics, see Chapter 5.

architecture (1984, 78–79). How, we might ask, is the shift from reproducing dream images or images from a changing world, to reproducing the processes of visual reproduction, charted in Greek poetry? What were the different social conditions that informed the visual narratives of Embirikos and Steriadis?

The key lies in the very issue of consumerism I have been discussing. While the surrealists through the 1950s could still give priority to production over reproduction and consumption, and imagine unmediated dream images that expressed desire, it was more difficult for poets of the 1960s and 1970s to ignore consumerism's appropriation of desire. It was not that advertising mirrored desires but that people often understood what they wanted by means of advertising. Surrealism in Greece may have accepted individual imagination as socially constructed, but it still described the dream images as coming from inside, as its reworking of the Oedipus complex as well as other psychoanalytic concepts suggests.[51] The more recent poetry no longer asks whether images come from inside or outside; there is no separation between the images of dreams and those of billboards, magazines, and television. Calas, in his article "Pop Icons" (1966), makes a similar distinction: the surrealist artist's conflation of art and life still relied on mimesis; that of the American pop artist no longer distinguished between the two. Calas describes the pop artists' images—Jasper Johns's lead flashlights or Robert Walls's hot dogs—as relics that, "subtracted from the superficial world of imitation, occupy a place in a reality from which identity has been excluded" (170).

This shift from production to reproduction and its ramification for poetry can be figured in terms of metaphor and metonymy, especially as Jacques Lacan has formulated them.[52] These tropes can then be shown to be fundamental in structural differences of the poetry of the generation of the 1930s and that of the 1970s. Metaphor substitutes one image for another and foregrounds similarity. It depends on mimesis and the ability to recognize an object's function from its appearance. Marinetti's automobile can stand for the speed of technology as well as for a poetry of the future. Engonopoulos's Σίγγερ (Singer) sewing machine poses a more complicated correspondence, and yet it also works metaphorically (1977, 11–12), standing for the odd state of surrealist poetry in Greece in the 1930s: on the one hand, imported like the Singer sewing machine, and yet on the other hand, indigenous inasmuch as the words *singer* and *sewer* are connected only in

---

[51] See, e.g., Embirikos's "Οιδίπους Ρεξ" (Oedipus Rex) (1980b, 145–52).

[52] I include synecdoche as a subset of metonymy rather than a different trope. The differences between metaphor and metonymy will never be firmly established, but for heuristic purposes I rely on Lacan's definition (1977, 146–78), drawing on Jakobson 1971b; Lodge 1977; S. Freud 1976, chap. 6; Genette 1982; Riffaterre 1978; White 1973; Gallop 1985b, 114–32; MacCannell 1986; Lemaire 1977, 191–205; and Lyotard 1983 to clarify his position.

the Greek word rhapsode ο ραψωδός—one who stitches songs together, ράπτω ωδή. In Lacan's system, metaphor allows for the immediate emergence of signification. The wheels and the streamlined appearance of a car signal speed. The needle and thread of a sewing machine signal the ability to connect something to something else. Metonymy, in contrast, mystifies, resisting and deferring signification (Lacan 1977, 146–78; Lemaire 1977, 191–205; Gallop 1985b, 114–32). Instead of calling attention to similarity and difference, metonymy emphasizes deformation and incompleteness. It refers to a whole range of processes—displacement, condensation, combination—and thereby foregrounds the *activity* of replacing something with something else, rather than the thing replaced or doing the replacing. Like Jameson's television shell that conceals its function, a metonym bears a less direct relation to that which it displaces or condenses. Even synecdoche, the most standard of metonyms, the part for the whole, a sail for a ship, focuses the reader's attention more on why this part and not another part has been chosen, than on the sail or the ship itself. In metonymy what is left out is always contiguous with what remains, and what something appears to be is never conclusive. In distinction to the sewing machine, machines such as the television, the video, and the radio do not look like what they do. Rather than producing meaning, they reproduce the process of producing meaning. It is not that metaphor cannot be used to mystify or metonymy to resolve meaning but, rather, that in following Lacan's lead, a useful distinction can be drawn between the poetic project of surrealist poetry and that of more recent poetry in Greece.[53]

To show how these tropes facilitate different visual and narrative effects, it is useful to distinguish between metaphor and the extended metaphor and between metonymy and the extended metonym. Michael Riffaterre (1978) suggests that the arch trope of surrealist poetry was not simply metaphor but the extended metaphor; that is, it was in the chain of metaphors that the signifying impulse of metaphor became clear. Whereas the surrealist poet's appeal to visual imagery and narrative ordering may appear illogical at first, on closer analysis a visual syntax is evident. He explains:

Surrealist images are arbitrary only in relation to our habitual logic and utilitarian attitude toward reality and language. In the reality of the text, they are rigorously determined by the verbal sequence and are, therefore, justified and appropriate within the framework of a given poem. Within this microcosm, a logic of words comes to be a logic that has nothing to do with normal

[53] Certainly metonyms can be found in surrealist poetry and metaphors in the poetry of the generation of the 1970s, but as Tziovas has pointed out, "A text is characterized as metaphorical or metonymic not according to the amount of metaphors or metonyms which it contains but mainly from the way it is structured and the way the narrative unfolds" (1987b, 148).

linguistic communication. This verbal logic creates a special code, a dialect within language, causing the reader to undergo the disorientation of the sense that the Surrealists saw as the essence of the poetic experience. (202)

He then analyzes certain extended metaphors to show how each metaphor in the series "expresses a particular aspect of the whole, be it a thing or a concept represented by the first metaphor in the series" (203). He quotes a line from a poem by Sainte-Beuve and analyzes how the primary metaphor ("a trickle of a poetic idea") is then connected to each subsequent metaphor so that all the vehicles, from "trickle" to "flow" to "river" to "lake" to "freezes" and "crystallizes" signify tenors that are all forms of poetic inspiration, whether "elegy," "meditation," or "sonnet." Repeatedly the vehicle—that which describes—and the tenor—that which is described—correspond to each other and relate back to the primary metaphor.[54] Riffaterre then adds that the surrealist extended metaphor differs only "in that it broadens the notion of acceptability" (204).

Embirikos's poems lend themselves to a similar analysis. "Η Αρχική Μορφή . . ." (The initial form . . .), for example, breaks down into tenors and vehicles that define "οι καιροί" (the times) in terms of the way women have changed. All the vehicles from "η αρχική" (the initial) to "έκτοτε άλλαζαν" (later times changed) to "έγινε" ([she] became) to "εποχές αλλάζουν" (the epochs change) correspond to tenors that are all different forms of woman:

Η αρχική μορφή της γυναικός ήτο το πλέξιμο των λαιμών δυο δεινοσαύρων. 'Εκτοτε άλλαξαν οι καιροί και άλλαξε σχήμα και η γυναίκα. 'Εγινε πιο μικρή πιο ρευστή πιο εναρμονισμένη με τα δικάταρτα (σε μερικές χώρες τρικάταρτα) καράβια που πλέουν επάνω από τη συμφορά της βιοπάλης. Η ίδια πλέει επάνω στα λέπια ενός κυλινδροφόρου περιστεριού μακράς ολκής. Οι εποχές αλλάζουν και η γυναίκα της εποχής μας μοιάζει με χάσμα θρυαλλίδος.

(1980d, 16)

The braided throats of two dinosaurs was the initial form woman took. Later, times changed and woman changed too. She became smaller, more lithe, more in keeping with the two-masted (in some countries three-masted) ships which float on the misfortune of an earned living. She herself floats on the scales of a cylinder-bearing dove of immense weight. The epochs change and the woman of our epoch resembles the gap in a filament.

In the content of the extended metaphor the imagery makes sense. Michael Chryssanthopoulos makes a similar case for the poems in Embirikos's Υψικάμινος (Blast furnace) ([1935] 1980d), though without using the term

---

[54] *Vehicle* and *tenor* are I. A. Richards's terms (1936, chaps. 5–6).

extended metaphor: "The unity that the critics could not find in the succession of individual words can be found in the succession of the poems. While the images appear unrelated if seen separately, they are a unified experience or apprehended as part of a complete poem" (Chryssanthopoulos 1979, 114). The extended metaphor works both visually and narratively: the vehicles invariably appeal to the eye, and each metaphor is connected to the next by conjunctions or verbs. The visual syntax remains intact. The narrative link supplied by the reader obeys the basic narrative convention whereby what comes first gets the status of "causing" what comes later. The transformation—the fact that one thing becomes another thing—is described rather than enacted.

The poetry of the generation of the 1970s is, in contrast, typified by what one might call an extended metonym, a trope that performs a transformation, displacement, deformation, or condensation. As the chain of signifiers is already a part of Lacan's formula for metonymy, one would actually have to conceive of a chain of already endlessly displaced signifiers for an extended metonym. The reader cannot fill in the gaps without constantly shifting terms. This is particularly evident in the early poetry of Vasilis Steriadis (but also of Pavlina Pampoudi) written under the dictatorship. Instead of constructing an internal logic of metaphorically connecting disparate images, as Embirikos's poetry did, their poetry resists meaning. The tenor is completely forgotten as one vehicle replaces another vehicle, to use I. A. Richards's terms, or the signifier is replaced by the next in an endless chain, to use Lacan's. The connections are not based on similarities but on less obvious relationships. Whereas the extended metaphor constructed a meaning for even the most surreal poem, the extended metonym has no pretensions to coherence. Roman Jakobson's description of metonymy is apt: "The reader is crushed by the multitude of detail unleashed on him in a limited verbal space, and is physically unable to grasp the whole, so that the portrait is often lost" (1971b, 256).

Steriadis's *Mr. Ivo* and *The Private Airplane* both describe and deploy this extended metonym. In one of his first poems it is not so much that the proper names have been replaced by pronouns but that the proper names have completely disappeared. The pronouns no longer refer to anything:

> Θα 'ρχότανε η φωνή πως χάσαμε τα ονόματά μας
> ανάμεσα σε μερικές εκατοντάδες λέξεις
> κι είμαστε μόνο "αυτός," "αυτή," "αυτό."
> (1970b, 11)

> A voice would say that we lost our names
> amidst some hundreds of words
> and we are only "he," "she," "it."

Here, as with Lacan's formula for metonymy, that which is signified, the names themselves, are no longer relevant. In *The Private Airplane* the unpredictability of metonymy is described and then deployed:

> Και λοιπόν πέφτοντας από ύψος ένα βράδι
> Χτύπησα κατά λάθος πάνω στο αρμόνιο, γι᾿ αυτό έγινα
> μουσικός.
> (1971, 16)

> And then falling from a height one evening
> I landed on a harmonium by mistake, and that's why I became
> a musician.

These descriptions of how metonymy works, that is, of how something is associated with something else through contiguity, are often accompanied by actual extended metonyms. In this same poem, after the above description, we find:

> . . . το καπέλλο μου ήταν λευκό προς το βάθος της τελετής
> και καθόλου περιστέρια.

> Τηλεοράδια και τανάπαλιν, τρυπητή μανιβέλλα
> φίλτατε, φίλτατε.
> (16)

> . . . my hat was white toward the back of the ritual
> and not at all doves.

> Tele-radios and vice versa, punctured crank
> my dear friend, my dear friend.

One image succeeds another and sets up a chain of signifiers whose only relation is one of contiguity and which have no connection to any signified. The reader cannot know what is meant. The reason something supersedes something else is more important than what has replaced it. The doves replace the hat because they are both white, whereas the alliteration of τηλεοράδια and τανάπαλιν and τρυπητή links these words by their sound.[55]

The poetry of Steriadis distinguishes itself from surrealist poetry by not allowing a single sentence or narrative structure to dictate the connections

---

[55] Anika Lemaire usefully outlines various of Lacan's metonymic rules such as the substitution of "the sign for the signifier," which would work for the substitution of white for the dove, and "the use for the thing," which helps explain the replacement of the sound for the alliterated word, the only use being its sound (1977, 193).

between all the images. The verbal logic is constantly shifting. As in Lyotard's theory of paralogy, the rules in Steriadis's poetry are constantly
being rewritten, and there is never recourse to a master narrative. Whereas
in the extended metaphor of the Embirikos poem there is one rule that connects all the images, in Steriadis's poem there is a new rule for every image.
Any attempt to make something appear logical is defeated. In another
poem in *The Private Airplane* Steriadis in fact distinguishes his poems from
those of the surrealists on exactly these grounds: "Things happened in an
idiosyncratic montage, just like in the olden times in surrealist poems" (10).
His description then of what exactly "happened" reveals that the surrealists' "idiosyncratic montage," though baffling to the uninitiated, is not in
the end illogical and that as soon as one figures out the particular order of
things, one can understand the poem. His own project, though, is different,
and he avoids using metaphors that serve as blueprints connecting a series
of implausibly related images.

In his poems inspiration and metaphysics are irrelevant because the
explanations and connections they furnish are no longer desirable. Paralogical times require paralogical verse:

> Ουδεμία σχέση με το λυχνάρι του Αλαντίν
> τους εξήγησα και τους γύρισα την πλάτη στο καινούριο
> ρεστωράν για να γίνη ατμόσφαιρα-ταμπαρατούμπαρα.
>
> (1971, 14)

> Not the slightest connection with Aladdin's lamp
> I explained to them and I turned away, my back to the new
> restaurant so that all hell would break loose.

The confusion of the times must be present in the language, not mitigated
by magic lamps. Jina Politi (1976) distinguished the new poetry from surrealism by calling it museless (ά-μουση). By this she seems to mean a
poetry without an extralinguistic element, whether Aladdin's lamp or a
specific signified. Whereas surrealist poetry ultimately presupposed a particular logic, in this new poetry, she explains, the reader is like another
Adam naming as he goes along. For examples she turns to two women
poets of the second postwar generation, Mando Aravandinou and Nana
Isaïa, whose work—unlike the poetry of Anagnostakis, Patrikios, and Alexandrou of the previous generation—foreshadows the younger poets'
metonymic resistance to meaning. She illustrates her point with a line from
a poem by Isaïa: "Αυτό και πάλι δεν σημαίνει τίποτα άλλο εκτός από αυτό το
ποίημα, που μόλις έχω τελειώσει να γράφω" (Once again this does not mean
anything except this poem, which I have just finished writing). Politi explains how this new poetry is not in the service of truth but, self-reflexively,

in the service of writing. As the titles of the books she is reviewing sug-gest—Γραφή Γ' (Writing 3) by Aravandinou and Ένα βλέμμα (One look) by Isaïa—it is the emphasis on the visual presence of the text that distin-guishes this poetry from its precursors.[56] She could as easily have drawn on the poetry of Sachtouris to make her point. Steriadis's poetry strips, where one image succeeds another in a paralogical fashion disrupting any illusion of coherence, constitute an important bridge between the poetry of the second postwar generation, especially that of the women poets, and the visual narratives of younger women poets in the 1980s. The postwar poets, among whom I would add Eleni Vakalo, Kiki Dimoula, and Katerina Anghelaki-Rooke, began to make readers aware of the materiality of the text; it then took the generation of the 1970s to carry the paralogical to such an extreme that the reader's attention is constantly led back to the medium itself—and the work of women poets in particular to fully exploit the possi-bilities of the extended metonym.

The medium of comics in his first two books, and that of film in his third, offer Steriadis ways of keeping images in motion and thus evading the fixity of meaning demanded by censorship. Even within a single frame of a comic strip there are lessons on how to create the illusion of motion. In comics, if a character hits another character, the hand that is hitting is reproduced again and again to signify movement through space; falling is visually reproduced by repeated images of the falling object. Steriadis invokes this process in the poem "Τα κακά μαντάτα" (The bad news), when he employs an idiom that figuratively means "to get sick" but literally means "to fall on the bed":

Βρε παιδάκι μου, της είπα, ξεσκονίζοντας τα μεγάλα φτερά
των αγγέλων. Τω καιρώ εκείνω έπεσα στο κρεβάτι απ' το στομάχι
μου, ένα από τα πολλά στομάχια δηλαδή . . .

                                          (1971, 22)

Hey kid, I said to her dusting off the large wings
of the angels. In those days I went to bed because of [I fell on the bed on]
                                          my stomach,
that is to say, one of my many stomachs . . .

The informal "Hey kid" and the reference to comic strips summoned up by falling on "one of my many stomachs" contrasts sharply with the image of

[56] I found a copy of Politi's article among Anghelaki-Rooke's papers; the latter's marginalia add an interesting perspective. For example, she puts a question mark after the article's title "Η απώλεια της μούσας" (The loss of the muse), suggesting that, at this point, she is not sure that poetry, hers or others', is becoming less prophetic and more self-reflexive. Sixteen years later, in an unpublished article (1992), however, she fully acknowledges a shift and concludes by focusing on women poets' attention to the self-reflexivity of language.

dusting off angels' wings. These phrases set the tone so that the poem can continue "αφήνοντας έξω εκείνο που έχει σημασία . . ." (leaving out that which is important . . .). Not only do images within a phrase replace each other in Steriadis's poems, but this continues from phrase to phrase and from poem to poem, much the way characters and objects are repeated in a comic strip from frame to frame. One odd detail leads to the next, connected only it seems by its inappropriateness as a topic for poetry—a peppermint from a woman's hand, unacceptable fantasies, minorities in Greece (i.e., Turks, Jews). Finally the poem concludes by admitting that this very activity of replacing one image with the next keeps the poem from finishing: "'Αλλώς θα είχα τελειώσει ένα καλό / ποίημα με αγγέλους" (Otherwise I would have finished a good / poem about angels). By modeling his writing on the "unpoetic" form of comic strips and writing about "unpoetic" things, he is freed from convention, and unlike the angel/messenger who is obliged to tell the truth directly, he can speak his truths at a slant.

In Steriadis's poetry, not only are the individual phrases and individual poems put into motion, but each of his first three books are divided into sections like comic strips, suggesting a larger-scale narrative motion. In the first book it is the last section, "Mr. Ivo," that seems to initiate this technique. "Mr. Ivo" is made up of an introduction, five different "cases" (περιπτώσεις), and a conclusion. His next book, *The Private Airplane* is divided into a prologue and five chapters. The publisher of this collection stresses its indebtedness to comics when he writes, in his introduction, "The poetry of Vasilis Steriadis is based on the idea that the spirit and the pace of our times have been registered in the cartoon and reactions of comic strip heroes" (6).

Steriadis's third book, *Pale Dick*, sustains this formal organization— certain images recur like characters in a comic strip: the heaven, the belly, Dick, Lulu. There are also numerous references to things that move: trains, airplanes, film. These objects, however, are not metaphors for motion or speed but, rather, models for sustaining images in motion. It is in this collection that the shift from comics to film is evident. Whereas in comics, images succeed each other frame by frame, here the speed gives the illusion that actions are replacing each other the way they do in film. Each frame contains an action rather than an image. This is effected by the abundance of periphrastic imperatives, for example, in the poem "Μαθητής Μιχαήλ" (Apostle Michael), in which one demand replaces another:

Να πης στη Λουλού
να βγη από την κλούβα
μη σκαλίζης τα αίματα Λουλού
δεν έχω άλλα κουφέτα να σου φέρω

μην παντρεύεσαι συνέχεια με άλλους
θα φύγω.

(1976, 34)

Tell Lulu
to get out of the cage
don't rummage around in the blood Lulu
I do not have any more sugar almonds to bring you
don't keep marrying others
I'll leave.

This shift of focus to film is also clear in a more recently published poem
that was written around the same time (1972–73) in which Steriadis makes
an analogy between the way his own book works on the reader and the
way a film works on him:

Λευκό φιλμ και μαύρο γαλλικό
μπαίνει και βγαίνει στο συναισθηματικό μου
κόσμο. 'Οπως ένα βιβλίο που έγραψα
μπαίνει απ' τα μάτια της και βγαίνει
από την κοιλιά της Ουρανίας, που είναι απούσα.

(1983, 23)

White film and black, french
weaves in and out of my emotional
world. The way a book which I wrote
enters her eyes and comes out
Ourania's stomach, who is absent.

Just as it was useful to look to Christianopoulos's essay for a connection
between advertising, anonymity, and censorship in Poulios's poetry, so it is
instructive to invoke film criticism again for the relation between poetry's
visual impact and censorship. What Rafaelidis said about film as an indecipherable language of pictures aptly describes Steriadis's poetry strips.
His poetry's appeal to the visual extended metonym is a subversive way of
making poetry more like film, detaching language from definitive meanings and defeating censorship.

Like Poulios, though, Steriadis does not sustain this project. His 1983
collection comprises poems most, and certainly the best, of which he wrote
years before. The collection is tellingly named Το χαμένο κολιέ (The lost
necklace) after the oldest series in the book, written in 1971–72, and the
poem that gives its name to the series is a perfect example of the poetry
strip he initiated but does not sustain. The most recent series in this collec-

tion, "Χιόνια στο καμπαναριό" (Snow on the bell tower), is peppered with acronyms and vain political strategies—see in particular "Τα χιόνια" (The snow) (51). Often foe and friend are indistinguishable. But instead of portraying this dissolution of boundaries as a potentially potent political strategy along the lines of the extended metonym, there is a nostalgia for a time when right and wrong were easier to determine, when the signifier belonged to a particular signified, a time when the "barbarians" were a "solution."

Steriadis's 1992 collection, Ο προπονητής παίκτης (The player coach), is also typified by a nostalgia, but this time for his childhood in Pelion, not his student years in Athens. The defeated, resolved tone of the book is set by the first poem:

> Η Αίγινα θα έπρεπε να είναι η Βενετία,
> όμως δεν είναι.
>
> Η Λήδα θα έπρεπε να είναι η Ουρανία,
> όμως δεν είναι.
>
> Κι αυτό το ποίημα
> θα έπρεπε να είναι το καλύτερό μου,
> όμως δεν είναι.
>
> (11)
>
> Aegina should be Venice,
> but it isn't.
>
> Leda should be Ourania,
> but she isn't.
>
> And this poem
> should be my best,
> but it isn't.

As in Poulios's *Things of Slight Importance*, everything is less than what it should be. Although the "linguistic idiom" of mixed affiliations makes for some memorable lines, especially those that draw on the language of soccer—"χτύπημα πέναλτι στην έρημο" (penalty shot in the desert) (Steriadis 1992, 13) or "πουλάω τη γωνία που συναντιόμασταν / και σφυρίζω ένα κόρνερ" (I sell the corner where we used to meet / and call a "corner") (14)—the game itself is not integrated formally the way comics and film were in his earlier collections, nor is the other televised event that informs this collection, the political scandals and trials of 1989–92, when "all of

Greece had turned into one big court room" (1994). The proper names of his childhood and the technical terms of soccer and law, his chosen profession, dominate these poems, but the narratives they refer to are missing. The visual suspense that characterized his earlier collections is gone, and the poems stammer and stop in a new self-consciousness. The reader, who was so crucial to the functioning of the extended metonym, is extraneous here. The poem as an experiment or a dare—so evident in his earlier brazen claim "Don't ask like a fool / this is a poem / it's not the bottom of your bottom" (in Ziras 1979, 153) has given way to "μαλακίες ποιήματα" (jerk-off poems) (Steriadis 1992, 18) and "μπάσταρδα ποιήματα / σαν αυτό που έγραψα απόψε" (bastard poems / like the one I wrote tonight) (32), poems that have already finished and failed before the reader gets to them. Even if such statements are ironic, after three or four of them it is hard for the reader not to begin to believe them.

I have now traced various poetic strategies that integrate the discourse of consumerism and censorship and shown how, in their reworking of the American loan of pop culture—whether it be, in Poulios's case, the redeploying of the effect of obscenities or the anonymity of the commodity or, in Steriadis's case, in taking the explosion of visual culture as an excuse to concentrate on poetry's connection to comics and film—the discourse of censorship is formative. Again and again it is what forces poetry to politicize the aesthetic and distinguishes this generation from both its American counterpart and previous generations of Greek poets. But in each of the two cases the poetic and political projects dwindle: Poulios with his political Beat and Steriadis with his poetry strip initiated an important poetics, but neither sustained it into the 1980s. Rather, it was the women poets of this generation—Galanaki, Laina, Mastoraki, Pampoudi, Papadaki, among others—who saw in censorship a productive matrix through which to explore power relations between the sexes after the colonels were gone. But before I explore how their visual narratives develop the poetic strategies I outline in this chapter, I want to discuss the uses of woman as a figure of resistance more generally under the dictatorship and connect this to the rise of feminism.

3

Women's Writing and the
Sexual Politics of Censorship

The realm of sexuality messes up what can be thought of in any straightforward sense as causality. Precisely, then, through its foregrounding of sexuality, feminism may be in a privileged position to challenge or rethink the dualities (inside/outside, victim/aggressor, real event/fantasy) which seem to follow any rigid externalization of political space.

—Jacqueline Rose

In her essay "Where Does the Misery Come From? Psychoanalysis, Feminism, and the Event," Jacqueline Rose situates feminism and sexual violence at the heart of the recurring dispute in psychoanalytic circles over the social or psychic origins of discontent.[1] She discusses how first Wilhelm Reich, then Jeffrey Masson, attack Freud for retreating from the real world. In both their arguments she finds a problematic externalization of violence and an inability to deal with ambiguity and relates these to their rigid conceptions of sexual difference. Her point is that, for Freud, violence was neither outside nor inside, social nor psychic, but an effect of these dichotomies and that feminism is useful in deconstructing such oppositions. The psychoanalytic object of Rose's inquiry may be different from my literary one, but the impulse and argument are similar. Although contemporary critical histories of psychoanalysis and of Greek literature have only a few proper names in common, the debate over "where the misery comes from" and its relation to feminism is central to both. In each case, feminism, with its attention to sexuality, accentuates the complexities involved in attributing blame or ascertaining origins. Neither woman as victim nor woman as agent of her own demise is a sufficient explanation of her subordination. Rose's story of how feminism helps psychoanalysis rethink violence as both external and internal to the subject finds an interesting parallel in Greece after the dictatorship, when feminism enabled contemporary literature, especially women's, to reconceive the strict division between censorship and self-censorship.

[1] I thank Anna Georgiopoulos for drawing my attention to the passage with which I have introduced this chapter.

The strength of postdictatorship Greek women's literature is linked to women writers' willingness to view in relation to one another the censorships of an authoritarian regime, of patriarchy, and of an author's self-critical gaze. To elucidate this linkage, I examine how the figure of woman was deployed under the dictatorship in relation to the regime's distrust of confusion. To the colonels' fear of linguistic ambiguity I add, here, the fear of sexual ambiguity. Poets, cartoonists, and novelists on the Left played off of these fears, often using the figure of woman to represent textual and sexual undecidability.[2] After discussing the cultural and theoretical landscape of the postdictatorship years, in particular the emerging discourse of feminism, I explore the ways in which a new formal concern with ambiguity, what I will specify as "undeliverability" in women's poetry after the dictatorship, is related to this gendering of undecidability under the dictatorship. My more general discussion of the representation of woman under the dictatorship in the first three sections of this chapter therefore provides the background for my overview of the social text of women's poetry after the dictatorship and the poetics it involves in the last two sections. In the final section and in the remainder of the book, I focus on the work of Rhea Galanaki, Jenny Mastoraki, and Maria Laina in order to call attention to a move toward a more visual and narrative poetry that incorporates the lessons of censorship and consumerism with the lessons of feminism, turning the generation of the 1970s' poetry of protest and doubt into a highly developed linguistic practice that continues to rehearse misunderstandings after the colonels are gone.

In keeping with the breakdown of the monolithic stature of poetry which I have outlined with respect to the generation of the 1970s, I broaden my own generic concerns, continuing to draw on a wide range of cultural productions—comics, films, and novels as well as poetry. Comparison with texts of contemporary European feminists such as that of the German writer Christa Wolf and that of the French philosopher Luce Irigaray make the Greek feminist issues more explicit as well as locate the cultural specificity of the Greek case. This is a pivotal chapter in that I shift from reading poetry in terms of the discourses of censorship, consumerism, and feminism to reading the Greek social context through the prism of women's poetry. It is in the formal structure of certain extended visual narratives written by women in the 1980s that I find a persuasive formulation of the role gender plays in defining subjectivity in Greece today.

---

[2] With the term *undecidability,* I recall this book's opening epigraph by Barbara Johnson and my discussion of it in my introduction's first footnote.

The Figure of Woman under the Dictatorship

The use of the figure of woman to represent different cultural and political agendas has a long tradition in the West.[3] The case of the surrealists provides an excellent example. As Bethany Ladimer points out, "By virtue of her political and social situation, woman symbolised for the surrealists a set of values contrary to the dominant social values against which they sought to rebel" (1980, 176). Ladimer then quotes the French surrealist poet André Breton: "The artist should emphasize to the fullest extent all that falls within the feminine mode of understanding as opposed to the masculine, and [he should] base his work exclusively on characteristic feminine perceptions: he should exalt and preferably even appropriate for his own personal use everything that distinguished the female from the male in matters of understanding and volition" (177). The Greek surrealists (so popular with the Greek poets of the generation of the 1970s) followed suit. The poem of Embirikos discussed in Chapter 2 illustrates how the figure of woman becomes the terrain for imagining social change. As in the case of Breton, Embirikos's desire to challenge the status quo relies on whether or not he can appropriate "the feminine mode of understanding." Woman in this context serves as the archmetaphor of flux and transformation. As times change, she changes: "Οι εποχές αλλάζουν και η γυναίκα της εποχής μας μοιάζει με . . ." (The epochs change and the woman of our epoch resembles . . .) (1980c, 16).

In the poetry of the generation of the 1970s the figure of woman is one of the primary sites for dealing with and challenging political oppression. By the same token, the interrelation between the discourses of consumerism and censorship is often mediated by reference to feminine experience. One of Poulios's earlier poems "Ερωτικό *Tank*" (Erotic tank), for example, acknowledges the repressive regime, and suggests the mixed political allegiances of the times by using the English word *tank* in the title, but frames its critique with reference to woman. She is the erotic tank linking military drive and feminine lust in lines such as "Τρέχεις μέσα μου κυνηγώντας . . ." (You run inside me hunting . . .), "Βαραίνει πάνω μου το μάτι σου και με γκρεμίζει . . ." (Your gaze weighs down on me and demolishes me . . .), and "στήθια μικρά αμπαζούρ, κοιλιά που κυβερνά πάνω . . ." (breasts small lampshades, belly which governs over . . .) (Poulios 1982, 31). But she is also the metaphor for the speaker's sense of emasculation, his feeling of

---

[3] Gayatri Spivak has outlined how the discourse of man, in particular the male philosopher, relies on the metaphor of woman. The titles of two of her articles are telling: "Displacement and the Discourse of Woman" (1983) and "Love Me, Love My Ombre, Elle" (1984). Woman has to be displaced or viewed as a shadow in order for men to get on with the (male) business of signification. See also Spivak's 1989 discussion of this topic.

being "entered" and "occupied." As in Embirikos's poem, woman is an attractive metaphor because she can stand for so many things.

Feminine experience also plays an important shifting role in the poem "Seascape" by another poet of the younger generation, Natasa Hatzidaki. In this poem, as we saw in Chapter 2, a foreign Triumph Spitfire is turned into a plausibly Greek image when it is put under surveillance. What I did not elaborate is how the Triumph and the spotlights are connected through the domestic image of the cooking pot. The phrase "in the slow boil" extends the metaphor of the cooking pots into the next line about the searchlights, relating the discourses of consumerism and censorship through the feminine experience of cooking:

> έχω ένα πυρίμαχο σπιτφάιρ της τράιομφ
> κι' όλα λάμπουν σαν κατσαρόλες
> μέσα στην αργή βράση των προβολέων.
>   (in Panayiotou 1979, 270)

> I have a fire-proof Spitfire by Triumph
> all shining like cooking pots
> in the slow boil of searchlights.

The terribly public experience of the dictatorship appears oddly intimate in this new configuration; conversely, the feminine experience of cooking becomes a public affair.

In Chapter 2, I also discussed how, in the cultural context of a regime that equated obscenities with subversive political action, sexuality became an important site of political resistance: if the censors were going to conflate sex and insubordination, then the resistance would too. Taking this analysis one step further, let me examine why reference to sex was invariably made in the name of woman. Why did protest against the mandatory voting in September 1969 take the form, in one instance, of a contraceptive rubber blown up and hung in Kolonaki Square with the word *Yes* in big letters and the name of Papadopoulos's mistress scrawled in cursive underneath (Andrews 1980, 10)? What is it about feminine experience that is so useful to Poulios and other poets of his generation? A clue is already to be found in the poems by Embirikos, Poulios, and Hatzidaki which I have just mentioned. It is not simply the claustrophobia and subordinate status of feminine experience that provide a way of describing life under an authoritative regime but the fact that feminine experience can be deployed to so many different ends. What is striking about the use of woman in all three poems is her ability to stand for more than one thing at the same time, even for the act of transformation itself. Her figural prominence in poetry produced under the dictatorship seems connected to her flexibility. But what were the more general cultural conditions in which woman emerged as a figure of undecidability and what was the character of this undecidability?

Not surprisingly, the regime sought to eradicate confusion and mixed messages not only through the press law but also through dress codes, curfews, and moral guidelines. The corollary of the censor's demand for a perfect fit between *what one said* and *what one meant* was the moralist's demand for a perfect fit between *what one looked like* and *who one was.* Any kind of undecidability, textual or sexual, was considered subversive. The Greek newspapers of 1969, when censorship was most severe, were full of references to the androgynous and gender-bending styles of hippies and male homosexuals. In an article entitled "Κι οι άντρες γίνονται γυναίκες" (And the men are becoming women) (1969) a columnist wrote: "This year's style in men's clothing allows the stronger sex to wear anything he pleases. There is not a single item in the woman's wardrobe which is exclusively woman's except perhaps her teensy . . . undergarments." Men's long hair, another sign of "men becoming women," was also the topic of much discussion.[4] The radical politics of the singer Savvopoulos was for years connected with his long hair. (It is worth mentioning that when he began to support the Right, he cut his hair and called his album "Το κούρεμα" [The haircut]). Costa-Gavras's film "Z," made in 1969, during the dictatorship, a thinly veiled account of the events surrounding the death of the leftist leader Grigoris Lambrakis, situates this suspicion of long hair in a political context. In one scene the police leap out of their van to break up a rally; a few grab a youth: instead of beating him up, they cut off his long hair. Homosexuality, another phenomenon that could naïvely be seen as a sign of "men becoming women," was also, of course, taboo.[5] As far as the regime was concerned, the disruption of conventional sexual distinctions by men with long hair and by homosexuals posed a threat similar to the one posed by the disjuncture between word and meaning. While Colonel Papadopoulos railed against metaphor and hidden meaning, another prominent member of the regime, Colonel Yannis Ladas, proclaimed long hair "the hirsute flag of nihilism" (Clogg and Yannopoulos 1972, 42) and closed down the magazine *Eikones* for publishing an article on homosexuality entitled "The Dark World of the Third Sex."[6]

[4] *Epikaira,* a popular weekly magazine, published just after the fall of the dictatorship the article "Τα μακρυά μαλλιά από τον Αδάμ ως τους Χίππυς" (Long hair from Adam to the hippies) which discussed how long hair had become associated with the counterculture in the 1960s and early 1970s in Greece and abroad (Zannidaki 1974).

[5] On homosexuality under and after the dictatorship, see the autobiography of Kostas Tachtsis 1989, 189–377, as well as Faubion 1993, 213–41.

[6] This conservative critique of long hair has a well-established precedent in the turn-of-the-

It was in the context of a regime trying to specify set gender roles that cartoonists, novelists, and poets focused on woman's figural flexibility.[7] Again and again, opposition to the regime is thematized through the sexually and textually undecidable figures of Kassandra, Little Red Riding Hood, Lysistrata, and Scheherazade, the heroine of 1,001 nights. Rarely do these women mean what they say or look like who they are. Lysistrata's puns are as bawdy as her plans; her scheme to put an end to war depends on seductive word play as well as a striptease. Similarly, Little Red Riding Hood's encounter with the wolf is as much a language game as it is a sexual initiation. Scheherazade's tales that forestalled death by seducing the king, her would-be killer, are a further example. Told in a harem, they also made language and sex into metaphors for deception. Whereas the regime's intolerance of undecidability focused on "men becoming women" and its weakening of the powerful, the resistance, in contrast, concentrated on the empowering of the weak, "women becoming men." They saw in characters such as Lysistrata and Scheherazade (and not, for example, the self-sacrificing heroines Iphigenia and Alcestes) women who intertwined sexual and linguistic wiliness in order to turn positions of weakness into positions of power. In Aristophanes's *Lysistrata*, for example, the women refuse to have sex until the men stop the war. Their feminine sexuality, that which turns them into the object of men's desires, in this case gives them their authority.[8] Little Red Riding Hood is known for duping her enemy. In one version she ties the string that is meant to restrain her to a plum tree, outwitting the wolf; in another version, she fills the wolf's stomach with stones so that he drowns. Writers and cartoonists of the times drew on women whose linguistic and sexual undecidability made them powerful. Two texts—Kyr's comic strip *Lysistrata* and Margarita Karapanou's novel

century critique of *malliarismos* (hairism) by the *katharevousiani* (the advocates of purist Greek) in the language controversy (Mackridge 1990, 30–31). This connection appears more than casual when one considers the colonels' attempt to reinstate Katharevousa.

[7] I should add, though, that just as the colonels' rhetorical force relied on the use of metaphor, which they prohibited others from using, so their attack on sexual undecidability did not stop them from manipulating gender roles to their own ends. While attacking popular culture for the "degenerate," effeminate styles of hippies and homosexuals, the regime frequently "feminized" its enemies. On September 21, 1969, the *New York Times Magazine* had a picture of a Greek man carrying water with the telling caption "Former Greek Official George Mylonas pays the penalty for differing with the ruling junta in Athens by performing household chores on the island of Amorgos where he lives in forced exile." The regime had degraded him by making him do woman's work. Pat Mainardi uses this as an example of why men do not do housework in her classic feminist article "The Politics of Housework" (1970, 509).

[8] See, for example, the exchange between Lysistrata and Calonice in which Lysistrata explains: "But don't you see, that's exactly what I mean to use to save Greece. Those saffron gowns and slippers and see-through dresses, yes, and our scent and rouge as well" (Aristophanes 1973, 181–82).

Kassandra and the Wolf—illustrate the figure of woman as the performative space in which undecidability is sustained.

Kyr's *Lysistrata*

The comic strip *Lysistrata,* published in thirty-seven weekly installments in the popular magazine *Epikaira,* beginning January 18, 1974, traces the shift from authoritarianism to democracy. The strip first appeared in the wake of the student uprising at the Polytechnic and Brigadier Dimitrios Ioannidis's take-over in November 1973, continued through Constantine Karamanlis's return as prime minister and the restoration of democracy in July 1974, and ended two months later, shortly before the first free elections in a decade on November 17. In the strip, the cartoonist Kyr reworks Aristophanes's story, using the classical figure of Lysistrata to address the contemporary issues of censorship, consumerism, and American military and political intervention in Greece. From the beginning, the figure of woman stands for everything desirable yet unattainable: peace, the lifting of censorship, and sexual freedom. She is the place where sexuality and politics are related: a provocative flapper with the word *Peace* written into the curve of her buttocks introduces the comic "instead of a prologue" (Figure 3). The fact that this comic's flagrant parody of censorship was not itself censored in the winter of 1973–74 reflects the rapid deterioration of the state apparatus after the Ioannidis coup.

Kyr sets the story in a time of war and international economic crisis, and it is clear from this first page that he is trying to make the most out of a dire situation. In a list of items that have suffered inflation—Persia has raised the price of petrol, Syros the price of Turkish delight, Chalkida the price of bricks—he includes the fact that *Epikaira* has raised the salary of the cartoonist: himself. But it is the figure of woman and her ability to transform one thing into another that enables him to oppose the regime and gain recognition as a resistance writer. "Yes, my dear readers! Just one thing! Lysistrata, a simple housewife, had a profound idea" (Figure 3). Aristophanes begins with Lysistrata complaining to her friend that though women rush to an orgy, none come to an organizational meeting for peace. Kyr's *Lysistrata* begins with a similar sentiment, but in his version, Lysistrata's friend tricks the women into coming to the meeting by shouting, "Attention! Attention! The sales have begun! Run! Run! . . . Discounts up to 50%" (Figure 4). Sales, women's weakness, are obviously the modern-day, capitalist equivalent of orgies. As in Adorno's critique of mass culture, in which woman is constructed as an Eve figure tempting man into capitalism, woman's sexual appetite is connected to her consumerism (Adorno

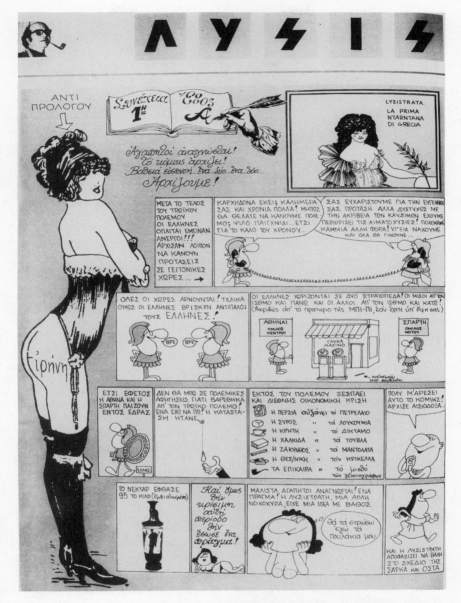

Figure 3. "Instead of a prologue" and "Lysistrata, a simple housewife, had an idea."

Figure 4. "Attention! Attention! The sales have begun."

Figure 5. Hanging out the laundry.

Figure 6. "You said male?"

1982, 279). But what is striking about both the classical and modern versions of Lysistrata is that the main plot is shaped by the fact that the very characteristic that disables women, their predilection for orgies or sales, can be turned into a constructive ploy. Even in this first encounter it is clear that what is attractive about woman is her ability to mediate between the discourses of consumerism and censorship, of excess and abstinence. Her double displacement, once by patriarchy, and once by the regime, equips her to take up different positions and reframe one sort of oppression in terms of another. Kyr accentuates this aspect of the Lysistrata story. On the cover of the issue of *Epikaira* in which the first installment appeared, Lysistrata is shown making a victory sign and carrying a spear with a pair of panties for a flag. To hang up laundry is certainly not unusual for a Greek woman, but to hang up laundry on a spear, or even more shockingly, between the columns of the Parthenon, is a radical act (Figure 5). Woman's transgressiveness seems connected with her ability to exorcize the claustrophobia of the dictatorship years by turning private acts into public ones.

It is this ability to bring one thing to bear on another which then allows the women to gain access to the citadel of power, the Acropolis. It is their use of ambivalent language and sexuality which enables them to get rid of the guards. In one episode, Parthenope, a cohort of Lysistrata, puts on poisonous lipstick in an attempt to kill a guard by seducing him (Figure 6). But the guard turns out to be gay. Parthenope exclaims, "Κρίμα που έβαλα στα χείλη μου αρσενικό" (Too bad I put arsenic on my lips). The guard overhears the word αρσενικό, which in Greek means "male" as well as "arsenic." Taking her for a man—"Αρσενικό είπες;" (You said male?)—he runs up to kiss her and meets his death. Being seen as something she is not and being understood saying something she does not mean make Parthenope an ideal figure of undecidability. Repeatedly it is the woman's ability to disguise and integrate opposing discourses which empowers her. She is the site of indeterminacy, both linguistic and sexual, in the form of puns and cross-dressing, and it is this indeterminacy in the context of a regime that wanted everything to be clear that turned her into the quintessential site of resistance.

As in a play within a play, Kyr dramatizes his own indebtedness to Lysistrata's wily ploys. Throughout the comics he has women resist censorship in a more open manner than men. By the end of the series, after the regime in fact has fallen, freedom is celebrated with sketches of women baring their bottoms to the censor, saying, "Now, if you can, cut it off [censor it]." Illustrating the awkward position writers found themselves in when, after preventive censorship was lifted in November 1969, they became their own censors, the most conservative character turns out to be Kyr, the fictional cartoonist who is introduced into the plot to keep order.

Figure 7. "Operation Magic Marker."

When things are getting out of hand, Kyr arrives on the scene to impose order, only to get beaten up by Lysistrata. When another character starts talking dirty, Kyr tries to cover over his words, warning him of censorship: "Shut up, buddy, or they'll close down the comics." And later when the man refuses to shut up, he shouts, "Stop it . . . if you don't close your mouth, I'll erase you." But Kyr's parodic collusion with the censors is short-lived because it is clear that he is behind Lysistrata's resistance tactics. She and her women, in what is called "Operation Magic Marker," capture the guards by drawing them into a little box (Figure 7) and then continue drawing the world the way they want it (Figure 8). They make men say what they want them to say (i.e., "Long live women") and draw all sorts of things that have no obvious connection to the plot. This "operation" is a blatant parody of the use of magic markers to blacken out the private parts on pornographic pictures at the time (Figure 2). In the middle of all this, Kyr has himself conveniently called away on business, giving him the excuse to hand over full control of the comics to women. Ultimately he can only undermine censorship and transform a bad situation into a good one by being in league with Lysistrata. Her sexual exploits provide a stage for his resistance.

In the same way that woman's sexual undecidability proves empowering, so does her ambivalence about national affiliations. Woman is a symbol of strength because of the way she stages transgressions and mixes allegiances of every sort. Up on the Acropolis, so as not to be noticed, Lysistrata and her women pretend to be American tourists. They say all the English words they happen to know—"Thank you . . . long play . . . CIA . . . Metro Goldwyn Mayer"—but because they are written in Greek, they "sound" Greek (Figure 9). The nationalist and racist call of "Greece for

Figure 8. Drawing the world the way women want it.

Figure 9. Lysistrata and her cohorts pretend to be American tourists.

Greeks and only Greeks" is associated with the regime, so the resistance foregrounds impurities and contamination: English with a Greek accent. At another point, the characters talk in English, and a note unabashedly states that it is because they are influenced by American comics. As in the poetry of Poulios and Steriadis, mixed affiliations are liberating rather than debilitating. But perhaps the most telling moment comes when peace is finally declared at the end. The women are running around celebrating, shouting things like "Finally we get to take off the plaster underwear"—this, referring to the dictator's favorite metaphor of Greece as a patient in a cast. Suddenly one shouts "KYP go home." A note from Kyr underneath explains that the woman does not mean him, the cartoonist, but ΚΥΠ the Greek Central Intelligence Service. This visual pun on the letter *R* in Greek, which looks like an English *P*, brings into focus again how it is woman who scrambles clear-cut distinctions. On the one hand, KYP, well known for its collusion with the CIA, is so American that it has to be written in English. On the other hand, if it is read in Greek, it spells the cartoonist's name.

But in the end, the undecidability touted throughout the comics in the figure of woman is no longer deemed necessary. With the regime over, the fear of censorship that has structured the comics is gone. Issues of control and subterfuge, and the subtle balance of power between Lysistrata and Kyr, seem beside the point. The final image is of a group of readers standing around wondering what Kyr will do next. Then suddenly he appears seated on a tank (Figure 10). His authoritative presence high above his readers is the only answer the comics offer to the question written underneath: "The End?" Kyr's inability to find an alternative solution to that of the dictator's seems connected to the faltering of Poulios's and Steriadis's poetic projects when the dictatorship fell. The mood of the times was succinctly summed up by Alexandros Kotzias in his acclaimed novel Αντι-ποίησις αρχής (Usurpation of authority). The novel's action takes place over three days during the student occupation of the Polytechnic in 1973 and ends with the words "and now what?" (1979, 289). Without something concrete to fight against, without Cavafy's barbarians, Kyr, Poulios, Steriadis, Kotzias all seem unsure how to proceed. Censorship had provided a

Figure 10. Kyr appears seated on a tank.

framework. Without it, writers, and particularly men, found themselves at a loss.[9]

Ritsos grapples with the gendered nature of this hesitation in "Πειστή-ρια" (Tangible proof), written in 1975. The poem presents a frozen world that needs a new kind of poetry, a new way of seeing, to set it in motion:

> Η γυναίκα είταν ακόμα πλαγιασμένη στο κρεββάτι. Αυτός
> έβγαλε το γυάλινο μάτι του, το ακούμπησε στο τραπέζι,
> έκανε ένα βήμα, σταμάτησε. Τώρα με πιστεύεις—της είπε.
> Εκείνη πήρε το γυάλινο μάτι, τόφερε στο μάτι της· τον κοίταξε.
>
> (1979, 118)

> The woman was still lying on the bed. He
> took out his glass eye, set it down on the table,
> took a step, stopped. Now do you believe me?—he said to her.
> She picked up the glass eye, brought it close to her eye; she looked at him.[10]

The poem depicts a changing of the guard in which the man comes to a complete stop, and the next step is left up to the woman. It is her responsibility to animate the scene. Though in the beginning she is still lying

---

[9] This "what now?" attitude echoes a comment the German writer Heinrich Heine made: "Ach! I can't write anymore. How can I write when there's no longer any censorship? How should a man who's always lived with censorship suddenly be able to write without it?" (quoted in Levine 1994, 1). Levine's discussion of Heine and censorship provides a useful comparative backdrop to my analysis here (1–20).

[10] This is Edmund Keeley's translation except for the title, which he translates as "Court Exhibit" (Ritsos 1979, 119).

passively on a bed, in the end she is the active subject of the last three verbs. The glass eye, which is useless to the man, in her hands is enabling; and her strength is related to her flexibility—she is both what is seen and what sees, both the object and the subject, both passive and active. The poem's narrative structure—with its shift from a male to a female subject—suggests that perhaps it is this ability to incorporate the other, the barbarians, the confusion and deceit of the times, which enables her to continue, while her male counterpart is left waiting for her answer. As Rose suggests, women may be in a privileged place to negotiate the co-implication of opposing positions because feminism as a social movement is well versed in challenging the clear-cut roles of victim and victor. Let us turn now to how woman is figured in a woman's text written at the same time.

Kassandra's Wolf and Wolf's *Cassandra*

Although in Kyr's representations of Lysistrata as a figure of undecidability there is an interesting tension between the struggle against the regime and the struggle for women's rights, the latter inevitably is subordinated to the former; on the whole, the resistance uses the figure of woman to underwrite an emancipation that has little to do with women's liberation. Karapanou's *Kassandra and the Wolf*, in contrast, is a work, written under the dictatorship, in which the feminist project is granted a certain autonomy. The novel contrasts with most of the texts thus far considered in other ways as well. Valtinos's short story "The Plaster Cast" undermined Papadopoulos's metaphor by inverting the master/slave relation and speaking from the position of the patient; Kyr's comic undermined the existing power relation in order to take command. In both cases the distinct categories of victim and victor were retained. *Kassandra and the Wolf*, however, uses the figure of woman to sustain undecidability; Karapanou asks whether there might be a response to censorship which does not view the figure of woman or puns and double entendres as one-way streets whereby one either effaces difference in the name of truth, as Papadopoulos did, or uncovers difference in the name of another truth, as Valtinos and Kyr do. The figure of Kassandra can be read as a negative response both to Kyr's question "The end?" and to the man's query in Ritsos's poem, "Now do you believe me?" Whereas Kyr's story ends in defeat—in the sense that parodic inversion of victim and victor is impossible to sustain—Karapanou's tale deconstructs this opposition and attempts to sustain the inversions through stuttering, cross-dressing, and other modes of deferring fixed definitions. As far as Kassandra is concerned, resolution is always undesirable because, whether in the form of tanks or "tangible proof," it reproduces similar power structures.

The figure of Kassandra is even more prominent than that of Lysistrata during the dictatorship. Although Kassandra's incomprehensible speech is usually a sign of despair,[11] Karapanou turns Kassandra's babble into a survival strategy. Throughout the series of short fragments which makes up Karapanou's text, two figures repeatedly appear who, in different ways, have power over the child: the General, who is a friend of Kassandra's grandmother, and Peter, Kassandra's butler and baby-sitter. Impatient with hierarchy, Kassandra sometimes makes fun of them; other times she feels sorry for these authorities. In one piece, Kassandra, parodying the regime's desire for identity and unequivocal meaning, confesses:

Την ξέρω τη Γιαγιά. Συχαίνεται τις αγγινάρες και τους Κομμουνιστές. Αγαπά πολύ το Στρατηγό. . . .

Κι εγώ τον αγαπώ το Στρατηγό. Σε κάθε-του επίσκεψη τρέχει να μου δείξει το κάδρο-του (αυτό με τις τρυπίτσες) και με το δάχτυλο τεντωμένο πάνω στα παράσημα: "Νάμαι," μου λέει, σαν να μου δείχνει το μέρος όπου έκανε πιπί.

"Νάσαι," του λέω κι εγώ. (26)

I know Grandmother well. She's crazy about politics. She detests artichokes and Communists. She loves the General very much. . . .

I love the General too. Every time he calls on us, he trots off to where his portrait is hanging (the one with the little holes in it) and, with his finger quivering at the row of medals, says: "There I am," as though he's pointing to the spot where he's done his pipi.

"There you are," I sing back. (48)

While the General gloats over this unmediated reflection of himself and his power—the row of medals—the little girl notices that the portrait is full of tiny holes. By calling attention to the imperfect surface of the canvas, she challenges the whole mimetic project on which his self-satisfaction relies. According to Kassandra, he is neither powerful, nor potent, but is riddled with holes and ridiculous.

In another passage, Kassandra takes a kind of ironic pity on the one in power:

'Ετρεχε στο δωμάτιό-του με το βιβλίο κάτω από τη μασχάλη και του το έδινα με τρυφερότητα.

Η πρώτη εικόνα είχε ένα λύκο που άνοιγε το στόμα και κατάπινε 7 ζουμερά γουρουνάκια.

---

[11] The postwar writers' letter of protest I referred to in Chapter 1 expressed the hope that Seferis's warning would not, like Kassandra's, fall on deaf ears. Kassandra's unheeded prophecy was also invoked in Seferis's poem "The Cats of St. Nicholas"; see Chapter 2.

Το λύκο λυπόμουνα συνήθως. Πώς θα τα καταπιεί τόσα γουρουνάκια μονο-
μιάς; (6)

I'd run to his room with the book under my arm and give it to him
tenderly.
The first picture was of a wolf opening his mouth to swallow 7 juicy
piglets.
It was the wolf I usually felt sorry for. How could he gulp down so many
piglets at one go? (9)

Her shifting sympathies disturb the simplicity and neatness of saying what
one means and looking like who one is.

When politics enter the home, Kassandra's body becomes an arena of
resistance. At every turn her language and behavior undermine the regime's censorship and puritanism. She stutters and stubbornly refuses to
do her math correctly; she does not conform to her grandmother's moral
conception of "a good little girl." Kassandra's stuttering, for example, is a
parody of the regime's censorship. The impediment that threatens to eradicate her words instead only defers or displaces them: "Ka-ka-ka-ka-s-s-
s-sandra" (134; 112). The words survive but break apart and form significant puns (κακά is a children's term for excrement and more generally
anything bad or naughty).[12] By not letting the censor conclusively delete
her words, Kassandra promotes the textual undecidability that is anathema to the regime. Similarly, on her first day of school, as I discussed in my
introduction, she exasperates her teacher by refusing to understand the
rudiments of subtraction. She is sure that even if her schoolmate Yannis
eats one of the four pears, it will still be there, just in his stomach (136; 114),
but in another fragment, "Το δώρο της Μαμάς" (Mother's present), Kassandra blatantly implicates herself as the censor. She recounts getting a
doll from her absent mother:

Την κοίμησα στο κουτί-της, αφού πρώτα της έκοψα τα πόδια και τα χέρια για
να χωράει.
Αργότερα της έκοψα το κεφάλι για να μην είναι βαριά. Τώρα την αγαπώ
πολύ. (11)

I put her to sleep in her box but first I cut off her legs and arms so she'd fit.
Later I cut off her head too, so she wouldn't be so heavy. Now I love her
very much. (8)

[12] One could also examine the masturbation scenes with regard to Sigmund Freud's theory
that masturbation is the internalization of beating; see Elisabeth Young-Bruehl's discussion
(1989, 396) of his "A Child Is Being Beaten" and Anna Freud.

In a monstrous parody of Freud's *fort-da* in which a child imitates his mother's departure by throwing a toy out of his crib (1984, 283–87), Kassandra alleviates the pain of separation from her mother by enacting the severing herself. By taking into her hands that which is being done to her, she acknowledges the ways in which redeploying censorship can be empowering. Nonetheless, the heavy irony of the conclusive "Now I love her very much" suggests that simply inverting victor and victim, censor and censored, is not a satisfactory solution. As with the displaced syllable or pear, the irony here reminds readers of the violence they may have forgotten.

While reworking the discourse of censorship, Kassandra also reworks assumptions of gender; she parodies the General's need for order by feminizing him, turning him into the maid: "Φαντάζομαι το Στρατηγό να συγυρίζει την Ελλάδα και να βάζει Κύριους και Κυρίες στα συρτάρια" (I imagine the General tidying up Greece, putting Gentlemen and Ladies in drawers) (8; 5). Just as Kassandra's puns and stutters defer meaning indefinitely, her imaginary cross-dressings postpone gender distinctions. This effect is illustrated by a passage in which the wolflike Peter and Kassandra "play doctor" in a rather unusual fashion. Like many things in this novel, the incident begins as a word game. Peter asks:

"Τι σούμαθε σήμερα η Miss Benbridge [sic];"
"Να καθαρίζω μπανάνες."
"Σαν Κύριος;"
" 'Οχι, σαν Κυρία." . . .
Τιγρεύουν τα μάτια-του.
"Σαν Κύριος;"
" 'Οχι, σαν Κυρία, όχι σαν Κύριος, σαν Κυρία."
Αυτό δεν θα με κάνει να το πω. (19)

"What did Miss Benbridge teach you today?"
"To peel a banana."
"Like a Gentleman?"
"No, like a Lady." . . .
His eyes go tiger.
"Like a Gentleman?"
"No, like a Lady. Not like a Gentleman, like a Lady."
He'll never make me say it. (28)

A few pages later Kassandra finally finds a way out. She answers, "Σαν Κύριος" (Like a Gentleman), and then adds, "Μα σαν Κύριος με φουστάνι, με στήθια και κοιλιά σαν μετάξι, και με χέρια βελούδινα" (But like a Gentleman in a frock, with breasts and a belly like silk, and velvety hands) (23; 31). She both gives in to the wolf and withholds exactly what he wants. By the end of the scene it is impossible to tell who is the victim and who the victor.

The feminist implications of Karapanou's resistance to authority come into relief in relation to Christa Wolf's *Cassandra*. Wolf's volume, containing a novel and four lectures, is much more explicit about the uses and abuses of the figure of woman. Written while Wolf traveled through Greece in 1980, the work is an attempt to re-create Cassandra, the ancient prophetess, as she existed in oral culture, before she was written about (287). Wolf outlines how Cassandra became the archetypal woman-as-object, robbed of her autonomy by a culture that began to fear mothers and privilege fathers. The task Wolf sets herself is "to retrace the path out of myth into its (supposed) social and historical coordinates" so that the personal drama of the myth is never the last word (256). Repeatedly she inverts the public and private spheres, showing, for example, how what the male mythologist mourned (i.e., Cassandra's "unfortunate" fate for not reciprocating Apollo's lust) is not a private affair but a public, political one. It was not simply that Apollo rendered her gift of prophecy ineffective by spitting in her mouth but, rather, that all over Greece the seeress was subordinated to the male priest and slowly forced from the public sphere. Cassandra's babble is not the symptom of one woman's madness, but of a historical moment that, for many interrelated economic and political reasons, inaugurated a new and widespread form of oppression. Wolf's insights about Cassandra are also meant as meditations on the challenges facing contemporary women writers. By fashioning a Cassandra whose subjectivity straddles the public and private sphere, Wolf suggests an alternative position from which East German women might write.[13]

Karapanou's *Kassandra and the Wolf* can be seen as delineating an analogous space for Greek women writers. In light of Wolf's refashioning of Cassandra, Karapanou's Little Red Riding Hood can be read as offering a domestic stage on which the public drama of an authoritarian regime is enacted. Less interested in the origins of myth than Wolf, Karapanou traces the Little Red Riding Hood story into the "(supposed) social and historical coordinates" of the contemporary moment.[14] The undecidability staged by

[13] That in the former German Democratic Republic this text was printed with certain passages censored attests to its political impact.

[14] *Kassandra and the Wolf* could also lead to an alternative reading of Wolf's volume, one that challenges her search for origins. Talking in an interview about the danger of letting myth efface history, Wolf mentions how an event that takes on mythical proportions, such as the Trojan War, "tends to push the organization of the material in the direction of a certain closure," but, she adds, "the structure of the lectures . . . helps to force open this closed form" (1988, 117). Karapanou's contemporary Kassandra might be used to deconstruct this distinction between novel and lectures by exposing the transhistoricizing slips in the lectures themselves. For example, while referring in one lecture to the modern Greek partisan in a novel by

Kassandra's and the wolf's word games and cross-dressing can be read both as a parody of the regime's rage for order and as a step toward an alternative feminist poetics in which the censoring and censored subjects are not binary oppositions.[15]

It is striking that Karapanou was willing to challenge the strict distinction between victor and victim, censor and censored, at a time when the difference was clear in the political sphere. For generations Greek writers responded mainly in two ways to oppressive regimes: either by taking the "disinterested" position in which elliptic usage and ambiguity were literary techniques, or by writing explicitly "engaged" prose or poetry, in which clarity was crucial. But Karapanou, like many young writers of her generation, takes an alternative route. Undecidability and multiple subject positions in this novel are not transhistorical, postmodern strategies of evasion but culturally specific modes of challenging the relegation of private and public, personal and political, female and male, to separate spheres. The claim of this approach is not simply that it is possible to make a political intervention indirectly but also that the struggles of previously less visible subjects such as women can be taken into consideration only indirectly. Expanding the political realm to include areas such as sexuality and the body finally permits women's needs to be addressed.

By blurring distinctions, this novel allows one form of oppression to act as a metaphor for others and bridges the concerns of writers under an authoritarian regime to those of women writers after the regime falls. Kassandra's unwillingness to deliver what is expected of her is a response both to the General and to the only male authority figure at home, Peter. It is also a reminder that one way to challenge a system is to use its tools to different ends, as Kassandra redeploys the censor's tactics so that they destabilize rather than fix meaning: she points out that the pear is still present, even if in Yannis's stomach, and concedes "like a Gentleman," but gives the Gentleman a dress, breasts, and smooth belly and hands.

Christa Wolf's writing offers a parallel case for undecidability as political intervention,[16] and her Cassandra is also defined in terms of multiple subject positions: "There is something of everyone in me, so I have belonged

---

Thanasis Valtinos, Wolf conflates the character with Orpheus, assuming exactly the kind of romantic continuity from ancient to modern times that many contemporary Greek writers question (184–85). Wolf's demythologization of Cassandra is at times premised on the very myth of continuity that it denounces.

[15] Karapanou's novel also offers a frame for examining Wolf's undermining of the authoritarian demands of social realist dogma in East Germany. Debate over Wolf's relationship to the regime serves to illustrate how precarious resistance is (Huyssen 1991; Hafner 1993).

[16] On the cultural context of such a strategy, see John Borneman's description of how education in the former East Germany prepared students to read between the lines and to internalize contradictions (1991, 220–25).

completely to no one, and I have even understood their hatred to me" (1984, 4). In an interview Wolf recounts that it was through her interest in contradictions and how contradictions provoke fear in readers that she arrived at the figure of Cassandra. She explains how the effeminate traits in the Kleist character in her earlier book *No Place on Earth* unnerved readers ("I had deformed him by giving him effeminate characteristics"), and she goes on to explain readers' unease about "anything hybrid, about fluid transitions, about things not being simply one thing or the other: friend or foe, male or female; a fear of learning to live with rather than against one another" (1988, 102). Like Karapanou, Wolf is careful to emphasize that the breaking of taboos is also an internal process: "Of course, I do not sit down at the typewriter, every time I tackle a new subject, with the intention of offending anybody. No, I want to make *myself* aware of the things which offend and hurt me. . . . Before the violent reaction from outside arose, I had to go through my own violent reaction. Like my readers, I am split" (122).

The contradictions that disturb authoritarian rule are the stuff of both Wolf's and Karapanou's work. If the choice to internalize difference which these texts endorse was exceptional, it might not be of much interest. But in both cases this choice is a symptom of shifting cultural climates. In Berlin during the 1980s, the members of Frigga Haug's women's collective initiated a project similar to Wolf's. They mapped their own stories of growing up onto particular social and historical coordinates. These women's simple yet groundbreaking hypothesis was that, "in girls, the process of individual socialization is synonymous with the sexualization of the body and its parts" (Haug 1987, 203). In Greece this collective had its parallel in the feminist journal *Skoupa*, published from 1979 to 1981, which raised issues of socialization less systematically through a wide range of articles.[17] Wolf's preoccupations, more explicitly feminist than Karapanou's, help relate the Greek author's reworking of the figure of woman simultaneously to the regime and to the growing women's movement. In this light, Karapanou's Kassandra offers an alternative solution to the Catch-22 of undermining authority, whether the regime's or the patriarchy's. Instead of substituting the traditional position of power, the dictator's or the wolf's, for the traditional position of weakness, the woman's, Karapanou constructs a place from which to speak which is always both.[18]

[17] One issue, for example, carried an interview with Christa Wolf following an analysis of the Little Red Riding Hood fairytale (Avdela et al. 1981, 25–48).

[18] In other words, instead of calling for multiple identities, she insists that identity itself is split. Diana Fuss theorizes a similar position when she critiques certain social constructivists for not taking into account the Lacanian notion of the split subject. She writes, "What worries me . . . is that difference is relocated from the space within identity to the space *between* identities. Difference is seen as a product of the friction between easily identifiable and unitary components (sexual, racial, economic, national . . .) competing for dominance within the subject" (1989, 103).

The Social Text of Women's Poetry after the Dictatorship

Before I analyze the shift from the allegorical use of the subversive woman in comic strips and novels in the 1970s to the formal attention to censorship in women's poetry in the 1980s, I want to outline the broader context of cultural changes that occurred after the fall of the regime. Censorship and other restrictions on individual freedom were often conceived of, both before and during the dictatorship, as externally imposed by governments; after the dictatorship was over, with the waning of the memory of the civil war (1946–49), with the rise of the women's movement, and with the influx of foreign books, television, and radio, public and private spheres became less and less clearly demarcated. For the first time in Greek culture, Marx's political theory of oppression and Freud's psychoanalytic theory of repression were being generally talked about in relation to each other. The intellectual milieu was one in which strict distinctions between outside and inside, oppression and repression, "us" and "them," censorship and self-censorship, were being challenged. The events and trends I discuss here are those that were particularly important for the women poets whose work I focus on and for the circles of leftist intellectuals with which they were involved.

Under the dictatorship, writers and other intellectuals on the Left and the Right—those who during the civil war twenty years earlier had been political enemies—suddenly found themselves working together in opposition to the colonels. The fact that the centrist Rodis Roufos and the leftist Manolis Anagnostakis could coedit the resistance collection *Eighteen Texts* was a signal that times were changing. When in 1981 the socialist government accorded equal honor to veterans of both sides in the civil war and encouraged open discussion, there was consensus that the beginning of a new era was in sight; not that polarization had ceased to exist but dialogue, at least, had become possible. The Government of National Unity of November 1989, whose cabinet contained representatives of the three main parties (left, right, and center) among others, would have been inconceivable without two decades of less official collaboration and toleration.

The dictatorship also marked a time in which clear-cut gender roles were being challenged. For seven years the subaltern "experiences" of women— the enforced claustrophobia, the curfews, the silencing and censorship, the physical restraints—became those of men and women alike. The general population was in a sense "feminized." With the fall of the regime the women's movement gained strength from the public denunciation of these repressive measures.[19] Analogies were made between the censorship of

[19] On the rise of the women's movement in Greece in the 1970s and 1980s, see Cowan 1994, Papagaroufalis 1990, and Stamiris 1986. Papagaroufalis provides a useful overview of the relations between various women's organizations and political parties.

an oppressive regime and the censorship practiced in the subjection of women.[20] Although many women's groups, dissatisfied with the second-class status of their concerns within male-dominated parties, broke with those parties, feminists rarely treated sexual equality as an issue independent from other political struggles.[21] Margaret Papandreou (1983), an active feminist and the wife of the leftist political leader Andreas Papandreou, in an interview with Andrea Dworkin explained how it had become an acceptable political practice to take up different positions in different situations—to speak as a Marxist in one context and as a feminist in another. Private and public spheres had become less clearly gendered or delineated. Issues of sexuality, for example, were receiving public attention and being given political weight. Debate over obscenity rulings reached its height in the 1977 trial of the September 1975 issue of the underground magazine *Sima*, for which the editors, publishers, and Tasos Falyreos, the author of a particularly "offensive" piece, were charged with indecency ("Το εφετείο . . ." [Sima acquitted . . .] 1977).[22] By 1978, sexuality had become a matter of central importance for women's groups.[23] With this attention to "private" issues came certain feminist victories. From 1981 to 1983 the government legalized divorce by mutual consent, officially abolished the dowry, and established an equal-pay policy.

It was exactly in the period when these multiple aspects of censorship both as constitutive of one version of reality and as exclusive of other possibilities came to be addressed in political struggles and sexual politics that the Left became interested in psychoanalytic theory.[24] Before the dictatorship it was generally accepted in leftist intellectual circles that oppression, not repression, was the intellectual's nemesis and should be the battleground of cultural production.[25] The obvious oppression, for example,

[20] Jean Franco makes a similar point about women in Latin America when she describes how "authoritarian regimes often forced women to make connections between state repression and oppression at home" (1992, 68). For a historical contrast of women's empowerment through larger social movements, see Janet Hart's book on Greek women in the resistance during the civil war (1996).
[21] Nora Skouteri-Didaskalou (1979) offers a four-page bibliography on the women's question in relation to other debates. Jennifer Cavounides's article ([1982] 1983) poses the question of women's work in the context of capitalist developments.
[22] Gail Holst (1977) describes this trial and the Athenian drug counterculture it brought to light.
[23] This was generally true of the leftist splinter groups with which most poets of the generation of the 1970s were aligned, for example the Movement of Democratic Women. For the importance of sexuality for the MDW and the influence of younger members, many of whom had studied abroad in France, see Papagaroufalis 1990, 82–83.
[24] This would not be true of the majority of Soviet-aligned communists in the largest community party, however.
[25] In fact there are not even two different words in common usage in Greek: καταπίεση is used for both the Marxist term *oppression* and the Freudian term *repression*. The psychoanalytic term in Greek, however, is καταστολή (LaPlanche and Pontalis 1986, 290–92).

of the resistance fighters during the civil war was, for the Left, of more immediate concern than the repression of an individual's desires and memories. This distinction between oppression as external and real, and repression as internal and obscure, fit neatly with a nationalist ideology that put the collective and public ahead of the individual and private.[26] Such a ranking was also evident in literary criticism. Marxist and conservative critics alike embraced poetry that spoke for the nation, from Dionysios Solomos to George Seferis, rejecting the more "self-involved" poetry of Kostas Karyotakis and N. D. Karouzos.[27] In 1984, in a discussion about the influence of marxist thought on literature in Greece since 1920, the poet Manolis Anagnostakis pointed out that already in the 1940s there had been a need for the Left to expand its purview and integrate the lessons of psychoanalysis, but not until the 1970s was the need widely acknowledged (Κέντρο Μαρξιστικών σπουδών [Centre of Marxist Studies] 1986, 41). The context for the Left's utilitarian views of art, in particular for the Soviet-aligned communist party, was that of Zhdanovism and social realism: psychoanalysis was petit-bourgeois drivel.[28] As one critic in the leftist journal *Antaios* wrote in 1949, "We must not forget that all defenders of the psyche [ψυχοαμύντορες] (priests, psychoanalysts, sociologists, philanthropists) in attending to its health have but one aim: to mask social contradictions" (cited in Hartokollis 1984, 48). Even though a series of essays on psychoanalysis was published as early as 1927 in another leftist journal, *Anagennisi*, the consensus was that before the 1960s, marxism and psychoanalysis were incompatible (Κέντρο Μαρξιστικών σπουδών [Centre of Marxist Studies] 1986, 22).

The real move away from Zhdanovism was only realized on the Left during and after the dictatorship. Young people in leftist splinter group youth organizations such as Rigas Pheraios, lent one another the works of psychoanalysts such as Freud, Jung, Reich, Laing, and Lacan, as well as the more predictable classic leftist reading material of Marx, Engels, Trotsky, and Mao Tse-tung.[29] Thinkers who drew on both the psychoana-

[26] On the differences between the more collective Greek concept of self and the Western Enlightenment view of the individual, see Pollis 1965.

[27] Linos Politis's praise of Seferis is paradigmatic: "The narcissistic 'I,' prominent in poetry of this epoch, was not heard in this collection, but basically and insistently like a trumpeting motif, the 'we'" (1980, 282).

[28] Zhdanovism, named for Stalin's most famous censor, Andrey Zhdanov, referred to the social realist view of art whereby the base-structure determined the superstructure: literature's function was merely to reiterate the heroic deeds of the comrades who in the service of the revolution would overthrow capitalism. Oppression was what "they" did to "us." Revolutionaries were by definition outside and unimplicated in its machinations. To acknowledge the Freudian concept of repression, and therefore to complicate matters, would be to take attention away from more important matters.

[29] In this book, as may already be clear, I tend to draw more on Freudian and Lacanian psychoanalysis than on Jungian, Laingian, or Reichian, which also had widespread popularity

lytic and marxist traditions—Walter Benjamin, Pierre Macherey, Michel
Foucault, and most important, Louis Althusser—were particularly influential.[30] The materialist notion of determination was being replaced by
a more complicated notion of *overdetermination* by which base and superstructure, the economic and the cultural, were implicated in each other.[31]
The Freudian notion of censorship as "normal," as a necessary check on
the unconscious, came into use and with it a more complicated sense of
the dynamics of literary production. The generation of the 1970s grew
up at home with such cross-fertilization; the popularity and general acceptance of this conflation can be gauged by returning to Kyr's *Lysistrata*.
One scene explicitly mentions the theoretical importance of the meeting

---

in Greece in the 1970s, because I am interested in psychoanalysis as literary criticism. As in my
treatment of oppression in the discursive form of Papadopoulos's speeches, I am interested in
repression as a discourse. Lacan's rereading of Freud's theory of the unconscious as a language allows me to focus on the highly textual nature of Freud's theories. (It is telling that
Freud criticizes Jung in "On Narcissism" [1984, 73] not for the content of his argument but for
its style. Freud dismisses Jung's "non-sexual" libido on the grounds of Jung's "inapt analogy.") Freudian psychoanalysis always brings us back to the mechanisms of writing as it
brings us back to the mechanisms of dream. It is this preoccupation with how things work,
with the process, that is one of the things that differentiates his theories from Jung's and
makes them so appealing to poststructural literary critics. Although Jungian thought was
more easily assimilated to marxist doctrine in that it worked on an explicitly "collective"
unconscious, it is my contention that Freudian psychoanalysis, with its focus on defense
mechanisms, better equips us for reading Greek poetry during and after the dictatorship.
[30] In an interview, the politician Anastasios Peponis (1987) discussed how many activists,
himself included, took the time to read and write in those years of curfews, bans on public
gatherings, exile, and jail in a way they had not before or, for that matter, since. Foreign books
and translations were not as carefully monitored by the censors as texts written in Greek.
Social, political, and literary theory flooded the market. My account of what people were
reading is taken from my interviews with the poets Rhea Galanaki (1987), Jenny Mastoraki
(1987), Maria Laina (1987), and Yannis Kondos (1987) and with the publishers Phillipos
Vlachos (1987) and Lambis Rappas (1987); from my conversations with the poet Andia Frantzi
in February 1989 and with the publisher Stavros Petsopoulos in July 1987; and informal
communication with many others. For a list of literary theory that was translated into Greek at
this time, see Eratosthenis Kapsomenos's bibliography (1983, 189–210). Nasos Vayenas mentions this bibliography in support of the wealth of literary theory translated into Greek (1987,
70), adding that it has only increased since then. In a rebuttal to Vayenas's article, Michalis
Tsianikas (1987, 65) uses the same bibliography to suggest the slow import of theory into
Greece. Whichever side one takes, it is important to note that in Greece the circulation of ideas
does not depend wholly or even mostly on translations, as the majority of Greek intellectuals
have been trained abroad and know foreign languages.
[31] The two most important discussions that inform my understanding of *overdetermination*
are Freud's (1976, 388–89, 415–19) and Althusser's (1982). I discuss the term in detail in
Chapter 6, but, in brief, Freud introduced this concept in his *Interpretation of Dreams* to explain
the laconic and fragmentary nature of dreams. One word, phrase, or image in the dream's
manifest content is determined not by one word, phrase, or image in the *dream-thought's* latent
content but by many; conversely, many aspects of the dream-thought are represented in the
dream by one element. By mechanisms of condensation and displacement, overdetermination
complicates cause and effect (1976, 389).

of private and public spheres, of the related mechanisms of repression and oppression, of Freudian and marxist theories. Instead of explaining her scheme to end the war, Lysistrata shows an animated cartoon.[32] At intermission in the foyer the women are smoking cigarettes and discussing the film. One woman turns to another and says, "I think the director's point is the urbanization of the Freudian masses with regard to the intelligentsia of consumer society." Although this is first and foremost nonsense, a spoof of intellectual chitchat, it is revealing that the two theories conflated in phrases such as "Freudian masses" are that of Freud and Marx.

In marked contrast, then, to the previous generations of leftists who ranked class oppression and oppression by foreign powers over all other forms, many of the writers of the generation of the 1970s embraced the double framing of sexual politics in class politics and vice versa, the figure of woman becoming the site of this meeting. But whereas many male writers of the younger generation no longer found this fancy footwork necessary after the regime's demise, the women continued to develop evasive tactics. Power struggles, according to them, though perhaps more obvious under an authoritarian regime, did not disappear with a return to democracy. In the spirit of Kassandra's protest that nothing is ever what it seems, recent women's poetry challenges the *apparent* exteriority of political oppression in relation to the *apparent* interiority of repression. The public limits and restrictions imposed by censorship are reworked in the form of more personal struggles between lovers and exposed as being part of the actual writing process. Instead of censoring the censor in the name of another ideology or, at the other extreme, resorting to a completely uncensored stream-of-consciousness writing, their poetry experiments with an alternative method of resistance, one that introduces the effects of censorship into their own writing. Macherey's invocation to "realise that the work has no interior, no exterior; or rather, its interior is like an exterior, shattered and on display" (1978, 96) becomes for these writers a gendered as well as a formal issue. Lysistrata, Kassandra, and Scheherazade function less as symbols of resistance and more as rhetorical tropes for enacting resistance. Kassandra's undecidability and Scheherazade's procrastination become blueprints for negotiating the sexual as well as textual inevitability of not being able to say what one means. Through elliptic syntax, unorthodox punctuation, and deferral of signification these women formally incorporate the lessons of censorship.

[32] The self-referentiality of this scene is a result of the comics' reference not only to the process of drawing comics (the material references to the act of making cartoons often involve references to film or video as if to align the art with its high-tech cousins) but also to the theoretical concerns that inform the comics.

Sexual Politics and Poetic Form

I have examined how the poets of the generation of the 1970s set up
visual narrative strategies for incorporating the anonymity of consumer
culture and for evading censorship by overloading the reader with a multitude of images, in Poulios's case by "stealing" and in Steriadis's by deferring meaning through extended metonyms in his poetry strips. The
women poets of this generation—Rhea Galanaki, Natasa Hatzidaki, Maria
Laina, Jenny Mastoraki, Pavlina Pampoudi, and Athena Papadaki, among
others—have carried on developing visual narrative strategies of evasion
well into the 1990s. For them, the lens of sexual difference provided by
feminism brings into focus other forms of censorship: those of patriarchy,
homophobia, the literary canon, even the creative process itself. The poetry
of Katerina Gogou is more popular and more explicitly feminist, but the
formal component I find in the poetry of these other women is missing. My
concern is with the women poets from the generation of the 1970s whose
sexual politics are elaborated through their poetics. Although the visual
narrative is the trademark of the generation of the 1970s, some very important women poets of previous generations such as Eleni Vakalo, Kiki Dimoula, and Katerina Anghelaki-Rooke who began publishing slightly earlier, also begin exploring the gendered aspects of experience through
longer sequences of poems in the 1980s and 1990s.[33]

Critics began to discuss the rise of women's writing in the 1980s, but
none relate this tendency to the social text of the dictatorship and postdictatorship years. Although women's poetry is no longer regarded as a
timeless repository of feminine emotion, critics still overlook its cultural
specificity. In a review of Mastoraki's *Tales of the Deep* and Laina's *Hers*,
Maronitis addressed the visual and narrative preoccupation of the poetry
but failed to view it in the context of the years following the dictatorship.
For him the fact that both poets developed a similar strategy was pure
coincidence: "It's strange that two women poets of our times should discover simultaneously, each in her own way, what I shall call 'painterly
narrative'" (1985). He is more concerned with individual talent than with
cultural explanations for such a writing strategy.[34] My aim is to suggest
how the visual and narrative emphasis is connected to the sexual politics of
censorship. I begin by charting the shift from women's concern with censorship in their poetry written under the dictatorship to their gendering of

[33] See, e.g., Dimoula's Χαίρε ποτέ (Hail never) (1988, 1996) and Anghelaki-Rooke's "Μια
άνοιξη για τη Γιαννούσα" (Springtime for Yiannousa) in Επίλογος αέρας (The epilogue wind)
(1990). Vakalo in many ways pioneered the visual narrative, eschewing the lyric from early on;
her 1981 collection is titled *Before Lyricism*. For her, too, gender becomes an important factor in
her collections that chronicle the life and times of Mrs. Rodalina (1984, 1990).

[34] In a longer article about the whole generation of poets, Maronitis touches on the cultural
specificity of their project, though not with respect to gender (in 1987, 241).

censorship in their later visual narratives. I outline the main distinguishing characteristics of this poetry—its difficulty, its endless deferral of meaning, its visual and narrative preoccupations. Primarily with reference to the poetry of Jenny Mastoraki, I then illustrate some of the ways in which the effects of censorship are reworked as formal components in these women's texts. I concentrate on the increasing ellipticism and scrambling of fixed hierarchies because these strategies are easier to illustrate through a discussion of single poems. This poetry's need to take up more and more time and space, that is, its visual narrativity, can, however, become fully evident only when I read through complete collections in the later chapters. This section is therefore a miniature version of the last three chapters, mapping out in a comparative fashion the path poetry takes from under to after the dictatorship and then concentrating on the role of the visual narrative in the 1980s.

Censorship is an obvious formative influence in the early work of Rhea Galanaki, Jenny Mastoraki, and Maria Laina.[35] Ellipsis characterizes their poetry from the start. The epigrammatic poems in Galanaki's first two collections (1975, 1979) are almost impenetrable to the uninitiated, and her comments about her writing under the dictatorship stress this cryptic quality:

> I wanted my poems to take a strict form . . . so that the subjective element . . . wouldn't show, and I believe that . . . there was a strong element of censorship . . . which I worked at with great intensity . . . because I was on the Left, because my husband was in jail, and because of the various other insecurities of daily life that existed . . . insecurities about language . . . that is when the police come and read everything in your house, all your papers . . . rip them up . . . you have the feeling that if anything survives . . . if you let anything out into the open, it shouldn't be legible to the interrogator. (1987)[36]

Maria Laina's early poems, though more subjective, have a similar reined-in feeling to them. T. D. Frangopoulos's review (1972a) of Laina's book Επέκεινα (Beyond) (1970) raises the dynamic of legibility which Galanaki mentioned.[37] He quotes the Polish poet Tadeusz Rozewicz's definition of poetry as "the language which everyone understands, however cryptic its

---

[35] Of the three, Galanaki was the only one actively involved in the resistance.

[36] In a letter Galanaki commented on an earlier use of this quotation, saying that it came across sounding "very personal and dramatic" because, as she explained, I did not then go on to address her work in detail. In the next chapter, I discuss the problem of using information from interviews and questionnaires and then go on to provide the context. For another description of writing under censorship, see her interview with the magazine *Diavazo* (1983b, 21).

[37] One other collection, Ενηλικίωση (Coming of age) (1968), predates this one, but as Laina later revoked it from circulation, I begin my analysis with *Beyond*.

meaning may appear—except the policeman and the censor" (525). Mastoraki's first book Διόδια (Tolls) (1972) also introduces poetry in terms of censorship. The first poem of the collection concludes:

> Τότε ένα γράμμα
> γεμάτο κατάγματα
> ήρθε από πολύ μακριά
> και μας παράγγειλε να κλείσουμε τις πόρτες.
>
> (1972, 9)

> Then a letter came
> full of fractures
> from far away
> and ordered us to close the doors.

Over the course of the book, the title *Tolls* comes to stand for the various ways of negotiating this premature closure. At what expense, these poems ask, does one open the doors, say what one means, express one's desires? To what extent must one work within the system in order to outwit the toll collectors, policemen, and censors?

But what is interesting is how such issues of ellipsis and legibility become gendered. Galanaki, in the same interview I quoted above, uses terms of sexual freedom to describe writing after censorship was lifted. To illustrate the relative freedom of speech after the fall of the regime, she does not choose to use a politically loaded word such as *freedom*, which was suspect under the colonels' regime, instead she says, "You can call a vagina a vagina" (1987). She describes freedom to talk about politics as freedom to talk about female sexuality. This ability to see analogies between political oppression and sexual repression is crucial to an understanding of the direction these women's work took after the regime. The formal training that censorship had provided was not dismissed; for writing as a woman seemed to be related to writing under censorship.

In Steriadis's poetry I found a new poetic strategy of connecting images in a metonymic rather than metaphorical manner: the reader could no longer make sense out of the sequence of images; they seemed selected according to arbitrary criteria. Women poets continued to develop this strategy by relating the use of metonymy to a sexual politics. By keeping things in motion and never fixing meaning, the self-censorship of cutting out connections or flooding the reader with too many allusions turned the debilitating effects of censorship into an empowering poetics. Their collections with long series of interwoven poems transform ellipsis into a feminine survival strategy for recognizing how meaning is lost, disfigured, or denied. If Lysistrata is the figure of woman that feminizes resistance, and

Kassandra the one that gives it its full linguistic application, then Scheherazade, or Halima, as she is called in Greek, is the figure who stresses that these underminings are only successful if they are sustained.

Scheherazade's status as procrastinator, as the one who is always ready with another tale, becomes emblematic of what I term a "poetics of undeliverability." Mastoraki's second collection, Το σόι (Kin), foreshadows this poetics with its last section, titled "Τα παραμύθια της Χαλιμάς" (Tales of Halima). The title poem explains that little verses are no longer sufficient:

> Δε μου είναι πια εύκολο
> μήτε θελητό
> να γράφω στιχάκια.
> (1978, 46)

> It is no longer easy for me
> nor desirable
> to write little verses.

Poetry must take up time and space. The use here of the subjunctive imperfective "να γράφω" ([for me] to write) and then later in the poem "σαν να βουτάς" (as if you are diving), coupled with the continuous sense of the final line "Πιο έπειτα το συνηθίζεις και σ' αρέσει" (Later you get used to it and like it) (1978, 46) underscores this sense.[38] In Greek, verbs are inflected according to whether the speaker or writer thinks of the action as happening once, a certain number of times (the perfective), or repeatedly or continuously (the imperfective).[39] Although the perfective aspect is more frequently used in Greek, it is the imperfective aspect that is used with striking frequency in these women's poems. In fact the abundance of constructions such as the subjunctive imperfective and the future imperfective, which use the present-tense root (i.e., να γράφω and θα γράφω simply add the marker να and θα to γράφω), imbues the present of this poetry with an unusual sense of duration. Like a southern drawl, these constructions perform the procrastination Scheherazade represents.

Women's visual narratives of the 1980s defer meaning indefinitely, taking as their content and form that which is missing: Galanaki's *The Cake* defers the birth of the child; Mastoraki's *Tales of the Deep*, the delivery of the letter; and Laina's *Hers*, the return of the gaze. In each case the book is the place where the activities of transformation, pursuit, and escape become poetic practice. Each comments on the gaps between *what we mean* and

[38] In the second edition of *Kin*, Mastoraki broke the final line into two lines: "Later you get used to it / and like it" (1990, 43).

[39] For an extremely readable comprehensive survey of the Modern Greek language, see Mackridge 1985.

what we say, what we are and *what we appear to be,* in very different ways; but in all three, the displaced third term, that which is exchanged between the first and second person singular, rehearses the effect of censorship as self-censorship. What these three narratives suggest is that if matters are not as they appear, if nothing fits, then perhaps poetics should stop making sense, should stop trying to tell the truth or to intend an exact meaning or reflection. A kind of writing that addresses the impossibility of saying what you mean, or appearing as you are, might be a more constructive way of coming to grips with contemporary experience. As far as these poets are concerned, poetry cannot transcend linguistic and sexual confusion; it must partake of and participate in it. And practice over time and space builds stamina.

One illustration of how these texts include the linguistic and sexual confusion of the times is the conflation by women poets of personal pronouns. The title of Pampoudi's collection Αυτός εγώ (He I) (1977b) dramatizes such a conflation. Similarly, in Galanaki's *The Cake* (1980), feminine and masculine pronouns hopscotch across the text, turning masculine birds of prey into feminine ones and vice versa. Laina's poetic narrative *Hers* (1985a) interjects an unexpected "him" after pages of feminine pronouns (40) and switches from "she" to "I" without warning (48), leaving the reader uncertain who is speaking.[40] The gendered nature of the Greek language makes this conflation of pronouns even more striking. In Mastoraki's macabre prose poems of *Tales of the Deep* (1983b) the confusion of subject and object, victim and victor, man and woman, reader and writer, serves both as content and linguistic register. As one line explains, it is impossible to determine who is doing what to whom: "έτσι σου μοιάζουν όλοι κομματιάζοντας, και πάλι εσύ, κομμάτια όλοι" (so they resemble you, torn to shreds, and you them, again, in pieces) (17). Subject and object are thematically and syntactically implicated in each other. *Tales* begins with a hunter who has other hunters behind him, an image that undermines the opposition of victim and victor from the start: "Αλλά μόνος παντού ο κυνηγός και ξοπίσω του διώκτες" (But the hunter alone everywhere with pursuers on his trail) (11). The confusion is exacerbated by the unconventional placement of the adverb παντού (everywhere) between the adjective μόνος (alone) and the noun that the adjective describes, ο κυνηγός (the hunter). How can there be anyone behind someone who is everywhere?

This confusion is also true of sex roles. In the second poem, men are feminized: "Εκεί θα περιμένουν άντρες τρυφεροί με κλάματα. Και τα μακριά μαλλιά τους όρθια στο σκοτάδι, όπως των πνιγμένων" (That is where tender men will wait in tears, their long hair floating in the dark. The hair of men

---

[40] For an interesting parallel, see Jan Montefiore on the confused gender in Emily Dickinson's love poems (1987, 174–75).

who've drowned) (15). And this kind of gender scrambling is continually enacted in the syntax of the poems. In "Οι κακοπαντρεμένες" (The unfortunate brides) the women of the title seem to turn into the groom who has threatened them. A series of similes equates their departure with glittering gold, first that of the sacrificial cock in Hades, then that of a golden jaw, and finally that of a horseman, who recalls the groom (who fled), the molten gold perhaps referring to a stolen dowry:

... να μην τον δουν που φοβερίζει, φεύγουν—

όπως αστράφτει ο πετεινός στον 'Αδη, κι όπως χρυσή μασέλα στο βουβό της νύχτας, τετράποδο τρεχάτο που κουδούνιζε, κι ο αναβάτης μάλαμα κοχλάζει.

(18)

... so they won't see him threaten, they leave—

the way a rooster lights up Hades, or a gilded jaw the speechless night, a beast jangling on the run, and the rider bubbles up gold.

In the last poem "Τι έλεγε εκείνη η επιστολή" (What that missive said), the victor not only turns into the victim and changes gender but also inverts the relation of writer and reader. The producer of the text, the "I" that is qualified by groups of victimized women throughout the book—beautiful ladies of the underworld (16), abducted women (35)—turns into the victor, "he":

Μα όταν κάποιος σου μιλά με τρόμους, φωνές χαμένων σε απαίσια σπήλαια και βάλτους—

εσύ να σκέφτεσαι προπάντων τι μπορεί να εννοεί, ποιο διαμελισμένο πτώμα κρύβει στο υπόγειό του, τι δαγκωτά φιλιά και φόνους ...

(49)

But when someone talks to you with terror, with voices of those lost in ghastly caves and marshes—

above all you must consider what he might mean, what dismembered corpse *he* is hiding in his cellar, what biting kisses, murders. . . .

(emphasis mine)

This victor, through the shifting of pronouns and scrambling of syntax in the middle section of the poem, is smothered in order that the poem can conclude by asking us to feel sympathy for him:

ποιον κλέφτη, τέλος, σε βαθύ κοιτώνα χάλκινο, πνιγμένον στα λινά
και κλαίει—

και να τον συμπαθείς, προπάντων να τον συμπαθείς, αγαπητέ Αρθούρε
ή Αλφόνσε.
(49)

what thief, finally, in a deep, brass bedchamber, smothered in linen,
and cries—

and you must feel for him, above all feel for him, my dear Arthur
or Alphonse.

Through an odd kind of suicide, the plural storyteller becomes singular and lies on his death bed, and the reader, who up until this point is referred to in the singular "you," is made the generic recipient of the letter, "Arthur or Alphonse," and is handed responsibility for continuing the story. The plea to *Arthur* or *Alph*onse is an invitation to the readers to go back to the beginning, to the *alpha,* and write the letter themselves. In a sense, Mastoraki's poems start with Kassandra's doll already in pieces. That no one is ever completely in control—neither the victor nor the victim, the man nor the woman, the writer nor the reader—affects language's ability to organize itself around fixed objects and subjects. Whereas in Karapanou's *Kassandra and the Wolf,* censorship is challenged, for the most part at the level of plot, in Mastoraki's, Galanaki's, and Laina's poetry, language itself enacts Karapanou's shifting sympathies, cross-dressing, and stuttering. The victor and the victim perform in the guise of floating pronouns, contradictory statements, dashes, blank spaces, double entendres, and quotation marks.

The undermining of the authority of quotation marks in *Tales* and *The Cake* provides another example of how women's poetry of the 1980s formally explores power relations. Mastoraki's juxtaposition of phrases within and without quotation marks raises the question of who has the right to speak for whom. Like elliptic syntax and other modes of obscuring meaning in recent Greek women's poetry, this technique derives its specific subversive potential from its deployment within the political and cultural context of Greece over the two decades since the dictatorship. As a formal reworking of the co-implication of victim and victor, censored and censor, which woman had come to figure, this feature is further testimony that censorship is a problem not only under an authoritarian regime.

Words in quotation marks, much like proper names, have a certain weight that other language does not carry; quoting is one of the main textual practices by which writing is authorized.[41] Though *Tales* borrows from canonical sources of Modern Greek poetry such as folk songs, the Bible, the works of nineteenth-century nationalist poets, the adventure stories of Jules Verne, the short stories of Georgios Vizyenos (a prominent writer of the generation of the 1880s) and Byzantine and medieval chronicles such as Διγενής Ακρίτας (Digenis Akritas) and *El Cid*, more often than not the effect of these references is to undo the authority of the tradition. The volume's focus is on the heterogeneity of these intertexts, rather than on their literary origins. The epigraph of *Tales*, from the short story "Ποίος ήτον ο φονεύς του αδελφού μου" (Who was my brother's murderer), by Vizyenos (1973, 1988), is the most obviously suspicious, as the citation is the only one linked by a note to its author. The epigraph states:

> Τι σύμπτωσις, μοι είπε, κύριε!
> Τι παράξενος σύμπτωσις σας φέρει
> εις τον οίκον του φονέως;

> What coincidence, sir, he said to me,
> what strange coincidence brings you
> to the house of the murderer?

This passage signals to readers who know the Vizyenos tale that they should be cautious in interpreting the epigraph as a gesture of deference; things are never as they appear to be. Just as the speaker refers to an inversion (the moment in which the narrator of the tale, in pursuit of his brother's murderer, finds that what he thought was the victim's house is the killer's), so may the function of the quotation be inverted: instead of lending an air of certainty, the borrowed words may repeat the uncertainty and confusion that is present everywhere in the *Tales*. In the new context, for example, Vizyenos's "you" no longer designates only a specific character but encompasses anyone reading Mastoraki's poems. Again and again *Tales* undoes the authority of the quotations and the whole process of referentiality by recontextualizing them. Similarly, Mastoraki undermines the authority of the proper name. The alternative names at the end of *Tales*—Arthur or Alphonse—deprive naming of its proper function; a name is only authoritative if its referential status is determinate.

One poem in particular, "Οι βουτηχτές" (The divers), introduces the problem of taking something out of its context and making it exemplary.

[41] Deconstructive readings stress the difficulty of undermining the authority of quotations and of proper names. Lacan's, Derrida's, and Johnson's readings of Poe's "The Purloined Letter" provide an excellent showcase (Muller and Richardson 1988). I explore this phenomenon more fully later.

This poem, which recounts the way writers gather material for stories, begins with a list. The importance of the quotation marks in the first item is deflated by the pluralizing of the borrowed statement and by the juxtaposition of all sorts of other phrases:[42]

Τα "πάρεξ να σε ιδώ, καλέ μου", τα κρυφομιλήματα, μεσ' από δύσκολους καιρούς, σωσμένα λόγια των εξορκισμών, τις σιγανές πατημασιές, τα ποιήματα, απόπειρες αγνοουμένων προ πολλού . . .

(25)

Those "nothing, save to see you, my dear"s, hushed conversations, the words to exorcisms salvaged from difficult times, the quiet footsteps, poems, attempts of those missing for ages . . .

The poem seems to conclude with an even more striking undermining of the authority of quotations:

Για να γυρνάς και να 'ρχεσαι και να μιλάς, λόγια σπουδαίων ειδυλλίων που ήταν μια φορά, ίχνη λαμπρών καρατομήσεων, τα "σε φιλώ", αχ πόσο σε φιλώ, το δήγμα επίχρυσο, επιτέλους, απ' το χρόνο.

(25)

So that you will return and come over and talk, words from great romances that happened long ago, traces of glorious beheadings, those "I kiss you"s, oh yes I kiss you, and the bite, at last, gilded by time.

This time the citation is thrice stripped of its authoritative status, first by being modified by a plural adjective, "those," then by being repeated without quotation marks, and finally by the suggestion that what the quotation concerns is not a kiss at all but a bite. Like the conflation of victor and victim or man and woman, the dissolution of a quotation into language that is unmarked relies on a strategy of subversion. Beginning and ending with quotations that have been stripped of their authority, this poem urges the reader to acknowledge the way texts participate in the power dynamics they address. The more attention is paid to how writing is controlled, the more adept writers and readers become at disturbing authority—that of the censor as well as their own.

To draw out the feminist implications of the challenge to authority in *Tales*, Mastoraki's use of quotation can be read in light of Luce Irigaray's

---

[42] To discuss quotation in this poem, I have had to resort to a more literal rendering in English, thus partially losing the anapestic rhythm I retain in my other translations of poems from *Tales*. For my preferred version, see Van Dyck 1998.

strategy of subversive mimesis (1985a).[43] At the same time, this feminist reading needs to be combined with Mastoraki's own contradictory view of her use of quotation as homage to the Greek literary tradition. Like *Tales*, Irigaray's *Speculum of the Other Woman* formally overturns the authority of quotation by injecting uncertainty where certainty is assumed. The first section, "How Can They Immediately Be So Sure?" cites Freud's lecture on femininity but undoes the authority of the document by repeatedly interrupting and qualifying his meaning:

> "When you meet a human being," he says, they say, first of all, "the first distinction you make is 'male or female?' and you are accustomed to making the distinction with unhesitating certainty." How? This remains implicit and seems to require no remark among yourselves. Silence, then, on the subject of that extreme assurance which keeps you from being mistaken *at first sight* about the sex of the person you run across. The important point, it seems, is for you to be firmly convinced, without possible hesitation, that you cannot be in error, that there is no ambiguity possible. (13–14)

Like the words "I kiss you," which euphemistically cover up a bite in Mastoraki's poem, Freud's extreme assurance, in the context of Irigaray's text, sounds defensive, as if concealing a doubt. Both authoritative statements are not what they appear to be. But *Speculum*'s undermining of authority, in contrast to *Tales'*, has an explicitly feminist goal. Irigaray challenges Freud's phallogocentrism in the name of "the other woman," who does not constitute herself as lacking a phallus. Irigaray argues that for too long men have censored women by speaking among themselves about femininity; it is time for women to intervene. Irigaray thus genders censorship as masculine and advocates a "feminine" way of writing in response.

Rhea Galanaki, whose poetry I examine more fully in the next chapter, similarly uses quotation marks to question male assumptions, but whereas Irigaray parodies Freud's assurance that sexual difference is always with respect to the phallus, Galanaki acknowledges the equally suspicious practice of effacing the importance of sex as a determining category:

[43] Moi (1985, 127–49) and Gallop (1985a) provide insightful analyses of Irigaray's *Speculum*, Moi usefully introducing the term *subversive mimesis* to refer to her practice of citing an authority (Freud, Plato) and then undermining his logic (130). Irigaray's disrespect for proper syntax ties her earliest work to her later. For her, language has always been the place where subjectivity is constructed, and if one wants to construct subjectivity differently, language is where one must begin. This is clear from her work on the language of schizophrenics, where she analyzes how the split identity might manifest itself syntactically (1973), to the punning wizardry of *Speculum of the Other Woman* ([1974] 1985a) and *The Sex Which Is Not One* ([1977] 1985b), in which she elaborates a feminine grammar, and culminating in a series of interviews and conversations in *Je, tu, nous: Pour une culture de la différence* (1990), on alternative modes of communication between the sexes.

Στην τζαμαρία της εξόδου κρέμεται ένα μικρό χαρτόνι με τα λόγια:

"Μην ανησυχείτε. Αφήστε το πτώμα μέσα στο ξενοδοχείο. Το αναλαμβάνουμε εμείς. Το φύλο του, όπως και το δικό σας, δεν μας ενδιαφέρει. Ευχαριστούμε για την προπάθεια που καταβάλατε ώστε να επικρατήσει η σωστή γραμμή."

(1980, 36)

Hanging on the glass exit door is a small piece of cardboard with the words:

"Don't worry. Leave the corpse in the hotel. We take full responsibility for it. Its sex, like yours, is of no interest to us. Thank you for your assistance in ensuring that the correct policy was implemented."[44]

Her point is that unmarked language is male. Both Irigaray and Galanaki unsettle male confidence by recontextualizing men's words.

In light of Irigaray's positive inscription of the other woman, Mastoraki's and, as we will see, Galanaki's projects appear to be negative. Rather than a gesture toward new forms of feminine sexuality, Mastoraki's challenge to authority, like Karapanou's and other writers under the dictatorship, seems to be an attempt to feminize masculinity.[45] *Tales* teems with sensitive men and ends with a thief crying; the hunter in *The Cake* is also tender. The insistence on men who do not conform to stereotype is very close to the critique that Kaja Silverman reaches in discussing Irigaray. Silverman concludes that "what passes for 'femininity' is actually an inevitable part of all subjectivity: . . . what is needed here is . . . a 'feminization' of the male subject" (1988, 149). Mastoraki's formal reworking of woman's undecidability feminizes writing in the name of turning men into women. Instead of constructing a space for an alternative feminine imaginary, her use of quotation recasts the realm of the (predominantly male) Greek literary imagination to include female experiences.

Mastoraki's own discussion of her use of quotation in *Tales*, almost ten years later, helps clarify this difference, even if her observations, as we will see in Chapter 5, are not conclusive. She too views quotation as a way to use the literary tradition to her own ends, but instead of seeking to undermine the authority of the tradition, she concentrates on how citation enables her as a poet. For her, quotation is a necessary condition of writing in

---

[44] In Greek the phrase σωστή γραμμή means "correct policy" but also "party line."

[45] The attempt is parallel with the declaration of the MDW in which it was stated that they "were against male-defined structures and institutions, rather than against men, and declared that their 'ultimate' goal was to 'overturn' these institutions, liberate both themselves and men and create the conditions for the development of 'essentially human relations' " (Papagaroufalis 1990, 86–87).

Greek, because the unusually layered history of the language requires that
the Greek speaker always use others' words:

Αφού κανένας δεν μιλάει μέσα στα ποιήματα, όταν χρειαστεί να μιλήσει, τα
λόγια του πρέπει να μοιάζουν με παραθέματα, και μάλιστα "μεταφρασμένα"
στο ύφος μίας άλλης εποχής. Πρόσεξε όμως πώς βγαίνει το "σε φιλώ" και έξω
από το παράθεμα, τόσο δυνατό είναι. (1992c)

Since no one speaks in [these] poems, when someone has to speak, the
spoken words must resemble quotations, moreover quotations "translated"
from another time. Watch, though, how the "I kiss you" breaks out of the
quotation marks, it's so strong.

For Mastoraki, the repetition of the line "I kiss you" enacts an escape, but
rather than dismantling the master's house with his own tools, as I suggest, the line acknowledges quotation as a central means of taking posses-
sion of words and overcoming silence.[46] Whereas I relate the effects of
censorship in *Tales* specifically to the dictatorship and to the rise of the
women's movement in Greece, Mastoraki views them more generally as a
condition of writing. In fact she denies that the political struggle in her
poetry written under the dictatorship, of victor and victim, censor and
censored, is connected in *Tales* to the more personal struggle of lovers
trying to communicate. In response to my interpretation, she wrote, " 'Όταν
γράφονται οι ιστορίες, η δικτατορία είναι πια ένα παρελθόν που δεν με
αφορά" (When the tales are being written, the dictatorship is already a past
that doesn't concern me) (1992c). The question I am posing is Are these
issues about power struggles and communication not closely linked to
those raised by the discourses of censorship and feminism? Mastoraki's
comments imply that her poem "The Divers" can be read as building on
the structures of power I suggest it undermines. The reception of *Tales* by
the Greek critical establishment supports this impression; whereas Irigaray was expelled from the Ecole Freudienne for *Speculum,* Mastoraki
was lauded by one of Greece's most influential male critics (Maronitis
1985).[47] Certainly the author's intentions and the response of critics cannot
be ignored, but taking them at face value *is* less fruitful than reading them
in relation to other historical and theoretical claims, those of censorship
and of gender, in particular. By attributing a different author-function to

[46] Here, I am inverting Audre Lorde's famous title "The Master's Tools Will Never Dismantle the Master's House" (1981). Mastoraki's professed position is actually closer to the original
title, though with an opposite impulse. While Lorde's depressing comments under this title
are a feminist call to leave behind the Master's tools and his house, Mastoraki uses his tools
and in this case sees no need for dismantling his house.

[47] I discuss Mastoraki's poetry's relation to the literary tradition more fully in Chapter 5 in
the context of the reception her next collection, M' ένα στεφάνι φως (With a crown of light).

Mastoraki than the one she or her critics imagine, I can link the sexual politics of her recent poetry to the concern with censorship in her early poetry and relate this connection to a more general trend in recent Greek women's poetry.[48]

An additional way of contextualizing my discussion of quotation is to acknowledge the different academic environments in which Irigaray's and Greek women's texts circulate. It could be argued that *Speculum* and much of poststructuralist French feminist theory and experimental writing—calling, as it does, for interdisciplinary thinking—are critical responses to the relative autonomy of disciplines such as philosophy, political science, and literature in France. Because disciplines in Greece have always been less clearly demarcated than those in France, Mastoraki's linguistically heterogeneous text does not threaten the Greek critical establishment. Only recently has literature in Greece become an autonomous institution; literary histories have usually included a wide range of writings from folksongs to religious tracts to political manifestos (Lambropoulos 1988, 23–43; Jusdanis 1991, 108–13). The different receptions of Irigaray's and Mastoraki's texts could be further explained if subversive mimesis were placed in the light of contrasting attitudes toward the "new" held by French writers, who tend to esteem innovation, and by Greek writers, who are inclined to mistrust it. Whereas Irigaray participates in a culturally acceptable practice when, as an avant-garde writer, she undermines her predecessors, Mastoraki works in a milieu where breaking with tradition is less likely to be valued.[49] Irigaray certainly helps to reveal the feminist implications of Mastoraki's challenge to authority, but Mastoraki's reading of "The Divers" can be used to uncover Irigaray's investment in the avant-garde as a tradition. The critical approach I am advocating, therefore, requires that the ground of investigation shift continually, so that texts can be viewed both cross-culturally, in relation to each other, and intraculturally, according to the modes available for acknowledging social change in the author's culture.[50]

At the end of her last lecture on Cassandra, Wolf makes a parallel between this seeress and the soothsaying Pythia: "At first men had identified

[48] On the term *author-function*, see Foucault 1975.

[49] As Anghelaki-Rooke once explained, "I don't have the sense that I am 'being original,' nor that I am 'opening new paths' but that I am using a poetic language, a secure tool which was handed down to me. This sense of continuity or security and the faith that in this country good poetry has been written were for me always a great support" (in Niarchos 1980, 20).

[50] Such an approach also involves making explicit the ways in which my own cultural context influences the kind of questions I ask. In Irigaray's dialogue with various French, Italian, and American feminists (1990), it is the questions posed by the American feminists Alice Jardine and Anne Menke that mirror the issues of the canon and of interdisciplinary studies which I turn to in explaining Mastoraki's and Irigaray's different receptions. These concerns are distinctly those of North American feminists, not of French or Italian ones.

with women, mimed the birth process, castrated themselves so they could become priests. . . . At Delphi later . . . the woman becomes a tool in the hand of the men. . . . The woman, once the executant, has either been excluded or turned into an object." Wolf then addresses her fellow writers Ingeborg Bachmann and Heiner Müller and suggests that once again the time has come for women to set the agenda. She challenges Müller's comment "It is good to be a woman and no victor" by asking, "Do people expect, do we expect, how difficult and in fact dangerous it can be when life is restored to an 'object'? When the idol begins to feel again? When 'it' finds speech again? When it has to say 'I,' as a woman?" (1984, 292–93). Wolf's question is echoed in Karapanou's challenge to the fixity of the male subject and again in Mastoraki's display of this disintegration in her syntax and use of quotation. After the dictatorship, to say "I" as a woman became a desirably unsettling way of sustaining an analysis of power relations: this "I" is, as Karapanou's Kassandra insists, never either a gentleman or a lady but both and is, as Mastoraki's confusing syntax demonstrates, not definitively subject or object. By relating the censorship of the colonels to that of patriarchy and then internalizing the enemy, Karapanou and Mastoraki, Galanaki, and Laina are able to offer women, as well as men, a more complex notion of subjectivity in life and writing than was previously available.

4

Rhea Galanaki's *The Cake* and the Deferred Delivery

Greek cinema, foreign cinema, Seferis, Cavafy, the claustrophobia of city life, the Beat Generation, the comic strip, pop art, Solomos, Kalvos, Byzantine historiography, Marx, Barthes, Benjamin, Freud, Lacan, Trotsky, the civil war, the German occupation, kitsch, Jung, love, folksongs, French poetry, illness, Plath, American poetry, English poetry, the Bible, feminism, Vizyenos, Papadiamantis, German poetry, the murder mystery, motherhood, the nouveau roman, postmodern fiction, angels, financial pressures, Karaghiozis, death, Herodotus, Plato, Thucydides, theater of the absurd, Ancient Greek tragedy, the sea, Sappho, Orthodoxy, Heraclitus, Eliot, Pound, jail, biography, Mallarmé, Baudelaire, Rimbaud, novels, Lévi-Strauss?

In a questionnaire I gave to writers of the generation of the 1970s concerning their experience of the dictatorship and the postdictatorship years, I included a question about influence in which I listed the above hodgepodge of literary and other influences and asked: "How would you assess the effect of the following phenomena on your writing? Choose those that are in any way relevant to your experience as a poet and put them in order of importance." Rhea Galanaki responded: "From literature—Seferis, Cavafy, Solomos, Kalvos, Ancient Greek tragedy, Sappho, Heraclitus, novels, Vizyenos, Papadiamantis, French poetry, the Bible, Plath, American poetry. From theory—Freud, Marx, Lévi-Strauss, Trotsky, feminism. Generally—foreign cinema, love, death, jail" (1989b). My question, though prompted by reading the works of Galanaki and her peers—their poetry, novels, plays, and anthologies—and also the literature and criticism in their bookshelves, the newspaper and magazine clippings in their archives, was also a gloss on my own education and its cross-cultural vicissitudes. Questionnaires, interviews, letters, and informal exchanges provide a testing ground for hearing writers' reservations and confirming my own hunches. Censorship, consumerism, and feminism were recurring themes in the literature itself, but I had highlighted them in my critical analysis, and certainly stressing their interrelation was my contribution. As I pondered the significance of authors' views of their own works, it was also crucial for me to address the status of my views.[1] I found in working on contemporary poetry that I could not help but shift, even if only slightly, the scene of poetic production.

---

[1] On the question of authorial intention, see esp. Benjamin, "The Author as Producer" (1978, 220–38); Wimsatt and Beardsley, "The Intentional Fallacy" (1954); Barthes, "The Death of the Author" (1984, 142–48); and Foucault, "What Is an Author?" (1977b: 113–38).

By foregrounding my role as investigator I am signaling a switch in emphasis in the last three chapters—from a cultural study of literature to a literary analysis of culture. Whereas in the first three chapters I framed women's poetry in its social context, in the last three I more often use the poetry itself as the frame within which I address wider social issues. Although I have been reading the cultural scene through the lens of poems (Seferis's "The Cats of St. Nicholas," Anagnostakis's "The Target," poems by Poulios, Steriadis, and Mastoraki), I now extend this practice and read the period through the formal structure of whole collections of poetry. I am as interested in the poetic form of sexual politics as I am in the sexual politics of poetic form. Ambivalent gender and syntax in Galanaki's collection of prose poems *The Cake* becomes a model for understanding the particular relation of psychoanalysis and feminism in Greece in the decade after the dictatorship. My reading is the result of an exchange over the years between myself and the poets, an exchange illustrated in the question and answer that introduce this chapter. Galanaki's acknowledgment, for example, that Freud, Marx, Lévi-Strauss, Trotsky, and feminism were particularly important to her theoretical development led to long discussions with her about psychoanalysis and feminism; these in turn contributed to my analysis of *The Cake* as a feminist reading of Freud's *Beyond the Pleasure Principle*. Whereas before, I was interested in establishing the essential features of literary history, now, having already set the terms, I emphasize my theoretical concerns as a feminist literary critic.

At the end of Chapter 3, I briefly outlined a shift from the general concern with censorship under the dictatorship to the specific concern with the sexual politics of censorship in women's poetry in the 1980s. I begin the chapters on individual poets by discussing each author's work, extending the overview to the early 1990s and making their visual narratives of the 1980s pivotal pieces rather than end points. There are many reasons why I start with Galanaki's *The Cake* (1980). Not only does her text predate the other two collections I discuss in depth, Mastoraki's *Tales of the Deep* (1983) and Laina's *Hers* (1985a), but it explicitly inscribes in a feminist poetics the change in scale from the shorter lyric poems under censorship to the longer narrative cinematographic series of poems. Neither as excessive in its imagery and use of linguistic registers as *Tales of the Deep*, nor as minimalist as *Hers*, *The Cake*'s measured, straightforward style provides a map that we can use to read Mastoraki's and Laina's more hermetic texts. *The Cake* more openly asks the questions I find useful in my readings of all three collections: What is the cumulative effect of an assault on clarity? a suspicion of art as imitation? an attention to sexual difference? Galanaki's text makes clear that to write, women must address these issues over time and space.

Born in Crete in 1947, Rhea Galanaki emerged in the late 1980s as one of Greece's most highly acclaimed novelists. Her historical novels Ο Βίος του

Ισμαήλ Φερίκ πασά (The life of Ismail Ferik Pasha) and Θα υπογράφω Λουί (I shall sign my name as Louis) have been praised by literary critics and enjoyed commercial success.[2] For many readers, her fame as a novelist has eclipsed her beginnings as a poet. I choose to look at the pivotal role her poetry played in her development as a writer, especially her collection *The Cake*, which registers this shift from poetry to prose. *The Cake* (1980) is a bridge between Galanaki's early, epigrammatic poems Πλην εύχαρις (Albeit pleasing) (1975) and Ορυκτά (Minerals) (1979) and her prose pieces, Πού ζει ο λύκος; (Where does the wolf live?) (1982b), Ομόκεντρα διηγήματα (Concentric stories) (1986b), and her novels *The Life of Ismail Ferik Pasha* (1989a) and *I Shall Sign My Name as Louis* (1993). *The Cake* is, therefore, a transitional work, signaling a shift in genre from poetry to prose, but also a change in source material from myth to history. It is also Galanaki's most explicitly feminist text to date.

In *The Cake* the pregnant woman with her unborn child is the figure that embodies these shifts and this explicit feminism. Significantly she is not a mother who has already given birth to her child but a woman who *will* give birth. Everything is in process, incomplete and pending—poetry has not yet become prose, myth has not yet turned to history, the child has not yet been born. Even in the final poem the birth is projected into the future:

> Και θα φυτέψω τα ρούχα της μαινάδας κοντά σε μια πηγή και η πηγή σ' ένα χαρτί ζωγραφισμένη και το χαρτί σελίδα γλώσσας που αναβρύζει. Και δίπλα θα ξαπλώσω ήρεμη και γυμνή για να γεννήσω.
>
> (1980, 54)

> And I will plant the maenad's clothes near a spring and the spring drawn on paper and the paper a page of language which wells up. And next to this I will lie down, calm and naked, and give birth.

The pregnant woman, like the text she figures, is indeterminate. Let me first situate this figure of woman in the context of Galanaki's other works, then outline how I read *The Cake* to bring out the formal implications of the pregnant woman.

Figuring (Out) Woman

The pivotal role of the pregnant woman clearly emerges as we look at the figure of woman, its development and eventual disappearance, in Galanaki's work from early books of poetry through the historical novels.

---

[2] For an overview of Galanaki's works, see Frantzi 1993–94. On *The Life of Ismail Ferik Pasha*, see Beaton 1994, 290–93; Maronitis 1992, 225–36; and Thalassis 1991.

Her first two collections draw heavily on classical mythology. The figure of woman is often a mythical figure outside the text. Though distinctly lyric, these books demand that the reader expand tiny epigrams by invoking the narratives to which the mythical figure refers. Her first book, *Albeit Pleasing*, written under the regime, offers the reader cryptic fragments that— like scenes from vase paintings or frames of a film—suggest much longer narratives. For example in "Ελληνικό τοπίο" (Greek landscape), perhaps her best-known poem in the collection, a reference to the "Furies" draws the reader into the Argive narrative of matricide and shifting legal orders.[3] This poem, first published in the resistance journal *Continuity*, also draws a parallel between the ancient maenads playing hide and seek, shouting their condemnations through their laughter, and writers resisting the colonels.[4] In a review of this collection, Andia Frantzi stresses the role of the reader in animating these poems. For her, it is the act of reading which allows these poems to "break their shackle" and to assume a visual and narrative relation to each other, to become like a film rather than like still "pictures framed in strict groupings" (1975). Although this text requires an effort on the part of the reader, the interpretative framework is fairly clear. To invoke the Furies as a symbol of resistance, like the Cassandra invoked by Seferis and the postwar poets, is a familiar move.

Galanaki's second book, *Minerals*, makes the reader work harder. Her poem "Της Πρόκνης και της Φιλομήλας" (Of Procne and Philomela), for example, presupposes a knowledge of two myths of violence, one that ends in Procne's and Philomela's metamorphoses into birds, the other that leaves Prometheus at the mercy of a vulture forever feasting on his liver. The first epigram refers to the women who have been turned into birds and makes them victims of a violent act:

> Ραμφίζουν ήσυχα τις φυλλωσιές
> όπως μιλούν το σούρουπο στο καλοκαίρι.
> $\qquad$ (1979, 14)

> They peck calmly amidst the foliage
> while they talk at dusk in the summer.

The second recalls the bird as predator:

> Χαράματα το ράμφος κόκκινο
> και το σηκώτι φαγωμένο.

---

[3] See Aeschylus's *Oresteia*, especially the third play in the trilogy, "The Eumenides," in which the Furies' old moral order of revenge is replaced by the democratic court of the Areopagus.

[4] This epigram was printed with three others, and the title "Greek Landscape" which only refers to the first, was incorrectly assumed to be the title of all three.

The red beak at dawn
and the liver eaten-through.

Inviting the reader to dissolve the frame around each two-line epigram by relating them, the lyric gives way to narrative. Unlike the reference to the Furies, which kept the ancient myth intact, albeit in an implied modern setting, these references to two different myths require that the reader create a new composite myth that implicates victim and victor and bears little resemblance to the ancient tales. As we might have expected, the figure of woman in the form of Procne and Philomela becomes the vehicle for such role scrambling. Changed into birds "pecking calmly amidst the foliage," they are also metonymically the red beak that eats Prometheus's liver in the second epigram. In Greek the connection is even more obvious: the verb *to peck* (ραμφίζω) is cognate with the noun *beak* (ράμφος).

Woman as a figure of undecidability motivates the choice of the pregnant woman as figure for both reader and writer in Galanaki's next work, *The Cake*. Instead of asking the reader to "break the shackle" of the epigrams by referring outside the text, the reader finds herself already in the text, and the text itself somewhat "hors d'oeuvre." The use of the second person in the first five sections assures this. The first poem concludes:

Το σώμα σου μεσ' στο καλό του φόρεμα ζυγίζει, μέσα στο φόρεμα γιγαντιαία
και ακίνητη κρατώντας, είναι σαν ήδη να κρατάς στα χέρια σου το κέικ.
(1980, 11)

your body in its best dress is weighing, in its best dress gigantic, immobile,
it is holding, it is as if you were already holding the cake in your hands.

Rather than having the reader turn to other mythical figures, the reader as pregnant woman creates her own myth as she goes along. Galanaki, comparing her use of myth in her earlier books to that in the 1980s, writes, "A broadening of the 'mythic' leads me to different things. For example, then I referred to the closed mythological space of Ancient Greece almost exclusively. Now I 'mythologize,' or at least research, real stories, my own situations etc." (1989b, 6). This shift is even clearer in the final section entitled "Τώρα εγώ" (Now me) in which the pregnant woman becomes the writer subsuming all her readers:

Το σώμα μου όλα τα χαρτονένια σώματα των γυναικών και φτάνω στην άκρη
ενός άδειου πάρκινγκ· και φτάνω στην άκρη των μύθων.
(1980, 53)

My body is all the cardboard bodies of women and I arrive at the edge of an
empty parking lot; and I arrive at the edge of myths.

Both reader and writer, mother and other,[5] "I" and "you," "she" and "he," subject and object, singular and plural, transitive and intransitive, still and in motion, the pregnant woman provides a model of semantic potentiality rather than a stereotype.

As we have seen, the figure of woman under the dictatorship came to stand for the breaking down of barriers, the act of transforming one thing into another and of challenging the status quo. In the guise of Kassandra and Lysistrata, she was the site of resistance in the form of cross-dressing and punning. But the pregnant woman in *The Cake,* beyond standing for such sexual and linguistic undecidability, offers a model of how language can partake in this confusion. Like the birth of the child that has not yet occurred, the moment of signification is also put off. Phrases fall apart, circle around, elliptically displace each other, and resist agreement. The difficulty of communication is the form and content of these poems. It is impossible to separate what one says from how one says it. As one poem explains, "Το ρούχο του ορισμού είναι η ίδια η διατύπωσή του και κουρελιάζεται μαζί της" (The definition's clothing is the same as its wording and both are torn to shreds) (39). The feminine adjectives without referents and the transitive verbs with no object describe and perform the pregnant woman's indeterminacy.

Galanaki's next two books, *Where Does the Wolf Live?* and *Concentric Stories,* continue to explore formally the question of writing as a woman, but here the struggle is less evident. The central tensions of the earlier collections—whether prose will prevail over poetry, whether history or "real stories" will prevail over myth—are already, for the most part, resolved. At first glance, in terms of its explicit reference to the dictatorship and the central figure of a woman, *Where Does the Wolf Live?* appears to be the more appropriate choice for a discussion of censorship and women's writing. Its short prose pieces punctuated with two poems and finishing with two letters, one from jail and one to jail, are dedicated to her friends from 1967 to 1974 and tell the story of student life under the dictatorship.[6] But the problem of women's writing is secondary to the plot. The pregnant woman is replaced by the female character Paula, the word literally meaning "dash" in Greek—"Η Παύλα είναι μετά την κάθε πρόταση σε όσα κρύβουμε" (Paula follows every sentence in everything we hide) (1982b, 37). Her presence affects everything, but she is less prominent than the pregnant woman, who takes up space and time, "immobile and gigantic." It is as if in the process of figuring out the role of woman in writing, woman is, in a sense, figured out of the text. Whereas *The Cake* begins by defining

---

[5] On the mother/other dynamic in the feminist psychoanalytic terms that inform my reading, see Garner, Kahane, and Sprengnether 1985.

[6] For an analysis of this work, which, among other things, draws on my discussion of women's writing and censorship, see Georgiopoulos 1991.

male and female roles in order to implicate one in the other and complicate each, the *Wolf* reverses the process. The two concluding letters resort to stereotypical male and female roles: the man in jail refers to philosophy and public events; the woman at home recalls fairy tales and personal experiences. It is not that gender is not a formal issue; one has only to compare her use of a female protagonist as a dash with Chronis Missios's straight-forward first-person subject position in his memoir Καλά, εσύ σκο-τώθηκες νωρίς (Lucky you died young) (1985), which also covers this period.[7] Yet in contrast to *The Cake*, the narrative content has taken precedence over its form.

Her next piece, *Concentric Stories*, consists of short stories with more conventionally developed characters.[8] One of these stories, "Η ιστορία της 'Ολγας" (The story of Olga), is about a woman learning how to write.[9] Once Olga "achieves literacy," something that historically was not a woman's privilege, Galanaki leaves the feminine subject behind. Her next two works published after *Concentric Stories* are historical novels about men. The question of gendered language is posed only indirectly.[10] Both novels are based on the lives of historical persons—*The Life of Ismail Ferik Pasha* on the Greek commander of the Egyptian army during the Cretan-Turkish war of 1866, and *I Shall Sign My Name as Louis* on Andreas Rigopoulos, a romantic revolutionary poet and playwright born on a boat off the shore of Patras on the day the Greek War of Independence began who committed suicide by throwing himself into the sea on the one hundredth anniversary of the French Revolution. As with Mastoraki's feminized men, Galanaki's project here involves complicating stereotypes by constructing not female, but alternative male, subjectivities. In the progression from poetry to prose and from myth to history, the figure of woman disappears.

I concentrate on *The Cake*, therefore, because it registers most dramatically the interrelation between genre and gender. It is the figure of woman's final and finest performance. In the questionnaire Galanaki described how her writing changed after the dictatorship: "My writing became more analytical; the books with small epigrams became books with poetic series,

[7] "I'm not writing from the Corfu jail; I am writing from Athens, relatively free . . . I want to talk to you about the old times, the old friends" (1985, 7).

[8] See Polychrou 1989.

[9] Proof of the less experimental and more accessible quality of this collection is that this story was included in an anthology of women's short stories given free to subscribers of the Greek edition of *Marie Claire*, a popular women's magazine, in the summer of 1994.

[10] An issue for further discussion is whether the novels are giving in to the temptation to participate in patriarchal language, a temptation Galanaki mentions as early as *Minerals*—"the charm of a hard narrative finished unambiguous" (1979, 22)—and recalls in *The Cake*, when she writes of "a page of language which closed like a lake," or whether they are attempting to make Greek the lost mother tongue, as it is for the protagonist of her novel, *Ismail Ferik Pasha*.

or prose (very recently)" (1989b, 6). In a 1987 interview (also cited in Chapter 3), she connected this formal shift to censorship and sexual liberation: "it was a time of transition from a very closed, objective poem . . . to me talking [openly] as a subject. And language grew bigger without fear of censorship . . . that is to say, a vagina is called a vagina." I return to these comments to frame the problematic of *The Cake.* More than any other piece that Galanaki has written, it explores the formal implications of feminism.

Twenty-four prose poems in six interrelated sections make up *The Cake.* The first two sections draw on the roles and rituals of traditional society: a pregnant woman, a hunter, a sacrificial cock. The first, "Το ένα και το άλλο μέτρο" (One and the other kind of measure), interprets these roles and rituals through the "feminine" imagery of cooking and measuring; the second, "Οι παγίδες" (The traps), does so through the "masculine" imagery of hunting. In the third section, "Το παιχνίδι" (The game), male and female roles are completely scrambled as an eagle and a snake pursue each other in a strange, ancient rite. The fourth section, "Στο κρεβάτι" (In bed), creates its own modern myth of victor and victim out of the bedtime rituals of reading, turning off the light, rolling over, making love, sleep and dreaming. Through the transformative power of games and the bed, the pregnant woman and hunter become plural and potential. Finally, in the fifth section, "Ο θάνατος και η κηδεία" (The death and the funeral), strings of cardboard cut-out men and women are collapsed into one so that the first-person "I" of the last section, "Τώρα εγώ" (Now me), has a wealth of roles to draw on as she describes the time and place where she will finally give birth. Though such a description of *The Cake* can make it sound like a rather schematic deconstruction of traditional gender roles, its hypnotic repetition of phrases and metonymic stringing together of images create a different effect. *The Cake* teaches that the figure of woman is a poetically as well as politically charged figure—the deferred birth is as much a writing style as a feminist manifesto.

In the remaining three sections of this chapter, I look at *The Cake* from three perspectives, slicing it three different ways, focusing each time on different sections in order to outline the theory of women's writing embedded there. First I analyze how *The Cake* deconstructs the purported supplementarity of gender by posing the pregnant woman as both male and female, masculine and feminine. I then examine the formal implications of the pregnant woman as a figure of subversive mimesis, and I explore the sexual politics of imitation and repetition by reading the third section, "The Game," and *The Cake* more generally, in relation to Freud's *Beyond the Pleasure Principle.* Finally, I combine my discussion of the pregnant woman as a figure of undecidability and as a way of figuring undecidability in my analysis of writing as a (pregnant) woman.

The Cake **Is Pink**

The first thing one notices on picking up this collection of poetry is that the cover is pink.[11] *The Cake* is feminine. Like pink clothes on a newborn, this cover, enclosing the reading experience, genders the text and its readers. Reading the first poem, the reader finds herself implicated, addressed as the second person, not only feminine, but pregnant. The pink cover and the feminized, pregnant second person turn women's experience into everyone's. Western literature, generally, has a long history of implying that male experience is everyone's, but women's experience is rarely given this status;[12] *The Cake*'s explicit feminism is even more shocking in the Greek context. As I discussed in my introduction, the term *women's writing* has a history of negative, or at least restrictive, uses in Greece. Even more so in the leftist circles in which Galanaki was involved, φεμινισμός (feminism) and φεμινίστρια (feminist) carried strong overtones of American imperialism and were doubly taboo. Even after the dictatorship and the rise of the women's movement, the term still carried the connotation of sentimental poetry and American intervention. Women in the private sphere were meant to keep things running smoothly by reproducing sons and writing about domestic life, so that men in the public sphere could get on with what Rilke had called "the serious motherhood of men," that is, artistic production.[13] For the most part Greek women writers in the late 1970s did not call attention to gender, not wishing to be excluded from this other motherhood. With its pink cover, pregnant protagonist, and the blatantly American word *cake* for its title, then, Galanaki's book takes a very different approach. Not only does this text represent women's experiences, but it does so in a way that challenges their marginality. "Pink," "reproduction," and "women's writing" are reinterpreted as central, productive, and serious. As Galanaki writes in her essay "Η γυναικεία γραφή και η καταραμένη Πανδώρα" (Women's writing and the cursed Pandora), "A person who writes, when she is a woman, opens her burden with all the small everyday objects that are useless to other people and that define her system of life and puts them in a different light" (1982a, 364).

On first reading *The Cake*, it seems that the suspenseful twenty-four books of the *Odyssey* with its male protagonist have been replaced by a

---

[11] An experimental feminist filmmaker and friend of Galanaki's, Antoinetta Anghelidi, designed this cover, as well as the one for *Minerals*.

[12] The Irish poet Medbh McGuckian, at a November 6, 1991 reading during a festival of Greek and Irish poetry, made a similar move. She introduced one poem by referring to her desire to have a fifth child as if everyone had had such an experience: "You know how it feels when. . . ." In a mixed audience at the Poetry Society of America, perhaps few of whom had been pregnant four times, her use of the second-person pronoun was arresting.

[13] I refer here to Maurice Blanchot's discussion of Rilke in *The Space of Literature* (1982, 125).

more prosaic twenty-four hours at home, where a pregnant woman is making the bed, baking a cake, getting dressed, trying to sleep. But on closer inspection these banal, "useless" details of everyday life turn out to be as significant as any of Odysseus's adventures. The strict divisions of private and public spheres, useless and useful, ephemeral and substantial, are undone. Life "at home" is as wild and gory as life "out there"; life at home in fact never was anything but wild, and it is the hunter's antics, if any, that are supplementary. The first section presents two contradictory ways of measuring worth, the feminine mode of reproduction and the masculine mode of killing. The productiveness of the woman in the first two poems is compared with the destructiveness of the man in the second two poems. She is making a cake and bearing a child, while he is hunting. But even in the first poem this opposition does not hold. *The Cake* tampers with the traditional scene, altering the terms so that neither role remains stable in its gender identification, and woman becomes the one who can survive and even thrive on this instability. The bed in the first poem sets the tone. It is the scene of a Greek ritual in which the butchered cock is used to bless the foundations of a new building. But in this case, the sacrificial blood is also the blood of birthing, and the blessing is not only for some male construction but for the female act of bearing a child as well. On the one hand, the productiveness of woman is contrasted with the destructive-ness of man: the pregnant woman "touches the blood on the clothes as if she were giving birth" (1980, 11), while the cock climbs onto the bed to die. On the other hand, and at the same time, the maleness of the cock is deflated by his association with the birthing woman. A quintessential ritual of culture turns out to be an imitation of the natural act of birth. This collection repeats this double move of contrasting male and female and then collapsing them by feminizing the male or masculinizing the female.

If men's rituals mimic women's, so their scientific discoveries are also derivative. The second poem tells us that the pregnant woman challenges our expectations of space and time "before Galileo"; her body already is both the stillness and the motion he discovered in the pendulum:

Το σώμα σου κινείται, τίποτε άλλο δεν κινείται από το σώμα σου σαν εκκρεμές κι ορίζεις πριν από τον Γαλιλαίο.
(12)

Your body is moving, nothing else is moving except your body like a pen-dulum and you define motion before Galileo.

Not only does the pregnant woman prefigure the male scientist's un-orthodox position, but she anticipates Galileo's resistance to censorship.[14] She can accommodate contradiction, "the one and the other kind of measure." Her body dissolves strict distinctions so that nothing is absolutely outside or inside.[15]

Whereas the man needs the pregnant woman to complete himself, she is already complete. She already contains what she needs. As we see in the quotation below, for example, her body constitutes the scales she is using to weigh the ingredients for the cake. This self-sufficiency is also true linguistically. She commands the transitive and intransitive use of verbs, whereas he is limited to the transitive. One example is the verb *to hold* (κρατώ). The pregnant woman, as we have seen in Poem 1, holds the child and holds the cake. But hidden in this transitive sense of the verb is the intransitive sense of duration, of being able to last and ultimately to outlast men. In Poem 2, we read of the pregnant woman:

Στα χέρια σου κρατάς ένα μεγάλο κέικ κι αφήνεις σ' όλες τις επέτειους ένα κομμάτι σαν να εγκαταλείπεις σ' όλες τις παγίδες ένα ίχνος από τη διάρκειά σου· μέχρι πότε;
(12)

In your hands you hold a big cake and you leave a piece at every anniversary as if you were abandoning in every trap some proof of your ability to last; for how long?

The man who enters as the hunter holding a sword in the third poem, however, has access only to the transitive sense. He can hold the sword; he cannot hold out:

Ο κυνηγός κρατά σπαθί αντί για δίκαννο· ο κυνηγός δε θα μπορούσε· ο κυνηγός κρατώντας το σπαθί δε θα μπορούσε να 'χει άλλο τρόπο να ζει κοντά σου από το κυνήγι.
(13)

[14] Popularly, Galileo is best known as a heretic censored by the Inquisition for geokinetic theories that could not be supported by a literal reading of the Scripture. See Galileo's letter to Castelli, in which he explains the problem of basing one's scientific claims on the Bible (Finocchiaro 1989, 50) and his sentence in which he is condemned for "interpreting Holy Scripture according to [his] own meaning in response to objections based on Scripture which were sometimes made to [him]" (288). In the Μεγάλη Ελληνική εγκυκλοπαίδεια (Greek grand encyclopedia) the picture in the middle of the entry is of Galileo in front of the Inquisition. This scene of censorship was also the one that intrigued Brecht in his play *Galileo*, a text read by many during the dictatorship. On Brecht's *Galileo* and the issue of censorship, see Bentley's introduction (Brecht 1966, 15–18).
[15] This dissolution of opposites could also be read in terms of Heraclitus's philosophy. In his fragments, antitheses are viewed in continuous flux, blending with each other, forming a unity of sorts. Galanaki claims Heraclitus is an important influence (see her list of influences at the beginning of this chapter).

The hunter holds a sword instead of a shotgun; the hunter has no other means, the hunter holding the sword has no other means of living near you besides hunting.

The repetition of the debilitating phrase "δε θα μπορούσε" (the hunter has no other means) emphasizes his transitive need for an object, his need for her. Her feminine cycle determines his every action. He is stuck, chasing her in circles, imitating her cycles with his motorcycle as he drives around the circle of Omonia Square as if riding "the circle of death" (13).[16]

The last poem of the first section compares once again his method of killing and her method of reproducing. Her method wins because it includes his. The poem begins with the hunter killing ancient myths and hanging them from meat hooks. In the course of the poem they become hares. He will have to keep killing because she will always produce:

θα ήθελε να ζει, θα ήθελε πολύ να ζει απαραμύθητος κι ελεύθερος. Δεν έχει άλλο τρόπο για να ζει· να ζει κοντά σου από το κυνήγι και δεν μπορεί, δε θα μπορούσε να σκοτώσει όλους τους λαγούς γιατί θα μέναν δυο και θα γεννούσαν έναν τρίτο, σαν να σε κουβαλά και να σε γονιμοποιεί ο ίδιος απ' ό,τι θα θυμάται. Ανελεύθερος θυμάται.

(14)

He would like to live, he would so much like to live without the consolation of myth and free. He has no other means of living; of living near you besides hunting and he cannot, he could not kill all the hares since two would survive and they would give birth to a third, as if he were carrying you, impregnating you himself with all that he will remember. Unfree, he remembers.

His dependency is poignantly underscored by the fact that he would like to live απαραμύθητος—meaning "without consolation" and also, literally, "without myths"—but cannot. He can hang up the old myths, but he needs her to create new ones.

The second section, "Traps," begins with the hunter imitating the woman, trying to make a cake.

Το δόκανο μιας επετείου. Είπε ο κυνηγός τόσο αλεύρι, τόσο βούτυρο και τόση ζάχαρη μου φτιάχνουν ένα σιδερένιο κέικ.

(17)

---

[16] This is the Greek term for the hair-raising amusement park ride in which a motorcycle climbs the walls of a high, metal cylinder so that the rider is ultimately parallel to the ground. Galanaki discusses the importance of circular imagery in her work (see Polychrou 1989).

An anniversary snare. The hunter said this much flour, this much butter and this much sugar make me an iron cake.

But whereas the woman's cake is versatile and can coexist with the unborn child, the man's cake is a trap that supplants the cake. Whereas for the pregnant woman the cake is a part of her, just as the child is a part of her, for him it is a snare, metal, inhuman. Time more generally, whether measuring years through anniversaries or hours with alarm clocks, is not something that comes naturally to him. He relies on external reminders:

Θα χτυπήσει· το ξυπνητήρι θα χτυπήσει. Στα υπόλοιπα κρεβάτια πρέπει να σε κυνηγήσει, γιατί κάθε κρεβάτι είναι μια επέτειος και κάθε επέτειος είναι παγίδα. Όπως μοσχοβολά.

(20)[17]

It will ring; the alarm clock will ring. He must hunt for you in the rest of the beds, because each bed is an anniversary and each anniversary is a trap. The way it smells sweet.

In another poem (to which I return in my next section), the pregnant woman's self-reliance is reflected in the fact that though the hunter seeks shelter, she can be a shelter and, "like a spell," protect herself simultaneously:

Ένα καταφύγιο. Σαν ξόρκι. Η νοσταλγία ενός καταφύγιου και αγκαλιάζεις με τα δύο σου χέρια τη μεγάλη σου κοιλιά· βυθίζεσαι στη μήτρα του παλιότερου μύθου· να σε κυοφορήσει, έμβρυο που κυοφορείς εν' άλλο έμβρυο.

(21)

A shelter. Like a spell. The nostalgia for a shelter and you hug your big belly with both hands; you bury yourself in the womb of the older myth; to be pregnant with you, an embryo pregnant with another embryo.

Similarly she can have a son and by never letting go of him, by never delivering him, also have him as her lover. In the last poem of this section the world has become completely "pink." She encompasses everything. Even the son-lover's snare turns out to be a figment of the pregnant woman's imagination:

[17] The hunter's dependence on the alarm clock could also be read as a gloss on Poulios's poem "Το ρολόι" (The watch). Whereas time is already internalized for Galanaki's pregnant woman, Poulios's speaker has to internalize the actual time pieces: " Έχω ένα μικρό ρολόι στο κεφάλι μου / που δουλεύει δουλεύει άπαυτα δουλεύει / μετρώντας τον εσωτερικό χρόνο ρυθμίζοντας / την αρμονία του είναι μου. / είναι ένα μαγαζάκι με ρολόγια το κορμί μου" (I have a small watch in my head / which works works unceasingly works / measuring my inner time, keeping / my being in tune. / my body is a shop of watches) (Poulios 1980, 11).

Αν η δική σου φαντασία είναι το δόκανο, αυτό που έκρυψε σε μιαν επέτειο ο κυνηγός σα σιδερένιο κέικ· τότε και το δικό σου το παιχνίδι παγιδεύει στην τελετουργία του τον κυνηγό: ο μικρός κυνηγός παίζει.

(23)

If your own imagination is the snare, the snare the hunter hid on an anniversary like an iron cake; then your game also traps the hunter in its ritual: the young hunter is playing.

Whereas woman traditionally was the supplement to man, Galanaki's pregnant woman supplants this division. Through a deconstruction of the oppositional relation between man and woman, her supplementarity is undermined culturally and biologically. She can bless a building *and* give birth, weigh *and* already encompass the scales, hold her child *and* hold out simultaneously, protect *and* be protected, have her son *and* have him as her lover. Man must abandon one thing in order to get another; woman ultimately can have her cake and eat it too.

The Sexual Politics of Mimesis

The pregnant woman's self-reliance and versatility involve an important revision of mimesis as social and artistic practice. For Aristotle, as for his mentor Plato, mimesis, meaning both imitation and representation, is an integral part of human nature (Aristotle 1973, 1448b5–9). Poetry for both is first and foremost an imitative art.[18] From the ancient tragedy to which Aristotle refers to the realist fiction of today, writers have taken seriously the goal of verisimilitude.[19] In Galanaki's formulation, however, in keeping with twentieth-century avant-garde traditions such as surrealism, mimetic representation—both at the level of content and that of form—is impossible. Nothing can be like anything else. The last four sections of *The Cake* are full of acts of cross-dressing and role playing which challenge the traditional mimetic relationship between art and life. The figure of the pregnant woman not only deconstructs the binary opposition of gender but destabilizes gender itself as a cognitive and social category while presenting the activity of deconstruction as an alternative poetic practice to mimesis. Imitation is never in the service of the real and final delivery, but as with Irigaray's and Mastoraki's subversive mimesis, it uses the master's tools to different ends.

Although for the most part in the first two sections *The Cake* is hers and he is imitating her, the strict opposition that imitation incurs between an

[18] On the differences between Plato's and Aristotle's views, see, e.g., Genette 1982, 128–33.
[19] The classic work of criticism on this topic is Auerbach 1968.

original and a copy, and the reliance on metaphor it traditionally upholds, are challenged from the start. Imitation, whether the male imitating the female or art imitating nature, presupposes a clear-cut hierarchy, which *The Cake* undoes. *The Cake* is interested not in likenesses and perfect matches but rather in the arbitrary contiguity of one thing with another. Even in the first poem we find that the shadow of the cock, the symbol of male virility, and the pregnant woman's hands are inextricably intertwined:

Γέρνει ο δίσκος που βαραίνεις με το δικό σου δάχτυλο και τη σκιά του κόκορα· ακίνητη γιγαντιαία σ᾽ ένα τοίχο η σκιά του και κοντά στο φως τα δάκτυλά σου ακίνητα μπλεγμένα.

(11)

The tray tips when you push down with your finger and the shadow of the cock; gigantic and immobile, his shadow on the wall and near the light your fingers, folded and immobile.

Her fingers are near the light, so it would seem that the cock is the shadow her fingers make on the wall, yet is her finger play not also an imitation of a cock? It is not clear who is imitating whom.

This confusion is self-referentially true of the language of the poems. The mimetic presumptions of language are undermined simultaneously. Each metaphor is a metaphor of another metaphor, an embryo pregnant with another embryo. Nothing is like anything else. It is as difficult to establish the syntactical structure of the poem as it is the relationships among the objects being described. In Greek the noun σκιά (shadow) in the first line is in the accusative case, suggesting that it must be the object of a verb or follow a preposition. The strongest possibility is the preposition "with" in the sentence "you push down with your finger," so that the sense becomes "you push down with your finger and *with* the shadow." This odd formulation makes object and reflection equally active, neither one the reflection of the other. The back and forth—from "your finger" to "the shadow" in the first line, both in the accusative, to "his shadow" and "your fingers" in the second line, both nominative—confirms this; having both objects in the accusative and then both in the nominative disturbs the sense that one is the subject and the other the object, that one is the reflection of the other. Both imitation *in* the poem and the poem *as* imitation are under attack.

The third and fourth sections of *The Cake* bring up the sexual politics of mimetic representation as explicitly social and artistic practice. In Section 3, "The Game," the woman who until this point has been imitated becomes the imitator and embraces the quintessentially male role of the hunter. In

the final poem of this section the woman is a she-eagle (αετίνα) preying on
a snake. At first it seems that gender has not affected the plot: the hunter
may be female but the scene is familiar. The victor imitates the victim in
order to kill it:

Το πέταγμα της αετίνας και του φιδιού το πέταγμα που είναι μίμηση · η μίμηση
της φύσης για το θάνατο της φύσης είναι.

(29)

The flight of the she-eagle and the flight of the snake which is imitation; the
imitation of nature is for the death of nature.

The aesthetic theory implied is also predictable. By imitating nature, the
artist conquers nature. The twist comes at the end of the poem, when the
imitation of nature no longer brings the death of nature because no one can
remember who killed whom:

Στο τέλος η αετίνα θα πει "καληνύχτα" στό φίδι και θα γυρίσει στη φωλιά της.
Το φίδι θα πει "καληνύχτα" στην αετίνα και θα γυρίσει στη δική του τρύπα.
Κανένας δε θυμάται ποιος σκότωσε σήμερα ποιον.

(29)

In the end the she-eagle will say "goodnight" to the snake and return to her
nest. The snake will say "goodnight" to the she-eagle and return to his hole.
No one remembers who killed whom today.

Imitation, in particular of violence and death, has traditionally been the
domain of men.[20] Whether it is an ancient war epic such as *The Iliad* or a
more modern version such as Seferis's meditation on the suffering of his
country in "The Cats of St. Nicholas" or Dimitris Dimitriadis's apocalyptic
Πεθαίνω σα χώρα (*I die like a country*) (1980), men have often sought solace
and protection from death through their literary representations of death.
By shuffling roles, Galanaki poses the question of what happens when
women assume this subject position, when they stop writing love poetry
and write about death instead.[21] Anghelaki-Rooke addresses this role
change in her poem "Μοναχικό" (Monkish), in which the polar bear who
imitates death in order to survive is female:

---

[20] Irigaray suggests that women merely service men's working out of the death drive owing
to the lack of recognition of woman's desire (1985b, 53).
[21] This feminist angle on the question of representation and violence is explored in Johnson
1989, 184–99.

Κι όπως η πολική αρκούδα
με το λίπος—όραμα του κορμιού της
αντέχει το κρύο γιατί στην παγωμένη τρύπα της
μιμείται το θάνατο
(1990, 55)

And like the polar bear
who with the vision-fat of her body
withstands the cold because in her icy hole
she imitates death

But whereas Anghelaki-Rooke continues to deploy metaphor ("and like the polar bear"), Galanaki suggests that woman-as-the-imitator-of-death demands a different, more metonymic kind of writing.[22] *The Cake* asks what happens to writing if imitation has no set outcome, if subject and object, essence and covering, inside and outside are no longer distinct— what happens if *who one is* and *what one looks like* and *what one means* and *what one says* are indistinguishably scrambled. As an alternative to imitation and metaphor, she offers the obscure syntax, the imperfect repetitions, and the prominence of metonymy found in *The Cake*.[23]

Galanaki's particular form of subversive mimesis rewrites Western, male views of representation by taking to task the theory of mimesis and its relation to death as we find it in Freud's *Beyond the Pleasure Principle*. Here we can find the precise structural framework for *The Cake*, as well as the gender bias it sets out to deconstruct.[24] Formally, Galanaki follows Freud's movement from the analysis of games to that of dreams and finally to a discussion of death in the third, fourth, and fifth sections of *The Cake*: "The Game," "In Bed," and "The Death and the Funeral." Her pregnant woman also seems to echo Freud's interest in embryology. Throughout the collection she touches on the ideas Freud addresses in his essay: the relation of stability and excitation (276–77), the postponement of satisfaction (178), repression and censorship (279), artistic imitation and children's play (287), Aristophanes's example of an apple cut in two (331), and his final quotation from Ruckert about flying and limping as modes of self-expression (338). In these references and rewritings Galanaki's central im-

---

[22] Also see Matsi Hatzilazarou's poem "ψυχανάλυση" (Psychoanalysis) (1985, 26–28) for another eloquent attempt by a woman to grapple with the sexual politics of repetition and the death drive.

[23] An important intertext for Galanaki's use of metonymy is Baudelaire's prose poem "The Cake"; see Johnson 1983, 79–84, for a reading of it.

[24] Leo Bersani's reading of *Beyond the Pleasure Principle* and the representation of male violence in Pasolini's Salò and Assyrian reliefs (1986, 51–79) provides an important background to my reading of this text as a gendered reworking of the problem of mimesis.

pulse seems to be to scramble clear-cut oppositions and challenge the perfect fit sought by imitation.

According to Freud, the compulsion to imitate and to continue doing so, that is, to repeat, is a defense mechanism by which one overcomes fear. Freud's most noted example of this is the child's fort-da game (discussed in reference to Kassandra in Chapter 3), which he introduces in *Beyond the Pleasure Principle* (1984, 283–87). The child, displeased by his mother's departure, makes up a game in which he imitates and therefore controls the fort ("go away") and da ("come back"), transforming danger into pleasure. But most of *Beyond the Pleasure Principle* examines a different example, the dreams of traumatic neurosis and the dreams patients have during psychoanalysis which bring to memory the psychical traumas of childhood (304). Unlike the child's game or dreams of wish fulfillment, these dreams are determined not by the pleasure principle but by something preceding its dominance. "These dreams," he writes, "are endeavouring to master stimulus retrospectively, by developing the anxiety whose omission was the cause of the traumatic neurosis" (304). Imitation and repetition are an attempt to protect oneself from a danger that has already passed, to replace the shock and surprise associated with fright with the belated preparedness of anxiety (282). In Freud's examples, at one level, it is very clear who is imitating whom and what is happening when: the son is imitating the mother, or the patient is repeating in a dream, or through transference in analysis, the childhood trauma. In Galanaki's "Game" and "In Bed" the issues of trauma and memory are the same, but neither protagonist serves as the figure to be imitated, and the temporality is confused. Originally, the fear of death, the attempt to evade death through imitation, may have set the plot in motion, but by the time the reader comes on the scene, there is no apparent motive for the repetitive game she or he witnesses. Galanaki's parody of imitation suggests a more dynamic, less hierarchical relationship between subject and object, past and present. If the woman in these poems can indefinitely defer birth, why not also death? In her hands, imitation in order to overcome and kill becomes less conclusive. Killing, which is meant to eliminate options, is turned into a mode of multiplying possibilities.

Although Freud's psychoanalysis opened the interior realm to the gaze of the outside world, it is noteworthy how distinct the two categories of inside and outside sometimes are in his work. He continually attempts to complicate the relationship between them, but it is telling that in his most "scientific" descriptions, subject and object are kept as opposites.[25] In

---

[25] Bersani describes the normalizing tendency of Freud's biologically grounded dualism in terms of "the tension between certain radical speculative movements and the wish to practice and even to institutionalize the speculative process itself" (1986, 3). Nicolas Abraham (1994,

Chapter 4 of *Beyond the Pleasure Principle*, Freud turns away from the conscious activity of games to the unconscious activity of dreams in an attempt to understand the repetition compulsion.[26] Though the dream may be an internal game, for Freud, the two players, the brain and the external stimuli, are kept as separate and distinct as the son and the mother of the fort-da game. He tries to explain why consciousness "should be lodged on the surface of the brain," "on the borderline between outside and inside," "instead of being safely housed somewhere in its inmost interior," why it "must envelop the other psychical systems" (1984, 295). He introduces the example of the embryo, in which the nervous system originates from the ectoderm and continues:

> It would be easy to suppose, then, that as a result of the ceaseless impact of external stimuli on the surface of the vesicle, its substance to a certain depth may have become permanently modified. . . . A crust would thus be formed which would at last have been so thoroughly 'baked through' by stimulation that it would present the most favourable possible conditions for the reception of stimuli and become incapable of any further modification. (297)

This crust, for Freud, is the brain's or embryo's protective shield:

> It acquires the shield in this way: its outermost surface ceases to have the structure proper to living matter, becomes to some degree inorganic and thenceforward functions as a special envelope or membrane resistant to stimuli. In consequence, the energies of the external world are able to pass into the next underlying layers, which have remained living, with only a fragment of their original intensity; and these layers can devote themselves, behind the protective shield, to the reception of the amounts of stimulus which have been allowed through it. By its death, the outer layer has saved all the deeper ones from a similar fate—unless, that is to say, stimuli reach it which are so strong that they break through the protective shield. *Protection against* stimuli is an almost more important function for the living organism than *reception* of stimuli (298–99).[27]

---

80) reads Jean LaPlanche and J.-B. Pontalis's *Language of Psychoanalysis* with a similar tension in mind, also referring to Chapter 4 of *Beyond the Pleasure Principle*. Michael Levine (1994, 100) on this topic refers readers to Freud's later piece "A Note upon the Mystic Writing-Pad," in which the division is more complicated. Also see Derrida's "To Speculate—on Freud" (1987) and "Freud and the Scene of Writing" (1978).

[26] Freud argues that games, "which have a yield of pleasure as their final outcome . . . are of no use for our purposes, since they presuppose the existence and dominance of the pleasure principle: they give no evidence of the operation of tendencies beyond the pleasure principle, that is, of tendencies more primitive than it and independent of it" (1984, 287).

[27] Jung also views the brain as a protective shell; see his discussion of Picasso: "He is the

Freud stresses that memory-traces have no place in this layer of conscious-ness. A memory-trace by definition is something that is too strong to be assimilated by the protective crust. One is either conscious of something or not: if not, then one houses memory-traces under the protective surface. Consciousness arises instead of a memory-trace, never as a result of a memory-trace. Freud separates the conscious from the unconscious both functionally and spatially. A childhood trauma permeates the crust and leaves a memory-trace. Dreams, then, repeat the trauma in an attempt to reconstruct a protective inorganic layer in the present that might have eased a pain in the past.

Walter Benjamin (1983) develops in his Arcades Project this idea of in-organic crusts, barriers, cases, envelopes, and coverings in his discussion of the poet Charles Baudelaire. Benjamin's language suggests that he is bringing Freud's private concerns to bear on the more public concerns of civilization and its discontents. He reinscribes Freud's distinct separation of inside and outside in terms of the bourgeoisie's obsession with protect-ing its riches and covering its traces. Boxes, velvet pouches, and so on become, in his analysis, ways of dealing with the shock of the city. They materially manifest the compulsion to repeat and imitate:

> Since the days of Louis-Philippe the bourgeoisie has endeavoured to com-pensate itself for the inconsequential nature of private life in the big city. It seeks such compensation within its four walls. Even if a bourgeois is unable to give his earthly being permanence, it seems to be a matter of honour with him to preserve the traces of his articles and requisites of daily use in per-petuity. The bourgeoisie cheerfully takes the impression of a host of objects. For slippers and pocket watches, thermometers and egg-cups, cutlery and umbrellas it tries to get covers and cases. It prefers velvet and plush covers which preserve the impression of every touch. For the Makart style, the style of the end of the Second Empire, a dwelling becomes a casing. This style views it as a kind of case for a person and embeds him in it together with all his appurtenances, tending his traces as nature tends dead fauna embedded in granite. (46)[28]

---

greater personality who bursts the shell, and this shell is sometimes—the brain" (1966, 141). But Jung is concerned with how individual genius bursts the shell from inside, whereas Freud is more interested here in how extenuating circumstances affect the individual from the outside.

[28] Benjamin returns to this topic at the end of the book: "The interior was not only the private citizen's universe, it was also his casing. Living means leaving traces. In the interior, these were stressed. Coverings and antimacassars, boxes and casings, were devised in abun-dance, in which the traces of everyday objects were moulded. The residents' own traces were also moulded in the interior" (169).

For Benjamin, the casings of commodities, like the brain's crust, imitate death in order to stave off death.[29]

Unlike Freud's "crust" and Benjamin's "cases," which mediate and soften the blows of "external stimuli" and "capitalist alienation," Galanaki's cake offers no such protection. Whereas Freud criticizes an analysand's premature interruption of treatment before the fissure has healed, or before projection has run its full course, suggesting that it is best to plug the gap with an imaginary substitute (the analyst), and Benjamin portrays the bourgeois fetishism of objects as a similar attempt to seal over the gap, the constant deferral in Galanaki's texts makes substitution impossible and calls attention to the gap; to the riddled, porous walls; to the holes in her own text. The crusts and cases are there, but always infiltrated by smoke, penetrated by daggers, riddled with holes. Her text questions the solid consistency of the crust and asks what happens if the memory-traces are on the surface of consciousness, unprotected. Her project consists of deconstructing the difference between the cover and what it covers or the case and what it encases, rather than reconstructing the latent content and then taking off the cover.[30]

If for Freud the surface of the embryo provided an example of a crust "so thoroughly 'baked through,'" so "incapable of further modification" that it formed a neat partition between inside and outside, for Galanaki the example of the embryo proves the circular inseparability of inside and outside. The hidden term in both these texts may well be the etymology of placenta, πλακούς in Greek, meaning a flat cake. In one poem I mentioned earlier in terms of the pregnant woman's versatility, the crust constantly makes and unmakes itself, turning itself inside out:

Εδώ που στέκεσαι, ένα κομμάτι κέικ αχνιστό εδώ, σ' αυτό το τρίστρατο ένα κομμάτι κέικ βουτηγμένο στο δικό σου αίμα γιατί φοβάσαι, τη γέννα όπως φοβάσαι και τον κυνηγό κι όπως εσκέφτηκες τον άσπρο θάλαμο με φόβο. 'Ενα καταφύγιο. Σαν ξόρκι. Η νοσταλγία ενός καταφύγιου και αγκαλιάζεις με τα δύο σου χέρια τη μεγάλη σου κοιλιά· βυθίζεσαι στη μήτρα του παλιότερου μύθου· να σε κυοφορήσει, έμβρυο που κυοφορείς εν' άλλο έμβρυο.

(21)

[29] Terry Eagleton explores the interrelation between Freud's and Benjamin's theories: "Death . . . is the ultimate aura, in which the organism can at last discover secure refuge from the shocks that batter it; and it is possible to speculate that the erotic enthralment to the commodity provides a foretaste of this condition" (1981, 34).

[30] Galanaki's project might be seen to have its psychoanalytic analogue in what Lyotard has called "writing the dreamwork," a process that entails paying more attention to the mechanisms of displacement and condensation than to their effect and thereby scrambles interiors and exteriors, latent and manifest contents (1983, 3–34). See also Chapter 5.

Here where you are standing, a piece of steaming hot cake here, at this crossroads; a piece of cake drowning in your own blood because you are afraid, of the birth the way you are afraid of the hunter and the way you thought about the white hospital ward with fear. A shelter. Like a spell. The nostalgia for a shelter and you hug your big belly with both hands; you bury yourself in the womb of the older myth; to be pregnant with you, an embryo pregnant with another embryo.

Not only is the cake, the external substitute for the unborn child, soaked in blood, the most internal of substances, but the surface of the belly that contains the embryo simultaneously protects from fear and is the fear itself; it is the memory of a shelter and the fear of the inevitable loss of that shelter with the birth of the child. You are outside hugging your belly and yet you are also inside, an embryo. This double invagination becomes *The Cake*'s modus operandi.

In light of Freud's and Benjamin's texts, *The Cake*'s game of hide and seek, its permanent veiling and unveiling, and its endless deferrals can be read as a feminist deconstruction of mimesis and of the kind of protection Freud's model presumes. To Benjamin's reading of Freud in terms of the shock of the big city rather than individual trauma, *The Cake* adds a gendered reading, asking how women's writing might provide an alternative scenario in which survival depended more on rehearsing disintegration than in building barriers. In the last half of *The Cake*, imitation as a form of protection is no longer valid. Whereas the snake in the first poem of "The Game" protects himself by imitating the eagle, in the next section the Ariadne snake, which is likened to an umbilical cord, is both inside and outside; her strategy of survival involves shedding and moving on, not imitating and covering up.

Writing as a Pregnant Woman

Now, having shown the way the figure of the pregnant woman undoes the clear-cut oppositions implied by sexual difference and mimesis, I want to show how writing as a pregnant woman involves sustaining both oppositions over time and space. For Galanaki in *The Cake*, scrambling, shedding, and other metonymic practices provide models for an alternative feminist writing. After the dictatorship, it was women who insisted on drawing parallels between the censorship of patriarchy and that of authoritarianism. It was women who continued to find strategies of deferral and digression necessary. Poetry for them was still a forum for exploring that which could not be said. In her essay that draws on the myth of

Pandora's box, Galanaki describes women's writing as that which brings the unconscious to the surface and exposes it: "Perhaps we could say that the important thing in feminine writing is the appearance of her unconscious and its uncensored combination, the more the better, with the conscious through the symbolic language of art" (1982a, 366). Instead of protecting the interior from the exterior, the various surfaces in *The Cake* exhibit their interpenetration. No surface, whether skin or a steel baking pan or clothing, is left intact. The pregnant woman is the embodiment of such porous surfaces and trespassings.

Like Hélène Cixous, Julia Kristeva, and other French feminists, Galanaki calls this kind of writing "feminine" (γυναικείο), not only because it is written by women—much of the experimental writing Kristeva calls feminine is written by men—but because it summons up a prelinguistic babble.[31] Where Kristeva talks about a semiotic *chora*, as the place in memory where this infantile babble is stored, Galanaki uses the image of Pandora's pocketbook. Both writers describe an unstable, reversible receptacle defined by the double stricture of mother-holding-child-holding-mother as the source of style. The semiotic *chora* bubbles forth and disrupts symbolic discourse;[32] all the things in Pandora's bag fly out and wreak havoc. The rhetorical figure of metonymy is the trope that best exemplifies the lessons of this double stricture.[33] It formally enables scrambling and shedding and does so in the name of circumventing censorship.[34] I have already discussed the intimate connection between metonymy and censorship under the dictatorship in Steriadis's cinematographic poetry strips in Chapter 2. Metonymy challenged censorship's presumed separation of the proper from the improper, the admissible from the inadmissible, its insistence on univocal meanings, and its exclusion of multiple interpretations. His re-

[31] For what Anglo-American scholars mean by French feminism, see Jones 1986. Two useful readers are Marks and de Courtivron 1981 and Moi 1987. On "écriture féminine," see introductions to Cixous 1991a and 1991b. For a Lacanian analysis of how French feminism has revalued the term *feminine*, see Rose 1986, 78–81. She writes: "For Lacan, men and women are only ever in langue ('Men and women are signifiers bound to the common usage of language'). All speaking beings must line themselves up on one side or the other of this division, but anyone can cross over and inscribe themselves on the opposite side from that to which they are anatomically destined" (73).

[32] Kristeva's most vivid expression of this is in "Stabat Mater" (1986, 160–86), where she juxtaposes semiotic babble and symbolic analysis typographically. For the distinction between semiotic and symbolic in feminist theory after Lacan, see the glossary entries in Cixous and Clement 1986, 167–68.

[33] For a parallel analysis of metonymy in feminist terms, see Stanton in N. Miller 1986, 157–82.

[34] Freud singles out metonymy as the mechanism of the unconscious best equipped to foil censorship (Lacan 1977, 160; Freud 1976, 414–19; MacCannell 1986, 91). Lacan formulated the relation between metonymy and censorship more generally when he wrote: "What does man [*sic*] find in metonymy if not the power to circumvent the obstacles of social censure?" (1977, 158).

liance on metonymy was in many ways what distinguished his paralogical writing project of the 1970s from the surrealist writing project of the 1930s. Whereas in an Embirikos poem I discussed, the emergence of a coherent signification was possible, in Steriadis's it was incidental. In *The Cake*, Galanaki genders this metonymic resistance to censorship and takes it to Scheherazadean and "pregnant" proportions.

The Cake can be read as a struggle to make the relationship of the cake and the as-yet-unborn child metonymic rather than metaphorical. If the cake is a metaphor for the child, then the whole series of poems and women's writing more generally would be in the service of reproduction, the "natural," "feminine" activity. But if the cake is a metonym, then no activity has priority over another: baking, weighing, hunting, giving birth, killing, writing are all equally valid feminine experiences that must be read through one another. And, even more important, if the cake is a metaphor, the relationship between the two signifiers is immediate; but if the cake is a metonym, then the relationship takes up time and space.[35] Metonymy, protracted into a strategy for constant elliptic displacement, creates a world out of useless things, redeeming that which has been rejected and recycling the censored. By defining babble as metonymic, Galanaki grants Pandora's outpouring the status of an alternative kind of writing.

Galanaki's first book of poems, *Albeit Pleasing*, creates a sense that metonymic displacement is necessary under an authoritarian regime but that it ultimately frustrates the transparent aims of poetry. Galanaki makes her poems "difficult to decipher" but imagines a time when things will have real meanings again, when the object and its imitation will be distinguishable. In one poem she writes: "Σου δίνω μήλο δεν τ᾿ αγγίζεις κόβεις μόνο τη σκιά" (I give you an apple you do not touch it you cut only the shadow) (1975, 24). The "only" (μόνο) suggests that the real apple is more substantial than its shadowy imitation. In *The Cake* there is no place for such a hierarchy; the object and its shadow are all mixed up in each other (μπλεγμένα) (1980, 11) in surprising ways. The apple is no longer the site of a lost authenticity and wholeness but rather, a meditation on the impossibility of imitation as protection and on the positing of metonymy as a different response to prohibition. In "In Bed," the two halves of the apple in Poem 17 do not work by metaphorical identity, the way the apple and its shadow do, but instead constantly displace each other and refocus on the cut. There is no determining which is real and which is not; for either one can stand in for the other, and they are both part of the same thing. The poem opens by

---

[35] Metonymy takes time. Anika Lemaire has written with reference to Lacan's definition of metaphor and metonymy, that in metaphor "the emergence of signification is immediate, being effected by a sort of speech in the mind which, from the start establishes the relationship between the signifiers substituted for each other. Metonymy, on the other hand, necessitates a longer mental trajectory, in search of the links uniting the signifiers" (1977, 198).

highlighting "the first white fibers," the severed connections that, like the umbilical cord, are in between:

Οι πρώτες άσπρες τρίχες ενός μήλου, όταν το μήλο σκίζεται σε δύο κομμάτια. Το ένα κομμάτι πρόσωπο του νικητή. Το άλλο, επίσης πρόσωπο του νικητή. Το πρόσωπο πάνω στο τζάμι. Η τζαμαρία της εξόδου πάντοτε καθρέφτης. Μετέωρα μάτια διαβάζουν τα λόγια της επιγραφής· μετέωρο στόμα συλλαβίζει τα λόγια της επιγραφής.
(37)

The first white fibers of an apple when the apple is cut in two. The one piece, the face of the victor. The other, also the face of the victor. The face in the window pane. The glass exit door is always a mirror. The eyes in mid-air read the words on the notice; the mouth in mid-air pronounces the words on the notice.

Hierarchy in this poem is undone. Though one face reflects the other we do not know which is which. Both halves of the apple are the face of the victor. Mimesis is not the axis along which things are divided. Similar to the subversion of imitation in Poem 1, in which the fingers and the shadow of a cock were inseparable, here also the object and its reflection are not clearly differentiated. Instead, the two eyes of the face, either face, are divided. One eye, it turns out, is feminine and the other, masculine:

Το πρώτο μάτι είναι βουβό και θηλυκό και στείρο, όμως, αν γεννήσει, το παιδί του θα 'χει τη δόξα της μητροκτονίας. Το πρώτο μάτι φοβάται μέσα σε μαλλιά που ασπρίζουν κι αθέατο ακολουθεί το άλλο μάτι. Ο νικητής δείχνει μόνο το δεύτερο μάτι του.
(37)

The first eye is mute and feminine and barren, however if it gives birth, its child shall have the glory of matricide. The first eye is scared, hidden in hair which is turning white, unseen it follows the other eye. The victor only shows his second eye.

Although at the level of content the feminine eye is always effaced by the masculine,[36] there is a sense that the metonymic mode suggested by the white fibers, the umbilical cord, and the shed skins of the Ariadne snake is

---

[36] The comprehension of the feminine eye by the masculine eye is more generally reinforced in Greek by the grammatical subsumption of the feminine gender in the plural by the masculine—e.g., if one is pointing to three good people, two of whom are women and one of whom is a man, one says "Να, οι καλοί" (Here are the good [men]) rather than "Να, οι καλές" (Here are the good [women]).

the dominant mode of these poems and that it is feminine. The masculine eye may have access to the language of the sign hanging on the door, the language that gets things done, the language that conquers and rapes,[37] but this is not the language of these poems. The language of *The Cake* is more hesitant, interrupted, undecidable, like a loosely woven fabric. It is the mother tongue the feminine eye tries to imagine as she hides behind her hair:

Το ένα μάτι κρύβεται μέσ' στα μαλλιά: κάτι δεν είναι η γλώσσα του, ή αυτό που ακούει, ή εκείνο που διαβάζει· αλλά και τα δυο μαζί δεν είναι η γλώσσα του, μια γλώσσα μητρική.

(37)

One eye hidden in hair: something is not its language, either what it is hearing, or what it is reading; even the two together are not its language, a mother tongue.

Galanaki's meditation on cutting an apple in half recalls Freud's reference in *Beyond the Pleasure Principle* to Aristophanes's sorb apple myth. In Plato's *Symposium*, Aristophanes uses the image of severing an apple to describe how man and woman, though rent apart, long to be one. Freud draws on this incident to confirm the conservative nature of instincts (1984, 331). In *The Cake*, Galanaki refutes Freud's message of stability and integration and focuses more on his language. His narrative at this point falters: "But here, I think, the moment has come for breaking off" (332). What seems to intrigue her are the severed threads of his text, not the need to restore a previous totality. For her, the apple fibers, along with the other loose strands, the hair that intervenes between the eye and the world, the threads that trail off, are about the way in which we cannot say what we mean, that metonymic "veering off of signification."[38] Cumulatively, as we will see, they create a space for rehearsing misunderstanding. They provide a context for the verbs without objects; the odd, inexact repetitions; cycles that in circling back do not come full circle but return to another point; and the words that seem out of place or misused in these poems.

A mother tongue—or more to the point a m(other) tongue—emerges: a way of writing as a pregnant woman (the child is not born yet), whose reader collects the various feminine, threadlike images and relates them to the idiosyncratic use of repetition and the privileging of metonymy. The Ariadne snake, the feminine eye hidden behind the hair, and the embryo

[37] The verb used, διακορεύει, means to deflower, to deprive of virginity. Galanaki is playing on the fact that κόρη is both the virgin/daughter and the pupil of the eye. Vision in these poems, as for the French feminists, is masculine and alienating.

[38] This is how Lacan retranslated Freud's term *Verschiebung* (displacement) in his discussion of metonymy (1977, 160).

within an embryo can be read as models of linguistic estrangement and
obfuscation. The Ariadne snake, for example, provides a feminine antidote
to the usual consolidating function of imitation and repetition. The shed
skins offer an apt description of how again and again in this text the
repetition of a word, phrase, or large chunk of the poem recycles meaning.
In Poem 2, the same verb "you cross" (διασχίζεις) is used twice in a row. It
makes perfect sense the first time, but it is difficult to understand the
second time because of the poem's syntax:

> Βαδίζει σ᾿ ἕνα τοίχο η σκιά σου όπως εσύ διασχίζεις το ταψί· άδειο ταψί κι εσύ,
> ασύλληπτη να το διασχίζεις από μάτι.
>
> (12)

Your shadow is walking across the wall as you cross the pan; you are an
empty pan too, difficult to grasp, you move across it with your eyes.

The phrase I translate as "difficult to grasp, you move across it with your
eyes" is broken in half in Greek so that the adjective ασύλληπτη (invisible,
difficult to conceive of) is separated from "από μάτι" (with your eyes) by
the verb διασχίζεις (you cross). Greek is a highly inflected language, so this
kind of ordering is not unusual, but here, because of the breaking up of the
idiomatic phrase "ασύλληπτη . . . από μάτι" (invisible to the eye), it is
disconcerting. Is the phrase "with your eyes" connected to the verb *cross*
rather than the early phrase "difficult to grasp"? Through repetition the
verb *cross* loses its original meaning, even if only momentarily. In the context of imagery such as the Ariadne snake and her shedding skin, this
formal move comes into focus: what was vital becomes difficult to grasp,
extraneous, inessential.[39]

The effect of repetition is similarly jarring and "unconstructive" when in
Poem 4 and Poem 15 the same terms of disintegration are used to opposite
ends, the first time to describe a hare, a vital, real hare, and the second to
reveal a lack. In Poem 4, Galanaki writes:

> Θα ήθελε να μάθει τι κάνει τον λαγό λαγό: τα δάχτυλα μέσα στα σπλάχνα, το
> σκούρο παγωμένο αίμα, τα έντερα και το συκώτι κι η καρδιά και το ανύπαρκτο
> σημείο σήψης κι η ζέστα της ζωής στην τελευταία ετοιμόρροπη σταγόνα.
>
> (14)

He would like to know what makes a hare a hare: the fingers inside the
entrails, the dark congealed blood, the intestines and the liver and the heart

---

[39] The fact that the pan is empty and the choice of the word ασύλληπτη, which means both
"inconceivable," she who cannot be conceived, and "unconceived," she who has not been
conceived, further supports this sense of barrenness and insubstantiality.

and the absent sign of decay and the warmth of something living in the last pendulous drop.

In Poem 15 there is no longer anything inside:

Η αετίνα ξεκουμπώνει τ᾽ άδεια ρούχα· τα δάχτυλα μέσα στα ρούχα που δεν έχουν σπλάχνα ούτε σκούρο παγωμένο αίμα, έντερα συκώτι και καρδιά κι ανύπαρκτο σημείο σήψης και τη ζέστα της ζωής στην τελευταία ετοιμόρροπη σταγόνα ...
(34)

The she-eagle unbuttons the empty clothes; the fingers inside the clothes which have no entrails, no dark congealed blood, intestines, liver, or heart, no absent sign of decay, nor the warmth of something living in the last pendulous drop ...

One thing replaces another until the original is forgotten. What one meant is no longer as important as how one says it. The process of substitution is emphasized over either the old or the new state of affairs. Metonymy as the evasion of censorship has become a poetics in its own right.

Poem 19, the final poem of "In Bed," discusses explicitly the way in which words are torn from their contexts, from their meanings. The twist we have witnessed repeatedly by which an object and its reflection become less important than an object and some other arbitrarily related object, is finally analyzed in terms of language. In the beginning the woman and the man are locked into an equation of mutual replaceability. The focus is on the positions, not the act of switching positions:

Κάθεσαι στο κρεβάτι. Ο κυνηγός είναι έξω στο μπαλκόνι, κάθεται σε μια πολυ-θρόνα πάνινη μασώντας ένα κομμάτι από το κέικ που βρέθηκε στο κομοδίνο. Αν είσαι το βουβό νερό γεμάτου ποτηριού εκείνος είναι το βουβό ποτήρι του νερού, ή το αντίθετο. Αν είσαι ο κώδικας του ερωτικού μαρκήσιου στη φυλακή, ο κυνηγός μιλά τη γλώσσα του πατριαρχικού αφορισμού της επανάστασης, ή το αντίθετο. Αν είσαι η ματωμένη απεργία του Σικάγου, αυτός στο Μεξικό δολο-φονεί τον Τρότσκυ, ή το αντίθετο. Αν είσαι ισορροπιστής, ο κυνηγός δεν έχει άλλο τρόπο για να ζει κοντά σου κι ορίζει την πόζα στερεότυπης φωτογραφίας και με το δεξί πατά ένα μεγάλο σώμα, το δικό σου, σωριασμένο παράλληλα στ᾽ όρθιο σώμα της μοτοσικλέτας, ή το αντίθετο.
(39)

You sit on the bed. The hunter is outside on the balcony, he sits in a deck chair chewing on a piece of the cake that was on the bedside table. If you are the mute water of the full glass, he is the mute glass of water, or the other way around. If you are the code of the erotic marquis in jail, the hunter speaks the patriarch's language of excommunicating revolutionaries, or the other way around. If you are the bloody strike in Chicago, he is in Mexico murdering Trotsky, or the other way around. If you are the one in a balancing act, the hunter has no other means of living near you and he sets up a stereotypical photograph pose with his right foot on a big body, your body, in a heap parallel to the upright body of the motorcycle, or the other way around.

But the repetition, "or the other way round," draws the reader's attention away from the oppositions to the process itself, away from what a phrase signifies to *how* it signifies. By the fourth "or the other way round," the reader is more concerned with the mechanism of substitution than with what is being substituted. The last half of the poem has the reader meditating on the act of substitution itself:

Ζυγίζεις πόσος ορισμός και πόσο σώμα: οι ορισμοί δεν ανταλλάσσονται, όπως δεν ανταλλάσσονται τα σώματα ποτέ. Τα σώματα δανείζουν κάποτε τις φορεσιές. Το ρούχο του ορισμού είναι η ίδια η διατύπωσή του και κουρελιάζεται μαζί της. Τα σώματα μένουν γυμνά και όρθια και πέφτοντας τρυπούν την ατσαλένια επιφάνεια του νερού. Ένα ταψί γεμάτο τρύπες ξαφνικές εφήμερες, ένα ταψί των επετείων γεμάτο τρύπες των σωμάτων. Και ξαναζυγίζεις πόσοι ορισμοί και πόσα σώματα.

(39)

You weigh the amount of definition and the amount of body: the definitions never replace each other, just as the bodies never replace each other. Sometimes the bodies lend their costumes. The definition's clothing is the same as its wording and both are torn to shreds. The bodies remain naked and upright and falling make holes in the water's steel surface. A baking pan full of sudden, ephemeral holes, an anniversary baking pan full of bodies' holes. And again you weigh the amount of definitions and the amount of bodies.

As with the examples of repetition I have mentioned, the progression in this poem is also from essence to surface. Whereas this poem begins as an analysis of the relation between the signifier and the signified, between the word and the thing, between the definition and the body, or in terms of the snake, the skin and the snake, it becomes more and more interested in the relation of signifier to signifier, the skin and skin. The poem first declares the subject is "οι ορισμοί δεν ανταλλάσσονται όπως δεν ανταλλάσσονται τα σώματα" (the definitions never replace each other, just as the bodies never replace each other). But by the end, everything is interchangeable and indistinguishable—"Το ρούχο του ορισμού είναι η ίδια η διατύπωσή του και κουρελιάζεται μαζί της" (The definition's clothing is the same as its wording and both are torn to shreds)—and this is followed by a final metonymic flight of signifiers from the costume to the shredded clothing to the steel surface of the water to the pan full of holes that disappear and to the baking pan full of holes made by bodies. The concluding refrain, "Και ξαναζυγίζεις πόσοι ορισμοί και πόσα σώματα" (And again you weigh the amount of definitions and the amount of bodies), connects the pan with yet another surface, that of the pan of the scales of the first poem, and reminds us who the blueprint of all this metonymic undecidability is: the pregnant woman with her unborn child.[40] Despite a certain nostalgia for real bodies and referents in the very poem that demands their evacuation, it is clear by the end of Poem 19 that metonymy in all its excess (note the shift from singular to plural, "how much definition" [πόσος ορισμός] to "how many definitions" [πόσοι ορισμοί]) is the rhetorical trope of *The Cake* and that it is conceived of as feminine. Writing as a pregnant woman involves never privileging one or the other kind of measure but substituting one for the other ad infinitum, keeping things in motion, in flux, strung out.

The greatest threat to this digressive practice would be the birth of a son because he would substitute for her and deny her signification. The work of "The Death and the Funeral" and "Now Me" is to find a way to give birth which will not efface this alternative mother tongue. Laura Mulvey in her essay "Visual Pleasure and Narrative Cinema" summarizes the problem for women in the same psychoanalytic terms Galanaki seems to have taken on: "Woman's desire is subjected to her image as bearer of the bleeding wound; she can exist only in relation to castration and cannot transcend it. She turns her child into the signifier of her own desire to possess a penis (the condition, she imagines, of entry into the symbolic). Either she must gracefully give way to the word, the Name of the Father and the Law, *or else struggle to keep her child down with her in the half-light of the imaginary*" (1989, 14–15, emphasis mine). Galanaki's solution involves keeping the child down in the half-light of the imaginary, but simultaneously turning this half-light into a public space, the loose weave of feminine threads that we as readers share, the book we hold in our hands.

In the penultimate section, metonymy's ability to connect the most improbable things reaches almost parodic heights when the dead woman's hand is the living hunter's and vice versa. Death is not prefigured here by Freud's inorganic crust but rather by a deconstruction of such barriers.

---

[40] When Galanaki was discussing my translation of *The Cake*, she noted that this poem about metonymic replacement was particularly "ριψοκίνδυνο" (risky) (1988). This comment echoes Lacan's formulation that metonymy is subversive: metaphor with its selectivity—this, not that—is the trope of institutional identity, of marriage, whereas metonymy is the trope of transgression, of breaking down boundaries.

Death is a way of preserving the reliance of inside on outside and vice versa, not of separating them definitively. In a now familiar move, this undecidability is once again figured by a feminine thread—first, as we will see, a pistil (the feminine supplement to stamen); then the syrupy rope of feminine domesticity from which she will hang, or already has hung, herself or possibly will not hang herself after all:[41]

Η πεθαμένη έχει ώρα που έφυγε και πάει στο διπλανό οικόπεδο να κρεμαστεί στην ανθισμένη κερασιά. Αφού δοκίμασε αν έδεσε το σιρόπι και το βρήκε εντάξει.

(45)

It has been awhile since the dead woman went to the neighboring lot to hang herself in the blooming cherry tree. After she tested the syrup to see if it had set and found it adequate.

The contiguity suggested by the umbilical cord, the shedding snake, the two halves of the apple, and the two eyes is reinforced in Poem 21, when the pistil and pollen create new cherries; these in turn become the syrupy rope, which in Poem 24 turns into twelve "κερασένιες ερωτήσεις" (cherry questions), the dots on a speedometer in a motorboat providing a getaway. By connecting this imagery to the metonymic poetics of censorship inscribed in the elliptic poetry itself, the text becomes a heterotopia, a place that organizes social relations differently.[42]

In "Now Me," the gendered materiality of this alternative reality becomes clearer. In Poem 23 a pitch-black vagina appears from within white-satin strips of material:

Έτσι κοιτάζοντας τις βδέλλες να κολλάνε τη βεντούζα και θ'ασελγήσουν για στερνή φορά, άσπρες σατέν λουρίδες υφασμάτων. Στην ανοιχτή ντουλάπα τα σκισμένα ρούχα θα μοιραστούνε ξαφνικά όπως τα βλέπω κι ανάμεσά τους ένα κατάμαυρο αιδοίο χωρίς ίχνος κόκκινου. Καπνοί και τους χαζεύω καθώς φεύγουν διάφανοι απ' το μπαλκόνι.

(52)

In this position I watch the leeches stick on with suction cups and rape for the last time, white satin strips of material. In the open wardrobe the

---

[41] The syrupy rope is not only feminine because of its connection to cooking, i.e., women's work, but also because of its sweetness. See Cowan's chapter "Everyday Sociability as Gendered Practice" for the gendering of bitter and sweet in Greece. Sweet liquor in Northern Greece is referred to as "το γυναικείο" (the feminine) (in 1990, 65–67).

[42] Foucault defines heterotopias as those places that exist in every culture "that are something like counter-sites, a kind of effectively enacted utopia in which the real sites . . . are simultaneously represented, contested, and inverted" (1986, 24).

shredded clothes will separate suddenly before my eyes and among them a
pitch-black vagina appears without a trace of red. I stare at the smoke as it
leaves diaphanously from the balcony.

Her vagina is no longer a sign of lack, but of self-sufficiency, of being able
to express things about feminine experience without fear of censorship:
"That is to say, a vagina is called a vagina" (1987). And this is possible
because the very fabric of the text has become feminine. There is no longer
any other measure; the whole context is pink. Like the hairs, pistils, and
snakes in these poems, the shredded clothing is feminine. It is yet one more
excessive, fibrous remainder exposing the metonymic contiguity of the
mother tongue.

But before this metonymic contiguity is actually christened feminine
writing, Galanaki revisits the question of myth. Having set up the priorities
and terms of her personal mythology, she returns to classical myth, mining
it for her own purposes. As with the repeated words that lose their meaning in new contexts, her use of myth does not provide the consolation the
hunter wants. Out of context and excessive, ancient references such as
"Ariadne's thread," "thyrsus," and "Phrygian" are combined with the
nonclassical allusions of international capitalism conjured in the foreign
words *cake, Ping-Pong,* and *parking* to create a myth that opens up, rather
than solidifies, meaning. Even when referring to a particular mythical
figure the allusions are impure. Galanaki, for example, mixes two versions
of the classical Ariadne story, one in which Ariadne dies a death by hanging (Adler 1967, s.v. Αιγαίον πέλαγος) and the other in which she is taken to
Naxos and abandoned, only to be found by Dionysos and married (*Oxford
Classical Dictionary*). Neither version cancels out the other. Both are present
simultaneously. The thread by which the pregnant woman might hang
herself turns into the labyrinthine narrative thread that connects the myths
of Theseus and Dionysos enabling a final poem, which rewrites Euripides's *Bacchae*.[43] Myth is feminized and then used for other purposes.

The final poem turns the threatening child of the hunter into a Dionysian
child that will not kill woman's desire with its birth. The cherries, which
heretofore decorated the cake, now appear on the child's head:

Το κέικ μέσ' στο φρυγικό ταψί κι εγώ μέσ' στην κουζίνα μου βαδίζω
κουβαλώντας ένα κεφάλι λιονταριού στα χέρια. 'Ενα κεφάλι λιονταριού μέσ'
στην κοιλιά μου. Αυτό τ' ασώματο και στρογγυλό κεφάλι που θα δοκιμάσει το
γλυκό μου. Το λιονταρίσιο του κεφάλι, που θα ξεράσει το γλυκό μου. Εγώ θα το

---

[43] This both/and approach has its analogue in the folk belief in which the diagnosis and the
cure are often the same. On homeopathic cures in Ancient Greece, see Eva Cantarella's analysis of swings, which both signify death by hanging and are a magic deterrent that exorcises
the ill effect of hanging (in Suleiman 1986, 57–67).

γεννώ και θα το θανατώνω. Αυτό το λιονταρίσιο κεφάλι κυνηγού. Και θα σταλάξω δώδεκα κερασένιες ερωτήσεις γύρω-γύρω.

(53)[44]

The cake is inside the Phrygian pan and I am inside my kitchen, I walk
around carrying the lion head in my hands. A lion head in my belly. That
round, bodiless head that will try my sweet. The lion head that will vomit
my sweet. I will give birth to it and kill it continuously. The hunter's lion
head. And I will drop twelve cherry questions in a circle around the top.

By making the son Dionysian—outside the realm of social censure, beyond
the law of the Father—the feminine metonymic mode can prevail. For the
first time, the cake and the child, like the two halves of the apple, are
referred to in the same poem, neither one replacing the other. The metonymic relationship suggested by the scales that began the whole sequence does, in the end, hold true for the child and the cake. Instead of
pulling the poems together, like the two halves of Aristophanes's sorb
apple, the metonymic relation of the cake and the child keeps them apart,
deferring resolution and creating a text that takes up space and time. Ultimately Euripides's tragedy is denied by putting off birth and death. Both
of the mother/son dyads—Semele and Dionysos at the beginning of the
play and Agave and Pentheus at the end—are left intact. Semele is not
killed as she gives birth to Dionysos, and Agave does not kill her lion-
headed Pentheus. The ancient myth is opened up and undone as the pregnant woman gives birth and kills continuously.

At the end of Poem 24, this Scheherazadean mode is finally given the
status of a kind of writing. First, masculine writing, which belongs to the
hunter's son, the unborn child, is abandoned:

Αυτό το λιονταρίσιο κεφάλι κυνηγού. Και θα σταλάξω δώδεκα κερασένιες
ερωτήσεις γύρω-γύρω. Να μοιάζει με ρολόι ταχυτήτων. Ο δείχτης μιας βεν-
ζινακάτου κι εγώ στη βενζινάκατο θα δραπετεύσω τραβώντας βίαια τον άλλο
δρόμο, αφού υποκλιθώ και χαιρετίσω βελανιδιές κι ελάτια τις ξύλινες κα-
ρέκλες με τους μεγάλους και με τους μικρότερους· αφήνοντας τη βάρκα δεμένη
σ' ένα πάσσαλο της λίμνης, τη λίμνη στο χαρτί ζωγραφισμένη και το χαρτί
σελίδα γλώσσας που έκλεισε σα λίμνη.

(53–54)

This hunter's lion head. And I will drop twelve cherry questions in a circle
around the top. To look like a speedometer. The indicator on a motorboat
and I will escape in that motorboat taking a violent turn and going the other

---

[44] This passage refers to the end of the *Bacchae*, when Agave tears her son's head off
thinking he is a lion.

way, after I bow to myself and bid farewell to the oaks and the firs, the
wooden chairs with the grownups and the children; leaving the boat tied to
a stake in the lake, the lake drawn on paper and the paper a page of language which closed like a lake.

Then, leaving behind the hunter's son's writing "which closed like a lake,"
The Cake embraces a feminine text. All the loose ends—the umbilical cord,
Ariadne's snake, the severed fibers, the pistil, the syrupy rope—are metonymically replaced by the maenad's shredded clothing which, having
exposed the vagina, now exposes a kind of feminine writing:

Θα αράξω σ' ένα τόπο ζεστό και πράσινο με κίτρινη αμμουδιά και φρούτα στα
δέντρα με τα εξωτικά πουλιά. Και θα φυτέψω τα ρούχα της μαινάδας κοντά σε
μια πηγή και η πηγή σ' ένα χαρτί ζωγραφισμένη και το χαρτί σελίδα γλώσσας
που αναβρύζει. Και δίπλα θα ξαπλώσω ήρεμη και γυμνή για να γεννήσω.

(54)

I will moor in a hot green country with yellow sands and fruit-laden trees
and exotic birds. And I will plant the maenad's clothes near a spring and the
spring drawn on paper and the paper a page of language which wells up.
And next to this I will lie down, calm and naked, and give birth.

Rather than a closed lake, writing is a self-renewing spring, a place defined
by its endless deferrals. This digressive text circumvents censors and ordinary expectations by turning the surface of the text into a fluid, ever-
changing dissolution of outside and inside. Birth and death are put off, and
the place of procrastination is the book the reader holds.

By reading through Galanaki's whole series of poems, *The Cake*, it is
possible to illustrate the cumulative effect of its elliptic deferral of meaning—the space and time it takes up. Although I discuss the visual aspect of
women's poetry's narrativity in more depth in my discussion of Mastoraki's *Tales* in the next chapter, the visual impact of this poetry should
already be clear. Galanaki's spatial and temporal project depends on a
reader who will connect one image to the next image in a cinematographic
fashion—the apple fiber to the pistil to the syrupy rope to the maenad's
rags. *The Cake* most obviously teaches us, however, that this visual narrative is feminist. Galanaki turns the sexually and textually undecidable
figure of woman, which men had used for their resistance under the dictatorship, into a feminist mode of writing that promotes sexual and textual
undecidability. For Galanaki, feminism provides a way to read the lessons
of marxism and psychoanalysis together so that no form of authority—
whether that of a dictator, husband, or self—is definitive. Like Mastoraki's
and Irigaray's use of citation (discussed in Chapter 3), Galanaki's figure of

the pregnant woman completely alters the traditional, "original" sense: rather than a figure of social reproduction, she is one of social transformation. Writing as a pregnant woman models an ongoing process of subversion whereby narratives of exploitation become maleable processes that can be taken apart, reversed, and reworked. By enlisting its readers in its feminist practice of repeating and imitating *otherwise*, *The Cake* becomes a resource for thinking in alternative ways about social relations.

5

Jenny Mastoraki's *Tales of the Deep* and the Purloined Letter

We have seen how, under the Metaxas dictatorship, George Seferis lamented the censoring of the size of angel wings in El Greco's paintings. The Spanish Inquisition "ordered all those who happened to find angels with large wings beautiful, to sacrifice something they liked and to accept in its place something they didn't like, for the sake of Christian dogma" (in Seferis and Tsatsos 1975, 77). For Seferis, the angel with large wings was a symbol of art untrammeled by the effects of history.[1] Under the more recent dictatorship, Jenny Mastoraki and other poets of the generation of the 1970s turn to the angel to suggest a less transcendent model of art, one that figures poetry's worldliness. For them the clearly delineated distinctions that Seferis's criticism and poetry assume—between El Greco and the Inquisition, between the poet or the critic and "dogma," between us and them, between inside and outside—are impossible. They view cutting and trimming not from a distance, as ideology's impingement on personal freedom, but from much closer to home, as poetry's modus operandi.[2] In a

[1] See Chapter 1 for my discussion of this passage. Although I focused there on the function of the angel in Seferis's criticism, his poems containing angels suggest a similar transcendent role. There, too, the angel is outside history. In Seferis 1976, see "Τον άγγελο" (The angel) in Μυθιστόρημα (Mythistorema) (43), "Les anges sont blancs" (180), and "Αγγελικό και μαύρο, φως" (The light is angelic and black) in Κίχλη (Thrush) (228). For how angels function as "the fiction of complementarity which closes the great gap," see Kermode 1967, 89, as well as Docherty on Kermode (1987, 133–36).

[2] Foucault in another context captures an attitude similar to theirs when he writes: "Knowledge is not made for understanding; it is made for cutting" (1977b, 154). The context of this quotation is his discussion of *effective* history, a concept that provides a useful alternative to traditional critical approaches. Effective history takes into account the effects history has on writing. It works psychoanalytically along the lines of Fredric Jameson's account of history as the *political unconscious* in his book of the same title (1981, 101–2). Both Foucault and Jameson talk about history as the experience of necessity. History is a record not of what was inevitable

confusion of personal pronouns and scrambled syntax their poetry dissolves the binary opposition that Seferis's implied sentence *"They* censor *you"* presumes. As the already quoted line from Mastoraki's *Tales of the Deep* illustrates—"έτσι σου μοιάζουν όλοι κομματιάζοντας, και πάλι εσύ, κομμάτια όλοι" (so they resemble you, torn to shreds, and you them, again, in pieces) (1983b, 17)—we are all cut up and cut into each other. The processes of censorship and self-censorship are intermeshed.

Over and over in literature and art in Greece in the early 1970s one finds angels deflated, grounded, mangled, or drowned. The wings of Yiorgos Himonas's angels are shivering and dirty in his novel Ο γιατρός Ινεότης (Dr. Ineotis) (1971), excerpted in the resistance collection *Eighteen Texts* (1970, 100–101; 1972, 84). Yannis Tsarouchis's twelve angels painted at this time, one for each month, are slumped over, bored—angels without a message or a vision. Steriadis's angel poem "The Bad News" discussed in Chapter 2 also deflates this symbol. His poem parodies Seferis's passage in his monologue, leaving no room for ideal figures. It flaunts the angels' out-sized, dirty wings: "Βρε παιδάκι μου, της είπα ξεσκονίζοντας τα μεγάλα φτερά / των αγγέλων" (Hey kid, I said to her dusting off the large wings / of the angels) (Steriadis 1971, 22). The epigraph to his later collection *Pale Dick* predicts freedom will come only after the "Angels of God" fall to the ground, quoting a line from a novel by the detective writer John Le Carré. Women poets of Steriadis's generation also remove angels from the realm of the sacred. The early books of Athina Papadaki and Pavlina Pampoudi, written under the dictatorship, are entitled respectively Αρχάγγελος από μπετόν (The archangel of concrete) (1974) and Τα μωρά των αγγέλων άσπρα και τυφλά (The infants of angels, white and blind) (1974). The cover of Pampoudi's collection shows an angel diving head-first earthward. One of Mastoraki's first poems, explicitly called a "dictatorship" poem,[3] likens a sinking sovereign bearing a naked sword to an angel (1974, 343). The angels that figure in the writing at this time, like Walter Benjamin's angel of history, are completely caught up in the storm, registering the effects of history down to the most unimportant details.[4]

---

or necessary but of what we experience as necessary. Not a fixed object, it is constantly subject to our desires. My own argument contrasting Seferis's and Mastoraki's poetics, and their different views on the relation of poetry to history, draws on this distinction between traditional and effective history.

[3] This poem appeared only in the resistance collection *Deposition*, not in her published collections.

[4] "This is how one pictures the angel of history," Walter Benjamin writes. "His face is turned toward the past. Where we perceive a chain of events, he sees one single catastrophe which keeps piling wreckage upon wreckage and hurls it in front of his feet. The angel would like to stay, awaken the dead, and make whole what has been smashed. But a storm is blowing from Paradise; it has got caught in his wings with such violence that the angel can no longer close them. This storm irresistibly propels him into the future to which his back is turned, while the

Fallen angels with their hope of resurrection subside, for the most part, as cultural icons in the 1980s in Greece. A reference to angels and wings in Mastoraki's poem "Αναπαράσταση σπανίου εθίμου: χρώματα έντονα και απαθείς μορφές, σαν μέσα σε ακίνητο νερό" (Depiction of a rare custom: vivid colors and impassive faces as seen in still water) (from *Tales*, 1983b) reveals a shift. Here the implication of writing and censorship, only alluded to by Steriadis, becomes the ground zero of poetic practice. Steriadis parodies Seferis's objective view that censorship affects art but is not a part of the original artistic process; Mastoraki's critique a decade later goes a step further. Instead of simply mocking the need to keep art pure, her poem deconstructs Seferis's passage on angels by exposing the violence of the poem's own figural language. The reference to angels in the first line "... και τους ετσάκιζαν καλά καλά για να τους δώσουν σχήμα αγγέλου" (... and they would break their limbs giving them the shape of angels) (1983b, 37) comments on censorship, as well as on the formal practice of writing poetry more generally: if force is necessary "[to give] them the shape of angels," this should be exhibited in the poetry. To challenge accepted views, the language in which such views are couched must also be challenged. Poetry and politics cannot be kept separate. Mastoraki's poem maps a very different attitude to censorship onto the figure of the angel from that found in Seferis's El Greco passage, or poetry written in the 1970s.

"Depiction of a Rare Custom..." is prefaced by the mention of a bandy-legged man hanging upside down, spitting coins (36). This figure, with its disregard for any accepted system of values, sets the stage for an outpouring of fragmentary phrases that break down neat distinctions. The poem reads:

... και τους ετσάκιζαν καλά καλά για να τους δώσουν σχήμα αγγέλου, κι έπειτα τους εξέθεταν σε τόπους οχυρούς και σε αλάνες, όπου με σύναξη μεγάλη και μυσταγωγία τους γλυκοκουβεντιάζαν και τους φώναζαν. 'Ωσπου με τα πολλά

---

pile of debris before him grows skyward" (1968, 257–58). If this chapter had an epigraph it would be this quotation, but for various reasons that become apparent as the chapter unfolds, I have chosen to bury the traces of my debt and leave the authoritative space of the epigraph blank. For another attempt to use Benjamin's angel to talk about the relation of poetry and history, see Forché 1995. Cultural critics have quoted certain passages from Benjamin so often they have become clichés. Those in Modern Greek studies are no exception: seminars on topics as different as the Greek economy and Greek-American literature have cited this very passage. When discussing contemporary culture, the angel, it seems, especially in Benjamin's seductive guise of worldly, yet messianic, is difficult to do without. As Wallace Stevens suggests, it is "the necessary angel." See his collection of essays of the same title (1951) and his poem (1982, 496) in which he introduces this concept. The Italian philosopher Massimo Cacciari's wide-ranging study, also titled *The Necessary Angel* (1994), places Benjamin's and Stevens's modern angels in the context of the Christian, Islamic and Judaic philosophic traditions and helps explain the image's appeal.

Υπερυψούτε, γονυπετείς και μεγαλεία, σκεπάστηκαν οι θόλοι με νεκρούς ιπτάμενους, εξαρθρωμένα μέλη και βαριά κατάγματα, στάσεις μεγάλης αγωνίας, αλλά και ωραιότατα φτερά, φωτάκια (που τα έτρεμαν οι παλαιοί), ανθρώπινους τροχούς που διάβαζαν το μέλλον—κεφάλια με οχτώ ποδάρια σαν βελόνια—και άλλα θαύματα, οδυνηρά και αξιοθέατα.

Γιατί εκείνες τις ημέρες, όπως λένε, έβγαιναν κήρυκες με το ψαλίδι και λαλούσαν.

(37)

. . . and they would break their limbs giving them the shape of angels, and then exhibit them in fortified places, and in abandoned lots, where with great assembly and secret rites they would placate them, call them back. Until, with all the holier-than-thous, genuflection and adoration, the domes covered over with flying corpses, dislocated bones, and awful fractures, postures of extreme agony, but also the most beautiful wings, tiny lights (so dreaded back then), human wheels that could tell the future—heads with eight tentacles like needles—and other wonders, harrowing but spectacular.

For, in those days, it is said, heralds appeared with scissors, proclaiming.

Each word, phrase, sentence is rife with ambivalent meanings, making the one-to-one correspondence of symbolic representation impossible. Instead of presenting the clipped wings as synecdochic reminders of the whole that is lost—of the angel that is altered, as Seferis does—Mastoraki gives the part (beautiful wings) and the whole (the angel) equal significance and attributes originality or totality to neither. The disfiguring process of censorship is spectacular and overwhelming, and nothing can escape its effects. This poem is as much the handiwork of the heralds, who go out with scissors proclaiming, as of the poet herself. The butchered angel is the symbol not of a transcendental escape that is inhibited but of the figural terrain of an alternative poetics.

Mastoraki, in a comment on an earlier draft of the above analysis, insisted that *Tales* had nothing to do with the dictatorship that had ushered her generation onto the literary stage a decade earlier:

When these tales are being written, the dictatorship is already a past which doesn't concern me. The terrain of the tales is *clearly that of the emotions.* Only on an erotic plane does the hunted become the pursuer, and vice versa. Only on an erotic plane do "the terrible things" happen, which are described from poem to poem in one way or another: the pillagings, the slaughterings, the abductions. . . . *nothing is parodied.* The climate is nightmarish, full of darkness which, sometimes, as [in the poem just discussed], is reminiscent of the darkest tales in the Bible. There, the angels marked people's doors with blood before the great catastrophes. (1992c)

Mastoraki views the politics of censorship and the dictatorship as belonging on a different plane from that of feminine sexuality and emotions, and she uses the distinction to separate her clearly political early poetry of *Tolls* from her more recent work. Yet, even as she attempts to do this, the two planes merge: if the terrible things happen in the private realm of the emotions, then why does she describe the climate in terms of the public disasters of the Old Testament? And why does she refer to the angel as a public messenger marking people's doors with blood? Though the dictatorship may no longer directly concern her, its effects are still felt in *Tales*. Reading against the grain of her comment, I suggest that in their insistent rehearsal of misunderstandings, her prose poems rework the experience of censorship in terms of gender relations and the self-censorship of writing.

Harold Bloom once wrote that "criticism is the art of knowing the hidden roads that go from poem to poem" (1973, 96). I am attempting to offer another map of postdictatorship Greece, one that charts some of the roads "less traveled," both between poems and between poems and other discursive practices under and after the dictatorship: from Seferis's passage on El Greco's angels to Steriadis's and Mastoraki's angels, and from Mastoraki's early poems to her later poems, and even among the poems in *Tales*. Drawing on Freud's discussion of the dreamwork in his *Interpretation of Dreams*, I read *Tales* for its radical approach to intertextuality and literary influence. By introducing the notion of intertext as a "purloined letter," I further explore the concept of undeliverability already discussed in terms of Galanaki's unborn child. In obliging the reader to string image to image cinematographically or to place image over image in the manner of a palimpsest, the endless deferral of the arrival becomes, in Mastoraki's poems, a physical space in its own right: the place of writing "where terrible things happen."

The Place Where Terrible Things Happen

Mastoraki, born in 1949, is regarded as one of Greece's leading poets and translators.[5] I concentrate on *Tales* because, like Galanaki's *The Cake* and

---

[5] Mastoraki has published four volumes of poetry to date—*Tolls, Kin, Tales of the Deep*, and *With a Crown of Light*—and numerous translations of European and American fiction. Greece's most influential critics, Maronitis and Savvidis, praise her poetry. She is well known for her

Laina's *Hers*, it raises questions about the formal implications of writing as a woman. The poetics of deferral deployed in all three of these long visual narratives tells an important story about the relations among women's writing, censorship, and the literary tradition under and after the dictatorship. Putting *Tales* in the context of Mastoraki's other works shows why *Tales* is her most useful collection for tracing the hidden roads of women's writing in postdictatorship Greece.[6] With each collection Mastoraki has written, censorship has progressively become a more private affair; women's experiences have figured more and more prominently, and references to Modern Greek literature have become more pronounced. *Tolls* is explicitly about the difficulty of writing under censorship and the ways in which history, from its ancient mythological past to the present, shapes poetry. *Kin* takes up similar issues with respect to personal history, family genealogy, and feminine sexuality. *Tales* and *With a Crown of Light* (1989) deal almost exclusively with the sufferings of those cut off from their histories, communities, and families: self-absorbed lovers, abandoned children, fugitives. What one can and cannot say has gone from being an explicitly political matter in *Tolls* to being more of an aesthetic and intra-subjective issue.[7] If *Tolls* addresses censorship and *Kin* rethinks censorship in terms of domestic power struggles, then *Tales* adds a third concern, language: what is it that the Greek language, and more particularly the Greek literary tradition, allows and does not allow her to say? *Tales* flaunts its linguistic crimes, calling attention to how censorship, sexual difference, and literary influence are inscribed in the text.[8]

Let me outline this progression from *Tolls* to *Crown* in more detail, concentrating first on issues of censorship and sexual difference and finally on the question of intertextuality. Vladimir Mayakovsky has argued that poets cannot "gaze skywards in search of inspiration while waiting for the celestial spirit of poesy to descend." They must "give up isolating it from

---

translations, esp. J. D. Salinger's *Catcher in the Rye*. In 1989 she received the Thornton Niven Wilder prize from the Columbia Translation Center. N. 26 lists her translations.

[6] *Cake, Tales,* and *Hers* predate their authors' success and definitive entry into the canon of Greek literature: both Galanaki and Mastoraki achieved wider recognition in 1989, Galanaki for *The Life of Ismail Ferik Pasha* and Mastoraki for *Crown*; and it is Laina's 1992 book, Ρόδινος φόβος (Rose fear), that earned her the National Prize for poetry.

[7] It is telling that on the cover of the first edition of *Tolls* the title is printed in red like a censor's stamp across a toll ticket creating an ominous atmosphere of public surveillance. The historical context is clear. On the cover of *Crown* the reader is greeted with the luminous face of a drowned maiden, a golden halo hovering above her, all her secrets concealed in the privateness of death. The original painting, *La jeune martyre* (1855) by Paul Delaroche, has been clipped, leaving out the male figure in the distance. There is no context for the crime.

[8] The term *linguistic crimes* refers to Susan Stewart's work in *Crimes of Writing* (1991). I thank Deborah Tanner for including me in her December 1992 Modern Language Association panel of the same title, where I had the chance to think about the specificity of censorship in the context of other linguistic crimes such as plagiarism and forgery.

all the other aspects of human toil as light work" (1987, 179, 181). In *Tolls*, Mastoraki, following Mayakovsky, insists that poets take up the tools of their oppressors.[9] They must not grant hope celestial status but must instead ground it in the material world:

> Ο ποιητής στις σκαλωσιές και στα γιαπιά
> στεριώνει με καρφιά και δόντια
> την ελπίδα
> (1972, 22)

> The poet on ladders and scaffolding
> secures hope
> with nails and teeth

The question is never how to transcend the oppressors' systems of meaning; it is how to work within them to displace them. That which disempowers must be transformed into a tool of empowerment:

> Η πέτρα που ξεκίνησε
> για να χτυπήσει ένα παιδί
> θα γίνει χελιδόνι κάποτε
> (24)

> The stone which set out
> to hit a child
> will become a swallow someday

And these are similarly the terms by which the silence of censorship can be turned into poetry:

> Τούτη η σιωπή που την ανάθρεψα
> μέσα στους τέσσερις τοίχους
> ήτανε από νωρίς προορισμένη
> να γίνει τραγούδι
> (26)

> This silence which I nurtured
> between four walls
> was destined early on
> to become a song

[9] Mayakovsky, mainly through Ritsos's translations (Ritsos 1964), was an important influence on poets in Greece under the dictatorship.

Although Mastoraki's poetry follows a trajectory whereby censorship assumes ever more private dimensions, censorship and self-censorship are implicated from the beginning. Already in *Tolls* one's ability to effect change is contingent on participation in the language of one's oppressors and on their transactions. Keeping dreams alive requires paying tolls. The first poem, as we have seen, ends with an invocation from outside to close the doors:

> Τότε ένα γράμμα
> γεμάτο κατάγματα
> ήρθε από πολύ μακριά
> και μας παράγγειλε να κλείσουμε τις πόρτες.
>
> (9)

> Then a letter came
> full of fractures
> from far away
> and ordered us to close the doors.

Mastoraki refers here to a poem by Leonidas Zenakos, a poet of the postwar generation, to suggest that closing the door and shutting out the world is not just a way of following orders, that this self-censorship is a form of self-protection. In the Zenakos poem, closing the door keeps one strong:

> κλείστε τις πόρτες, κλείστε καλά,
> μην τύχη κ' έμπη ο θάνατος,
> μην τύχη κ' έμπη η φρίκη
> μην τύχη κ' έμπη το ψωμί,
> και μαλακώσουν τα σαγόνια,
> και δεν μπορούν τα δόντια μας
> να σφίξουν το μαχαίρι!
> (in Apostolidis and Apostolidis 1970, 1:376)

> Close the doors, close them well,
> so that death won't come in,
> so that terror won't come in,
> so that bread won't come in,
> and the jaws grow soft,
> so our teeth are unable
> to grasp the knife!

The letter in Mastoraki's poem is already full of fractures, already censored by time.

The necessity of transforming through poetic expression that which incapacitates into that which enables is even more obvious in *Kin*. Drawing on material from the Arabian *A Thousand and One Nights,* she genders this practice of transformation. Halima forestalls her death by telling the Pasha stories. To survive she must devise different ways of articulating and rearticulating her hopes and dreams, and as long as Halima tells stories she is out of danger: "Λέγαμε ιστορίες να κρατηθούμε ξάγρυπνοι" (We told stories in order to stay awake) (1978, 37). Though death may ultimately inhibit the story, it is first and foremost what enables it. *Kin* expands the discussion of censorship to include that of sexual oppression. The plain beige skin-colored cover of the first edition sets a tone that brings sexual politics to the fore. The feminine narrator, like Halima, is more clever than her male counterpart. In the poem "Θανάσης" (Thanasis), the woman is not tricked by Thanasis's discussion of revolutionary politics. She knows he only wants to have sex with her:

Εμένα πάντως δε μπορείς να μου το βγάλεις απ' το νου, πως όταν μου μιλάς για Μαρξ είναι που θέλεις να με βάλεις στο κρεβάτι, και τέλος πάντων κρίμας που φορείς και κόκκινο πουκάμισο.
(1978, 45)

As for me, you can't get it out of my head, that every time you talk about Marx you just want to get me in bed, and it really is too bad you're wearing a red shirt.

Over the course of the collection, the lens of feminism allows for certain connections between issues of censorship and self-censorship to be magnified and observed. The poet/narrator begins to implicate herself in the act of censorship and to enjoy what she used to consider dangerous. "They" do not come from outside to shut the doors; instead the poet sets up the barriers herself, and this internalization of censorship becomes pleasurable. In the last poem of *Kin* she ironically describes writing as diving off a wall:

Στην αρχή μοιάζει λίγο
σα να βουτάς με το κεφάλι
απ' τον τοίχο.
Πιο έπειτα το συνηθίζεις και σ' αρέσει.
(1978, 46)

In the beginning it seems a bit like
you are diving off a wall
head-first.
But then you get used to it and like it.

But there is a sense of resignation, as there was in *Tolls,* that has to do with an inability to enact this internalization at the level of grammar and syntax. The final poem admits that, even with the various strategies for transforming impediments into strengths, the poet has exhausted poetry in verse:

> Δε μου είναι πια εύκολο
> μήτε θελητό
> να γράφω στιχάκια.
> (1978, 46)

> It is no longer easy for me
> nor desirable
> to write little verses.

In the prose poems of *Tales,* censorship becomes a poetics rather than simply the subject matter of poetry (as in *Tolls*) or the pretext for poetry (as in *Kin*). Censorship, violence, and prohibition are rehearsed and reinvented at every level of language. Whereas censorship in her early poetry came from the outside and had obvious origins, in *Tales* it is diffuse, something as likely to happen between lovers or in one's own dreams as in a press office. Instead of resisting the censor in the name of another ideology or, at the other extreme, resorting to the fiction of a completely uncensored stream-of-consciousness writing, these poems experiment with a formal method of resistance: *Tales* deploys censorship's displacements as a poetics and offers metonymic chains of signifiers that break syntactic and semantic rules and make definitive interpretations impossible.[10] The overarching poetic strategy of deferral, which I have analyzed in terms of the unborn child, is also present in Mastoraki's purloined letter. As in Galanaki's *The Cake,* communication is difficult and misunderstandings abound. In *Tales,* signifier and signified are forcibly disengaged from each other; the letter as the bearer of meaning, like the angel, never arrives at its destination intact; inside and outside, victim and victimizer, public and private are shuffled together. Two crucial words that appear in *The Cake* also show up in *Tales:* αυτόχειρας meaning the person who commits suicide, but, literally, one's own hand, and αναβλύζω meaning to churn up, gush forth. Both in their specific contexts suggest the confluence of inside and outside, of oneself and other.[11] Both underscore writing's own complicity in making the terri-

[10] I use the word *displacement* in the psychoanalytic sense to describe the process whereby an image, a person, or a fragment of speech is replaced by another in an attempt to foil the superego (Freud 1976, 414–19). This concept becomes clearer after I discuss the dreamwork.

[11] In *The Cake:* "If, on the other hand, the snake manages to hide in the bushes, it quickly sheds its skin and shines like a sword; it is a sword. The hilt, where the handle ends and the blade begins, becomes wings. It takes off and cuts the she-eagle's throat. Here the hour of

ble things happen. As in *The Cake,* the Scheherazadean practice of deferral
offers an arena for rehearsing how and when connections are not made.
And as in *The Cake,* what becomes clear over the course of the text is that
this violence of misunderstanding involves a sexual politics. It is "the sufferings of love" (the title of one of the sections)—sealed mouths, bruised
necks, and hymenal blood—that provide the material of this writing. Although not as explicitly feminist as *The Cake, Tales* also suggests that writing that internalizes sexual and textual undecidability is feminine.

Before focusing on *Tales,* the place where the terrible things happen, let
me finish establishing its context by turning briefly to her later collection,
Crown. The fourth collection includes sealed mouths and other signs of
inhibited communication, but issues of censorship and feminine sexuality
seem less urgent. Instead, it is the question of literary influence that takes
center stage. Mastoraki's poetry from *Tolls* through *Tales* draws on a wide
range of material, but up until *Crown,* the concern is mainly with challenging accepted modes of redeeming one's debts. References to ancient mythology in *Tolls* or to personal history in *Kin* have little of the clout one
expects.[12] The first poem in *Tolls* refers to tales that are not usually told, the

---

death is the swift bullet of the suicide (αυτόχειρας)" (1980, 27); and in *Tales:* "I say beware the
suicides (αυτόχειρες) who wrote" (1983b, 35). The word αναβρύζει appears in Galanaki's text
in the last poem: "And I will plant the maenad's clothes near a spring and the spring drawn on
paper and the paper a page of language which wells up (αναβρύζει). And next to this I will lie
down, calm and naked, and give birth" (54); in Mastoraki's text it is also near the end: "Just as
the devious beggar outside the walls, carefully mantles his wounds which bloomed by some
miracle. And the ancient geometrist deadens behind him huge expanses with his oars and
wells up (αναβλύζει)." N.B.: The liquid phonemes ρ and λ are often interchangeable in Greek.
[12] In one poem in *Tolls* the inability to say what one wants to say under an oppressive
regime is expressed in terms of the symbolic impotence of the ancient deities Justice and
Hermes:

> Μένεις λοιπόν με το κέρμα στη χούφτα
> και το κοιτάς, που έχει από τη μια
> ένα τραχύ προφίλ της Δικαιοσύνης
> και το κηρύκειο του Ερμή στην άλλη
> σύμβολα που δεν το μπορείς
> όσο κι αν θες
> να τα εξηγήσεις.
>   (1972, 28)

> You are left with the coin in your hand
> and you look at it, on one side
> the stern profile of Justice
> and the herald's wand of Hermes on the other
> symbols which you cannot explain
> no matter how much
> you would like to.

The meaning of ancient myth is not simply unfathomable but bankrupt. The ancient heroes,
like the coins on which they are stamped, no longer have value. No matter how much one may
want to explain them, one cannot. Whereas the early poems take on some traditional myths—

excess of history, the stories, for example, that were not translated into Greek from the Old Testament:

> γεμάτο παραμύθια, σαν την Παλιά Διαθήκη
> πριν απ' τους Εβδομήντα.
> (1972, 9)

> full of fairy tales, like the Old Testament
> before the Septuagint.

Non-Greek traditions and noncanonical texts are just as likely as classical myths to inform *Tolls* and *Kin*. Mastoraki's attention to underprivileged historical figures and moments is not an attempt to turn the tables and establish an alternative canon; it is a way of internalizing in writing the activity of being disempowered.[13] Whereas *Tales*, as we will see, can be read as an emptying out of explicit references to the classical mythology of *Tolls* and the family history of *Kin*, *Crown* may be read for how it reestablishes the importance of influence by referring to the nineteenth- and twentieth-century Modern Greek literary tradition. There is a striking contrast between the relative lack of explicit reference to other texts in *Tales* and the notes at the end of *Crown*.[14]

In Chapter 3, I read *Tales*'s relation to the literary tradition in two contradictory ways. First, through the optical illusion of Irigaray's speculum, as an undoing by which the authority of a quotation was completely effaced and overcome, and second, through the poet's own admission (1992b), as a tribute to the rich linguistic history of Greek. I now want to suggest that Mastoraki's reading of *Tales* as an unproblematic part of the Greek literary canon may in fact have more to do with *Crown* and the high critical praise it received. Mastoraki once said that *Tales* and *Crown* were siblings. And as with siblings, one might add, the birth of the second seems to have affected the life of the first. In *Crown*, Mastoraki draws profusely on the poetry of the nineteenth-century national poet Dionysios Solomos.[15] She acknowledges his and other Greek poets' influence on her in her notes and adds that she hopes that other references are "ευανάγνωστα" (easily recogniz-

---

the Trojan horse (1972, 11, 40) and Prometheus (39)—in *Kin*, the classical tradition plays a less important role. "Iphigenia," for example, is simply her old-fashioned name that needs revamping in "Σημείωση" (Note) (1978, 13). And when the ancient myth of sacrifice is worked into another poem with the actual title "Ιφιγένεια" (Iphigenia) (1978, 25–27), the demotic tone of apartment gossip only reveals how little the tradition has to tell us about who Iphigenia really was.

[13] The most important precedent for this is found in Cavafy's poetry; see Jusdanis 1987, 107–10.

[14] See Mastoraki's list of literary debts in *Crown* (1989, 63).

[15] On Solomos's work and his importance as a national poet, see Mackridge 1989.

able) (1989, 63). Her collection is then praised for its masterly use of the Greek language (Savvidis 1989) and mythopoeic tradition (Maronitis 1992, 154–67).[16] In *Crown*, Mastoraki may well have become the strong poet Bloom recommends, skillfully rewriting Solomos and others; but the reception of *Crown* should not efface the different relation to influence and the literary tradition embedded in *Tales*.[17] My point is that in *Tales* there is a feminist critique of Bloom and, even more important, of the conservative notion of literary tradition prevalent among Greek poets and critics. Unlike *Crown*, *Tales* makes it nearly impossible to locate origins of any sort. For Mastoraki's *Tales* are not determined by any particular text; they are over-determined by a plethora of texts—Byzantine romances, murder mysteries, detective and adventure tales, *ithographies* (ηθογραφίες),[18] folksongs, case studies, dreams, spells, prayers. They focus on the activity of burying and digging, covering and uncovering, submerging and surfacing. The issue is neither the anxiety of influence nor the pleasure of influence which comes with overcoming one's poet-father; it is instead the activity of influence itself, how it functions. As one poem of *Tales*, "Οι βουτηχτές" (The divers), illustrates, the attention is not on the diver encumbered by his prize but on the activity of dredging everything up, of revealing the violence involved in making writing "the place where terrible things happen":

να τ᾽ ανασύρεις όλα απ᾽ τα βαθιά, από μεγάλα σκότη, ανέπαφα, απ᾽ τις σιωπές ερειπωμένων μητροπόλεων, την άλωση, τη θεομηνία, τη ρομφαία: όπως τρο-

[16] Mastoraki's exquisite command of the Greek literary tradition even prompts Savvidis to rebaptize her with her Greek name Iphigenia: "Jenny," which had seemed adequate for her first three volumes, was no longer appropriate for a Greek poet of such stature. For a discussion of this and other issues regarding *Crown*'s critical receptions, see Patilis 1990. To my knowledge his is the only negative review *Crown* received. For her own discussion of the relation of "Jenny" to "Iphigenia," see *Kin* (1978, 13).

[17] The anxiety of influence, as Harold Bloom has formulated it, stems from the desire to outdo the father. In Bloom's Oedipal narrative, the poet-son is weighed down by the influence of the poet-father (1973). Strong poets overcome this anxiety in various ways, what Bloom terms "revisionary ratios," such as misreading, completion, or self-purgation (5–16). In the winter and spring of 1989 and 1990, while *Crown* was being lauded, a number of pieces were written by Greek scholars on Bloom's theory of literary influence, *The Anxiety of Influence*. The pretext for these articles was Dimitris Dimiroulis's Greek translation (1989). Highlights include Vayenas 1989, 1991 (now in 1994); Kapsalis 1989; Veloudis 1989; Dimiroulis 1990; and Berlis 1990, 1991. For a comprehensive bibliography see Vayenas 1991. Attention in these articles is focused on the accuracy or inaccuracy of Dimiroulis's terminology. The main criticism was that he had not taken into consideration the psychoanalytic terms that Greek psychoanalysts had laboriously created: he had not paid homage to his precursors. This debate over influence and originality provides a context for the overwhelmingly positive reception of Mastoraki's *Crown* with its well-documented allegiances.

[18] *Ithographia* is a Greek term used to identify a genre of nineteenth-century realist writing that describes the customs of rural Greece, usually employing stereotyped characters to convey a moral point. For a brief definition of the genre, see Beaton 1994, 72–73; on the complex debate surrounding the term, see 72 n.

παιοφόρος βουτηχτής βαραίνει στ᾽ άπατα, ή ευπατρίδες πελεκάν την ώρια
κόρη, κι ο πιο καλύτερος της παίρνει το κεφάλι—

(1983b, 25)

you must dredge it all up from the depths, from the great darkness, intact,
from the silence of a ruined metropolis, the fall, the plague, the flaming
sword: like the diver encumbered by his prize in the bottomless sea, or
patricians who hack the fair maiden and the best takes her head—

One comparison between *Crown* and *Tales* should suffice to illustrate
their different relation to literary influence. In *Tales,* walls are riddled and
porous, boundaries transgressed, and everything out in the open: writing
itself is in the service of trying to capture this fluidity.[19] In *Crown*, by contrast, walls and writing are meant to be permanent. *Crown* begins with a
quotation from the poet Lorenzos Mavilis's "Πόρτα Ριάλα" (Porta Reale), a
sonnet written in 1895 lamenting the tearing down of the Venetian gate
and walls in his home town of Corfu in the same year. It is a harsh indict-
ment of the "slaves" who have no concern for art. The sonnet's final tristich
expresses the hopes that Mavilis's verses might survive as long as the walls
had, and, indeed, avenge the walls' destroyers:

> Να μπορούσαν να ζήσουν τουτ᾽ οι στίχοι
> 'Οσο εσύ θάχε ζήσης, να σε κλάψουν
> Και κείνους που σ᾽ εχάλασαν να κάψουν.
> (Mavilis, 1990, 67)

> O, that these verses could live
> as long as you would have lived, to mourn you
> And to burn those [who] destroyed you.[20]

In Mastoraki's revision in her epigraph, the second line is left out:

> Να μπορούσαν να ζήσουν τουτ᾽ οι στίχοι,
> κι εκείνους που σ᾽ εχάλασαν να κάψουν.
> (1989, 7)

> O, that these verses could live,
> And to burn those [that] destroyed you.

---

[19] One homonym that recurs in *Tales* reinforces this connection between walls and writing.
The phrases "Πίσω απ᾽ τους τοίχους" (Behind the walls) (1983b, 15) and "τρυπώντας τους
βρεγμένους τοίχους" (breaking through damp walls) (31) both carry the homonym στίχους
meaning the lines or verses, recalling the way the lines of verse homonymically build walls
around the poet in Cavafy's poem "Τείχη" (Walls) (1993, 1:117). See Nehamas 1983 on this
effect in "Walls."
[20] The Greek conjunction που can mean "who" or "that."

Though readers who know the Mavilis poem may connect the demonstrative pronoun "those" to the workers, in its new context the only referent is "verses." The more likely reading is that old verses must be burned for new ones to flourish.[21] In Mastoraki's rewriting of the Mavilis poem, the walls are no longer the issue; they have been completely subsumed by the verses of poetry, making Mavilis's wish come true. In *Crown*, poetry, like a fortress, is a matter of immortality, aspiring to permanence like Mavilis's sonnets.[22] If Mastoraki's reading of *Tales* as a homage to the Greek literary tradition suggests a direct path to *Crown*, mine discovers a detour and, leaving prizes, crowns of light, and other redemptive measures aside, stops to explore the feminist implications of the violence involved in writing poetry—of *how* terrible things happen.

In my analysis of *Tales*, I first draw on Freud's *Interpretation of Dreams* to illustrate how Mastoraki's tales with their heterogeneous sources occupy an in-between zone analogous to the dreamwork. I focus on how the constant movement back and forth from depths to surface gives writing, in all its materiality, a certain precariousness. Writing the dreamwork, it turns out, entails exhibiting the cracks, the frayed edges, the worn or crumpled surfaces of the text. In the penultimate section I return to my discussion of intertextuality, by way of Poe's purloined letter, to show how, even in the more explicit intertexts of *Tales*, the goal is to call attention to writing's destabilizing tendencies, not to establish hierarchies, literary debts, or legacies. I conclude by underscoring the feminist implications of this treacherous kind of writing by implicating myself as a feminist reader, comparing its uncertainty to the conclusiveness usually associated with the murder mystery.

Writing the Dreamwork

In his review of *Tales*, Yannis Patilis, another poet of the generation of the 1970s, made a list of the heterogeneous linguistic registers and styles he found and concluded by complaining, "Μα πού συγκλίνουν όλα αυτά" (But where do all these things converge?) (Patilis 1985). This collection with its scrambled syntax and buried references, indeed, belongs to the nether

---

[21] This is Maronitis's reading. Neither Maronitis (1992) nor Savvidis (1989) in their reviews mention Mastoraki's ellipses in this epigraph. Maronitis refers to the epigraph as a distich, not a tristich, leaving Mavilis's workers out, and sums up its significance in terms of the question of literary production: "In order for the new verses to live, they must burn the old. Mastoraki promises self-conflagration, therefore, not arson, *With a Crown of Light*" (1992, 154).

[22] This is true not only of Mavilis's "Porta Reale." For Mavilis, on the model of Shakespeare, the sonnet generally is a form of consolation; it brings back what has been lost, capturing it for posterity. This, in essence, is his definition of the sonnet in his early poem "Σονέττο" (Sonnet), which contrasts fleeting passion and spoken words with the epitaphic quality of his own written text on the page (1990, 53).

lands of dreams, nightmares, and the unconscious. It is in between, neither in the depths nor out in the open. To try to make sense of these poems is to miss the point. Patilis's desire for closure, though no doubt a common response to these difficult poems, is not as productive as tracing the poems' own refusal to make sense. *Tales,* with its practice of burying traces, demands a different model of interpretation than elucidation or explication, one that takes into account the functioning of the unconscious.[23] Freud's *Interpretation of Dreams* with its radical hermeneutics of overdetermination provides one way of grappling with *Tales.* In his account, the dream is not a riddle in need of a key, as dream interpretation since Artemidoros's dream book would have it, but a rebus with its own complex syntax. The process of semiosis is not a matter of one-to-one correspondences but one of transference, triangulation, displacement, and condensation. Approaching *Tales* through Freud's psychoanalytic model of the unconscious as it is theoretically unpacked in his *Interpretation of Dreams,* that is, as if they were dreams, means focusing on how these poems work and not on whodunit or why.

For Freud, dreams are not an exception but an exemplary showcase in which to present a more general theory of interpretation. In talking about dreaming, he constantly draws analogies with other processes such as writing poetry and translation. He is interested in how one system of signs can be transposed onto another and how the function of censorship is constitutive of these signifying processes. For Mastoraki, too, writing poetry and translating share a poetics with dreaming, one that relies heavily on censorship. As one of Greece's best poets and foremost literary translators, writing in the wake of surrealism and first publishing under an authoritarian regime, this perhaps should come as no surprise. As in Freud's *Interpretation of Dreams,* in Mastoraki's *Tales* the inability to say anything directly focuses important attention on the activities that lie between what we read and what we write, what we dream and what we remember, any original and its translation. Reading *Tales* through the interpretive structure laid out in Freud's text brings this indirectness into relief.

In his discussion of dreams, Freud distinguishes between the latent *dream-thought* and the manifest *dream-content.* The first we experience while we are asleep; it is the result of all sorts of stimuli—physical sensations, recent conversations, things we have seen during the day, memories, aspirations, traumatic experiences—and can only be retrieved through analysis. The second is what we remember when we wake up. Freud describes

---

[23] Geoffrey Hill's *Mercian Hymns* (1985) provide an interesting cross-cultural comparison because its dense medieval prose poems resist interpretation in a similar way. On reading Hill's poetry, see P. Robinson 1985.

these two texts in terms of translation: "The dream-content seems like a transcript of the dream-thoughts into another mode of expression, whose characters and syntactic laws it is our business to discover by comparing the original and the translation" (Freud 1976, 381). In between the dream-thought and the dream-content there is a set of functions Freud calls the *dreamwork,* which scramble, condense, and displace the former, producing the latter. It is in this in-between area of the dreamwork that censorship is enacted. For an image or phrase to be present in the manifest dream-content, it must pass through the censorship imposed by the ego and its resistances (419).[24] It is here that overdetermination complicates cause and effect—a look, a phrase, an itch can mean so many things. By introducing the dreamwork as the mediator, Freud shifts the hermeneutic terms of dream analysis away from emblem and essence to a more complex tripar-tite schema of dream-content, dreamwork, and dream-thought. The man-ifest dream-content is not determined by the latent dream-thought but is overdetermined in relation to it through the activity of the dreamwork. To describe the dreamwork, Freud then makes an analogy between dreaming and the creative process of writing. He quotes a passage from Goethe's *Faust* about weaving: "Unseen the threads are knit together, / and an infinite combination grows" (Freud 1976, 388 n). By referring to translation and to writing poetry in his discussion of dreams, he suggests that these processes are analogously tripartite.

Similarly for Mastoraki it is the in-between process, not the product, that interests her in both her translating and her writing. She describes transla-tion as a process: ". . . that ready-made material which someone else thought of and laid down before me, offers a boundless field for exercises of self-discipline and the pleasure of a lifetime apprenticeship to the Greek language" (1982a, 65). She has not chosen to be the definitive translator of any one literature or author but to translate many genres, from many languages—German, Spanish, Italian, and English.[25] For her, translation is not simply a matter of producing a translation but of theorizing difference. The act of translation involves occupying a world analogous to that of the dreamwork, in which each word or phrase is uprooted from its normal sense. In her own poetry Mastoraki also gives priority to the place between latent and manifest texts. In another interview she discusses literary influ-

[24] For the most in-depth analysis of this process, see A. Freud 1986.

[25] Mastoraki's body of translations comprises a heterogeneous assortment of essays on Marxist thought (Paul Sweezy, Agnes Heller, Erich Fromm) and on art (Leonardo da Vinci); of plays (Kleist, Carlo Goldoni, Federico García Lorca); of poems (Allen Ginsberg); and of novels (Salinger, Upton Sinclair, Carson McCullers, Elias Canetti, Giorgio Manganelli). Translation prizes are usually given for a substantial contribution to the translation of one literature into another; thus a unique case had to be made for Mastoraki when she was awarded the Wilder prize.

ences in the *Tales* as if they occupied the space of the dreamwork: "References to other texts exist, very buried . . . no, they don't surface, not that I didn't let them surface, it is just that they did not surface" (1987). As with the dream one remembers in the morning and the completed translation, a poem also contains the scrambled remnants of other texts. As Freud's quotation from Goethe suggests, the poem is the product of a combinatory process that severs, condenses, displaces a wealth of narrative threads.

Although *Tolls* and *Kin* addressed the in-between realms of dreaming, translating, and writing, the question of how to *write* the in-between only becomes pressing in *Tales*. This collection asks how one might write the dreamwork rather than reconstruct the latent dream-thought.[26] The title Ιστορίες για τα βαθιά displays the difficulty of *writing* an activity at the same time as one is *writing about* an activity. This title can mean "tales for the deep," tales that belong in the depths, in other words, tales that are not meant to see the light of day; or it can mean "tales about the deep," in the sense of an objective account of the doings of the unconscious or of the depths of the sea. The first interpretation involves the reader in an act of indiscretion; for merely by witnessing the title of the book, he or she is proof that these stories are not in the depths, where they belong, but out in the open, for all to read. The second keeps things neat and clean by suggesting an objective report. That two such different meanings are suggested by one title is paradigmatic of this collection. The conceptual tension between these two senses is heightened by the picture that accompanies the title on the cover of the book. Instead of the dark tunnels of the repressed, we are greeted with the luminous, eerie openness of a painting by Joseph A. Smith—sheets, shredded and clinging to branches, strung across a pale blue sky. The title says that these tales are "for" or "about" the deep, and yet the picture says that everything is out in the open—like the dowry "thoughtlessly sown by someone on the run" in Mastoraki's poem "Τα Ενδύματα" (Garments). Writing the dreamwork involves a paradox, a constant shifting of terms. Nothing can stay in any one place for long. And the plea in one poem to "dredge it all up from the depths" (1983b, 25) is a call for the reader to participate in this game and keep writing in motion.

Throughout this series of poems, full of lost objects, unexplained horrors, murders, and misunderstandings, the tension between depth and surface, between that which is hidden and that which is out in the open, is evident at the level of word, phrase, poem, and entire series. Nothing is ever what it purports to be. Proof—"σαν βούλλα αυτοκρατορικής επιστολής

[26] Lyotard (1983) reads Freud in a similar way. His first step is to frame the spatial transgressions the dreamwork commits in the terms of the paper on which the primary text (dreamthought) is written. He asks if grammar enables us to transcribe activity, what kind of metagrammar—typographic or other—does the actual activity of transcription or writing have?

που εκλάπη καθ' οδόν, κακόπεσε" (like a seal on an imperial missive, stolen en route, gone astray) (41)—is elusive. The collection is divided into an introduction, "Συντομοτάτη περιγραφή του τόπου εκείνου όπου τελούνται όλα τα φοβερά" (A brief description of the place where terrible things happened); a conclusion, "Τι έλεγε εκείνη η επιστολή" (What that missive said); and three main sections, two long ones of eleven poems each, "Τα Πάθη της Αγάπης" (The sufferings of love) and "Μικρές παράξενες ιστορίες" (Strange short stories), bridged by a shorter section of three poems, "Τρία τραγούδια για ώρα μεγάλης ανάγκης" (Three songs in case of emergency). The structure of the series is striking: the first section has one poem, the second eleven, the third three, the fourth eleven again, and the last concludes with one, like the first section. If the sequence is written out numerically, 1.11.3.11.1, three is clearly the pivotal number. As in Galanaki's poetry, binary oppositions do not structure these poems. Instead it is the tripartite schemes of dreams, translations, and poems, the process of getting from one place to another, that is foregrounded.

Although the two longer sections differ in subject matter, the formal structure of the poems is similar and corroborates the sense that everything is in flux. The first paragraph (and the second, when the poem has three paragraphs), sets the scene with a collage of pasted fragments of dreams, mad ravings, and stories, whereas the last paragraph sums up the scene "objectively," foregrounding the arbitrariness of analytic conclusions and of explanations of any kind. This shift of tone, from subjective to objective, rehearses the shift from latent to manifest content in dreams. *Tales*'s structure also reveals, at the level of poem, that individual, subjective experience and objective analysis of it, like depths and surfaces, are implicated in each other.

The poem "Του γάμου" (Wedding song) begins inside the scrambled grammar of the latent dream text:

'Οπως στους ύπνους των αγρίων καταποντίζεται το πλοίο-φάντασμα, ή φαρμάκι τρώει το κύπελλο του αφέντη—μακριά ο δεμένος ρουθουνίζει σαν να ξέφυγε, ή σαν λυμένος από χρόνια και με βόγκους—έτσι σου μοιάζουν όλοι κομματιάζοντας, και πάλι εσύ, κομμάτια όλοι.

(17)

Just as the phantom ship sinks in the sleep of savages, or poison cankers the master's cup—far off the captive moans, just escaped, perhaps untied for years and unaware—so they resemble you, torn to shreds, and you them, again, in pieces.

It then concludes outside, as if the narrator is reporting at a distance:

Με κρότους και μυστήρια φωνάγματα, με λιθοβολισμούς και αλληλούια κοι-
μούνται οι συζυγοκτόνοι.

(17)

Through crashes and mysterious cries, stonings and alleluias the spouse-
killers sleep.

In the first paragraph the contradictions of dream are present at the level of
grammar. The two sides of each metonymic equation are left in: in the
savages' sleep either the phantom ship sinks *or* poison cankers the master's cup. Instead of choosing, the poem includes both possibilities. Similarly "the captive moans, just escaped, perhaps untied for years"; no priorities are made. The indecision is even more startling in the final phrase of
this paragraph, in which the "either/or" is no longer restricted to two
halves of a clause but is present in almost every other word. In the phrase
"so they resemble you, torn to shreds, and you them, again, in pieces," it is
impossible to tell who is resembling whom because each resembles the
other. The pronouns, distinguishing two different parties, ultimately do
not distinguish anything. There is no way to tell the simulacrum from the
original.[27] By the end of the phrase, the possibility of objectivity has been
destroyed. *They* resemble *you*, but *you* are just what *they* are: in pieces. The
predictable grammar of the second paragraph, then, provides a striking
contrast. The novelty is not merely the confusing syntax of the first section
but the tension between that and the grammatically traditional conclusion.
The framing and analyses of the event, the reader's task, happens not
outside the poem but inside, in between the first and last paragraphs. The
leap from one kind of language to another, from latent dream-thought to
manifest dream-context, cannot happen afterward but must take place in
the process of reading. The white space between the paragraphs draws
attention to the dreamwork, to the activity of internalizing different influences, rather than to the dream's meaning.

In another example, the first stanza of "Garments" brings together fragments from various stories:

Τα τεκμήρια έμεναν πάντοτε στου φονέως τον κήπο, ξεσκισμένα από τέλειο
φάσγανο, σαν προίκα βουλιαγμένα στα έλη, σαν να τα 'σπειρε κάποιος αλό-
γιστα στο φευγιό του απάνω. Πελερίνες, μετάξια, και δίμιτα, με την αίγλη που
έπρεπε τότε, χλιαρές αλλαξιές που ποτίστηκαν μυρωδιές και θορύβους, ζι-

---

[27] A literal translation would read: "in this way *they* resemble *you they* all, breaking into
pieces, and *you*, pieces *they* all." I use the phrase "they all" here instead of "all of them" to
preserve the fact that the *you* and the *they* (except for the first "*they* resemble *you*" in which the
you is the object) are always in the nominative and so always subjects.

πουνάκια λευκά και στηθόπανα μ' αραιές μαχαιριές και φεστόνια, και τα
εύθραυστα εκείνα ενδύματα που τα λέγαν το πάλαι ποτέ καμιζόλες.

(24)

The evidence stayed in the murderer's garden forever, shredded by a perfect
blade, like clothes from a dowry sunk in marshes, thoughtlessly sown by
someone on the run. Velvet cloaks, silk and dimity, with the splendor of a
bygone era, warm changes of clothing, saturated with smells and noises,
white vests and corselets scattered with stabs and festoons, and those fragile
garments they used to call camisoles.

Then there is a space, and the poem concludes:

Ονειρώδεις οι θάνατοι, και ο δράστης αθώος. Μ' ένα τραύμα τυφλό, σαν παρά-
θυρο που πατιόταν μονάχα τις νύχτες.

(24)

Deaths are dreamlike, but the agent is innocent. And his wound like a
window that only gets trespassed at night.

In the first paragraph we are at the scene of the violence in the dream,
whereas in the second we have stepped back and are aware that all this is
dreamlike. The formal achievement of these poems lies in how the space
between the two paragraphs acts out and deconstructs the shift from subjective to objective, focusing the reader's attention on the activities of the
dreamwork itself, rather than on the latent dream-thought that is disfigured by the dreamwork. In Mastoraki's tales the blank spaces between
paragraphs and between the poems scramble signifiers and disengage
them from signifieds, writing the dreamwork in their relentless repetition
of this typographic move.

Consider how differently Seferis handles the question of latent dream-
thought and other "original" texts in Poem 3 of *Mythistorima*:

Μέμνησο λουτρών οις ενοσφίσθης

Ξύπνησα με το μαρμάρινο τούτο κεφάλι στα χέρια
που μου εξαντλεί τους αγκώνες και δεν ξέρω πού να τ' ακουμπήσω.
Έπεφτε στο όνειρο καθώς έβγαινα από το όνειρο
έτσι ενώθηκε η ζωή μας και θα είναι πολύ δύσκολο να ξαναχωρίσει.

Κοιτάζω τα μάτια· μήτε ανοιχτά μήτε κλειστά
μιλώ στο στόμα που όλο γυρεύει να μιλήσει

κρατώ τα μάγουλα που ξεπέρασαν το δέρμα.
Δεν έχω άλλη δύναμη·

τα χέρια μου χάνουνται και με πλησιάζουν
ακρωτηριασμένα.
   (Seferis 1981, 6)

Remember the baths where you were murdered

I woke with this marble head in my hands;
it exhausts my elbows and I don't know where to put it down.
It was falling into the dream as I was coming out of the dream
so our life became one and it will be very difficult for it to disunite again.

I look at the eyes: neither open or closed
I speak to the mouth which keeps trying to speak
I hold the cheeks which have broken through the skin
I haven't got any more strength.

My hands disappear and come toward me
mutilated.
   (7)

Here the reader is not implicated in the activity of dreaming. The confusion of dream and reality has already been carefully worked out and translated into proper grammar. Whereas Mastoraki enacts the conflation with her confusing syntax, "so they resemble you, torn to shreds, and you them, again, in pieces," Seferis describes the confusion clearly: "It was falling into the dream as I was coming out of the dream." Seferis's poem transcribes a nightmare; Mastoraki's takes the reader through the nightmare. This ability to describe the dream in an undreamlike fashion seems connected to Seferis's use of a line from Aeschylus's *The Libation Bearers* as an epigraph to the poem. For Seferis the activity of dreaming and the activity of literary influence are processes that happen before writing. The manifest dream-content of a dream and the epigraph, like "this marble head," are burdens we must live with in the present. They are severed from the contexts that created them, but the contexts are known, traceable. In Mastoraki's texts, writing is not secondary to dreaming or the activity of being influenced. It does not happen when we wake up, or after we read Aeschylus. Writing, like dreaming or being influenced, is a process of mediating, and for Mastoraki all the stages of the mediation must be performed and exposed on the surface of the poem. Although Seferis is interested in the process of dreaming and influence, his poem does not feel implicated in the working of the dream or of the influence. His writing fixes a relation between the dream-thought and the dream-content, but it does not rehearse it within the poem itself. There is the sense that meaning can be determined. The quotation refers to specific contexts, suggesting that a "correct" reading is possible. In Mastoraki's text most of the quoted texts are not set apart but integrated into the fabric of the poem. Seferis gives credit to others and marks out what belongs to whom through references or typographically, through italics. Mastoraki's signals in the *Tales*, in contrast, are oblique.[28]

Seferis's transcription of dreams conflates dream-thought and dream-content and thus effaces his role as transcriber. In forcing the illogical dream language into proper grammar, he writes himself out of the picture.[29] Mastoraki's *Tales*, in contrast, tries to acknowledge a qualitative difference between *writing* the dream and *writing down* the dream and admits her own complicity. For Mastoraki, if the dreamwork is present on the page, then the violence of madness and nightmares is not a private affair, not mediated, but acted out in broad daylight and shared by readers, at least potentially. The conclusion to "Garments" suggests that the agent gets away with murder, if sleep is the only time we deal with violence. If, on the contrary, we make our writing into a window, into a nonsolid, impermanent space that opens and closes, if we perform the dredging for all to see, dragging everything up from the depths, then there is the possibility of confronting the violence in broad daylight. The cumulative effect of rehearsing misunderstanding by writing and reading the dreamwork is an ability to recognize how terrible things happen.

The Exhibition of Prohibition

One of Mastoraki's central messages in *Tales* seems to be that prohibition can be productive, if we are willing to turn prohibition into an exhibition of what has been prohibited. We come across a palimpsest of unsettling images that suggest this. Over and over again, fear and horror are associated with places that have depth, such as wells, lakes, seas, cribs, mouths, wounds, and tombs, but attention is focused on their surfaces—on the wax sealing the mouth, the dough wrapped around wounds. These surfaces

[28] Another example from *Mythistorema* would be the reference to Solomos's *The Woman of Zakynthos*, when Seferis writes, "τα δάχτυλα στο φιλιατρό, καθώς έλεγε ο ποιητής" (the fingers on the rim of the well, as the poet said) (Seferis 1981, 4). Of course Seferis's poetry contains traces of his reading far beyond those he explicitly acknowledges, but his careful notes, like Eliot's at the end of *The Waste Land*, suggest the desire to make his readings known, whereas Mastoraki in *Tales* seem to have the opposite in mind.

[29] Likewise Freud's transcription of a patient's analysis, his "talking cure." In shaping hysterical and schizophrenic language into proper grammar, Freud's own role is erased. The act of transcription is conflated with the transcription itself; the transcriber is forgotten.

are then connected to an attempt at written communication. The dough, for example, is "σαν απ᾽ το ψιλούτσικο χαρτί που δένονται οι αστροκαμένοι κι οι εξωμότες" (as fine as the paper that binds the star-crossed and the apostates), an image that recalls the vellum "με αμνημόνευτα χαράγματα" (with immemorial marks) in an earlier line (1983b, 39). What becomes clear as we examine these images in more detail, and place them in the context of the whole series, is that moving back and forth between the depths and the surface is a highly textual activity. Writing the dreamwork is a material practice of physically exhibiting that which prohibits self-expression, an activity in which we as readers are intimately involved; for we are the ones responsible for crossing the typographic space and connecting one image to another.

Tales begins deep in the heart of a forest: "Σκιερός ο δρυμός για να χάνο-νται βασιλείς νυχτοθήρες" (Let the forest be dark, so that kings on night-prowl lose their way) (11). And from here on, terrible things continue to happen in the depths: "τα υπόγεια" (the underground) (15), "στον Άδη" (in Hades) (18), "στον πάτο λιμνοθάλασσας" (at the bottom of a saltwater lake) (23), "στο βαθύ χωράφι" (in a deep field) (41), or "σε βαθύ κοιτώνα χάλκινο" (in a deep, brass bedchamber) (49). The metonymic contiguity of things with vertical depth—beds, wounds, and tombs—and their proximity to horrible mishaps suggests a conflation of sleep and death. The postman lying in the deep field is very likely dead (41), for example,[30] and the thief smothered in linen in the deep, brass bedchamber is unlikely to fare any better (49). The only hope of survival is to drag everything up and out into the open. The insistence that everything is at the bottom, in the depths of the unconscious, and must be brought to the surface, is complicated by the movement through space from *behind* to *in front*. The other most prominent group of images in *Tales* deals with this horizontal motion, suggesting a connection between walls, doors, and, self-referentially, the rectangular pages the reader is turning. Whereas the first group of images provides a nonlinear vision of constant motion from the depths to the surface and back again, this second group actually progresses apace with the narrative. The series begins "Πίσω απ᾽ τους τοίχους" (Behind the walls) (15), moves to the walls themselves ("Οι τοίχοι γερά και μαγκωμένοι") (20), then to the door half open ("την πόρτα, μισή βυθισμένη, μισή ανοιχτή με αντικλείδι") (22), then to disintegrating walls ("τρυπώντας τους βρεγμένους τοίχους") (31), and to a collapsing gate ("Και πέφτοντας η πύλη") (42), and ends "προ των τειχών" (outside the walls) (45).

The penultimate tale brings the two series of images together and offers a less than definite conclusion. The phrase " 'Οπως επαίτης ύπουλος προ των

---

[30] His probable death is enforced by an intertextual reference. As we have seen in Chapter 3, the postman/brother in Vizyenos's "Who Was My Brother's Murderer?" is murdered.

τειχών" (just as a devious beggar outside the walls) combines the tension of depths-to-surface and behind-to-in-front: ύπουλος means "underhand" or "devious" and contains the prefix υπό (under), which implies concealment, as well as the word ουλή, which means "scar" and refers to a wound that has been covered up, while προ means "in front." Just when we think we have arrived "out in front," the same revealing/concealing activity is re-enacted:

'Οπως επαίτης ύπουλος προ των τειχών, καλύπτει επιμελώς με το μανδύα του πληγές που άνθισαν, με κάποιο θαύμα. Κι όπως αρχαίος γεωμέτρης λάμνοντας, νεκρώνει πίσω του τεράστιες εκτάσεις κι αναβλύζει.

(45)

Just as a devious beggar outside the walls, carefully mantles his wounds which bloomed by some miracle. And an ancient geometer deadens behind him huge expanses with his oars and wells up.

Surface and depths are implicated. The beggar covers his wounds, which, like beds and tombs, are images of vertical depth, while the geometrist leaves behind him expanses of still water, an image of horizontal motion. And yet in both cases the concealment is undone: the wounds have bloomed and are exposed for everyone to see; the ancient geometer is the subject of the verb αναβλύζει (to gush or spurt forth).

This shuttling between depths and surface can also be read as a shuttling between the voice and the page. The forms of expression referred to in *Tales* trace a trajectory from speech to writing and back again. *Tales* begins by setting the scene, "Συντομοτάτη περιγραφή του τόπου εκείνου όπου τελούνται όλα τα φοβερά" (A brief description of the place where terrible things happen) (11). The repeated and implied periphrastic imperative suggests spoken directions—"Να χυθεί . . . ο αέρας" (Let the air first spill over), "Σκιερός ο δρυμός" (Let the forest be dark). In the second section *Tales* describes the sufferings of love in which rituals and events such as marriage and abduction are given the titles of folksongs: "Του γάμου" (The wedding song) (17), "Η απαγωγή" (The abduction) (22). The third section introduces experiences that call attention to themselves as spoken, such as spells, "Μαγικό ξόρκι να σε φυλάει . . ." (A magic spell to protect you . . .) (29). Only in the fourth section do we get to the written form of stories such as "Περί των αφηγήσεων εν γένει" (About narratives in general) (35) and "Δια χειρός αγνώστου, πραγματεία" (Treatise, written by an unknown hand) (41). And finally, in the conclusion, we are told the contents of an epistle, which we have been pursuing throughout the fourth section. Just when we are about to get the evidence that would secure writing a new and privileged place, the letter itself evades us and we find ourselves with our attention drawn to the voice: "Μα όταν κάποιος σου μιλά με τρόμους, φωνές χαμένων σε απαίσια σπήλαια και βάλτους—" (But when someone talks to you with terror, with voices of those lost in ghastly caves and marshes—) (49). At the moment when we think the progression from speech to writing is complete, it is reversed. Yet the fact remains that the poems come to us in a written form. Writing the dreamwork seems to involve writing that can retain the immediacy and ephemerality of speech and that constantly works out the relationship between speaking and writing.

Even before the written word becomes the dominant form of expression in *Tales* there are marks that herald writing by acting as the record of an event or transaction. We find bruises ("μελανιές"), a stain ("ένα φαρδύ, σαν φύλλο σκοτεινό ματώνει") (16), wounds ("λαβωματιές") (19), knife slits ("μαχαιριές") (24), snake bite ("δάγκαμα φιδιού") (29), the burn ("το έγκαυμα"), and a seal ("σαν βούλλα αυτοκρατορικής επιστολής") (41), among others. Although in the first three sections, speech not writing is the privileged form of communication, during the course of the series these marks become more and more connected to the activity of writing. The first bruises and stains the reader comes across are connected with song:

Ωραία θηλυκά του Κάτω Κόσμου, με μακριούς ποδόγυρους κι ερεθισμένα μάτια. "Εύμορφα, εύμορφα!" τους λέγαν και τα στρίμωχναν. Αργότερα τα έκαναν τραγούδια. Διδακτικές γυναίκες. Με λαιμά γεμάτα μελανιές. Με ζαρωμένα μεσοφόρια. Κι ένα φαρδύ, σαν φύλλο σκοτεινό, ματώνει στις λινές τους βράκες.

Αυτά να μείνουν από τους αρχαίους καημούς. Τους έρωτες.

(16)

Beautiful ladies of the Underworld, with long hems and eyes sore from crying. "My fair ones!" they would call them as they cornered them. Later they turned them into songs. Exemplary ladies. With bruised necks. Crumpled petticoats. And on their linen pantalets, a stain of blood, a dark leaf, spreading.

Let that be what is left of ancient longings. And of ancient loves.

The men sing about the exemplary ladies with their bruises and stains; and the men's songs, then, are what is remembered. The visible marks of these women's violation are subsumed by the voice and turned into songs.[31]

In another poem the forgotten promise of an extra dowry, now over-

[31] The word τραγούδι (song) here can also mean poem, and usually does for the older generation of poets such as Palamas, and later for Sikelianos. This conflation is yet another sign of how intertwined poetry and orality are in Greece.

grown with moss, is framed in terms of the transience of orality—sad ballads, sobs and glorias, wild laughter:

Σαν από τα λυπητερά τραγούδια, και διωγμένες με λυγμούς και δόξασοι, με τα μακριά τα κόκκινα και τα ποδήρη, ψηλά ποδήματα των κυνηγιών, κι ο λόγος πανωπροίκι μαλακός και χορταριάζει, με φλόγες και φρυάζοντας και γέλιο ακράτητο, να μην τον δουν που φοβερίζει, φεύγουν—

όπως αστράφτει ο πετεινός στον Άδη, κι όπως χρυσή μασέλα στο βουβό της νύχτας, τετράποδο τρεχάτο που κουδούνιζε, κι ο αναβάτης μάλαμα κοχλάζει.

(18)

As in sad ballads, chased with sobs and glorias, in dresses, long and red, and ankle length, in hunting boots, the dowry promised once, now soft and moss grown, with flames and fuming and wild laughter, so they won't see him threaten, they leave—

the way a rooster lights up Hades, or a gilded jaw the speechless night, a beast jangling on the run, and the rider bubbles up gold.

All the images—a rooster glistening, a gilded jaw—are subsumed grammatically by the tenor of the metaphor, "a beast jangling on the run" in which the sound of the bells and the galloping rhythm of the phrase *tetrápodo trecháto pou koudoúnize* (τετράποδο τρεχάτο που κουδούνιζε) take over. The written text is again subsumed by the oral, the permanent by the transient. In the last image, gold is not only molten, and therefore unstable and outside the system of exchange, but bubbling—the reader is left with the sound of this bubbling in the onomatopoeic word *kochlazi* (κοχλάζει).

Throughout the second section of this collection the marks connected with the female body (whether physically, as in the bruises of the women of the underworld, or metaphorically, as in the extra dowry of the unfortunate brides) are associated with speech. For example, all the tokens of affection in the second paragraph of "Οι άπιστοι" (The unfaithful) are turned into sounds in the third paragraph:

Με πένθη αιώνων να πνέουν οι άνεμοι, σέρνοντας τρόμους λαθραίων ερώτων, εγκόλπια, μαύρους πλοκάμους, μικρά ευσεβή αναθήματα, νέους που βράχηκαν μέχρι το κόκαλο σε μπόρα αιφνίδια, ώρα εσπέρας.

Και πολλοί ποταμοί παρασύροντας στέγες αθλίων, αγγελίες μικρών αποστάσεων, προτροπές, νουθεσίες και όρκους, ασπασμούς, και τα κλάματα. Παρασύροντας κλίνες απίστων συζύγων, και τις άνανδρες λέξεις "λαχτάρα μου."

(21)

While winds heave with ages of sorrow, dragging fears of clandestine love,
amulets, black locks, small, pious oblations, young men soaked to the bone
by a sudden storm at dusk.

And many rivers carrying away the roofs of the wretched, messages that
never went far, urgings, oaths, admonitions, embraces, and tears. Carrying
away the beds of unfaithful spouses, and the unmanly words "I need you."

Perhaps most telling are the ephemeral "messages that never went far"
and the words that are carried away by rivers; they have none of the
permanence one normally ascribes to the written text. In another poem in
this section the little girls bite their sheets "tittering" (με χάχανα), again a
sound (22). In another, the loved ones fill "your" mouth with wax so "you"
won't scream (23). It is the voice, not the written text, that is inhibited. But
the materiality of the marks (the bloodstains on the linen underwear, the
sheets, the wax) raises the question of whether writing might also be implicated in, even a function of, this oppressive situation. As with Philomela,
who managed to weave her story after her tongue was cut off, writing in
Tales turns out to be a way of transforming prohibition of speech into a
visual exhibition of this prohibition.

The shift to writing specifically as a viable model of expression does not
take place until after the third section. In the last poem of this section there
are two important references, first to the great storyteller "Θείο Ιούλιο"
(Uncle Jules [Verne]) "για να έρχεται τα βράδια σφυρίζοντας" (so he'll come
by at night whistling), second, to the related act of "τρυπώντας τους βρεγμένους τοίχους" (breaking through damp walls) into the private home, the
space of the bourgeois reader. Both herald a new status for writing. In the
fourth section, titled "Μικρές παράξενες ιστορίες" (Strange short stories),
writing is the main form of expression. It is the materiality of written texts,
rather than the transience of sobs, songs, and laughter, which affects us.
The terrible things are now written, not sung, wailed, or moaned. The first
poem, "Περί των αφηγήσεων εν γένει" (About narratives in general), warns
us to be suspicious of any kind of narrative, particularly those that are
written:

Τις γραφές τους να τρέμεις τις άπατες κι όλο
πατήματα—
        (35)

You must fear their bottomless scriptures which echo with
footsteps—

Instead of writing being overtaken by speech, as we have seen in the first
three sections, the opposite happens. All the sounds of the second and

third paragraphs of this poem, for example, are taken over by writing in the last line:

... και βουνά που χαράζονται, όπως γκρεμίζει πανάρχαιο ικρίωμα, ή κλαψού-
ρισμα ζώου που βρέθηκε νύχτα στο ρέμα να 'χει έξαφνα δύο κεφάλια—

Με φωνές στρατευμάτων σε ώρα επίθεσης, μουγκρητά και ανάθεμα, με βαθιές
βασκανίες και ξόρκια, με γητειές, μαγγανείες,

να φυλάγεσαι, λέω, τους αυτόχειρες που έγραφαν.
                                                    (35)

... and mountains scored, an ancient scaffold ready to collapse, or late at night, deep in some gully, the whimper of a beast that found itself, all of a sudden, with two heads—

With battle cries at the hour of attack, howls and curses, with exorcisms and incantations, hexes, charms,

I say beware the suicides who wrote.

The poem juxtaposes written and oral evidence of horror, but it is the materiality of "the suicides who wrote," not the whimpering beast or the howls, that turn out to be most threatening. Here the literal sense of "one's own hand" embedded within the word αυτόχειρες (suicides) implicates the medium in the message: writing is dangerous because it does not simply record violence, in the manner of a battle cry or a howl, but participates in it, exhibiting its own complicity.

From this poem on in *Tales*, writing is foregrounded over speech; that is, the medium of signification is more and more often the material stuff of writing. The mouth spits concrete objects (coins) rather than ephemeral words:

Και πίσω πίσω κρέμεται ανάποδα ο στραβοκάνης πρησμένος από τ' ασημένια
τάλιρα και φτύνει.
           (36)

And further off the bandy-legged man hangs upside down, swollen with silver coins, and spits.

Speech and song are like a text:

Έλεγαν όμως και τροπάρια μελωδικά, σε γλώσσα μάλλον δυσανάγνωστη και
αυστηρή, σαν κείμενο ανεπανόρθωτα φθαρμένο που όλο πάει να τραγουδήσει

και λυγίζει. Πώς κράζει φτερωτό σκυλί, αδιάβατο πρωινό, χάσκει ψηλά το στόμα του και ξεματώνει.

(38)

But they were also chanting melodious hymns, in a rather indecipherable, and strict tongue, like a text irreparably worn, which is always about to sing, but falters. The way a winged dog howls, impenetrable dawn, its jaw wide open and bleeding.

It is the reference to the text which is new, though this text is hemmed in by metaphors of sound—"which is always about to sing, but falters," "the way a winged dog howls." That which heals is no longer spoken (a spell, an ode). Instead the soothing paste they put on arrow wounds *is like* paper:

κι οι τοίχοι έφεγγαν καθώς από λεπτότατη διφθέρα, παλαιική, με αμνημόνευτα χαράγματα. Και πέρα, στα πολλά τα χώματα, είχε ξασπρίσει η γης κι αραίωνε, σαν το ζυμάρι που φασκιώνουν τις σαΐτιές, και σαν απ' το ψιλούτσικο χαρτί που δένονται οι αστροκαμένοι κι οι εξωμότες.

(39)

and the walls aglow as if made of the finest vellum, antique, with immemorial marks. And way off, by a pile of dirt, the earth so pale and thin, like the dough they wrap wounds in, as fine as the paper that binds the star-crossed and the apostates.

Yet, in each of these examples that illustrate the materiality of writing, writing's materiality is also being questioned: texts are *irreparably* corrupt or worn out (38); the paper is *very* thin (39). And the next poem, according to its title "Από σπαράγματα βραχέος χρονικού . . ." (From the fragments of a brief chronicle . . .), is comprised solely of fragments from a text that has fallen apart. The first two fragments break off after a reference to silencing, equating censorship with the ravages of time:

Ευλόγησον, ξεφωνητά, και βουτηγμένοι στο μετάξι να δαγκώνουν το βαρύ λεπίδι
Μη Μιλάς

. . . .
ή πάλι σέρνοντας μνηστή δεμένη κι άλαλη, ονόματι

(40)

Blessed Be, screams, and buried in silk, let them bite the weighty blade
Be Silent

. . . .
or again dragging a fiancée bound and gagged, by the name of

Though Philomela's predicament—"let them bite the weighty blade Be Silent," "a fiancée bound and gagged"—may turn our attention to the material attributes of writing, this materiality can in no way be equated with permanence. This is only a tentative solution.

It is not surprising, then, in the last section, "What That Missive Said," to discover that the written letter has disappeared and that we must be *told* of its contents. The pattern I identified above, whereby the double motion from the depths to the surface and from *behind* to *in front* is never complete and always includes its inversion, is also true of the movement from speech to writing. The person who speaks—"Μα όταν κάποιος σου μιλά με τρόμους . . ." (But when someone speaks to you with terror . . .) (49)—and the persons who do not speak but instead prove themselves with visual evidence—"Δεν το μιλούν, μα το επιδεικνύουν" (They don't talk about it, but they show it) (41)—coexist. Writing and visual proof carries with it the transience of speech; speech relies heavily on a letter that has already been written. The two forms of expression, speech and writing, are inextricably bound up and *Tales* registers this—in writing.

In the context of a Greek critical tradition that often privileges poetry's oral components, I want both to call attention to other attributes of writing, and—in the particular case of Mastoraki's poetry, to its self-reflexive materiality—and also, and more important, to suggest that writing and speaking are not as distinct in Modern Greek culture as they were (some critics have argued) in ancient Greece and in Western culture more generally (Ong 1982). By constructing her book as a workshop for transforming one mode of expression into another, Mastoraki challenges the supremacy of any one mode and stresses their interdependence. Flexibility, the virtue that is prized above all in *Tales,* is not constitutive of either oral or written culture exclusively. When contemporary composers such as Theodorakis and Hatzidakis set Greece's best modern poetry to music, turning writing back into the oral tradition it draws on, or when villagers in the northern town of Sohos consult the folklorists' texts to make sure they are performing their carnival tradition correctly, or when a group of men in a *kafeneion* (coffee shop) break into a fight as they watch an anthropologist's video of a local brawl in the same place a year earlier, secondary orality—that is, orality deeply informed by the technology of writing and transcription—is in full swing.[32] *Tales* shows that this give and take between the oral and the written has never been a one-way street. In a culture in which folk songs and the memoirs of a self-taught general are the founding literary texts, and demotic Greek the preferred language of so many nineteenth- and

---

[32] The last two examples are drawn from discussions with the anthropologist Jane Cowan regarding her fieldwork in Sohos (1990). For a more complicated analysis of secondary orality than Ong gives, see Kittler 1987.

twentieth-century writers, a neat division between the spoken and the written has never been easy to uphold. *Tales* suggests that it is neither the original orality of the folksongs, *nor* the written collections that school children read, but the relation between the song and the transcription which counts. Similarly it is not the seeming orality of the memoirs of General Makriyannis, a self-professed illiterate, who wrote down his experience of the Greek War of Independence in 1829, *or* the literary value ascribed to them by the poet Seferis that made them a canonical text, but the struggle between these two forms of expression which this text demonstrates.[33] In *Tales* we may find that the undoing of the difference between depth and surface, speech and writing, for which Derrida equips us, is often already undone.

The Purloined Letter and the Woman Reader

In this section I want to explore further the material instability attributed to writing in *Tales* and, in particular, its feminist implications, by returning to the discussion of subversive mimesis and the literary tradition which I set forth in Chapter 3. As I have suggested, *Tales* is written under the sign of a letter that never reaches its destination, a purloined letter, a letter for which the reader is handed over the responsibility of writing. The letter is introduced in the penultimate section of *Tales* in a line that compares the need to prove something to the seal on a letter that gets stolen:

Δεν το μιλούν, μα το επιδεικνύουν—σπανίως ειν' η αλήθεια, όποτε το καλεί η ανάγκη—σαν βούλλα αυτοκρατορικής επιστολής που εκλάπη καθ' οδόν, κακόπεσε, κι ενόσω αμέριμνος ο αυτοκράτωρ γευματίζει, ο ταχυδρόμος του λιμνάζει στο βαθύ χωράφι και βραδύνει.

(41)

They don't talk about it, but they show it—hardly ever, it's true, only when necessary—like a seal on an imperial missive, stolen en route, gone astray, and while the insouciant emperor dines, his postman lies in a deep field of blood and is late.

Then, in the final section and poem, we are told "what that missive said." Not only is the original letter missing, and its contents only related, not read, but the poem ends with the appropriate beginning of a letter—"My dear Arthur or Alphonse." The concept of a purloined letter is useful for illustrating Mastoraki's poetics of deferral more generally and for under-

---

[33] For how Seferis "created" Makriyannis, see Lambropoulos 1988, 44–65.

scoring its sexual politics. Like the proper names "Arthur or Alphonse," which lose their specificity and "properness" by being doubled, a letter that never arrives forfeits its raison d'etre. It cannot prove anything. Yet, as we saw with Galanaki's unborn child in *The Cake,* the purloined letter of *Tales* takes its loss as its gain, turning undeliverability at the level of word, phrase, sentence, poem, section, and collection into its mission.

One of the keys to the poetics of *Tales* is found in its particular brand of intertextuality, its mode of severing ties, scrambling syntax, and burying traces, which I have discussed in terms of the dreamwork. The purloined letter with its ineffectual seal and signature, lying with the postman in a pool of blood,[34] offers an evocative image of the effects of the dreamwork as well as of its materiality. Everything is caught in the act of being diverted, altered, buried, stolen. Nothing can mean what it was meant to mean, and this resistance to meaning must take up space. In my discussion of intertextuality in *Tales,* I have thus far mostly referred to those sources not explicitly mentioned in the text but inferred by the reader, the hodgepodge of incongruous discourses—murder mysteries, Byzantine chronicles, folksongs, odes, and idylls—hinted at, but hidden. There is, however, another kind of intertext, referred to briefly in Chapter 3: direct quotations and proper names taken explicitly from somewhere.[35] In *Tales* there are few of these—the epigraph from Vizyenos's "Who Was My Brother's Murderer," a few scattered phrases from nineteenth-century romances, the proper names "Jules" in the middle, and "Arthur or Alphonse" of the oral epic at the end. Even in these cases, however, each is progressively less definite: "Jules" is probably Jules Verne, but are Arthur and Alphonse from the oral epic of Arthurian romance and the *Poem of the Cid?* It is the dearth of explicit intertexts, in the context of a poetic tradition that prides itself on literary allusion, which makes *Tales* more interesting to me than *Crown,* with its "easily recognizable" debts. In Chapter 3, I showed how even the most attributable lines, those from Vizyenos's short story, lost their air of authority in their new context in the *Tales.* I now want to continue this argument, illustrating how Vizyenos's tales not only repeat the uncertainty already established in *Tales* but confirm the specific interdependence between orality and textuality I have been analyzing, offering their fragile in-between status as support for the alternative kind of writing proposed by *Tales.*

Vizyenos and other writers of his generation inaugurated the short story in Greece by drawing on the heterogeneous linguistic registers available to

[34] Mastoraki suggested adding the more explicit reference to blood in the English translation, though this is only inferred in the Greek by the verb λιμνάζει (to stagnate) and the general context.

[35] Riffaterre usefully distinguishes these two types of intertexts as "aleatory" and "obligatory" (1983a, 123).

writers in the 1880s: dialect, loan words, folksongs, and folktales.³⁶ His short stories highlight the transcription of an oral culture into a written medium. His story "Το μόνον της ζωής του ταξείδιον" (The one and only journey of his life) contrasts the oral tradition of storytelling and the importance of plot (πλοκή) to the written tradition with its preoccupation with style (ύφος). By juxtaposing a grandfather seated on a hill knitting and his grandson, a tailor, this story highlights another sense of the ancient word plot (πλοκή), knitting, and suggests a connection between the word for style (ύφος) and the trade of the tailor who spends all day with material (ύφασμα), in Greek a cognate of style (ύφος).³⁷ And yet, though Vizyenos's tales call attention to the interrelation of writing and speaking, Mastoraki's *Tales*, as a reading of Vizyenos's tales, reveal the full implications of such hybridity.

Tellingly the Vizyenos tale Mastoraki cites also has as its premise a purloined letter. The narrator, Yiorgis, whose name is diminutive for the author's own name Georgios, and who also shares other biographical details with the author, has returned "από τα ξένα" (from abroad), to accompany his mother on a search for his brother's murderer. Although many outside factors have contributed to the mysterious death of his brother, the narrator is driven by a personal sense of guilt; for it was the hope of securing his letters "from abroad" that convinced his mother, against her better judgment, to let his brother take the job of postman. In an attempt to assure that his letters arrive safely, his brother's life had been endangered. This subtext is clear in the following exchange between his brother and his mother earlier on in the story:

—Ε! καλά, είπε τότε. Δεν την παίρνω. Άφησε να μείνης καναδύο μήνες χωρίς γράμμα και να διής πως εσύ θα το μετανοιώσης.

Αυτό μ' έγγιξεν εκεί που με πονούσε. Τα γράμματά σου δεν ήρχοντο τακτικά, γιατί τα άνοιγαν στον δρόμο. Και δεν φθάνει που δεν άφησαν μέσα τίποτε, μόνον ύστερα εντρεπόντουσαν να τα φέρουν ανοιγμένα και έτσι έμενα εγώ χωρίς ειδήσεις σου κι εκαθόμουν κι έκλαια. (Vizyenos 1973, 48)

— "'Well, all right!' he said then. 'I'm not taking it. You just wait a month or two without a letter, and then you'll see how sorry you'll be.'

"That hit me right where it hurt. Your letters didn't come regularly because they opened them on the way. And it wasn't enough that they didn't

---

³⁶ On Vizyenos and intertextuality, see Chryssanthopoulos 1994. For an overview of Vizyenos criticism, see the October 1995 special issue of the *Journal of Modern Greek Studies*.

³⁷ It is interesting to note that Papadiamantis also transforms material from oral literature (folksongs and tales) into a written form. In "Η Νοσταλγός" (The homesick wife), for example, he models the plot on a few lines from a folksong the heroine of his story is singing. The simple imagery of the folksong is spun out into an undisputably written form involving all sorts of subordinate clauses alien to oral tradition.

leave anything inside, but they didn't dare deliver them once they'd been opened. So I went on without news of you and merely sat and cried." (Vizyenos 1988, 61)

The narrator's own writing, it seems, is one of the more plausible answers to the story's title question Who was my brother's murderer?[38] Although for Vizyenos the ambiguity of the murderer was at the level of plot, it is not difficult to see how Mastoraki found support for her more formal use of undecidability in *Tales*. The direct references to "Jules" and "Arthur or Alphonse" similarly refer to an enmeshing of orality and textuality.[39] Like the reference to Vizyenos, they trouble the border between speech and writing, lending only more credence to the claim that intertextuality is a destabilizing force in *Tales*.

The deconstructive logic proposed by Mastoraki's purloined letter becomes even clearer when examined in the context of Edgar Allan Poe's short story "The Purloined Letter" and the numerous critical responses it has prompted in recent years.[40] Poe's tale of ratiocination unfolds as a series of conversations and encounters between the narrator, his friend

[38] Although, at the level of plot, Kiamil the Turk is the most likely candidate, when the narrator, Yiorgis, returns home and finds him tending his brother's grave, he does not turn him in to the authorities (Vizyenos 1973, 97–99, and 1988, 92–94).

[39] The tales of Jules Verne have been a favorite of children in Greece for generations but also have a specific linguistic association for Greek writers. The main translation until the 1960s was in very flowery, purist Greek, creating an odd disjuncture: stories that were meant to be read aloud in a language removed from the spoken idiom. I am indebted to Pavlina Pampoudi for her account of the linguistic influence Verne exerted on her generation (1994). Beaton (1994, 220) also mentions this in his discussion of the influence of Verne on Embirikos, who, as I have already mentioned, is in many ways an honorary member of the generation of the 1970s. The reference to "Arthur or Alphonse" can also be read in relation to the question of orality and textuality. The only place they appear together is in medieval epics: King Arthur in the Arthurian romances, and King Alphonse in the *Poem of the Cid*. Again, one of the distinguishing characteristics of this genre is its hybrid status as oral or written literature.

[40] I refer the reader to the collection of critical essays *The Purloined Poe: Lacan, Derrida, and Psychoanalytic Reading* (Muller and Richardson 1988), which includes the short story and the three essays I discuss. The pretext for my discussion of obligatory intertexts is actually an aleatory intertext: *Tales* never mentions Poe. Though I have drawn connections between the Arthur of *Tales* and the Arthur of Arthurian legend, a case could also be made for the Arthur of Poe's *The Narrative of Arthur Gordon Pym of Nantucket*. No doubt such a doubling of Arthurs in an already doubled reference to "Arthur or Alphonse" is plausible. T. S. Eliot once wrote, "One cannot be sure that one's own writing has *not* been influenced by Poe" (cited by Shoshana Felman in Muller and Richardson 1988, 135). And this is even more true of the Greek scene, where Poe is a very important reference point. As in France, where he was translated by Baudelaire, in Greece he was translated by one of the most influential writers and critics of his times, Immanuel Roidis. On Poe's influence with respect to Bloom's theory, see Felman in Muller and Richardson 1988, 135–37. For Poe's influence on Mastoraki, see Maro Douka's tribute to Mastoraki "Ποιος φοβάται τον 'Αλλεν Πόε" (Who's afraid of Allan Poe) (in 1992, 25–29). For another Greek post-Poe use of the purloined letter motif, see Mitsakis's 1895 novella (1988) and Maronitis's discussion of it (1992, 169–82). For a comparison of Poe's "The Man of the Crowd" and Mitsakis's novella, see Gotsi 1996.

Dupin, the Prefect who is trying to locate the Queen's stolen letter, and the thief himself, a certain Minister D-----. In the end it is Dupin, not the Prefect, who finds the letter, because the latter is unable to accept the obviousness of where the Minister has placed it. The final conversation occurs between the narrator and Dupin after the Prefect has purchased the letter from Dupin and is on his way to deliver it to the Queen. Dupin is explaining how he put a facsimile where he found the letter in order not to incur the immediate wrath of the Minister. He admits to wanting to know the Minister's reaction when he does eventually discover he has been duped. The narrator then asks if Dupin included anything in his facsimile. Poe's tale concludes with Dupin's confession that he had indeed left a signature of sorts, a quotation in his own manuscript:

> "Why—it did not seem altogether right to leave the interior blank—that would have been insulting. D-----, at Vienna once, did me an evil turn, which I told him, quite good-humoredly, that I would remember. So, as I knew he would feel some curiosity in regard to the identity of the person who had outwitted him, I thought it a pity not to give him a clue. He is well acquainted with my MS., and I just copied into the middle of the blank sheet the words—
>
> —*Un dessein si funeste,*
> *S' il n' est digne d'Atrée, est digne de Thyeste.*
>
> They are to be found in Crébillon's 'Atrée.'" (in Muller and Richardson 1988, 23)

Barbara Johnson, in "The Frame of Reference," reads Derrida's reading of Lacan's seminar on Poe's story to show how a quoted text is repeatedly used as a signature in both the story and the criticism of "The Purloined Letter." Through the act of quotation, each text (Poe's, Lacan's, Derrida's) inevitably bears the stamp of the quoted author which determines the newer text's meaning, whether or not the quoting author acquiesces. Dupin cannot refrain from filling in the blank and including a clue to his identity—the Crébillon quotation—in the letter. Lacan points this out and then falls into the same trap by turning the letter's lack of meaning into *the* meaning of the letter. Each of these texts exposes and glosses the repetition-compulsion at work in the act of quotation. Like the child who overcomes his mother's departure through repetition, for each of these writers, quotation is a symbolic form of mastery. Poe's character Dupin quotes Atreus's avenging of Thyestes in his own attempt to get back at the Minister. Lacan and Derrida cite Poe and each other in an attempt to get back at each other, a rivalry all the more tricky because, as Johnson points out, it is "over something neither man will credit the other with possessing" (in Muller and Richardson 1988, 219–20). Johnson suggests that the logic of the purloined letter is that each subsequent reader's attempt at mastery, "one-upmanship," turns into failure, "one-downmanship." "It is as though," she writes, "any attempt to follow the path of the purloined letter is automatically purloined from itself. Which is, as we shall see, just what the letter has always already been saying" (214).[41]

What becomes clear in the context of Johnson and company's reading of the purloined letter is that *Tales* also "operates as a text which evades every assignable destination, and produces, or rather introduces by deducing itself, this unassignableness at the precise moment when it narrates the arrival of a letter" (204).[42] The direct references to Vizyenos, "Jules" Verne and "Arthur or Alphonse" function, I argue, as Mastoraki's signatures, in a fashion similar to the quotation in Poe's tale and in its criticism. Rather than offer conclusions, they simply confirm the inconclusiveness about which *Tales* has already taught us a great deal. The questions remain, however, what the specific function of this unassignableness is in the Greek context[43] and why contemporary Greek women's poetry is preoccupied with the plural signature and the inability to trace the signifier to a referent?[44]

I have pointed out the ramifications of the purloined letter in *Tales* and suggested that *Tales* plays off the detective genre, with its emphasis on whodunit. It now remains for me to draw out the importance of the reader,

[41] Derrida continues this discussion of purloined letters, quotation, and signature in *The Postcard: From Socrates to Freud and Beyond*, being more explicit than in his Poe essay about how signatures are never authoritative and how writing and speaking rely on each other. The book cover reproduces an etching in which Plato is looking over Socrates's shoulder as he writes, rather than the more familiar scenario in which Plato is the scribe and Socrates, the orator. By referring to so many different positions, Derrida's flagrant signing of his own initials and proper name decenter, rather than consolidate, our sense of an author. As he explains, "I regret that you [tu] do not very much trust my signature, on the pretext that we might be several. This is true, but I am not saying so in order to make myself more important by means of some supplementary authority. And even less in order to disquiet, I know what this costs. You are right, doubtless we are several, and I am not as alone as I sometime say I am when the complaint escapes from me, or when I still put everything into seducing you" (Derrida 1987, 6). He deploys a plural signature in order to deconstruct the belief that every letter has one sender and one receiver and will arrive at its destination—what he calls the "postal principle." See Nehamas 1987 which places this work in the context of Derrida's other texts.

[42] The question remains whether, by framing her discussion of Lacan's and Derrida's differences in the theoretical writings of Lacan and Derrida, Johnson anticipates her own reader's attempt to one-up her and shifts the terms or whether she simply fills in the blank like one of the boys. I come back to the feminist implications of this reliance on "the boys."

[43] For a different approach to this question and Derrida's *Postcard*, see Moullas 1992.

[44] As I have already mentioned, there are other visual narratives that illustrate this unassignability besides the three discussed in this book. Pavlina Pampoudi's 24-poem series *Postcard* (1980), written in the same year as Derrida's *Postcard*, just when Mastoraki was beginning *Tales*, is a particularly interesting example.

and the female reader, in particular, to this process. In *Moses and Mono-theism*, Freud discusses the detective story in terms of how the reader/analysand reconstructs the suppressed murder from memory-traces.[45] Walter Benjamin is interested in how the reader compensates for high capitalism's alienation through the satisfaction of figuring out whodunit.[46] In both formulations the reader is crucial. Contemporary Greek women's poetry undoes the bourgeois detective story by taking the role of the reader one step further. Not only do texts begin where Benjamin predicts the detective story will no longer be necessary, when everything is out in the open, but they implicate the reader as murderer. Prose poems and, in Laina's case, fragments offer multiple endings, multiple victims, multiple criminals, and multiple returns to the scene of the crime. Near the end of *Tales* we find "Και τι απέγινε ο δολοφονημένος" (And what happened to the man who was murdered). Despite the title's claim to elucidate matters, the text obfuscates them; and instead of eliminating options until a solution is found, each line multiplies the possibilities. The first paragraph begins with a list of all the things people thought happened to the murdered man:

'Αλλοι τον θέλουν, χρόνους έπειτα, έπαρχο, νόθο παιδί μιας παρακόρης· ρου-φιάνο οι τρίτοι, να υπηρετεί δυσώνυμη μεγαλειότητα· και κάποιοι—πώς δι-χάζονται ξανά οι γνώμες—οπλουργό, συλλέκτη πολυτίμων λίθων, ανατόμο, και πάντως χήρο από γυναίκα πόρνη, εκπάγλου καλλονής, σε μια επιδημία που έφεραν τα καραβάνια εμπόρων.

(1983b, 44)

Years later some want him a prefect, others the maid's illegitimate son, and still others a pimp serving ignominious nobles; and a few—once again how opinions differ—a swordsmith, a collector of precious stones, an anatomist, and most certainly a widower whose harlot wife of astounding beauty died in an epidemic that the trade caravans brought over.

This list is followed by another list of all the places the murdered man hid, which, like Galanaki's final poem, concludes with the fact that hiding is impossible because everything is out in the open:

[45] Freud writes: "In its implications the distortion of a text resembles a murder: the difficulty is not in perpetrating the deed but in getting rid of the traces. . . . Accordingly, in many instances of textual distortion, we may nevertheless count upon finding what has been suppressed and disavowed hidden away somewhere else, though changed and torn from its context" (1985, 283–84). See also Lyotard's discussion of this passage (1983, 6).

[46] Benjamin, recalling the lessons of Poe's tale "The Man of the Crowd," writes: " 'It is almost impossible,' wrote a Parisian secret agent in 1798, 'to maintain good behavior in a thickly populated area where an individual is, so to speak, unknown to all others and thus does not have to blush in front of anyone.' Here the masses appear as the asylum that shields an asocial person. Of all the menacing aspects of the masses, this one became apparent first. It is the origin of the detective story" (1983, 40).

Το θύμα θα μεταναστεύει διαρκώς: στο λίκνο νήπιου ηγεμόνος ή στο ξέφωτο, εκεί που μακελεύουν τον φυγάδα, στο άντρο των συμμοριτών, στους πατριώτες που τρυγούν κλεμμένο αμάξι στη χαράδρα, στη μυστική ετοιμασία του εκδικητή, στα φώτα πόλης, εκθαμβωτικά ύστερα από ετών συσκότιση, ...

(44)

The victim will always be on the move: to the infant ruler's crib or the clearing with the butchered fugitive, to the robbers' den, the ravine where patriots loot a stolen carriage, to the avenger's secret preparation, to city lights that dazzle after years of black-out, ...

The poem then ends by connecting the issue of multiple persons and places with the murdered victim in numerous disguises, on the move:

από παντού, με πολλαπλές μεταμφιέσεις θα περνά, συστασιώτης, εραστής και ποντοπόρος, πανούργος κάπελας, αιχμάλωτος ανιχνευτής, με δανεικές ζωές ακόμη.

(44)

he'll travel all over under various disguises, fellow-conspirator, lover and seafarer, wily innkeeper, captive explorer, with borrowed lives to spare.

This manifesto of unassignability and infinite digression is as much about reading as it is about writing. As we have seen, one group of images in the *Tales* charts the vertical movement from the depths to the surface, and another charts the horizontal movement from behind the page to in front of the page. The first group gives us information about the relation that the violence has to the inhibiting of speech or writing and examines where the violence is perpetrated; the second tells us how the reader is implicated. Setting the two groups against each other, as the penultimate tale about the beggar and the geometer suggests (45), it becomes clear that the speaking subject has been killed by her own language but that the death is not quite suicide because it only happens if the reader reorganizes the images. Reading, it turns out, is what makes the indeterminacy of writing possible.

In the last section I used Poe's detective story to foreground the deconstructive logic of the letter that appears at the end of Mastoraki's *Tales* and its implications for a less permanent kind of writing, but I want to conclude by following its cues about the importance of the reader. In an interview Mastoraki discussed choosing the Vizyenos passage as an epigraph: "*Tales* was already done when I reread Vizyenos, and I put in that little passage ... I never do that. ... But I suddenly felt that all of me came from inside there ... it was the key to the decoding of the *Tales* ... about the murderer who returns to the scene of the crime ... that phrase referred to me" (1987). In her account, literary influence is not about overcoming one's predecessors but about turning oneself in. The call for forgiveness at the end—"and you must feel for him, above all feel for him, my dear Arthur or Alphonse"—recognizes that these references to other texts only serve to implicate the author further. But, tellingly, it is the author *as reader* who admits culpability. It is in *reading* Vizyenos that she recognizes herself as murderer and thief and her text as the scene of the crime. But just as I am about to point the finger and make her the reader—that is, (as Derrida would say) to narrate the arrival of a letter—I find myself implicated in the text. It is *my* reading, after all, that has been equally instrumental in creating the place where terrible things happen; it is my reading that has dredged up the corpses and purloined letters. The "you" of Vizyenos's "What coincidence brings you to the house of the murderer?" momentarily affixes itself to the author, only to come loose and stick to each subsequent reader. If we feel for the thief, buried deep in his bed, it is because, in the end, we too have no alibi for our presence at the scene of the crime, no excuse for why we insist on filling in the blank with our own reading.

Here and there in this chapter I have posed questions about the feminist ramifications of *Tales*. In my discussion of Bloom's theory of literary influence I raised the question about whether the different relation to literary influence proposed in *Tales* might have something to do with the fact that Bloom's poet-son is, in our case, a daughter.[47] Johnson's reading of Poe raises a similar issue: might her reading differ from Lacan's and Derrida's in its willingness to admit that it never had the kind of authority they try to relinquish? Might writing from the feminine subject position further deconstruct the assumptions of Derrida's postcard, addressed as it is to a woman?[48] Though Johnson does not treat these questions in her piece on Poe, she does so in the more recent *A World of Difference* (1989). Here she expands the terms of deconstruction to include the politics of race, gender, and class and shows how feminism gave her a different take on the fraternal rivalry and masculine logic of the purloined letter. In *Tales* the purloined letter also invites me to fill in the blank, to reread and rewrite Mastoraki's text. In following Johnson, I can begin to formulate a response by implicating myself not only as a reader but as a woman reader.

Reading Mastoraki's poetry as a woman turns her poetry into women's writing. From Mastoraki's first book, *Tolls,* the poet's ability to write can be connected to her position as a woman. The four walls of jail and of the home under curfew to which resistance writers refer have a double mean-

[47] For other examples of how women's writing challenges Bloom's theory, see Gilbert and Gubar 1979, 46–53.
[48] Spivak's work is, among other things, a feminist response to Derrida; see esp. 1983, where she asks whether the double displacement of the feminine subject position suggests alternative writing strategies, and her 1989 elaboration.

ing for women writers: they are also the four walls of the domestic space.[49] Her "song" is shaped by both these experiences of incarceration:

> Τούτη η σιωπή που την ανάθρεψα
> μέσα στους τέσσερις τοίχους
> ήτανε από νωρίς προορισμένη
> να γίνει τραγούδι.
>
> (1972, 26)

> This silence which I nurtured
> within four walls
> was destined early on
> to become a song.

Rather than rejecting the claustrophobic domestic sphere and inscribing her poetry in the realm of production, Mastoraki transforms domestic work into a "productive" activity, making it a metaphor for her writing. She likens her song to her mother's apron pocket, in which she places the economic power of the daily wage:

> Τραγούδι βαθύ και σκοτεινό
> σαν τ᾽ αμίλητο νερό
> και σαν την τσέπη της ποδιάς
> της μάνας μου.
> Να δώσει καθενός το μερτικό του.
>
> (26)

> Song deep and dark
> like speechless water
> and like the pocket
> of my mother's apron
> To give to each their daily wage.

Halima's storytelling in *Kin* serves a similar function. Women's "natural" talents are used to very different ends. Like Galanaki, Mastoraki challenges certain assumptions about women's poetry by turning feminine sexuality and reproduction into production.

But it is in *Tales* where the reader's role is so important that writing becomes formally associated with the feminine subject position. By tracing the hidden roads between poems in *Tales*, between different collections,

---

[49] On how writing is affected by the four walls of jail, see Mangakis 1984. For an evocative portrayal of the claustrophobia of the domestic sphere, see Katy Drosou's collection of poetry Οι τοίχοι τέσσερις (The four walls) (1985).

and between her collections and other discourses, it is possible to view woman's violated body—her speechlessness, her bruises, the blood on her underwear—as actually heralding writing. No one is immune to the terrible things that happen in *Tales,* but more often than not women are the victims. It is on *her* metaphorical body, whether the beggar's or someone else's, that wounds bloom and that the exhibition of prohibition creates a surface on which to write. As with Galanaki's pregnant woman, it is the female body that figures a new kind of writing. Galanaki's early epigrams that conceal the truth from specific censors and Mastoraki's earlier explicit discussions of censorship give way in their visual narratives of the 1980s to metonymic sequences that constantly displace meaning and connect censorship to the experience of writing as woman.

In conclusion, through a reading that loses the letter, defers conclusion, and multiplies options, it is possible to view Mastoraki's text as an alternative writing style to traditional modes, whether modernist poems or detective tales with their emphasis on whodunit. Though the deferral of signification and the prominence of metonymy in her poetry is not radically new, what is noteworthy is the way such strategies are sustained and implicated in larger cultural trends. Like the unborn child in *The Cake,* the purloined letter in *Tales* signals a shift in Greek poetry whereby the surrealist appeal to the feminine and to the irrational as a poetic reservoir is reinscribed as the material practice of everyday life. In the context of a new willingness on the part of feminism and the Left more generally to relate the mechanisms of oppression and repression, the public and the private, *Tales* draws on the activity of the unconscious, the dreamwork, with its intricate poetics of censorship, as a political model for rethinking causality and determination in her writing. By rewriting the experiences of censorship in terms of the emotional terrain of private misunderstandings, *Tales* offers deferral and indirectness as political intervention. In this chapter, by giving feminism a role in Mastoraki's work, I can provide a link between her early and later poems, and a politics for her continued hermeticism. Writing as a woman is often only possible after one has been read as a woman.

6

Maria Laina's *Hers* and the Unreciprocated Look

άλλωστε στην αφήγηση αυτή
φαίνεται η αδυναμία
να βρεθεί ένας χώρος

besides in this narrative
the difficulty
of finding a space is clear
—Maria Laina

I have analyzed the ways in which women's poetry has reacted to, made use of, and appropriated censorship as a matrix for poetic innovation since the fall of the dictatorship in 1974, and I have isolated two key collections of poetry which allowed me to show a change in the relationship between censorship and poetry. Through Galanaki's *The Cake* and Mastoraki's *Tales of the Deep* I have traced a larger, primarily feminist, paradigm shift whereby the disciplinary and normative workings of censorship are seen as extending into all spheres of life, especially into what had previously been considered the private sphere of women's lives. With the work of Maria Laina, I can now show how this understanding of censorship as both restrictive and productive of discourse and behavior is then applied to the very core of how subject formation is modeled, to the look of love, the specular confirmation sought in another.

Galanaki's and Mastoraki's generalized model of censorship emphasizes the interruptions and incompletions involved in making sense. In Galanaki's *The Cake* and Mastoraki's *Tales*, deferral and displacement were enacted in the overarching tropes of the undelivered child and the letter. Metonymy was not only thematically important to these collections but formally constitutive. By never giving birth, the mother and, by analogy, the mother tongue were not restricted to one role and could embody a plethora of functions; and by never delivering the letter, meaning was deferred and the reader implicated in its peregrinations. Laina's poetry also takes up metonymy as a mode of circumventing social censure and involving the reader. The simple, laconic phrases of *Hers* create and comment on the gap between what we *mean* and what we *say* in a fashion very different from the more excessive manner of Galanaki's and Mastoraki's texts, but here too the deferral of the desired object emphasizes process over product and exposes the page as the only place certain connections can be made. In *Hers,* instead of the child or the letter, it is the look of the other that is always just out of reach.

In Laina's poetry, however, the concept of censorship relates less clearly to the experience of censorship under the colonels. From the beginning her poetry situates itself outside the sphere of leftist politics and resistance. Whereas Galanaki's first poem, though elliptic, is about the plight of Greece and came out in a resistance journal, and whereas Mastoraki's first collection, *Tolls,* is about censorship and has a picture of a toll receipt written in the oppressors' purist Greek on the cover, Laina's first two collections, *Coming of Age* (1968) and *Beyond* (1970), are concerned with metaphysical questions of love and death and make no reference to the dictatorship.[1] Censorship in Laina's poetry is rooted in a lack of recognition which inhibits the possibility of articulation, not in some external force that alters something already articulated. It denies agency not by rewriting one's words but by blankly ignoring the possibility that one has words. It is only in the 1980s that the brutal privateness of Laina's poetry finds an analogue in Galanaki's and Mastoraki's poetry and the projects of these three poets converge. Women poets have not become less political; instead the political itself has been redefined by and through women's poetry. The private sphere of personal relations, language acquisition, and identity formation, which Laina explores from her early poetry on, has become a national concern.

Born in 1947 in Patras, Maria Laina is widely regarded as one of the best writers of her generation. Her collection *Rose Fear* (1992) received the National Prize for Poetry in 1994, and her theatrical pieces have been important events in Athenian intellectual life.[2] I concentrate on the collections leading up to *Rose Fear,* in particular *Hers* (1985a), though, because it is their search for "a place of her own," a place that is "hers," which, one could argue, enables the public acceptance of her more recent work.[3] The

---

[1] In her third collection Αλλαγή τοπίου (Change of scene) (1975), in the first section, "Τα πουλιά" (The birds), Laina tentatively attempts a more explicitly political poetry, drawing on the rhetoric of the times. There are apparent references to the Christian dictum Papadopoulos appropriated, Love your neighbor as you love yourself (7) and to Papadopoulos's desire for order (8) and assurances of peace (15). But in this collection too the experiment is short-lived and the sequence is, on the whole, more productively read as writing as a lesbian than as writing under an authoritarian regime. The dead birds alluded to in these poems are not a general symbol of compromised freedom; rather, they draw on a particular lesbian experience. In one poem the birds' blood is the sand between her legs as she makes love (11); a few poems later, it has become the small, black signs of a new kind of writing (15).

[2] I do not address Laina's dramatic pieces Ο κλόουν (The clown) (1985b) and Η πραγματικότητα είναι πάντα εδώ (Reality is always here) (1990), though the latter with its female protagonist and minimalism is closely connected to *Hers* and could be fruitfully read in relation to it.

[3] *Hers* raises questions about writing as a woman which *Rose Fear* takes for granted. In *Rose*

central problem in Laina's poetry seems to be how to come to grips with a look that censors by ignoring her, how to describe a woman who, as she explained in an interview, "βρίσκεται σε ασυμφωνία με το περιβάλλον της" (finds herself at odds with her environment) (1987), how to find a way to talk about a kind of love that others neither recognize nor approve of, a love that is "strange" (1970, 17), and "awkward" (1985a, 20). Whereas Galanaki and Mastoraki define feminine sexuality in relation to the opposite sex, Laina hardly ever mentions men. The love she wants to describe, at times lesbian, at other times autoerotic or narcissistic, or nonexistent, is never heterosexual and therefore never socially acceptable. Repeatedly her inability to find a place that is hers is connected to the absence of any support for her kind of loving. As the introductory poem of *Hers* explains, "Λείπει το έδαφος του έρωτα" (The ground of love is missing) (1985a, 9).[4] Like Galanaki's *The Cake* and Mastoraki's *Tales,* Laina's *Hers* is a pivotal piece that lets me analyze the relations among censorship, gender, and poetry in the 1980s and to construct another map of postdictatorship Greek culture.

Laina's concern with the unreciprocated look and the difficulty of finding a space of her own ties in to feminist debates in Greece and abroad since the 1960s regarding the question of censorship and the patriarchal gaze. Before addressing Laina's particular contribution in *Hers,* and its more explicit elaboration of Galanaki's and Mastoraki's position in *The Cake* and *Tales,* let me outline the broader context. In 1982 the poet and critic Katerina Anghelaki-Rooke introduced a collection of translations titled *Ten Women Poets of Greece* (including Mastoraki's and Laina's poetry) by stating that women have been more severely objectified than men (Siotis 1982, 7). She then quoted a longer version of the following passage from John Berger's *Ways of Seeing,* a materialist critique of art history, which drew on British and American feminist thought and had just been translated into Greek: "To be born a woman has been to be born, within an allotted and confined space, into the keeping of men. The social presence of women has developed as a result of their ingenuity in living under such tutelage within such limited space. But this has been at the cost of a woman's self being split into two. . . . Men look at women. Women watch themselves being looked at" (Berger 1972, 46–47). In doing so she continued a line of argument put forth by previous generations of Greek women poets such as Zoë Karelli in her poem "Η Άνθρωπος" (Man, femi-

---

Fear, the writer is the ungendered "poet," and finding a space for writing is not an issue, but given: "Τι είδους μοναξιά χρειάζεται ο ποιητής / άσπρο στο άσπρο του μυαλού του η σελίδα" (What kind of solitude does a poet need / the page, white on the white of his mind) (1992, 7).

[4] In Greek the word έρωτας refers to erotic love but is not limited to this sense. It is, therefore, often translated more broadly as "love."

nine gender) (in 1957, 61–62) and Kiki Dimoula in "Σημείο Αναγνωρίσεως" (Mark of recognition) (in 1971, 42). In both widely anthologized poems, woman is the sex traditionally under surveillance, captive, his. In her essay Anghelaki-Rooke explores how contemporary Greek women poets negoti- ate this subordination and self-division and come up with their own em- bodied way of seeing. She concludes optimistically: "Young women poets today have through their craft and their consciousness been able to con- ceive of an image of the woman to come. As a complete being, containing and contained, acting and acted upon and not as a half-entity where the one half is desperately looking for the other half which is always situated somewhere outside herself" (in Siotis 1982, 16).

Ioanna Zervou, another of the poets whom Anghelaki-Rooke intro- duced in the same anthology, also stresses the importance of a newly born woman free from surveillance in "Το κορμί και ο λόγος" (The body and the word) (1981), though she relies more on the work of French feminists than on British or American.[5] Rather than attempt to appropriate the gaze, the suggestion is that women should draw on their different relation to it. They should rewrite the myth and history of patriarchy by writing the body. Zervou's own 1978 collection of poetry Ίχνη (Traces) is a nuanced explora- tion of this trajectory beginning with poems such as "Ο βασιλιάς-φαλλός" (The king-phallus) (15), in which the feminine subject cannot speak but is spoken, cannot write but is written, and concluding with poems such as the title poem "Traces," in which a new mother tongue emerges from the breath, hair, and womb of the female body (45).

Clearly this project of embodied writing that Anghelaki-Rooke and Zer- vou describe is one direction contemporary Greek women's poetry has taken, one of which Anghelaki-Rooke's own poetry is perhaps the best and most sustained example.[6] But in Galanaki's, and even more so in Mas- toraki's or Laina's, narratives of the 1980s, another response to the censor- ship of the gaze is apparent. As opposed to the emphasis on retrieving the subject's wholeness, the subject in their poetry is shattered.[7] Writing is not

[5] French feminists discuss the gaze in their theories of "écriture féminine." They contrast women's materiality with the disembodiment associated with the male gaze. See esp. Irigaray 1985b, 23–33, esp. 25–26, and Cixous 1976, 877n. On concepts such as "écriture féminine," "writing the body," and "newly born woman," see Jones 1986. For a comparison of French and American feminisms in the 1970s, see Marks and Courtivron 1981, ix–xiii.

[6] Anghelaki-Rooke comes back to the issue of the body repeatedly in her poetry and even titles her selected poems Όταν το σώμα (When the body) (1988). On her conception of the body, see her collection Μαγδαληνή το μεγάλο θηλαστικό (Magdalene, the vast mammal) with its epigraph from Seferis, "Κατά βάθος ο ποιητής έχει ένα θέμα: το ζωντανό σώμα του" (At bottom the poet has one topic: his own living body), and her often anthologized poem "Το σώμα είναι η νίκη και η ήττα των ονείρων" (The body is the triumph and the defeat of dreams) (1974, 27). On the role of the body in the poetry of Anghelaki-Rooke and Sylvia Plath, see Bohandy 1994.

[7] The contrast I am making finds a useful analogy in the work of contemporary Irish

a therapeutic act of reassembling the pieces but a complicitous practice of disintegration. In psychoanalytic terms, the former and latter positions might respectively be allied with object relations theory and a more Lacanian approach.[8] For Lacan the shattering effect of the gaze is not something one can do without or remedy. Indeed, wholeness is always already an illusion. In his influential essay "Le stade du miroir" (The mirror stage) (1977, 1–7), he analyzes the infant's misrecognition (*méconnaissance*) of himself-as-coordinated-whole as the founding moment of the ego. Unable even to stand on his own, the six-month infantile bundle of turbulent movements held in front of the mirror is anything but intact or in control. For Lacan it is the disjuncture between what the infant sees and what he is that is crucial. The point is that the mother or the *trotte-bébé* holding the child in place, as well as the mirror itself, all get in the way, mess up the ideal, and that it is this instance of disintegration that is formative.[9] In his analysis, then, the censorship of the gaze cannot be ameliorated by any loving look but represents the fundamental lack all looks involve.[10] Lacan introduces a temporal sense to the more obvious spatial claustrophobia of the gaze: it is what always already lies in wait for us (1991, 224); it is "presented to us only in the form of a strange contingency, symbolic of

women poets. Eavan Boland's poetry takes a line similar to Katerina Anghelaki-Rooke's with regard to the gaze, myth, and the male tradition, and the work of Medbh McGuckian with its elliptic private language is much closer to that of the poets I address. For a comparison of Boland's and McGuckian's work, see Wills 1993, chap. 2.

[8] Feminist theorists have been influenced by and have reworked both positions. By "object relations theory" I mean the broad spectrum of work done in the wake of psychoanalysts such as Melanie Klein and D. W. Winnicott which gives priority to intersubjective relations between self and other (i.e., the importance of bonding with the mother) over the intrapsychic theory of the unconscious. See esp. Chodorow 1978, Dinnerstein 1976, and J. Benjamin 1988. For an analysis of mothering in Greece which draws on this body of literature, see Christea-Doumani 1983. By "Lacanian approach" I mean the return to early Freud initiated by Jacques Lacan. On Lacan on subject formation, see Silverman 1983, 126–93. Lacan's position, in particular his views on the gaze, has been important to feminist film theorists. See, e.g., the debate in the British film journal *Screen*, esp. Laura Mulvey, "Visual Pleasure and Narrative Cinema" (1975) and her "Afterthought" (1981), both republished in her 1989 collection, as well as E. Ann Kaplan's response "Is the Gaze Male?" (1983) and de Lauretis, "Rethinking Women's Cinema" (in 1987, 127–48).

[9] The difference between Lacan's position and that of object relations theorists is neatly illustrated in Winnicott, "Mirror-Role of Mother and Family in Child Development" (1991, 111–18), a response to Lacan's "The Mirror Stage." Whereas Lacan's essay insists that the mother is just another prop, Winnicott gives her a much more important role by inscribing the face of the mother as the precursor of the mirror. Jacqueline Rose poses the Lacanian difference this way: "The mother does not (as in D. W. Winnicott's account) mirror the child itself, she grants an image to the child, which her presence instantly deflects" (1986, 53).

[10] Lacan distinguishes between the gaze and the look much the way he separates the meaning of the phallus from that of the penis. The gaze and the phallus, on the one hand, are resources of cultural power and do not adhere to any one body. The look, like the penis, on the other hand, belongs to specific bodies. In other words, the gaze surrounds us, whereas the look emanates from a particular source. For a clear exposition of this distinction, see Silverman's discussion of Fassbinder's film: "Ali: Fear Eats the Soul" (1992, 125–56).

what we find on the horizon, as the thrust of our experience" (1986, 72–73). Its all-pervasiveness has to do with its evasiveness; it is that which "slips, passes, is transmitted" (73). In keeping with this account of subjectivity, Galanaki, Mastoraki, and Laina, are not looking for a place beyond the patriarchal gaze where they might be whole again—an ancient matriarchy or a future utopia—but instead seem set on exhibiting the spaces available in the midst of its criss-crossing trajectories.[11]

The nature of this shattered and decentered writing position becomes clearer if we look briefly at the relation of the gaze to censorship in the poetry collections already analyzed. In one poem in *The Cake* the slippage Lacan associates with the gaze is acted out in a series of metamorphoses: the eyeball becomes a mouse, then a spermatozoon, an aborted fetus, and finally a mouse again, which is flung into the street (Galanaki 1980, 38). Its disembodiment, like Ritsos's glass eye, which the woman picks up in the poem "Tangible Proof," allows it to be redeployed to other ends. In *Tales*, too, the disabled eyes become the site of a different kind of vision. Like Galanaki's grotesque eyeball, the eye in Mastoraki's poems is irritated, sore (1983b, 16). The word for wounds, "λαβωματιές," in one poem contains the word for looks or glances, "ματιές," and in the next stanza the connection suggested by this compound word materializes: a nail is inserted into the eye (19). In both Galanaki's and Mastoraki's texts, the eyes continue to function in spite of infirmity. The wounded eye in *Tales*, for example, ultimately supports an alternative way of seeing. It is from the nail in the eye that a picture is hung (19). The aim of these texts is not to heal or seal over the effects of the censoring gaze but to adopt the wounded, fragmented subject as a position from which to write. Deferral and displacement create a space that, though not "outside" patriarchal systems of meaning, is not fully within their control either.

Of the three women poets whose work I examine in detail, Laina most explicitly addresses the problem of the gaze. In taking the look of love as

[11] Galanaki's, Mastoraki's, and Laina's decentered subject-position could also be usefully explored in terms of Foucault's analysis of the gaze. In *Discipline and Punish* (1977a) in his discussion of the Panopticon, Bentham's ideal prison, he emphasizes the impossibility of disengaging oneself from the gaze. Surveillance is not something one can get "outside of." Since the 1980s a growing number of feminists have used Foucault to show how women participate in the discursive production of the male gaze. One example is Frigga Haug and her collective's "memory-work" project, which I mentioned in Chapter 3. In *Female Sexualization* (1987), she and her collaborators exhibit their coimplication in their socialization. The titles of their chapters suggest the fragmented body they inhabit: "The Hair Project," "The Leg Project." In the American context, the controversial 1982 Barnard conference that addressed alternative sexual practices such as lesbian S/M charted a shift to a more self-implicating reading of the male gaze; see Vance 1984 as well as the minutes of the planning committee and other memorabilia collected in Vance 1983. This is a move parallel to the one outlined in n. 8 with regard to feminist film theory after Lacan.

the deferred object par excellence, *Hers* can be read as an attempt to re-define subjectivity in Lacanian terms.[12] Repeatedly in her poetry specular imagery—the mirror, Narcissus, the mother's face, the lover's smile—serves to frustrate and split rather than consolidate the self. But whereas in her early collections, in particular *Beyond,* there is an attempt to put the halves back together, in her later collections the shattering effect of the gaze is viewed with less regret. The Cartesian view of the self as a unified, knowing subject is no longer definitive. In *Hers* another model of the subject has taken over, one that acknowledges a fundamental lack of cohesion. Laina's protagonist finally finds a place for herself where the unreciprocated look is not debilitating but just the existing state of affairs. The ego ideal, the mirror image she has striven to live up to, is worn thin, frayed, reduced to a tain, and this very texture of illusion has become the ground of an alternative kind of subjectivity and writing.

Before examining *Hers* in depth, however, I want to trace the function of the look in Laina's early work. I am interested not only in how a different model of subject formation takes hold in her later work but also in the material reworking of this model in the Greek context, how the censorship of the unreciprocated look is reproduced as an evasive typography.[13] The title of my first section, "The Look of Censorship," refers both to the specular moment of unrequited love, the censored look, and to the materiality of this process—the way it structures a relationship between the look of the reader and the look of the text. Whereas *Tales* made a significant formal departure from Mastoraki's previous volume, in Laina's case we find that the visual narrative of *Hers* is already initiated in *Change of Scene* and Σημεία στίξεως (Punctuation marks), her collections written in the 1970s. I therefore spend considerable time discussing these collections in the first section. In the other two sections I apply the double sense of the look of censorship to *Hers,* first reading it for the kind of writing subject the censored look engenders and, second, for the visual narrative this censored look then entails. Although I divide my discussion of *Hers* into two parts, the interrelation of the unreciprocated look and the look of the text should

---

[12] Love poetry more generally lends itself to a Lacanian analysis because the lyric tradition usually insists on an I who is looking for confirmation in the thou. On love poetry and the mirror stage, see Montefiore 1987, 97–134. See also Collecott 1986 for a comparative discussion of mirror images in the poetry of Sylvia Plath, Adrienne Rich, Denise Levertov, and H.D. informed by Lacan and Irigaray.

[13] In the case of Laina, I only occasionally refer to anything that could be called concrete poetry. I am more interested in the typography of the unconscious such as that which Jean Starobinski (1979) uncovers in his work on Saussure or Gaston Bachelard (1964) and Maurice Blanchot (1982) theorize more generally. Nonetheless, my discussion of the look of her poetry does owe something to accounts of typographically experimental poetry such as Drucker 1994, Janecek 1984, and Sayre 1983.

by this point be clear: the challenge of *Hers* is to structure the reader's gaze so that the deferred reciprocation of the look becomes the physical space that writing occupies, creating, in the end, a place that is hers, "δικό της."

The Look of Censorship

In Laina's early collection *Beyond,* it is clear that the kind of love the narrator wants is inaccessible and unacceptable: "Κάτι μοιάζει με έγκλημα στον τρόπο που μ' αγάπησες" (Something about the way you loved me resembles a crime) (1970, 16). What troubles her is not the transgression, though, but the fact that the woman, the object of desire and the excuse for the crime, has left her:

> Κι ήταν μια πράξη αφοσίωσης που μ' άφησες. Όμως εγώ, χτυπημένη απ' το ακαριαίο σου χαμόγελο, ένα ολόκληρο, ανώφελο καλοκαίρι κατοικώ την ερήμωσή μου και σε ικετεύω να μ' αγαπήσεις πάλι μ' αυτό τον τρόπο που μοιάζει με έγκλημα.
>
> (16)

it was an act of devotion that you left me. I, however, beaten by your instantaneous smile, one whole useless summer, inhabit my desolation and beg of you to love me again in that way that resembles a crime.

The problem is that the lover's smile of recognition is instantaneous, unretrievable. Whereas in her later collections, censorship, fragmentation, and loss become the conditions of love, in *Beyond,* all efforts are made to find the lost object and make the divided subject whole.

The narrator, incapacitated by another woman's absence, first and foremost her mother's, to whom these poems are dedicated, demands a justification. In one poem, addressing her in the terms Winnicott suggests, as the precursor of the mirror, she implores:[14]

> Δικαιολογήσου για την απροειδοποίητη ημέρα
> που 'φυγες με τον τρόπο που γλυστρούν οι χιονοδρόμοι
> από τα μέρη που συνήθισαν στα ίχνη τους.
> Μεγάλη φίλη, που καθρέφτιζες το πρόσωπό μου . . .
>
> (30)

> Find an excuse for the day you left
> without warning the way skiers glide away
> from places used to their tracks.
> Older friend, who mirrored my face . . .

[14] See n. 9.

But whether in the mother's face or the lover's smile, the look of confirmation is nowhere to be found; the "other" is self-consumed and absent:

Σήμερα, ή έστω αύριο, μια απ᾽ αυτές τις νύχτες τελοσπάντων, θα με καταπιεί το κάτω πάτωμα και συ δε θα καταλάβεις τίποτα από το έγκλημα στις πρωινές εφημερίδες. Μόνο θα κοιταχτείς στον καθρέφτη και θα περηφανευτείς για την ομορφιά σου.

(33)

Today, or even tomorrow, in any case one of these nights, the downstairs will swallow me and you will not notice a thing when the crime is written up in the morning newspapers. You will just look at yourself in the mirror and admire your own beauty.

The other's narcissism leaves the narrator unable to love herself. The mythical figure Narcissus, in one poem in this collection, is tellingly both someone who "was never loved" and someone who "was never able to love himself"—in Greek the passive and reflexive senses of the verb have the same form: Ο Νάρκισσος ποτέ δεν αγαπήθηκε (24). The persistent question in this collection is how to get "beyond" the crippling effect of the unreciprocated look. Rather than imagining the self differently, *Beyond* is caught in the illusion of a possible wholeness, as if there were an origin to which one could return. The collection ends with an oddly unsubstantiated confidence that the narcissism of the mother and the mirror can be exchanged for the functional self-reflexivity of the boomerang. Finally the narrator will be able to replace the lost smile with her own: "Θα ξέρω ακριβώς πώς λειτουργεί το μπούμεραγκ και θα χαμογελώ!" (I will know exactly how the boomerang works and I will smile!) (44).[15]

This optimism, however, is short-lived, and a very different response to the unreciprocated look is worked out in Laina's next collection. In *Change of Scene* the sense is not of transcendence but of working within the restrictions of the censoring look. The poem "Συνάρτηση όρων" (Interrelation of terms) maps out this shift—from a rejection of the male gaze, to a venera-

[15] It would also be interesting to explore the specifically lesbian reworking of the gaze with regard to the mother-daughter relationship in Laina's *Beyond* by comparing it to Karapanou's heterosexual version in *Kassandra and the Wolf*. Both texts are so markedly structured by the mother's look away. Karapanou's novel begins: "I was born at dusk, hour of the wolf, July, under the sign of Cancer. When they brought me to her, she turned her face to the wall" (1976, 3). In this respect Judith Roof's (1991) comparison of Kristeva's and Chodorow's heterosexual narratives of mothering with Rita Mae Brown's and Jane Rule's lesbian accounts would be particularly useful. To what extent do the two parables she introduces work for the Greek scene—the heterosexual one, in which the mother of "this is not for you" becomes "this was once for you," and the more ambiguous lesbian one in which "the mother is both there and not, sighted but always out of reach" (91)?

tion of the body, to a more complicated, self-implicating reworking of the gaze. In the epigraph to the poem the eyes are first dismissed as useless:

> Τα μάτια μας δεν είναι
> παρά για να μας γνωρίζουν οι άλλοι
> και κανένας δε βλέπει τους τυφλούς
> (1975, 35)

> *Our eyes are only*
> *so that others will recognize us*
> *and no one sees the blind*

But then blindness is understood to encourage a more material relation to the world. It enables women to bring the body into play. The first two lines of the epigraph are repeated with a different conclusion:

> Τα μάτια μας δεν είναι
> παρά για να μας γνωρίζουν οι άλλοι
> εμείς μ' άλλα μάτια κοιτάζουμε
> μοιράζουμε τον κόσμο μ' άλλους άξονες
> απλούστερους
> και τις περσότερες φορές
> εξασφαλίζουμε την ίδια απόσταση
> ψάχνοντας με τα χέρια.
> (35)

> Our eyes are only
> so that others will recognize us
> we look with different eyes
> we divide the world with other
> simpler axes
> and most of the time
> we secure the same distance
> searching with hands.

But ultimately touch is not privileged over vision. The poem continues and, as we have seen in Galanaki's and Mastoraki's later collections, suggests that disability might provide another way of seeing. In the final lines, the blind eyes become a darkroom for developing a different view of the world:

> Μες στους θαλάμους των ματιών μας
> αγνώριστα υγρά

περίεργες φωτογραφίες εμφανίζουν.
Μες από μας υπάρχουν τα πράγματα
αδυνατίζοντας το χρώμα της σκιάς μας.

(35)

In the chambers of our eyes
unrecognizably fluid
strange photographs develop.
Inside of us things exist
weakening the color of our shadow.

The italicized epigraph, which announces the failure of the gaze—"our eyes are only / so that others will recognize us"—"develops" into something else when it is internalized in the body of the poem. Deferral and displacement in form and content enable a different way of seeing, a way that ultimately changes how others see us, rendering our borders less distinct by "weakening the color of our shadow."

In *Beyond* the unreciprocated look is confined to the level of content, not internalized as a textual problem that also involves the reader. The shift in *Change of Scene* is striking: all the relationships that were structured in terms of external references in *Beyond* suddenly happen on the page, intratextually. Instead of quoting an intertext such as Psalms as *Beyond* does, *Change of Scene* quotes itself and relies on the reader to make the connection. In Chapter 3 I discussed the way Karapanou's Kassandra parodied the General's self-satisfaction at seeing his own image in his portrait. Kassandra first imitates his glee—"There I am"—and then points out that his reflection is imperfect; his glee is only possible if he ignores the tiny holes in the canvas. Kassandra undoes his infantile captivation with his own reflection by insisting that the relationship between *what you see* and *what is there* is not immediate but mediated by the materiality of whatever is used to create the illusion, in this case the painting's canvas. By drawing attention to the materiality of the text, *Change of Scene* takes a similar stance. The confirmation the protagonist of *Beyond* sought is impossible: something—the mother, the canvas, the page—always gets in the way.

This understanding of the self as a function of misrecognition engenders a different way of loving and writing. In *Change of Scene,* finding a way to love and a way to write about this love are intimately connected to a continuously shifting self. The title of the poem "Τροπικός" (Tropical) refers both to the "wet and red place" of lovemaking and to a writing that is full of tropes.[16] The title's double meaning relates the act of lovemaking to the act of writing about lovemaking. What both meanings of "tropical"

---

[16] In Greek the word τροπικός has both these meanings, although the first is by far the most common.

(deriving from the ancient Greek τρέπω, to turn) have in common is their dependence on a spatial relationship. In the first meaning, the adjective *tropical* has to do with a place's position vis-à-vis the turning sun, and in the second, it has to do with "turning a phrase," saying "this is like this," or "this is a part of this." Such turns are also enacted typographically in this poem. In response to the question "Στάση ή κίνηση είναι ο φόβος; ᾿Εξω ή μέσα;" (Is fear stillness or motion? Outside or inside?), the poem answers by turning back to the previous poem:

> Ανάμεσα στα πόδια μου τρέχουν
> μικρές σταγόνες άμμος
> το αίμα των πουλιών.
> (1975, 11)

> Between my legs run
> small drops of sand
> the blood of birds.

Though the blood is in motion here, the poem recalls the bird's blood in the previous poem, which was still:

> όταν θυμάσαι
> το αίμα των πουλιών
> δε στάζει
> στέκεται όπως μνήμη
> πάνω σ᾿ ένα πρόσωπο
> ξεχασμένο
> (10)

> when you remember
> the blood of birds
> stops dripping
> it stays in one place
> like memory
> on a forgotten face

Lovemaking and writing in this poem are about generating ambivalence, not securing answers. The unstable self engenders an unstable kind of writing. The importance of the page as a place in this collection is suggested repeatedly by the fact that certain lines require the reader to make a spatial connection with lines from across the page. "Tropical" is both the exotic place between her legs *and* the place of tropes that is the page. The conflation of feminine body and text suggests that there is something feminine about this shifting meaning and shifting typographic text; yet this is not the healing kind of writing the body which Anghelaki-Rooke imagines. No two halves have come together. The image of woman conceived here is not a complete being.

Another poem in *Change of Scene* dramatically calls attention to the fact that the movement and spatial relations described often refer to the poem on the page and that this poetics of shifting is feminine. Its title, "Μετατόπιση" (Displacement), refers both to the narrator's movement in space and self-referentially to the shifting of an earlier poem into the center of this one. The poem begins:

> Αν θέλω να φχαριστηθώ μεγάλους χώρους
> γυρεύω ένα διάστημα ανάστροφο
> μπροστά μου επιτρέπουν μόνο μια στιγμή κάθε φορά.
>
> > (24)

> If I want to enjoy big spaces
> I look for an inverted dimension
> in front I'm only allowed one moment at a time.

It then continues by taking a portion from an earlier poem (20), slightly expanded and repeating it in italics, in "an inverted dimension." The displacement and inversion of one text into another is granted the materiality of a pregnancy, and birth is placed in the narrator's own hands:

> Απ᾿ την κοιλιά μου ξετυλίγεται ο αφαλός που μ᾿ έκλεινε
> αυτή τη φορά θα γεννηθώ από μένα.
>
> > (25)

> From my belly the umbilical cord which locked me in unwinds
> this time I will give birth to myself.

In the poem "Συνουσία" (Intercourse) the body and the text are again confused. The typographic division of the text, by printing every other line in italics, once again connects the act of lovemaking with the act of writing and reading poetry. One time the regular print describes the act of writing and reading poetry—"Κόβοντας την συνέχεια σ᾿ αρχές" (Cutting the continuation into beginnings)—and the italics describe the act of lovemaking—"κλωστή σε σύντομες ανάσες" (thread in short breaths)—but in the next two lines the opposite is true, "with the head in the position of the feet" in regular type and "upside down enjambment" in italics and so forth:

Κόβοντας την συνέχεια σ' αρχές
κλωστή σε σύντομες ανάσες
Με το κεφάλι στων ποδιών τη θέση
ανάποδος διασκελισμός
Και δάχτυλα που δε μετρούν
αμέτρητες αφές
(29)

Cutting the continuation into beginnings
thread in short breaths
With the head in the position of the feet
upside down enjambment
And the fingers that do not count
uncountable touches

In all the cases I have just mentioned, in order for the poem to work, the reader must be willing to see the typographic shifts. In the poem titled "Παραλλαγές" (Variations), the reader's role is even more explicit (38–39). The eyes are connected with a freedom to order things as one wishes: "Η ελευθερία βρίσκεται στα μάτια" (Freedom can be found in the eyes). By pasting together bits of text and creating a different kind of pregnancy, it is possible to write about the love she feels is out of the ordinary. The page has been changed into the place where the lovemaking can happen:

'Ένα μικρό κομμάτι
που τρέχει
να ενωθεί
μ' ένα μικρό κομμάτι
στην ακαταστασία ενός απερίγραφτου γρίφου.

Μ' ένα διπλό σεντόνι σκεπάζεται η μοναξιά
έτσι ολοκληρώνεται η ομορφιά της.
(42)

A small piece
which runs
to join
with another small piece
in the disarray of an indescribable riddle.

Loneliness is covered over by a double sheet
this way its beauty is complete.

The sheet that covers the narrator's loneliness is both the double page of the book on which the bits of text are organized and the double sheet of lovemaking. Her way of seeing and the materiality of the text have tentatively set up a place for an alternative kind of love, one imagines a lesbian love, but, in keeping with the "indescribable riddle" in which the pronouns are always ambiguous, it could also be autoerotic. Does the feminine possessive pronoun της in the final line, which I translate "its," refer to her unmentioned lover's beauty or to the beauty of loneliness, the feminine noun in the previous line? The ambiguity of course is lost in English, where nouns are not gendered.

Punctuation Marks (1979), Laina's next collection, calls attention to its visual presentation even more than *Change of Scene*. The amount of white space is striking. The book is large and almost square, and the poems are as far away from their titles as possible. Whereas the visual articulation of space in *Change of Scene* was commanded by the switch to italics or the occasional period, *Punctuation Marks*, not surprisingly, is full of punctuation marks; semicolons and periods abound. It even embraces other, more experimental forms of organizing space. One poem, for example, in keeping with its title "Χιαστί" (Crosswise), is in the shape of an *X*. Just as one half of the *X* mirrors the other half, so this poem mirrors itself along the seam of the book. But this heightened attention to the visual composition of the poem does not neatly coincide with the elaboration of the alternative kind of loving and writing in *Change of Scene*. Instead, much of the collection seems concerned with the fact that the shifting place she thought she had established in *Change of Scene*, the birth she had inverted, is really not her's after all. The epigraph acknowledges this:

> Από μιαν άποψη δεν ονειρεύτηκα ποτέ
> κανένα πρωινό δεν αναγνώρισα δικό μου
> (1979, 7)

> In a way I never dreamed
> I never recognized a single morning as my own

Calling attention to the imaginary bases of identity, the inevitable mediation and loss, it seems, does not preclude nostalgia for a model of subjectivity in which the lost object can be found.

About halfway through the book, though, there is a shift of tone and an attempt to treat uncertainty and displacement as productive. The poem "Επιτέλους" (Finally) and the following three fragments, which propose an alternative punctuation, suggests that her unorthodox sexual preference, that which marks her as different, might finally be accommodated:

Επιτέλους ο εξευτελισμός μου
θα πάρει άλλο νόημα.

(26)

Finally my debasement
will take on another meaning.

On the next page she lists three symbols (□, ○, ——), each followed by a
short poem.[17] The first symbol, a square, seems to stand for the empty,
silent, stillness of the blank page. The square is an angular, closed shape
like the alpha privative that begins the first three lines, denoting negation:

□

'Άδειο[18]
Αθόρυβο
Ακίνητο
Ο χρόνος επιστρέφει λευκός

(27)

Empty
Noiseless
Motionless
Time returns white

The next symbol is a circle, which also acts as a negative force, the way the
alpha did, because it is the omicron that begins the word ούτε, meaning
"neither":

○

Ούτε λέξεις
Ούτε μουσική
Ούτε σχήμα
Γυμνό που αντέχει γυμνό

(27)

Neither words
Nor music
Nor form
Naked which endures naked

---

[17] In the second edition (1991) these are three poems on separate pages.
[18] "'Άδειο" is in fact distantly an alpha privative. Its root meaning is "free from fear"
(ancient α + δέος).

Neither the square nor the circle is sufficient; for both work by absolutely negating what comes after. The only possibility seems to be the line, the symbol that titles the last poem, that which is in between, that which promotes ambivalence, that which mediates:

─────

> Θαμπή πυκνή κι απρόβλεπτη
> στο φύσημα
> του νερού η απάντηση
> (27)

> Misty, dense, and unforeseen
> the ruffling
> of the water is the answer

The line calls attention to the materiality of the surface where two different elements, air and water, intermix without negating each other. This final symbol denaturalizes identity, acknowledging ambivalence and insecurity as constitutive of self. The shifting subject that was introduced through the typographic experimentation of *Change of Scene* resurfaces here in an alternative punctuation.

Though there are still moments of regret and relief that seem more in keeping with the project of salvaging a coherent, knowing self in the earlier *Beyond*,[19] for the most part in the second half of *Punctuation Marks* subjectivity is about not knowing, about the unavoidable stuff that comes between the reflection and that which is being reflected. A few poems later, in "Crosswise," for example, the narrator calls attention to her new conception of herself:

> Το περίεργο είναι ηως αυτό το σώμα ξεκίνησε με μιαν απαράμιλλη σιγουριά
> και τώρα υποχωρεί συνεχώς σε μιαν εξαντλητική άγνοια
> (32)

> The odd thing is that this body began with an incomparable certainty
> and now it retreats constantly to an exhausting ignorance

This exhausting ignorance is then connected to an unreciprocated look reflected in water, "ένα άγνωστο σχήμα με ξεχασμένα μάτια" (an unknown shape with forgotten eyes). But like the X shape of the poem that crosses

---

[19] The exclamation in one poem seems straight out of *Beyond*: "'Ωστε λοιπόν είχα κι εγώ μητέρα!" (So I also had a mother!) (1979, 39). Indeed it is the first exclamation point to appear in a poem since *Beyond*.

her out, puts her *under erasure,* and yet provides the formal structure of the poem, this blank look in its negation offers an alternative subject position. It is the apparatus of reflection, the means and materiality rather than the reflection, that matters.[20]

The final poem, " 'Ετσι" (Like this), before a five-poem epilogue, once again concludes, like the dash poem and the X poem, that the ebb and flow, the approach and retreat, the hovering in between, on the border, is the most apt description of how we are who we are. The self is not something already given; it is a shifting position that one is continuously entering:

> Έτσι θα μου συμβεί
> ολοένα
> μια είσοδος στον εαυτό μου
> (37)

> That is the way it will happen to me
> continuously
> an entrance into myself

And in the epilogue, titled "Συνέχεια" (Continuation), the narrator promotes an I in which speed, multiplication, and lack of attachment are the defining characteristics, rather than the coherent knowing, feeling, lyric I of *Beyond:*

> Σκέφτηκα πως είχα πεθάνει
>
> . . . .
>
> Μ' εκπληκτική ταχύτητα μέσα στο χώρο
> πολλαπλασιαζόμουν
> Θυμάμαι πως έβλεπα γύρω μου τον ουρανό
> να υψώνεται κι άλλο
> Δεν πρόσεχα καμιά ένταση.
> (1979, 40)

> I thought I had died
>
> . . . .
>
> In space I multiplied
> With surprising speed
> I remember I was looking at the sky around me
> rise up and one other thing
> There was no tension.

---

[20] This technique of calling attention to what gets in the way of the look over the look itself could be compared with Fassbinder's emphasis on shooting through windows, at mirror reflections, and so on; see Silverman 1992, 133.

It no longer bothers the narrator of *Punctuation Marks* that she is nothing but what others devise:

> Δε με πειράζει να πω πως έχω πεθάνει
> το ξέρω γιατί στέκομαι δίπλα μου
> κι έχω σιγά σιγά ξεχαστεί
> μέσα σε κάτι άλλο
> διαρκώ . . .
>> (42)

> It doesn't bother me to say I've died
> I know it because I am standing next to myself
> and I have slowly forgotten myself
> I exist
> inside something else . . .

This being "inside something else" is the basis for an alternative model of subjectivity. Complicating the famous feminist poem "Man, Feminine Gender" of Zoë Karelli (1957), in which the poet states that she will no longer be "his" moon, no longer belong to him, but instead stand alone, on her own,[21] Laina suggests that inhabiting the reflection, "any moon at all," is the only possible subject position:

> Δεν είχα προφτάσει
> Βρισκόμουν στο φως
> και μετατοπιζόμουν μαζί του
> Ένα οποιοδήποτε φεγγάρι
> μπορούσε να μ' ακουμπήσει
> Ένιωθα πως αυτό θα περνούσε
> πως τελικά
>> θα είχα ένα τόπο να μείνω
>>> ένα οποιοδήποτε φεγγάρι
>>> (1979, 44)

> I had not caught up
> I found myself in the light
> I was changing places with it
> any kind of a moon
> could touch me

[21] In Friar's translation of "Man, Feminine Gender" the part of the poem I refer to reads: "And I say that I am 'man,' completed / and alone. I could not have been formed without him / but now *I am* and am capable, / and we are a separated pair, he / and I, and I have my own light. / I was never the moon" (Friar 1973, 339).

I felt that it would pass
in the end
        I would have a place to stay
                any moon at all

There is nothing more real than a reflection. Whereas *Punctuation Marks* began seemingly troubled by the fact that "Από μιαν άποψη δεν ονειρεύτηκα ποτέ / κανένα πρωινό δεν αναγνώρισα δικό μου" (In a way I never dreamed / I never recognized a single morning as my own) (7), it ends at peace with the otherness of herself: "Το πρόσωπό μου ήσυχα δίπλα μου" (My face calmly next to me) (43). The reflection in the mirror, "any moon at all," provides a place to stay which is already double, divided, split and has no ambition of becoming one. If identity is a fantasy, then it is no longer a problem that the morning is someone else's.

As we have already seen, Galanaki's and Mastoraki's narratives constantly call attention to what makes illusion possible, whether it be the trope of metonymy, the dreamwork, or the physical page on which the poem takes place. Laina's poetry, from *Change of Scene*, to *Punctuation Marks*, to *Hers*, is particularly insistent about the physical space of the page. All three collections have titles that signal a preoccupation with space and an interest in delineating boundaries—changing scenes or landscapes, punctuating breaks and subordinating clauses, determining what is "hers." In each there is progressively more space and less text to the page. I have drawn on the earlier collections, therefore, not only to show the shift in the way Laina understands the censorship of the look from restrictive to productive of subjectivity but also to explore the ramifications of these different models of subject formation for loving and writing—how messing with identification might actually provide an alternative ground of sexuality and textuality.

Let me now turn from the relation between the unreciprocated look and the look of the page in *Change of Scene* and *Punctuation Marks* to how this relation is elaborated in *Hers*. I read twice through *Hers*, first to show how Maria, the protagonist of this collection, is set up in pieces and how this fragmented body becomes a blueprint for a poetics of inconclusiveness; second, to examine the role the reader plays in intervening between Maria and her reflection and constructing the page as the elusive ground of love which supports this alternative grammar of self. If the look in the mirror in *Beyond* was an attempt to become whole in the eyes of the other, and the look in the mirror in *Change of Scene* and *Punctuation Marks* was about recognizing the illusory nature of the other and therefore of the self, then the look in the mirror in *Hers* shifts attention from the dyadic relation of subject and idealized mother/lover to the triangular relation of Maria, the reflection, and the reader, focusing on the mechanisms of the mirror and on diverting the look, rather than on who is looking or being seen. In many ways my attention here to a poetics of indeterminacy and inconclusiveness returns to my comparative discussion in Chapter 3 of the formal undermining of authority in women's poetry of the 1980s. There I was concerned more generally with how power relations were explored in this poetry through the scrambling of pronouns and the use of quotation marks. In my reading of *Hers*, I am interested in the particular power dynamic of subject formation and in how the coimplication of self and other found in Lacan's account of the mirror stage—in Laina's terms, the fact that nothing is her own and that she seeks herself in everything—is displayed in the language of these poems. I am concerned with how shifting personal pronouns privilege misrecognition and disintegration over identification and coherency. By exploring this issue of fragmentation in depth and giving various examples of how the protagonist and the text are in pieces in *Hers*, I can continue my discussion of the interrelation of sexual politics and poetic form from Chapter 3 as well as pave the way for my reading of how the reader, and in particular the woman reader, is implicated in this process in the final section of this chapter.

Toward an Alternative Grammar of Self

Throughout *Hers*, censorship and claustrophobia are viewed as both restrictive and disabling as well as productive of a different kind of language and behavior. *Hers* critiques the attempt by the patriarchal order to keep woman intact and in place, subordinate and heterosexual, and offers the basis of an alternative grammar—hers, which the text suggests is not as monumental and totalizing as his. In *Punctuation Marks* the protagonist moved from fearing that nothing belonged to her, neither her dreams nor her mornings, to accepting that the disjuncture between dreams and reality is the only reality. In *Hers* the woman described in the epigraph takes this conclusion even further. If everything is plausibly someone else's, then she will find herself everywhere: "Σε όλες τις πράξεις γύρευε τον εαυτό της· / κανείς δεν πρέπει να της έχει εμπιστοσύνη" (In everything she did she sought herself; / no one should trust her) (1985a, 7). If representation is fundamentally an untrustworthy process of misrecognition, then her response will be to display this untrustworthiness. Instead of trying to salvage an ideal, this collection flaunts its disintegration.

Except for an introductory poem and an epilogue, the book is comprised of fifty-nine short fragments, from two to twelve lines each. Each fragment relays a gesture, a thought, or a memory of Maria's, a woman, seated for the most part, by herself. These fragments are roughly divided into eight sections. Each section begins by introducing Maria in the process of representing herself or being represented—in a mirror, in a votive offering, in a photograph. Attention is not on the reflection or representation but on the set-up that enables it—the position of Maria in front of the mirror, the act of developing the photograph, the kind of stone in which a relief is carved. And in each section's initial poem there is some gesture or word that suggests that things are not as one would expect—some fidgeting, fixing, rearranging, surprise, or discomfort. Laina here seems to take as her starting point the Lacanian lesson of coherency as misrecognition. What one sees in the mirror is never exactly who one is. The reader is not asked to sort out fragments and make Maria whole again; a different task is at hand. Like an unmarked box of old snapshots that tell a story without any particular order, these poems invite the reader to shuffle through all the different ways identification is interrupted and to leave Maria in pieces and in flux.

The first poem of the collection, "Τοιχογραφία" (Fresco), introduces the body and text in pieces with a description of a crumbling Minoan painting of a woman:

Σώζεται η αρχή απ' τους μηρούς
σε άτονο γαλάζιο
τμήμα ποδιού ακόσμητο προς τα αριστερά
και τμήμα απολήξεως φορέματος.
Στο δέρμα διακρίνονται γραμμές
κυρίως οξυκόρυφες.
Ο χώρος του λαιμού διακόπτεται
απ' τον αριστερό βραχίονα
που φέρεται προς τα επάνω
ενώ μονάχα το δεξί στήθος δηλώνεται
με ελαφρά καμπύλωση.
Από το κάτω μέρος του προσώπου
λείπει το μεγαλύτερο κομμάτι.
Κόκκινα τρίγωνα ή τόξα
σ' όλο το άσπρο του βολβού.
Σώζεται επίσης η κορδέλα των μαλλιών
και η στροφή του σώματος
που ασφαλώς προϋποθέτει
ανάλογες κινήσεις των χεριών.

Λείπει το έδαφος του έρωτα.
                                        (1985a, 9)

The beginning of the thighs still remains
a dull blue
to the left a section of foot unadorned
and a section from the hem of the dress.
On the skin lines are visible
mainly sharp angles.
The neck area is interrupted
by the left arm
which is raised up
while only the right breast is registered
by a slight curve.
Most of the lower part
of the face is missing.
Red triangles or arcs
cover the white of the eye.
The hair ribbon also remains
and the body's twist
which surely presupposes
similar movements in the hands.

The ground of love is missing.

This poem reads as if taken verbatim out of an archaeological textbook. Descriptive terms such as "to the left a section of foot unadorned / and a section from the hem of the dress" and passive verbs such as σώζεται, διακρίνονται, διακόπτεται, δηλώνεται ("is saved," "can be discerned," "is interrupted," and "is registered") abound. The authority of its formal, technical language, however, is undermined by the simple observation in the final line, "The ground of love is missing," as well as the rest of the collection, which is written, for the most part, in this plainer tone. The spatial break between the archaeological description and Maria's one-line conclusion further distinguishes the two discourses. Whereas archaeologists emphasize what remains, "The beginning of the thighs . . . remains. . . . The hair ribbon also remains and the body's twist," *Hers* will concentrate on what is missing. Reading against the grain, the reader finds the crucial parts are gone: "The neck area is interrupted" and "Most of the lower part / of the face is missing." As in Mastoraki's *Tales* where mouths are sealed with wax and necks are bruised, in *Hers* too, the place from which women speak is damaged. But as in Mastoraki's text this disabling representation of woman also suggests an alternative mode of representation, one that defines itself in contradistinction to the language of salvaging, nostalgia, and regret; the woman in the fresco in pieces projects a grammar

of self for which dissolution, incompletion, and disjointedness are necessary conditions of subject formation.

Before addressing the role of the reader in recognizing this fragmented
self and in helping to facilitate a space and time, a visual narrative, in
which she can be left that way, let me offer some more examples of how
Maria's body and text are in fragments. Although in the first poem after
"Fresco," Maria is introduced as "ολόσωμη" (full length, or literally "whole
body") (12), the cumulative sense of Maria as she is described over the
course of the collection is far from distinct and whole.[22] If Mastoraki deflated the authority of the proper name by doubling it, Laina does so by
giving her protagonist the most common of Greek proper names, Maria.
Not only does this name stand both for the most holy and the most promis-
cuous, the Virgin Mary and Mary Magdalene, but for thousands of women
in Greece, not to mention the author herself. The many different snapshots
of her in myriad positions—sitting, standing, lying down—and viewed
from many different angles corroborate this sense of Maria as many Marias
and Maria in pieces. But this kaleidoscopic approach breaks up Maria as
well as multiplies her. Descriptions of her, like filmic close-ups, often focus
attention on one part of the body or another, separating her into disjunct
areas. In one poem we read:

> Πίνει ένα φλιτζάνι τσάι
> και χαίρεται
> να ανάβει ένα τσιγάρο
>   (35)

> She drinks a cup of tea
> and gets pleasure
> from lighting a cigarette.

In another:

> Λοιπόν
> η Μαρία
> όταν κανείς δεν την προσέχει
> ταχτοποιεί τα χέρια της.
>   (45)

> So
> Maria
> when no one is watching her
> arranges her hands.

---

[22] I return to this poem in the next section.

Quite a few poems list actions that also break up the body: "να φορέσει τα ρούχα της / να χτενίσει τα μαλλιά της" (to wear her clothes / to comb her hair) (39). And in one poem, Maria is literally in pieces. She is missing her elbows and knees, the parts of the body that connect the limbs:

> Παρέσυρε μαζί της
> και τα πουλιά απ' το χαλί
> κι ύστερα βγήκε
> χωρίς αγκώνες
> χωρίς γόνατα.
>   (53)

> She even dragged with her
> the birds from the rug
> and then she left
> without elbows
> or knees.

But what is significant about Maria's fragmented body for my reading is that the language of the text, too, is in pieces. Throughout *Hers*, Maria's disjointed self is supported by a language without the usual connections and consistency of person, tense, and gender. In the same way that her body is missing elbows and knees, so too her text has lost certain connecting parts of speech. Conjunctions and adverbs, for example, are often out of order, free floating, and they seem unconnected to the phrases they are meant to tie together:

> Ενώ ολόκληρες φράσεις περνούν και τις δέχεται
> και διατρέχει συνεχώς μεγάλο κίνδυνο
> ακόμα το κορμί που θυμόταν
> αλλά υπήρχε κάτι που δεν είχε ξαναδεί.
>   (19, underscoring mine)

> While whole phrases pass by and she accepts them
> and she constantly faces great danger
> still the body she remembered
> but there was something she had never seen.

Pronouns also are left out so that objects and subjects are confused: "ακόμα το κορμί που θυμόταν" could mean that the body remembered or that she remembered the body.[23] At the rare moments when pronouns do appear, they tend to shift in an unorthodox fashion from "she" to "he" or "she" to "I." For example, at the point when Maria is taken away to "a room of her own," after pages and pages of the third person, she suddenly speaks in the first person:

> Είναι πολύ ευτυχισμένη εδώ
> κάθεται και κοιτάζει και
> όταν ο ήλιος πιάνει το δωμάτιο
> βλέπει καλά τις ώρες να περνούν.
> Δε συμμετέχει
> διαβάζω όμως και
> κοιμάμαι ήσυχα τα βράδια.
> Σκέφτομαι, καμιά φορά πετύχαινα γραμμές
> σχεδόν με μονοκοντυλιά.
>
> (48)

> She is very happy here
> she sits and stares
> when the sun fills the room
> she watches closely the hours passing.
> She does not participate
> I read however and
> sleep calmly at night.
> I think, sometimes I managed lines
> in one pencil stroke.

This shift between the third and first person in the fifth and sixth lines, rather than clarifying her subject position, gives equal value to different parts of Maria. It is the linguistic equivalent of showing us Maria from different angles. It makes Maria's subjectivity less, not more, fixed.[24] It seems significant that Laina, in discussing the English translation of this poem (1991), insisted that μονοκοντυλιά could not be a pen stroke—it had

---

[23] Person and number are signaled by the verb in Greek, so pronouns are less frequent than in English; but Laina takes their infrequency to an extreme, accentuating the ambiguity their absence creates.

[24] The other place where the "I" speaks directly has a similarly disorienting effect: "Εκεί, ψιθύρισε / εκεί την έβλεπα τη θάλασσα" (There, she whispered / There, I could see the sea) (54). Again we have no idea which one is Maria. These are the only places in *Hers* where Maria speaks directly in the first person, without the mediation of the narrator. I should note, however, that there are two points where she speaks in the first person in reported speech. On p. 20 we read, "όταν λέει / χαϊδεύω το κορμί μου" (when she says / I caress my body), and on p. 41, "απάντησε· / την επόμενη φορά / θα μπορούσα να μιλήσω με κάποιον / και ν' αγαπήσω, αν χρειαστεί" (she replied: / Next time / I will be able to talk with someone / and to love, if necessary).

to be delible, like those pencils school children used on slates. In this poem, writing and subjectivity are incapable of staying put.

This grammar of self, however, does not shift indiscriminately. Laina's pronouns are overwhelmingly in the service of the third person singular rather than the more traditional first person of much women's poetry in Greece. The distinction between the discourse of archaeology and her way of speaking in the introductory poem is not, as one might expect, supported by a move from third to first person. Maria's text, excepting the epilogue at the end, is also in the narrative third person. The shift is not between dry, objective discourse and a lyric, subjective mode but between this dry discourse and something else, as yet undefined. As *Hers* states, Maria's language is different: "Εντελώς άλλα λόγια σκεφτόταν" (She was thinking totally different words) (61). Looking back at the collections already discussed, a pattern becomes clear. Whereas Galanaki's, Mastoraki's, and Laina's earlier collections were written mostly in the more subjective first person, *Hers*, as well as *The Cake* and *Tales*, are written primarily in the objective third person. The third-person narrative allows the narrator to give voice to a plurality of positions, to a shattered self, to Maria in pieces scattered across many pages. In striking contrast to Laina's earlier collections, the protagonist of *Hers* is left a bundle of shifting pronouns, disconnected actions, memories, and intentions. Her disintegration of body and text presupposes not a lost order that could be salvaged, as in the archaeological discourse of "Fresco," but rather a freer way of defining subjectivity and of representing it.[25]

Finding the Ground of Love Elsewhere

I now turn to how this fragmented body and text is bound up with the censored look of love and how the role of the reader is not to give what the other (mother or lover) withheld but to continue to defer the look's reciprocation and focus attention on the physical space of the page. It may already be obvious that the ability to keep body and text in pieces is inti-

---

[25] Frigga Haug's women's collective in Berlin comes to similar conclusions: in reconstructing female sexualization as female socialization, the first-person "I" was not adequate. What they term "memory-work" required the distance of the third person: "Writing about past events is almost impossible, unless we have some way of distancing ourselves. The very fact that we learn not to take ourselves and our own interests into account has the effect, in memory-work, of reducing the time and trouble spent in writing about ourselves; large portions of experience are neglected, or motive and desires are attributed to our past selves that we would find inadequate as explanations for the actions of others. By translating our own experiences into the third person, we were enabled to be more attentive to our selves. Thus the gaze we cast today on ourselves of yesterday becomes the gaze cast by one stranger on another" (1987, 45–46).

mately connected to the vast empty space *Hers* consumes. The airy typography of this collection disperses Maria across more than eighty pages, keeping elbows, knees, conjunctions, and pronouns spread out and disconnected. After "Fresco" the reader finds a whole page devoted to the section number 1, and then on the next page, a short poem at the top of the page. Out of the fifty-nine poems, few cover more than a quarter of the page and each of the eight section numbers has a page to itself. Compared with Mastoraki's and Galanaki's books, Laina's is spacious. Even compared with Laina's earlier books the abundance of white space on the page in *Hers* is striking. Though the presence of white space may be self-evident, the way in which this visual poetics functions is not so clear. Let me first confirm its importance by comparing Laina's collection with a poem by the postwar poet Miltos Sachtouris and then move on to the more difficult task of analyzing how the visual poetics of *Hers* constructs a space that is hers.

The significance of space for the construction of a fragmented grammar of self in *Hers* is particularly clear in comparison with Sachtouris's poem "Η Μαρία" (Maria) from his 1958 collection Τα φάσματα ή η χαρά στον άλλο δρόμο (Spectral figures).[26] Sachtouris, a surrealist poet, and one of the more important influences for the generation of the 1970s, introduces many of the elements in this one short poem that are then developed and reworked in Laina's collection. Sachtouris's Maria, like Laina's, is described as contemplative and as doing small, insignificant tasks:

Η Μαρία σκεφτική
έβγαζε τις κάλτσες της
(1984a, 120)

Maria was pensively
taking off her stockings
(1982b, 61)

She is an amalgam of odd discourses, snatches of conversation, things overheard and remembered:

Από το σώμα της έβγαιναν
φωνές άλλων ανθρώπων
(120)

[26] John Stathatos included a selection from *Spectral Figures* under this name in his book of Sachtouris translations, *Strange Sunday* (1984b), but "Maria" is not in the selection. Another useful point of comparison for Laina's spatial project would be Cavafy's poetry, in particular his love poems, which also clear a space for an alternative kind of love; see, e.g., "Ο καθρέπτης στην είσοδο" (The mirror in the front hall) (1993, 2:87 and 1975, 161). For a cross-cultural perspective, see Ullman 1979, a collection Laina says influenced her.

Voices of other people
rose out of her body
(61)

She changes mood quickly and this is registered typographically, one sentence juxtaposed to the next:

Η Μαρία έκλαιγε έκλαιγε
τώρα η Μαρία γελούσε
(120)

Maria wept and wept
then Maria laughed
(61)

And finally, as we will see in Laina's poem, Sachtouris's poem concludes with an escape of sorts:

Τότε η Μαρία
σιγά-σιγά άνοιγε τα χέρια της
άρχιζε να πετάει
γύρω-γύρω στο δωμάτιο
(120)

Then Maria
slowly slowly opened her arms
and began to fly
round and round the room
(61)

But whereas Sachtouris's "Maria" takes up a page, Laina's, significantly, fills a whole collection. Sachtouris's Maria is still trapped within the traditional four walls of the domestic sphere; Laina's takes off. Laina's penultimate poem concludes with this apotheosis, "κι ανασηκώθηκε σε άλλη εποχή" (and [Maria] was lifted into another era) (80), and the final poem, "Επίλογος" (Epilogue), acknowledges that Maria has found an alternative time and space that is "έξω στο φως" (out in the light) (82) and "άσπρο" (white) (82), namely the page the reader holds open. As in Galanaki's and Mastoraki's collections, in Laina's *Hers* sexual politics is a formal project of taking up time and taking over space, of procrastination and occupation. And this project requires the involvement of the reader.

Returning to the beginning of *Hers*, let me trace how the page becomes the ground that supports the decentered textuality and sexuality of Laina's

Maria, first by highlighting the look of the reader in the text and its role in making the fragmented grammar of self possible, then by enumerating how the reader's look connects the disjointed body and text of Maria's writing to the awkward body and text of her loving. Section 1, as I have already mentioned, begins with Maria looking at herself in front of the mirror:

Η Μαρία μέσα στον καθρέφτη
ολόσωμη
στρώνει το φόρεμά της στο λαιμό.
Δεν έχει σημασία τώρα πού ξαπλώνει το κορμί της
αν έγινε σημύδα ή χορτάρι
η Μαρία μέσα στον καθρέφτη
στρώνει το φόρεμά της στο λαιμό.
                    (1985a, 12)

Maria in the mirror
full length
straightens her dress at the neck.
It does not matter now where her body lies
whether she turned to birch or grass
Maria in the mirror
straightens her dress at the neck.

Coming after "Fresco," a poem about a woman in pieces, and before a long series of fragments that offer another woman in pieces, this poem at first seems to present a different picture in which Maria sees herself as whole. But on closer examination this formative moment in front of the mirror is not about an unmediated reflection of an intact Maria. There is something unsettled: Maria is fidgeting; she "straightens her dress at the neck."

The structure of the poem, too, seems to support a sense of interruption. The poem on the page mirrors Maria looking at herself in the mirror, but attention is focused on what gets in the way rather than on the reflection. The first three lines describe Maria; the next two lines, a kind of dead substance, an empty signifier explaining that after death it does not matter any more what you become, "whether she turned to birch or grass"; and then the last two lines again repeat the description of Maria. By calling attention to itself, the mirror, that which enables the reflection, also obstructs it. Moreover, not only is the mirror an obstruction in this reading, but that which is mirrored—Maria fidgeting—is reflected formally in the typographic disturbance of the reflection: the two lines that are repeated, "Maria in the mirror" and "straighten her dress at the neck," do not mirror each other perfectly. The first time they are broken up by the line "full length"; the second time they are not. This poem is not so much about Maria looking for something in the mirror as it is about the mirror, the page, and the look of the reader that get in the way. The illusion of unmediated completeness which consumed the General in Karapanou's *Kassandra and the Wolf* and the narrator in *Beyond* is impossible. The dyadic relation of subject and desired object gives way to a triangular relationship of the woman looking in the mirror, the woman in the mirror, and the reader looking at the woman looking in the mirror.

The next poem, where Maria's position in front of the mirror is more explicitly described in terms of typography, further supports the reader's key role in turning the page into the place all these unreciprocated looks coexist:

> Τριμμένο με νερό και στάχτη παρελθόν.
> Η Μαρία γελάει
> γυρίζει και ξαναπαίρνει τη θέση της.
>
> Αντικριστά ο ίασπις κι ο ίασμος
> (13)

> The past scrubbed with water and ashes.
> Maria laughs
> turns and takes her place again.
>
> Jasper and jasmine opposed

This poem compares Maria's position to the position of two words: jasper and jasmine. The only place where jasper and jasmine are spatially related to each other, where they "oppose" or face each other, is on the Greek dictionary page, where they usually follow each other alphabetically.[27] Again, as in the mirror poem, it is the reader that establishes a typographic relation between Maria and her reflection. And again, as in the mirror poem, the reflection is not perfect. In Greek, ίασπις and ίασμος share the first three letters and their last, not their middle two. Someone or something always foils the possibility of a perfect correspondence. As in the mirror poem, it is the reader who calls attention to the importance of the page with its attention to the letter and its ability to accommodate such

[27] The dictionary of choice for the Greek poets whose work I address in this book is the three-volume Προΐας (Proias) (1970). These poets also use, as much as they do any dictionary, Vostantzoglou's Αντιλεξικόν (Antilexicon) (1990), a thesaurus-like reference book that groups words according to properties and oppositions. In both *Proias* and Vostantzoglou, ίασμος and ίασπις follow each other. The typographic use of the word αντικριστά is foreshadowed in *Change of Scene* where Laina used the cognate for "to look in the face" (αντικρίζει) to implicate the reader's look, but here her usage is even more obviously connected to the look of the page.

arbitrary connections. It is the look of the reader that deflects the possibility of any straight-forward identification.

If the first poem of the collection examined the question of representation and the role of the reader in terms of a fresco, and the first poem of the first section with reference to the mirror, the first poem of the second section does so with regard to some sort of stone carving, perhaps a votive stele or relief. Here, too, the reader is obliged to link what is being represented to the mode of representation and, in doing so, draw out connections to the actual look of the poem on the page. This poem, like the one above, also reads like a description of an archaeological discovery:

> Δεν υπάρχει καμιά αμφιβολία.
> Και η κατεύθυνση
> και ο προορισμός
> (μετωπικός κι αφύσικος)
> το μαρτυρούν.
> Λίθινο βέβαια
> αναθηματικό.
>
> (22)

> There is no doubt.
> Both the direction
> and the inclination
> (frontal and unnatural)
> prove it.
> Stone, of course
> anathematic.

The key word is "αναθηματικό" (anathematic), an adjective used by archaeologists to describe an object on which a votive inscription or visual depiction of a tribute has been carved.[28] Like the fresco and the mirror, the object described in this poem is meant for an audience; its function is to represent something for someone. The adjectives "μετωπικός" (frontal) and "αφύσικος" (unnatural) and "αναθηματικός" (anathematic) can be read as referring not only to the position of the representation on the stone but also to the reader's position looking at the poem. The reader's position is frontal, even anathematic in the sense that the reader is paying tribute to the poem. But the look of the reader does not stand in for the look of the

---

[28] In English the term *anathema* more commonly refers to a curse (ανάθεμα), but the earlier sense of an offering (ανάθημα) is a second meaning in the *OED*. I have retained the Greek adjective "anathematic" in my translation in part to focus attention on its contradictory meaning, that which damns and consecrates, but even more important, to call attention to its etymological roots in the ancient Greek verb ανατιθέναι "to put up," positioning and placement being so crucial to Laina's visual poetics.

lost one, the one in whose memory the tribute is made; rather, it focuses attention on the materiality of the votive offering. The words on the page— lined up stele-like in a tall rectangle—posit a place of unreciprocation which has its own physical presence. As in the fresco and the mirror, the surface of reflection, "Stone, of course," is more important than what is being reflected. The look of the reader grants the page a certain materiality. It is a place that can contain loss and otherwise untenable scenarios such as the surreal "Περνούσε με άμαξα μπροστά στο καλοκαίρι" (She passed in front of summer in a carriage) (25) or "διέσχιζε τον ψίθυρο και την σιωπή" (she walked across the whisper and the silence) (26).

In Section 3 the reader's role in directing attention to the medium of writing, or what Lacan has called "the letter of the discourse," is inten-sified.[29] In the first poem a term from literary scholarship, the verb "to be attributed to" is used to describe Maria: like a poem by an unknown au-thor, Maria cannot be "attributed" to anyone, "δεν μπορεί να αποδοθεί σε κανέναν . . ." (32). Then Maria's actual position is described in syntactic terms:

> Στέκεται με την πλάτη στο παράθυρο·
> το βάζο
> η πρόθεση των λουλουδιών.
> Λέει στον αμαξά να περιμένει.
>
> (37)
>
> She stands with her back to the window;
> the vase
> the intention of flowers.
> She tells the coachman to wait.

The vase is the "intention" of flowers because when it is empty its presence suggests the flowers that are not there, but it is also that which, like a preposition, "positions" the flowers. The crucial word here is πρόθεση, which means both "intention" and "preposition," the part of language that denotes spatial placement. The reader in acknowledging all these refer-ences to Maria's textuality—the alphabetical order of herself and her reflec-tion in the jasper and jasmine poem, her surrealisms, the fact that she cannot be attributed to anyone, the prepositional quality of her intention— not only suggests the conflation of grammar and self in a grammar of self but registers the materiality of its indeterminacy. Maria is made up of a language in which words are other, different (61), untimely (33), in which person, case, and gender are confused, a language in which the arbitrari-

---

[29] Lacan (1977, 159) uses this expression to refer to Freud's attention to the analysis of language in the *Interpretation of Dreams*.

ness of the sign is paramount. And this arbitrariness makes language itself the focus rather than any extratextual referent.[30]

But where does this linguistic turn in Laina's oeuvre get us with regard to the question of love? How does the material impact of language fashion an alternative ground of love? It is not surprising that in each of the fragments I have discussed with regard to how the look of the reader constructs an alternative grammar of self for Maria, there is the suggestion that this look is connected to the look of love. As this collection unfolds, the discourses of textuality and love become more and more difficult to disentangle.[31] The reader's making of a fragmented and disjointed text is increasingly connected with clearing a space for her kind of loving. The first poem introduces this project by announcing that, though the archaeologist may salvage much of the fresco of the woman, the ground of love is missing (9). Cued in this way, the reader, then, begins to connect what is missing, out of place, or awkward—the cracks in the fresco, the fidgeting in the mirror, the unnaturalness of inclination and direction, and the tentativeness of Maria at the window—to the missing ground of love. When the salvaging discourse of archaeology of the first poem resurfaces in the votive-offering poem, the reader, better versed in what is missing, is more

---

[30] See de Saussure 1966, 67–69, on the arbitrary nature of the sign. My poststructural attention to this, however, is indebted to Lacan's reading of Saussure (1977, 146–78). The idea that language does not represent experience but *is* experience is a position strikingly different from, say, Ritsos's credo in "Το νόημα της απλότητας" (The meaning of simplicity), written in 1946, where language is the medium by which one gains access to the poet's world:

> αν δε με βρείτε, θα βρείτε τα πράγματα,
> θ' αγγίξετε εκείνα που άγγιξε το χέρι μου,
> θα σμίξουν τα χνάρια των χεριών μας.
> (1979, 2)

> if you don't find me, you'll find the things,
> you'll touch what my hand has touched,
> our hand-prints will merge.
> (3)

Communication is possible if "often cancelled." His poem concludes:

> Η κάθε λέξη είναι μια έξοδος
> για μια συνάντηση, πολλές φορές ματαιωμένη,
> και τότε είναι μια λέξη αληθινή, σαν επιμένει στη συνάντηση.

> Every word is a doorway
> to a meeting, one often cancelled,
> and that's when a word is true: when it insists on the meeting.

In contrast, these women's texts postpone the meeting indefinitely.

[31] The intertext that the author suggested was useful was Peter Handke's film *The Left-Handed Woman*. Maria, like the protagonist of Handke's film, is at odds with her environment and cannot communicate with anyone. The film, instead of portraying the socialization of a misfit, like so many feminine Bildungsromans, provides a space for the left-handed woman where she can be as she is. Similarly, *Hers* does not make Maria fit in; rather, it creates a place where the reader must acknowledge her and her language as they are.

suspicious. What does it mean: There is no doubt? Both the direction and the inclination prove it? Stone, of course? Just as I discussed Irigaray's parodic citation of Freud's essay on femininity as a model for how Mastoraki deploys quotation to unsettle authority in *Tales*, I can make a similar point about the way Laina mimics archaeological discourse in *Hers*. In the context of Laina's poetry of fragmentation and loss, archaeology, the discourse of salvaging and of evidence, becomes insecure, dislodged. Over the course of the collection, rectangular spaces of reflection—the fresco, the mirror, the stele or relief, the window—come to frame an interrupted form of representation, one that rehearses misunderstanding and how things do not add up, rather than affirm a coherent whole. And it is this mode of representation which constitutes an alternative ground of love. The poem, as well as being about the unnatural, frontal, and nonmimetic relationship of reader and poem, is also about the awkwardness of a different kind of love. The descriptive terms—"There is no doubt. / Both the direction / and the inclination / (frontal and unnatural) / prove it. / Stone, of course / anathematic."—also underwrite an alternative sexuality. The noun "προορισμός" (inclination) could also refer to someone's sexual orientation. The adjective "αφύσικος" (unnatural) recalls the adjective with which she described her body in the preceding poem, "αδέξιο" (awkward). The cumulative effect of rehearsing misunderstanding suggests not only a poetry of fragments and distortion but a way of loving that has little to do with the compensatory, romantic love of a certain lyric tradition in which the woman reflects the man, playing moon to his sun, making him whole. The lover here is not looking for the perfect reciprocation of the boomerang in *Beyond* but has accepted the inevitable swerving off. And it is the page that accommodates this unreciprocation and makes it hers.

The relationship of textuality and sexuality is also evident in the vase poem. Here, too, there is a sense that this fragmentary grammar of self provides the terms for a different way of loving, a more open-ended, inconclusive mode in which intention overrides action. Whereas the readerly expectation in the archaeological poem "Fresco" is that the woman, the object of desire, can be made whole, in the vase poem there is no thought of completion—Maria, like the vase without flowers, is just there. One assumes that she is waiting for something, like the vase is for flowers, but the poem is about the waiting, not what she is waiting for. The contrast is all the more striking if one considers that whereas the desire for wholeness in "Fresco" only led to the news that the ground of love was missing, here the lack of any expectation means that the ground, though obviously a different kind of ground, is already there. The flowers may be missing, but the support, "the vase, the intention of flowers," is not. There is certainly not any assurance that she will be able to love, but the possibility, the ground, exists. As the last poem in Section 3 states:

'Όταν την ταρακούνησαν απάντησε:
Την επόμενη φορά
θα μπορούσα να μιλήσω με κάποιον
και ν' αγαπήσω, αν χρειαστεί.

(41)

When they shook her she replied:
Next time
I will be able to talk with someone
and to love, if necessary.

In the middle of Section 4, a story begins to unfold which further suggests that the censored look is actually providing an alternative ground of
love on the page. This story-within-a-story begins with Maria opening her
fan and ends when she lowers it at the conclusion of Section 6. Hiding
behind her fan has an effect similar to closing the window in an earlier
poem (36) and other acts of concealment: it gives her strength. The reader's
project of collecting modes of frustrated reciprocation and moments of
procrastination is beginning to pay off. Maria is starting to take up more
space:

Το απόγευμα
ενώ η πόλη ήταν χαμηλά
η Μαρία κατέλαβε ολόκληρο το σώμα της.

(58)

In the afternoon
while the city was down low
Maria took over her whole body.

But it is in Section 6 that the two different looks of censorship are de-
cisively connected—the censored look of love to the look of the page. Here
we find two poems mirroring each other. Instead of Maria looking at herself, we find the unreciprocated nature of the look itself being mirrored. On
the left hand page the poem begins:

Κρατούσε σοβαρή το σώμα της
στο χολ, στο δρόμο
ανάμεσα σε άλλους.
'Εβλεπε πράγματα να μεγαλώνουν·
μήπως μια άλλη που κοιτάζει έξω;

(64)

Serious, she held her body
in the hall, in the street
in the midst of others.
She saw things grow;
could it be someone else staring out?

Perhaps she is not staring at herself but rather at someone else. Then the question in italics mirrors the same question in regular print on the right-hand page:

Από τη μια στιγμή στην άλλη
έπεφτε έξω και της άρεσε
αλλά αυτό δεν την απασχολούσε τώρα πια
αν και παρέμεινε ευδιάκριτη
να απαντάει και να έρχεται.

Μήπως μια άλλη που κοιτάζει έξω;
(65)

From one minute to the next
she fell out of line and liked it
but this no longer concerned her
though she could still be seen
answering and approaching.

Could it be someone else staring out?

This poem explicitly makes the book the scene of the reflection, as one page mirrors the other. Through the work of the reader, the page physically gives us what the fresco, the mirror, the votive stele, or the window suggested: a space of nonreciprocation, a place in which otherness and interference have become constitutive of who Maria is.

It is the reader who enables this time- and space-consuming project. Maria can finally lower the fan when the reader has participated enough to know how difficult this process is of clearing a space. In the first poem of Section 7, we read:

άλλωστε στην αφήγηση αυτή
φαίνεται η αδυναμία
να βρεθεί ένας χώρος
(70)

> besides in this narrative
> the difficulty
> of finding a space is clear

At this point Maria can really take up more space:

> Το τελευταίο πράγμα που συγκρατούσε
> πιο χαμηλά
> λιγάκι δεξιότερα . . .
>   (71)

> The last thing she remembered
> a little lower
> a little to the right . . .

The next poem takes these same directions to grander proportions; they become geographical: "κι απλώθηκε νοτιοανατολικά" (and spread out southeastward) (72). . . . "πλημμύριζε τα πεζοδρόμια και φύτρωνε" (she flooded the sidewalks and sprouted) (74). Though in the first section it had to be stated that it did not matter where Maria put her body—the statement becoming a kind of mirror that kept Maria to herself—now, in Section 8, her position no longer needs justification; Maria is, and will be, where she is:

> θα κάθεται λοιπόν
> ή είναι ξαπλωμένη
>   (78)

> So she may be sitting
> or she is lying down

By constructing a topography of the unreciprocated look on the page, the reader names the counterspace of these poems the ground of love, giving Maria a space of her own.

The final section of this collection ends with two wild propositions that seem oddly plausible because the reader by now has grown used to the page as a place in which anything can happen. In the penultimate fragment, a dark blue lion passes by and Maria puts on her shawl (79). We are used to acts of concealment or restraint in order to gain or retain power (the closed window, the fan, the containment of the vase). In the final fragment, Maria then calls her own name and escapes to another epoch (80). The collection, however, does not end with this rather spectacular escape. It ends instead with an epilogue that contrasts sharply with the rest of the collection. It is written in the first person, not the third, and in prose, not verse; the tone is apologetic, not matter of fact. Like Mastoraki's beggar, who uncovered his wounds in front of the walls near the end of *Tales*, or like a curtain call at the end of a play, this radical shift is a demystification. Maria's apotheosis was too magical, too self-generated; too complete. The epilogue balances this out. Whereas Laina's previous collections ended optimistically, *Hers* concludes by explaining the necessity of lowering one's expectations, of not wanting anything, not waiting for the mother or anyone else to reciprocate the look:

Με βοηθάει να μην έχω το νου μου, να μην περιμένω τίποτα. Γιατί τότε τίποτα δε θα μπορούσε να συμβεί, εκτός από κάτι που ήδη το ξέρω. Και τι ξέρω εγώ; Τι ξέρω;
(82)

It helps if my mind is elsewhere, if I am not waiting for anything. Because then nothing can happen, except for something I already know. And me, what do I know? What do I know?

The epilogue posed as a question involves the reader and makes us realize that we too have come to expect nothing. We know the page will accommodate what there is, that it is a substitute for the meeting place our looks will never find, and that this is all we know. *Hers* is a strange narrative without suspense, completely lacking in overt emotion and intention, and this very indifference allows it to be the ground of love that is missing. The epilogue, no matter how disconcerting and even inelegant, fulfills a crucial function. It keeps the look in motion. It reminds us of the book we have in front of us. In the same way Galanaki offered her poem, *The Cake*, instead of the unborn child to its reader, and Mastoraki offered her *Tales* in lieu of the purloined letter, so Laina presents *Hers* in place of the unreciprocated look.

I have addressed Laina's poetics of censorship in terms of how her poems teach her readers to read differently. At one level her poetry seems to counter the excessiveness of Galanaki's and Mastoraki's poetry, but at another level it is quite similar: the unreciprocated look, like the procrastinated deliveries of child and letter, is rehearsed in language and becomes an excuse to defer meaning. By continuously deferring the look, and by making the page the scene of this diversion, *Hers* constructs a place where Maria is no longer at odds with her environment, not because she has become better socialized but because the place itself has become more heterogeneous and nonhierarchical. The ground of love, missing at the beginning of *Hers*, is tentatively found in the shifting materiality of the text we are reading. Though at points this collection suggests that the other epoch to which Maria escapes is centuries ago, when the fresco was (9), before metal and cotton (72), or in the future when the soft stone has crumbled (22) and writing has been wiped away because it was not indelible (48), more than anything, *Hers* insists that this other epoch is right now, right here—"έξω στο φως" (out in the light), the book in front of us, the place of our reading. Laina offers an alternative response to the question another contemporary Greek woman poet Ioanna Zervou poses in the article on writing and the body which I discussed in my introduction to this chapter. Whereas Zervou asks whether there has been in the past or will be in the future a cultural space in which woman moves freely (1981, 202), Laina points neither to some lost matriarchy, nor to a future-tense "newly born woman," but to the page in front of us, to a woman who was here all along, but misinterpreted.

Epilogue

In Greece since the mid-1980s, gender has emerged as a useful category for literary analysis. The more writing by women is read as women's writing, the less facetious Mastoraki's remark about being a woman poet seems: "Do you write women's poetry?" "Of course. Insofar as a doctor from Volos practices Voliot medicine and bakers from Piraeus bake Piraean bread" (1982a, 65). Maro Douka's novel *Fool's Gold* published in 1979 anticipates this by posing women's writing as a product of the dictatorship and postdictatorship years. In this rambling narrative, a young girl becomes a woman under the colonels' regime, as is true of the novelist herself and the poets whose work I have been discussing. Her story, however, is as much about writing becoming women's writing as it is about a girl becoming a woman. Over the course of the narrative there evolves an appreciation of the complex role gender plays in the construction of a text.

The catalyst for this memoir is a questionnaire that a woman friend in a leftist organization gives the protagonist to fill out in the wake of the dictatorship. Although at the end of the novel she answers the questions within the space provided—admitting, "So, finally, I fitted onto a single sheet of paper" (1991, 312)—for most of the novel she responds to these questions in a different fashion:

> I don't know how writers manage, what satisfaction they can feel, if indeed they do get satisfaction from writing. I've had the impression throughout of constantly leaving things half said, whatever I've wanted to say would involuntarily take off into vagueness, I can't help it, I suppose I was afraid to go the whole way, this is the best I could do. And so I've been left throughout with the bitter feeling that was all hot air. But at least I've been talking about real and immediate things. I've strayed a lot certainly, but never quite lost

the thread. And it was nothing like Ariadne's thread either—all I tried to do, quite simply, was to answer some specific questions. (309)

In this novel, as in the poetry collections from the 1980s, writing stumbles, halts, swerves. It does not guide the reader through the story the way Ariadne's thread leads Theseus out of the maze; it requires a reader willing to take detours.

As with much of the poetry I have been analyzing, the gendered nature of this undecidable kind of writing is not directly announced. When she is explaining how the questionnaire helped her, the issue of gender is raised through a reference to the military service:

But the encounter had done me good. The questionnaire most of all. It had given me a real shock, as though suddenly I'd seen my whole life simplified, implacably and absurdly, into a handful of questions. And allotted numbers, one, two, three, up to fourteen. There was even a fifteenth question, but that one didn't concern me, about whether I'd done my military service. (312)

In many ways the whole book can be read as an answer to this fifteenth question, which does not pertain to her. The book describes the experience of becoming a woman under the dictatorship, acknowledging her necessarily slant relation to the status quo inasmuch as she is constantly addressed as a man or ignored. Douka's conclusion is a fitting epilogue to this discussion of women's writing and censorship because it traces the same trajectory of writing under the dictatorship to the point where writing can be read as writing as a woman. By calling attention to the act of being gendered through reading—in this case, of being read as a man—she fills 271 pages writing as a woman. Like Karapanou's *Kassandra and the Wolf*, this is a story about the way the undecidable figure of woman provides an alternative mode of expression which acknowledges the indecision of the postdictatorship years—"and now what?"—but manages to turn this indecision into a viable form of writing.

In my analysis of Galanaki's, Mastoraki's, and Laina's poetry, it is clear that the third term each poet introduces, whether it is the child, the letter, or the look, depends on the reader for its deferral. The reader's feminine gender and plurality keeps the possibility of any delivery pending. In this way, the text can sustain its undecidability. Similarly, the idea that the page is the only place where certain relations can be enacted appears repeatedly in these visual narratives. The page becomes a place for an alternative ordering of space, what Foucault (1986) has called a heterotopia. The material analogue of the undecidability of meaning is the unstable page, made up of severed threads (Galanaki), damp walls (Mastoraki), and the unreciprocated look (Laina). Rather than insist on clear-cut answers, these collections rehearse misunderstanding over time and space. They take the slant, the swerving-off, the paralogical, the "irrelevant" as a formal as well as a thematic challenge. In their insistence on working within the constraints of censorship to produce a writing that acknowledges different forms of power struggle, their writing formalizes difficulty as feminine.

The question remains, however, what is the significance of women's poetry's hermeticism in the context of Greece's own recent estrangement from Europe and her other neighbors? In the years since these poets first began to publish, Greece has become more and more preoccupied with the idea that its language is a private language. At a discussion on Greece and the European Union, Katerina Anghelaki-Rooke voiced her fear that soon the only purpose Greek would have would be for dirty jokes between waiters serving tourists in Syndagma Square. Jokes are in fact one of the places the anxiety over the fate of the Greek language manifests itself most clearly. In the Kyr cartoon, Lysistrata and her cohorts speak in English, but written in Greek letters, while the ice cream man uses the Greek name written in English. Elsewhere a note admits that characters speak English because they are influenced by American comics. In the early 1970s there is the sense, however parodic, of an openness to international exchange and cosmopolitanism. But more recently such openness is hard to find; the interplay between Greek and English, more vexed. In 1994 the joke equivalent of Kyr's 1970s cartoon involved a young man going up to a kiosk to buy a drink. He begins his request mumbling Greek so that no one can understand him "Blah, blah, blah . . ." and ends with the clearly pronounced English word, ". . . Coca-cola." The vender then replies, having understood the muddled Greek, but not the clear English, "a bottle of . . . what?" Greek and the multinational English language of the rest of the world (Coca-cola) are mutually incomprehensible.

Does the critical attention to women's writing in Greece have anything to do with the fact that women writers are working on something everyone is worried about? Might women's problematizing of language in the form of poetry's hermeticism or Douka's digressions exemplify a concern that is being felt more generally in Greece? Is part of the reason Galanaki's novel *The Life of Ismail Ferik Pasha* was such a success because it is the story of a pasha for whom Greek is the forbidden, lost language? Could women poets' long-standing attention to the rhetoric of misunderstanding offer new ways of coping with the fear of inadequacy and irrelevance? Might these women poets' exploration of undecidability be viewed as a resource, a place for rehearsing the complex ways in which Kassandra cannot say what she means?

Works Consulted

Besides listing works cited in the text, I provide information regarding poetry collections, prose, and criticism published since 1967 by writers central to this book, as well as important reviews and translations of their work. I also include relevant critical work on women and gender in Modern Greek studies, as there is no bibliography yet available. The best general source in English of information on Modern Greek literature is Philippides 1990. The forthcoming annotated bibliography edited by Stratos Constantinidis for the Modern Greek Studies Association, will offer more interdisciplinary coverage. In translating Greek titles, I have used the wording of existing English translations wherever possible. This at times means the English strays considerably from the Greek. For the benefit of readers who do not know Greek, I have also included references to available translations of authors' works even when they are not the specific work I discuss.

Abraham, Nicolas. [1969] 1994. "The Shell and the Kernel: The Scope and Originality of Freudian Psychoanalysis." In *The Shell and the Kernel* by Nicolas Abraham and Maria Torok; ed., trans., and intro. Nicholas T. Rand. Vol. 1. Chicago: University of Chicago Press.

Adler, Ada, ed. 1967. *Suidae Lexicon*. Stuttgart: Teubner.

Adorno, Theodor W. 1982. "On the Fetish Character in Music and the Regression of Listening." In *The Essential Frankfurt School Reader*, ed. Andrew Arato and Eike Gebhardt. New York: Continuum.

Aeschylus. 1975. *The Oresteia*. Trans. Robert Fagles. New York: Bantam.

Alexandrou, Aris. 1978. Ποιήματα, *1941–1974* (Poems). Athens: Kastaniotis.

———. [1974] 1984. Το κιβώτιο (The mission box). Athens: Kedros.

———. 1996. *The Mission Box*. Trans. Robert Crist. Athens: Kedros.

Alexiou, Margaret. 1974. *The Ritual Lament in Greek Tradition*. Cambridge: Cambridge University Press.

———. 1982. "Diglossia in Greece." In *Standard Languages: Spoken and Written*, ed. W. Haas. Manchester: Manchester University Press.

——. 1983. "Sons, Wives, and Mothers: Reality and Fantasy in Some Modern Greek Ballads." *Journal of Modern Greek Studies* 1: 73–111.

——. 1993. "Greek and Black Women's Voices." *Point of Reference* 1: 35–44.

Alexiou, Margaret, and Vassilis Lambropoulos, eds. 1985. *The Text and Its Margins: Post-Structuralist Approaches to Twentieth-Century Greek Literature.* New York: Pella.

Althusser, Louis. [1969] 1982. "Contradiction and Overdetermination." In *For Marx.* London: Verso.

Anagnostaki, Nora. 1977. Η κριτική της παντομίμας (The criticism of pantomime). Athens: Kedros.

——. 1980. Μαγικές εικόνες (Magic pictures). Athens: Nefeli.

Anagnostakis, Manolis. 1973. "Poems by Manolis Anagnostakis." Trans. Kimon Friar. *Boundary* 2 1: 419–32.

——. 1980. *The Target: Selected Poems.* Trans. and intro. Kimon Friar. New York: Pella.

——. 1986. Τα ποιήματα, *1941–1971* (The poems). Athens: Stigmi.

Analis, Dimitri. 1979. "La poésie entre la lyre et le bouzouki." *Les Nouvelles Littéraires,* August 23.

Anastasopoulou, Maria. 1991. "Awakening and Self-redefinition in Greek Women Writers." *Modern Greek Studies Yearbook* 7: 259–85.

Andrews, Kevin. 1980. *Greece in the Dark, 1967–1974.* Amsterdam: Hakkert.

——. 1988. Private interview, Athens, July.

"And the Men Are Becoming Women," see "Κι οι άντρες γίνονται γυναίκες."

Angelou, Alkis, P. Ambatzoglou, T. Ioannou et al. 1972. "Συζήτηση για το βιβλίο" (Discussion about the book). *Chroniko 1972* 3: 30–41.

Anghelaki-Rooke, Katerina. 1963. Λύκοι και σύννεφα (Wolves and clouds). Athens: Zarvanos.

——. 1971. Ποιήματα, *1963–1969* (Poems). Athens: Ermis.

——. 1974. Μαγδαληνή το μεγάλο θηλαστικό (Magdalene, the vast mammal). Athens: Ermis.

——. 1975. *The Body Is the Victory and the Defeat of Dreams.* Trans. Philip Ramp. San Francisco: Wire Press.

——. 1976. "Φεμινισμός και νεώτερη γυναικεία ποίηση στην Ελλάδα" (Feminism and contemporary women's poetry in Greece). In Αφιέρωμα στη σύγχρονη γυναικεία ποίηση (Special issue on contemporary women's poetry), ed. Yannis Goudelis. *Kainouria Epoche* (fall): 53–59.

——. 1977. Τα σκόρπια χαρτιά της Πηνελόπης (The scattered papers of Penelope). Salonika: Tram.

——. 1978. Ο θρίαμβος της σταθερής απώλειας (The triumph of constant loss). Athens: Kedros.

——. 1982. Ενάντιος έρωτας (Beings and things on their own). Athens: Kedros.

——. 1983. "Sex Roles in Modern Greek Poetry." *Journal of Modern Greek Studies* 1 (1): 141–56.

——. 1984. Οι μνηστήρες (The suitors). Athens: Kedros.

——. 1986. *Beings and Things on Their Own.* Trans. Jackie Willcox with the author. Brockport, N.Y.: BOA Editions.

——. 1988. Όταν το σώμα: Επιλογή *1963–1988* (When the body: Selected poems). Athens: Ipsilon.

——. 1990. Επίλογος αέρας (Epilogue wind). Athens: Kedros.

——. 1992. "Towards a Private Vision: Notes on Greek Poetry Today." Typescript.

——. 1993. Άδεια φύση (Empty nature). Athens: Kedros.

———. 1995a. Λυπιού (Tristiu). Athens: Chirokinitos.

———. 1995b. Ωραία έρημος η σάρκα (The beautiful desert of flesh). Athens: Kastaniotis.

———. 1996. "Η Αλήθεια ως μεταφορικός λόγος στην Ελληνική γυναικεία ποιητική γραφή" (The truth as metaphorical language in Greek women's poetic writing). Paper given at the Symposium on Translating Greek Women's Writing, July, French Institute, Portocheli.

Apostolidis, Iraklis, and Renos Apostolidis. 1970. Ανθολογία της νεοελληνικής γραμματείας (Anthology of Modern Greek literature). Vols. 1–3, Η ποίηση λόγια και δημοτική από το μεσαίωνα ως τις μέρες μας (Learned and folk poetry from the Middle Ages to our day). Vols. 4–7, Το διήγημα από τις αρχές του στον 19ο αιώνα ως τις μέρες μας (The short story from its beginnings in the nineteenth century to our day). Athens: Ta Nea Ellinika.

Aravandinou, Mando. 1975. Μετα-γραφή ή εμπειρία συνόρων (Meta-writing, or the experience of borders). Athens: Ermis.

Argiriou, Alexandros. 1986. Αναψηλαφήσεις σε δύσκολους καιρούς (Retrials in difficult times). Athens: Kedros.

———, ed. 1979. Η ελληνική ποίηση (Greek poetry). Vol. 1, Νεωτερικοί ποιητές του μεσοπολέμου (Innovative poets of the interwar period). Athens: Sokolis.

———. 1983. Η ελληνική ποίηση (Greek poetry). Vol. 2, Ποιητές της πρώτης μεταπολεμικής γενιάς (Poets of the first postwar generation). Athens: Sokolis.

Argiriou, Alexandros, Takis Karvelis, Alexandros Kotzias, Christoforos Milionis, Kostas Steriopoulos, and Spiros Tsaknias, eds. 1992. Η μεταπολεμική πεζογραφία: Από τον πόλεμο του '40 ως τη δικτατορία του '67 (Postwar prose: From the war of '40 to the dictatorship of '67). Vol. 1, Εισαγωγή (Introduction) by Alexandros Argiriou. Athens: Sokolis.

Argiriou, Alexandros, Alexandros Kotzias, and Dimitris N. Maronitis. 1973. Συνέχεια (Continuity). 7 vols. (March–September). Athens: Kedros.

Aristophanes. 1973. *Aristophanes: Lysistrata/The Archanians/The Clouds*. Trans. and intro. Alan H. Sommerstein. Harmondsworth: Penguin.

Aristotle. [1947] 1973. *The Poetics*. In *Introduction to Aristotle*, ed. Richard McKeon. Chicago: University of Chicago Press.

Arseni, Kitty. 1983. Μπουμπουλίνας 18 (Bouboulina). Athens: Themelio.

Auerbach, Erich. 1968. *Mimesis: The Representation of Reality in Western Literature*. Trans. Willard R. Trask. Princeton: Princeton University Press.

Avdela, Efi, and Angelika Psarra, eds. 1985. Ο φεμινισμός στην Ελλάδα του μεσοπολέμου (Feminism in Greece in the interwar period). Athens: Gnosis.

Avdela, Efi, Fani Ziozia, Marianna Kondili, et al., eds. 1979–81. Σκούπα: Για το γυναικείο ζήτημα (Broom: On the women's question). 5 issues (January, June, December 1979; July 1980; July 1981).

Axelos, Kostas. 1986. Από τη μυθολογία στην τεχνολογία (From mythology to technology). Athens: Agra.

Axelos, Loukas. 1984a. Εκδοτική δραστηριότητα και κίνηση των ιδεών στη Ελλάδα (Publishing activity and the movement of ideas in Greece). Athens: Stochastis.

———. 1984b. "Publishing Activity and the Movement of Ideas." *Journal of the Hellenic Diaspora* 11 (summer): 5–46.

Bachelard, Gaston. 1964. *The Poetics of Space*. Trans. Maria Jolas. Boston: Beacon.

Bakalaki, Alexandra. 1986. "Κομμωτική: 'Ένα 'γυναικείο' επάγγελμα" (Hairdressing: A 'woman's' profession). *Dini* 1 (December): 98–103.

———. 1994. "Gender-Related Discourses and Representations of Cultural Specificity in Nineteenth-Century and Twentieth-Century Greece." *Journal of Modern Greek Studies* 12 (1): 75–112.

Bakhtin, Mikhail Mikhailovich. 1981. *The Dialogic Imagination: Four Essays.* Ed. Michael Holquist; trans. Caryl Emerson and Michael Holquist. Austin: University of Texas Press.

———. 1984. *Problems of Dostoevsky's Poetics.* Ed. and trans. Caryl Emerson. Intro. Wayne C. Booth. Minneapolis: University of Minnesota Press.

———. 1986. *Speech Genres and Other Late Essays.* Trans. Vern W. McGee. Austin: University of Texas Press.

Barbeito, Patricia. 1993. "The Poetics of Female Identity." *Point of Reference* 1: 45–49.

Barthes, Roland. 1973. *Mythologies.* Trans. Annette Lavers. London: Granada, Paladin.

———. 1974. *S/Z.* Trans. Richard Miller. New York: Hill & Wang.

———. 1975. *The Pleasure of the Text.* Trans. Richard Miller. New York: Hill & Wang.

———. 1984. *Image Music Text.* Trans. Stephen Heath. Oxford: Oxford University Press.

Bataille, Georges. 1980. Η ιστορία του ματιού (The story of the eye). Trans. and Intro. Dimitris Dimitriadis. Athens: Agra.

Baudelaire, Charles. 1982. Εγκώμιο του μακιγιάζ (In praise of make-up). Trans. Margarita Karapanou. Athens: Agra.

Bazin, André. 1967. "Για ένα μη–καθαρό κινηματογράφο" (In defense of mixed cinema). Trans. Vasilis Rafaelidis. *Ellinikos Kinimatografos* 3–4: 29–31.

Beaton, Roderick. 1994. *An Introduction to Modern Greek Literature.* Cambridge: Cambridge University Press.

Bekatoros, Stefanos K., and Alekos E. Florakis. 1971. Η νέα γενιά: Ποιητική ανθολογία, *1965–1970* (The new generation: Poetry anthology). Athens: Kedros.

Belezinis, Andreas. 1975. Review of Ποίηση 1, 2 (Poetry) by Lefteris Poulios. *Speira* 2: 200–239.

Benhabib, Seyla, and Drucilla Cornell, eds. 1987. *Feminism as Critique.* Cambridge, Mass.: Blackwell, Polity.

Benjamin, Jessica. 1988. *The Bonds of Love: Psychoanalysis, Feminism, and the Problem of Domination.* New York: Pantheon.

Benjamin, Walter. 1968. *Illuminations.* Ed. and intro. Hannah Arendt; trans. Harry Zohn. New York: Harcourt, Brace & World.

———. 1978. *Reflections.* Ed. and intro. Peter Demetz; trans. Edmund Jephcott. New York: Harcourt Brace Jovanovich.

———. 1983. *Charles Baudelaire: A Lyric Poet in the Era of High Capitalism.* Trans. Henry Zohn. London: Verso.

Berger, John. 1972. *Ways of Seeing.* Harmondsworth: Penguin.

———. 1986. Η εικόνα και το βλέμμα (Ways of seeing). Athens: Odisseas.

Berlis, Aris. 1990. "Η επάχθεια των νεκρών" (The burden of the dead). *Logou Harin* 1 (spring): 181–89.

———. 1991. "Ερμηνεύοντας και παρερμηνεύοντας τον Χάρολντ Μπλουμ" (Interpreting and misinterpreting Harold Bloom). *Logou Harin* 2 (spring): 162–66.

Bersani, Leo. 1986. *The Freudian Body: Psychoanalysis and Art.* New York: Columbia University Press.

Bien, Peter. 1985. "The Predominance of Poetry in Greek Literature." *World Literature Today* 59 (2): 197–200.

——. 1990–91. "Ritsos's Painterly Technique in Long and Short Poems." *To Yiofiri: Periodical of Modern Greek Studies* (Sydney) 11: 1–11.

Blanchot, Maurice. 1982. *The Space of Literature.* Trans. Ann Smock. Lincoln: University of Nebraska Press.

Blonsky, Marshall, ed. 1985. *On Signs.* Baltimore: Johns Hopkins University Press.

Bloom, Harold. 1973. *The Anxiety of Influence: A Theory of Poetry.* Oxford: Oxford University Press.

——. 1989. Η αγωνία της επίδρασης: Μια θεωρία για την ποίηση (The anxiety of influence: A theory of poetry). Trans., intro., notes, Dimitris Dimiroulis; afterword, Paul de Man. Athens: Agra.

Boatwright, James, ed. 1985. *Greek Writers.* Spec. issue of *Shenandoah: The Washington and Lee University Review* 27 (fall).

Bohandy, Susan. 1994. "Defining the Self through the Body in Four Poems by Katerina Anghelaki-Rooke and Sylvia Plath." *Journal of Modern Greek Studies* 12 (1): 1–36.

Bonaparte, Marie. 1944. Η λανθάνουσα νεκροφιλία στο έργο του Έδγαρ Πόε (Latent necrophilia in the work of Edgar Allan Poe). Trans. K. Alki Drakoulidi; intro. Andreas Embirikos. Athens: Koridalos.

——. 1984. Ταύτιση κόρης και πεθαμένης μητέρας (Identification of daughter and dead mother). Trans. Liza Petridi. Athens: Agra.

"Book Trade in Crisis!" see "Το βιβλίο περνάει κρίση!"

Borneman, John. 1991. *After the Wall: East Meets West in the New Berlin.* New York: Basic Books.

Bostantzoglou, Mendis [Bost]. 1973. "Το τέρας του ΛόχΝΑΙ" (The Lochyes monster). *Tachydromos*, July 20, 8–9.

——. 1975. 18 αντι-κείμενα ή υπέρ διχτατορείας λόγος (18 anti-texts or pro dictatorship discourse). Athens: Anti.

Bourdieu, Pierre. 1986. *Distinction: A Social Critique of the Judgement of Taste.* Trans. Richard Nice. London: Routledge & Kegan Paul.

——. 1991. "Censorship and the Imposition of Form." In *Language and Symbolic Power.* Ed. John B. Thompson; trans. Gino Raymond and Matthew Adamson, Cambridge: Harvard University Press.

Bowie, Malcolm. 1991. *Lacan.* Cambridge: Harvard University Press.

Βραδιά Σεφέρη (Seferis evening). 1972. Athens: Kedros.

Brecht, Bertolt. 1947. *Selected Poems of Bertold Brecht.* Trans. H. R. Hayston. New York: Reynal & Hitchcock.

——. 1966. *Galileo.* Trans. Charles Laughton; intro. Eric Bentley. New York: Grove.

Brooks, Cleanth. 1975. *The Well Wrought Urn: Studies in the Structure of Poetry.* New York: Harcourt Brace Jovanovich.

Bürger, Peter. 1984. *Theory of the Avant Garde.* Trans. Michael Shaw. Minneapolis: University of Minnesota Press.

Burke, Carolyn. 1981. "Irigaray through the Looking Glass." *Feminist Studies* 7 (2): 288–306.

Burroughs, William S. 1959. *The Naked Lunch.* New York: Grove.

Burt, Richard, ed. 1994. *The Administration of Aesthetics: Censorship, Political Criticism, and the Public Sphere.* Minneapolis: University of Minnesota Press.

Butler, Judith. 1993. "The Lesbian Phallus and the Morphological Imaginary." In *Bodies That Matter.* New York: Routledge.

Cacciari, Massimo. 1994. *The Necessary Angel*. Trans. Miguel E. Vatter. Albany: State University of New York Press.

Calas, Nicolas. 1966. "Pop Icons." In *Pop Art*, ed. Lucy R. Lippard. London: Thames & Hudson.

———. 1982. Κείμενα ποιητικής και αισθητικής (Texts on poetics and aesthetics). Athens: Plethron.

Calinescu, Matei. 1977. *Faces of Modernity: Avant-Garde, Decadence, Kitsch*. Bloomington: Indiana University Press.

Cammett, John M. 1995. "A Bibliography of the Works of Antonio Gramsci: Publications of His Writings in 27 Languages, 1930–1995." *International Gramsci Society Newsletter* 5 (November): 3–27.

Campbell, J. K. 1964. *Honour, Family and Patronage: A Study of Institutions and Moral Values in a Greek Mountain Community*. Oxford: Oxford University Press.

Cavafy, C. P. 1975. *Collected Poems*. Trans. Edmund Keeley and Philip Sherrard. Princeton: Princeton University Press. Rev. Ed. 1992.

———. 1982. Εις το φως της ημέρας (In broad daylight). Athens: Agra.

———. 1983. "In Broad Daylight." Trans. James Merrill. *Grand Street* 2 (3): 99–107.

———. 1993. Τα ποιήματα (Collected poems). Vol. 1, *1896–1918*. Vol. 2, *1919–1933*. Rev. ed. Ed. George P. Savvidis. Athens: Ikaros.

Cavell, Stanley. 1976. *Must We Mean What We Say? A Book of Essays*. Cambridge: Cambridge University Press.

Cavounides, Jennifer. [1982] 1983. "Capitalist Development and Women's Work in Greece." *Journal of Modern Greek Studies* 1 (2): 321–38.

Caws, Mary Ann, and Hermine Riffaterre, eds. 1983. *The Prose Poem in France: Theory and Practice*. New York: Columbia University Press.

Center of Marxist Studies, see Κέντρο Μαρξιστικών σπουδών.

Chambers, Ross. 1991. *Room for Maneuver: Reading the Oppositional in Narrative*. Chicago: University of Chicago Press.

Chase, Cynthia. 1984. "Models of Narrative: Mechanical Doll, Exploding Machine." *Oxford Literacy Review* 6 (2): 57–69.

Chioles, John. 1993. "Poetry and Politics: The Greek Cultural Dilemma." In *Ritual, Power, and the Body: Historical Perspectives on the Representation of Greek Women*, ed. C. Nadia Serematakis. New York: Pella.

Chodorow, Nancy. 1978. *The Reproduction of Mothering: Psychoanalysis and the Sociology of Gender*. Berkeley: University of California Press.

Chouvel, J. F. 1968. *La gréce à l'ombre des epées*. Paris: Laffont.

Christakis, Leonidas, ed. 1974. *Panderma*: Παντός τέρμα ή παντός δέρμα (Panderma: All finished or all skin) 10 (October): unpaged.

Christea-Doumani, Mariella. 1983. *Mothering in Greece: Collectivism to Individualism*. New York: Academic Press.

———. 1989. Η ελληνίδα μητέρα άλλοτε και σήμερα (The Greek mother then and now). Athens: Kedros.

Christianopoulos, Dinos. 1975a. "Γιατί το τραγούδι δεν σοκάρει εκεί που σοκάρει το ποίημα" (Why doesn't the song shock the way the poem does)? *Diagonios* 11: 137–38.

———. 1975b. "Ποίηση ή μεταποίηση" (Poetry or metapoetry). *Diagonios* 11: 168–69, 173.

Chryssanthopoulos, Michael. 1979. "The Emergence of Greek Surrealism: Literary and Intellectual Origins." M.A. thesis, University of Birmingham.

——. 1986. "Memory and Imagination in the Short Stories of Georgios M. Vizyenos." Ph.D. diss., University of Birmingham.

——. 1994. Μεταξύ φαντασίας και μνήμης (Between imagination and memory). Athens: Estia.

Cicellis, Kay. 1977a. Introduction to *Greek Writers and the Dictatorship*. Spec. issue of *Descant* 8 (2): 8–10.

——. 1977b. "Panagoulis: Two Photographs, Two Texts." *Boundary 2* 5: 461–64.

——. 1986. "Crossed Wires." Story in typescript.

Cixous, Hélène. 1975. "At Circe's, or the Self-Opener." *Boundary 2* 3: 387–97.

——. 1976. "The Laugh of the Medusa." Trans. Keith Cohen and Paula Cohen. *Signs* 1 (4): 875–93.

——. 1991a. *Readings: The Poetics of Blanchot, Joyce, Kafka, Kleist, Lispector, and Tsvetayeva*. Ed., trans., and intro. Verena Andermatt Conley. Minneapolis: University of Minnesota Press.

——. 1991b. *Reading with Clarice Lispector*. Ed., trans., and intro. Verena Andermatt Conley. Minneapolis: University of Minnesota Press.

Cixous, Hélène, and Catherine Clément. 1986. *The Newly Born Woman*. Trans. Betsy Wing. Minneapolis: University of Minnesota Press.

Clogg, Richard. 1979. *A Short History of Greece*. Cambridge: Cambridge University Press.

——. 1992. *A Concise History of Greece*. Cambridge: Cambridge University Press.

——, ed. 1983. *Greece in the 1980s*. London: Macmillan.

Clogg, Richard, and George Yannopoulos, eds. 1972. *Greece under Military Rule*. New York: Basic Books.

Collecott, Diana. 1986. "Mirror-Images: Images of Mirrors in Poems by Sylvia Plath, Adrienne Rich, Denise Levertov, and H.D." *Revue Francaise d'Etudes Americaines* 30 (11): 49–60.

Continuity, see Argiriou, Kotzias, and Maronitis.

Cowan, Jane K. 1990. *Dance and the Body Politic in Northern Greece*. Princeton: Princeton University Press.

——. 1994. "Women, Men, and Pre-Lenten Carnival in Northern Greece: An Anthropological Exploration of Gender Transformation in Symbol and Practice." *Rural History* 5 (2): 195–210.

——. 1996. "Being a Feminist in Contemporary Greece: Similarity and Difference Reconsidered." In *Practicing Feminism: Identity, Difference, Power*, ed. Nickie Charles and Felicia Hughes-Freeland. London: Routledge.

Crowder, Diane Griffin. 1983. "Amazons and Mothers? Monique Wittig, Hélène Cixous, and Theories of Women's Writing." *Contemporary Literature* 24 (2): 117–44.

Culler, Jonathan. 1982. *On Deconstruction*. Ithaca: Cornell University Press.

Dafnis, Grigorios. 1955. Η Ελλάς μεταξύ δύο πολέμων, *1923–1940* (Greece between two wars). Vol. 1. Athens: Ikaros.

Dallas, Yannis. 1979. Εισαγωγή στην ποιητική του Μίλτου Σαχτούρη (Introduction to the poetics of Miltos Sachtouris). Athens: Keimena.

Dalven, Rae. 1994. *Daughters of Sappho: Contemporary Greek Women Poets*. Foreword,

Andonis Decavalles; preface, Karen Van Dyck. Rutherford, N.J.: Fairleigh Dickinson University Press.

Daniels, Kate. 1991. "The Demise of the 'Delicate Prisons': The Women's Movement in Twentieth-Century American Poetry." In *A Profile of Twentieth-Century American Poetry*, ed. Jack Myers and David Wojahn; intro. Ed. Folsom. Carbondale: Southern Illinois University Press.

Daniil, Yorgos. 1980. Τα αδιέξοδα και τα τερπνά (Dead ends and amusements). Salonika: Egnatia.

——. 1984. Τα επίθετα: Ποιήματα, *1968–1983* (The adjectives: Poems). Athens: Prosperos.

Daraki, Zefi. 1973. Ο κήπος με τα εγκαύματα (The garden with the burns). Athens: Keimena.

——. 1976. Ο αρχάγγελος καθρέφτης (The archangel mirror). Athens: Kedros.

——. 1977. "Dark on Dark," "Freedom," "The Hanging Kites," "Suicide." Trans. Kimon Friar. *Coffeehouse* 5 (winter): 38–41.

——. 1978. Ο λύκος του μεσονυχτιού (Midnight's wolf). Athens: Kedros.

——. 1982. Το μοναχικό φάντασμα της Λένας 'Ολεμ (The lonely ghost of Lena Olem). Athens: Estia.

Davis, Natalie Zemon. 1990. "Rabelais among the Censors, 1940s, 1540s." *Representations* 32: 1–32.

Decavalles, Andonis. 1978. "Modernity: The Third Stage, the New Poets." *Charioteer* 20: 11–43.

de Certeau, Michel. 1984. *The Practice of Everyday Life*. Trans. Steven Rendall. Berkeley: University of California Press.

Δεκαοχτώ κείμενα (Eighteen texts). 1970. Athens: Kedros. *Eighteen Texts*. 1972. Trans. ed. Willis Barnstone, intro. Stratis Haviaras. Cambridge: Harvard University Press.

de Lauretis, Teresa. 1984. *Alice Doesn't: Feminism, Semiotics, Cinema*. London: Macmillan.

——. 1987. *Technologies of Gender: Essays on Theory, Film, and Fiction*. Bloomington: Indiana University Press.

Deleuze, Gilles, and Felix Guattari. 1986. *Kafka: Toward a Minor Literature*. Trans. Dana Polan; foreword Reda Guattari. Minneapolis: University of Minnesota Press.

de Man, Paul. 1989. "Dialogism and Absence." In *Rethinking Bakhtin: Extensions and Challenges*, ed. Gary Saul Morson and Caryl Emerson. Evanston, Ill.: Northwestern University Press.

Deposition, see Κατάθεση.

Derrida, Jacques. 1973. *Speech and Phenomena and Other Essays on Husserl's Theory of Signs*. Ed., trans., and intro. David B. Allison. Evanston, Ill.: Northwestern University Press.

——. 1978. *Writing and Difference*. Trans. and intro. Alan Bass. London: Routledge & Kegan Paul.

——. 1987. *The Postcard: From Socrates to Freud and Beyond*. Trans. Alan Bass. Chicago: University of Chicago Press.

——. 1991. *A Derrida Reader: Between the Blinds*. Ed., intro., and notes Peggy Kamuf. New York: Columbia University Press.

de Saussure, Ferdinand. 1966. *Course in General Linguistics.* Trans. Wade Baskins. New York: McGraw-Hill.

Digenis Akritas: The Two-Blood Border Lord: The Grottaferrata Version. 1985. Trans. and intro. Denison B. Hull. Ohio: Ohio University Press.

Dimaras, C. Th. 1972. *A History of Modern Greek Literature.* Trans. Mary P. Gianos. Albany: State University of New York Press.

———. [1948] 1975. Ιστορία της Νεοελληνικής λογοτεχνίας (A history of Modern Greek literature). Athens: Ikaros.

Dimen, Muriel. 1983. "Servants and Sentries: Women, Power, and Social Reproduction in Kriovrisi." *Journal of Modern Greek Studies* 1 (1): 225–42.

Dimiroulis, Dimitris. 1985. "The 'Humble Art' and the Exquisite Rhetoric: Tropes in the Manner of George Seferis." In *The Text and Its Margins,* ed. Margaret Alexiou and Vassilis Lambropoulos. New York: Pella.

———. 1990. "Ο Μπλουμ στην Ελλάδα: Οι αγωνίες, τα άγχη και τα συμπλέγματα της βιβλιοκριτικής" (Bloom in Greece: The agony, angst, and complexes of reviewing books). *Logou Harin* 1 (Spring): 169–80.

Dimitras, Panayote. 1987. "Changes in Public Attitudes." In *Political Change in Greece: Before and after the Colonels,* ed. Kevin Featherstone and Dimitrios K. Katsoudas. Kent: Croom Helm.

Dimitriadis, Dimitris. 1980. Πεθαίνω σαν χώρα (I die like a country). Athens: Agra.

Dimoula, Kiki. 1971. Το λίγο του κόσμου (The little of the world). Athens: Keimena.

———. 1976. "Jungle," "Dialogue between Me and Myself," "Incompatible Things." Trans. Kimon Friar. *Coffeehouse* 4 (summer): 39–42.

———. 1981a. "Φωνή σε αδειόδρομους" (Voice in empty streets). *Lexi* 2: 88–90.

———. 1981b. Το τελευταίο σώμα μου (My last body). Athens: Keimena.

———. 1983. "Έχουμε τερατώδη αύξηση του ποιητικού πληθυσμού" (We have monstrous inflation in the poetic population), interview. *Ta Nea,* April 28.

———. 1988. Χαίρε ποτέ (Hail never). Athens: Stigmi.

———. 1996. *Lethe's Adolescence* (includes *Hail Never*). Trans. David Connolly. Minneapolis: Nostos.

Dinnerstein, Dorothy. 1976. *The Mermaid and the Minotaur.* New York: Harper & Row.

Docherty, Thomas. 1987. *On Modern Authority: The Theory and Condition of Writing, 1500 to the Present Day.* Brighton, East Sussex: Harvester.

Douka, Maro. 1979. Η αρχαία σκουριά (Fool's gold). Athens: Kedros.

———. 1991. *Fool's Gold.* Trans. Roderick Beaton. Athens: Kedros.

———. 1992. Ο πεζογράφος και το πιθάρι του (The writer and his urn). Athens: Kastaniotis.

Doulis, Thomas. 1969. "Loula Anagnostaki and the New Theater of Greece." *Chicago Review* 21 (2): 83–87.

Drosou, Katy. 1985. Οι τοίχοι τέσσερις (The four walls). Athens: Keimena.

Drucker, Johanna. 1994. *The Visible Word: Experimental Typography and Modern Art.* Chicago: University of Chicago Press.

Dubisch, Jill, ed. 1986. *Gender and Power in Rural Greece.* Princeton: Princeton University Press.

Ducrot, Oswald, and Tzvetan Todorov, eds. 1983. *Encyclopedic Dictionary of the Sciences of Language.* Trans. Catherine Porter. Baltimore: Johns Hopkins University Press.

Eagleton, Terry. 1981. *Walter Benjamin, or Towards a Revolutionary Criticism*. London: Verso.

———. 1990. *The Ideology of the Aesthetic*. Cambridge, Mass.: Blackwell.

Eco, Umberto, and Thomas A. Sebeok. 1988. *The Sign of Three: Dupin, Holmes, Peirce*. Bloomington: Indiana University Press.

"Η ηθική του μαρκοδόρου" (The ethics of the magic marker). 1973. *Tachydromos*, June 29, 16–18.

Eighteen Texts, see Δεκαοχτώ κείμενα.

"Η λαϊκή μούσα" (The popular muse). 1969. Athens.

Ελληνική νομαρχία ήτοι λόγος περί ελευθερίας (The Greek rule of law or discourse on freedom). [1806] 1968. Athens: Kalvos.

Ellis, Keith. 1983. *Cuba's Nicolás Guillén: Poetry and Ideology*. Toronto: University of Toronto Press.

Elytis, Odysseas. 1978. Η Μαρία Νεφέλη (Maria Nephele). Athens: Ikaros.

———. 1981. *Maria Nephele: A Poem in Two Voices*. Trans. Athan Anagnostopoulos. Boston: Houghton Mifflin.

Embirikos, Andreas. 1969. *Amour, Amour: Writings or Personal Mythology*. Trans. Nikos Stangos and Alan Ross; intro. Nanos Valaoritis. London: Alan Ross.

———. 1974. Ο δρόμος (The road). Salonika: Tram.

———. [1945] 1980a. Ενδοχώρα (Hinterland). Athens: Agra.

———. [1960] 1980b. Γραπτά: Η προσωπική μυθολογία (Writings, or personal mythology). Athens: Agra.

———. 1980c. Οκτάνα (Oktana). Athens: Ikaros.

———. [1935] 1980d. Υψικάμινος (The blast furnace). Athens: Agra.

———. 1984. Η σήμερον ως αύριον και ως χθες (Today as tomorrow and as yesterday). Athens: Agra.

Empson, William. 1984. *Seven Types of Ambiguity*. London: Hogarth.

Engels, Friedrich. 1985. *The Origin of the Family, Private Property, and the State*. Intro. Michèle Barrett. Harmondsworth: Penguin.

Engonopoulos, Nikos. 1977. Ποιήματα Α': Μην ομιλείτε εις τον οδηγόν. Τα κλειδοκύμβαλα της σιωπής (Poems I: Do not converse with the driver. The pianos of silence). Athens: Ikaros.

———. 1983. Μπολιβάρ (Bolivar). Athens: Ikaros.

Η ποίηση σήμερα στην Ελλάδα (Poetry today in Greece). 1984. Spec. issue. *Grammata kai Technes* 35–36 (November–December): 3–32.

"The Ethics of the Magic Marker," see "Η ηθική του μαρκοδόρου."

Έξη ποιητές (Six poets). 1971. Intro. Kimon Friar. Athens.

Fakinou, Eugenia. 1982. Αστραδενή (Astradeni). Athens: Kedros.

———. 1983. Το έβδομο ρούχο (The seventh garment). Athens: Kastaniotis.

———. 1991a. *Astradeni*. Trans. H. E. Criton. Athens: Kedros.

———. 1991b. *The Seventh Garment*. Trans. Ed. Emory. London: Serpent's Tail.

Fallaci, Oriana. 1976a. Γράμμα σ' ένα παιδί που δεν γεννήθηκε ποτέ (Letter to a child never born). Trans. Eri Kandri. Athens: Papyros.

———. 1976b. *Letter to a Child Never Born*. Trans. John Shepley. New York: Simon & Schuster.

———. 1980. *A Man*. Trans. William Weaver. New York: Simon & Schuster.

Farinou, Georgia. 1984. "Narrative Techniques in Papadiamandis's Fiction, 1887–1910." Ph.D. diss., King's College London.

Farinou-Malamatari, Georgia. 1987. Αφηγηματικές τεχνικές στον Παπαδιαμάντη, *1887–1910* (Narrative techniques in Papadiamantis). Athens: Kedros.

——. 1988. "The Novel of Adolescence Written by a Woman: Margarita Limberaki." In *The Greek Novel: A.D. 1–1985,* ed. Roderick Beaton. Kent: Croom Helm.

Fatsi, Yannis. 1993. Πολυτεχνείο '73: Εξέγερση. Κατάληψη. Εισβολή (The Polytechnic '73: Revolt. Occupation. Invasion). Athens: Kastaniotis.

Faubion, James D. 1993. *Modern Greek Lessons: A Primer in Historical Constructivism.* Princeton: Princeton University Press.

Featherstone, Kevin, and Dimitrios K. Katsoudas, eds. 1987. *Political Change in Greece: Before and after the Colonels.* Kent: Croom Helm.

Fehervary, Helen. 1980. "The Gender of Authorship: Heiner Müller and Christa Wolf." *Studies in Twentieth Century Literature* 5 (1): 41–58.

Felman, Shoshana. 1993. *What Does a Woman Want? Reading and Sexual Difference.* Baltimore: Johns Hopkins University Press.

——, ed. 1982. *Literature and Psychoanalysis: The Question of Reading Otherwise.* Baltimore: Johns Hopkins University Press.

Ferlinghetti, Lawrence. 1995. Αυτά είναι τα ποτάμια μου: Νέα ποιήματα και επιλογή από το λούνα παρκ του νου (These are my rivers: New and selected poems from a Coney Island of the mind). Trans. and intro. Christos Tsiamis. Athens: Kastaniotis.

Finocchiaro, Maurice A., ed. 1989. *The Galileo Affair: A Documentary History.* Berkeley: University of California Press.

Fleming, Amalia. 1972. *A Piece of Truth.* London: Cape.

Fokkema, Douwe, and Hans Bertens, eds. 1984. *Approaching Postmodernism: Papers Presented at a Workshop on Postmodernism, 21–23 September 1984, University of Utrecht.* Utrecht Publications in General and Comparative Literature 21. Amsterdam: Benjamins.

Forché, Carolyn. 1995. *The Angel of History.* New York: HarperCollins.

Forrester, John. 1980. "Aphasia, Hysteria, and the Talking Cure." In *Language and the Origins of Psychoanalysis.* Basingstoke: Macmillan.

Foster, Hal, ed. 1983. *The Anti-Aesthetic: Essays on Postmodern Culture.* Port Townsend, Wash.: Bay.

Fostieris, Andonis, and Thanasis Niarchos, eds. 1975–81. Ποίηση (Poetry). 7 vols. Athens: Mikri Arktos.

——. 1987. Δικτατορία και διανοούμενοι (Dictatorship and intellectuals). Spec. issue of *Lexi* 63–64.

Foucault, Michel. 1977a. *Discipline and Punish: The Birth of the Prison.* Trans. Alan Sheridan. Harmondsworth: Penguin.

——. 1977b. *Language, Counter-Memory, Practice: Selected Essays and Interviews.* Ed. and intro. Donald F. Bouchard. Ithaca, N.Y.: Cornell University Press.

——. 1980. *The History of Sexuality.* Vol. 1, *An Introduction.* Trans. Robert Hurley. New York: Random House, Vintage.

——. 1986. "Of Other Spaces." Trans. Jay Miskowiec. *Diacritics* 16 (1): 22–27.

Fourtouni, Eleni, trans. 1978. *Contemporary Greek Women Poets.* New Haven, Conn.: Thelphini.

——. 1982. *Four Greek Women: Love Poems.* New Haven, Conn.: Thelphini.

Franco, Jean. 1992. "Going Public: Rehabiting the Private." In *On Edge: The Crisis of Contemporary Latin American Culture,* ed. George Yúdice, Jean Franco, and Juan Flores. Minneapolis: University of Minnesota Press.

Frangopoulos, T. D. 1972a. Review of Επέκεινα (Beyond) by Maria Laina. *Books Abroad* 46: 525–26.

——. 1972b. Review of Σχεδόν χωρίς προοπτική δυστυχήματος (Almost without the prospect of misfortune) by Pavlina Pampoudi. *Books Abroad*. 46: 719–20.

——. 1974. Δίαυλοι (Channels). Athens: Diogenis.

——. 1976. Review of Τα μωρά των αγγέλων άσπρα και μαύρα [sic] (The babies of angels, white and black) by Pavlina Pampoudi. *Books Abroad* 50.

——. 1982. "Η γυναίκα και ο κόσμος της" (The woman and her world). In Η Προσφορά της γυναίκας στον πολιτισμό (The contribution of woman to culture). Spec. issue of *Nea Estia* 1331 (Christmas): 2–10.

Frangoudaki, Anna. 1973. "Και πάλι για το γλωσσικό πρόβλημα" (And again on the language problem). *Continuity* 6 (August): 277–81.

Frantzi, Andia. 1975. Review of Πλην εύχαρις (Albeit pleasing) by Rhea Galanaki. *Anti*, December 13.

——. 1978. Η περιπέτεια μιας περιγραφής (An adventure of a description). Salonika: Egnatia.

——. 1984. Review of Ιστορίες για τα βαθιά (Tales of the deep) by Jenny Mastoraki. *Anti*, March 16.

——. 1988. Ούτως ή άλλως (In any event). Athens: Politipo.

——. 1993. "Ο ευάλωτος ρυθμός" (Corruptible rhythm). In spec. double issue on Manolis Anagnostakis, *Anti*, July 30.

——. 1993–94. "Ρέα Γαλανάκη: Από τις φωτογραφίες του ιστορικού στην 'ποιητική' της ιστορίας" (Rhea Galanaki: From the photographs of the historian to the "poetics" of history). *Simio* 2: 259–64.

Frantzi, Andia, Katerina Anghelaki-Rooke, Rhea Galanaki, Athena Papadaki, and Pavlina Pampoudi. 1990. Υπάρχει, λοιπόν, γυναικεία ποίηση; (So does women's poetry exist?) Athens: Scholi Moraitis.

Freud, Anna. 1986. *The Ego and the Mechanisms of Defence.* London: Hogarth.

Freud, Sigmund. 1976. *The Interpretation of Dreams.* Ed. Angela Richards; trans. James Strachey. Pelican Freud Library 4. Harmondsworth: Penguin.

——. 1984. *Beyond the Pleasure Principle* and "A Note upon the 'Mystic Writing-Pad.'" In *On Metapsychology: The Theory of Psychoanalysis,* ed. Angela Richards; trans. James Strachey. Pelican Freud Library 11. Harmondsworth. Penguin.

——. 1985. *Moses and Monotheism.* In *The Origins of Religion,* ed. Albert Dickson, trans. James Strachey. Pelican Freud Library 13. Harmondsworth: Penguin.

Friar, Kimon. 1978. "The New Poets." *Charioteer* 20: 42–115.

——. 1982. "Eleni Vakalo: Beyond Lyricism." *Journal of the Hellenic Diaspora* 9 (winter): 21–27.

——. 1985. *Contemporary Greek Poetry.* With intro., bios., and notes. Athens: Ypourgio Politsmou.

——, trans. 1973. *Modern Greek Poetry: From Cavafis to Elytis.* With intro., essay on trans., and notes. New York: Simon & Schuster.

Friends of *Anti.* 1984. Κάτι το ωραίον: Μια περιήγηση στη νεοελληνική κακογουστιά (Something beautiful: A tour of Modern Greek kitsch). Athens: Anti.

Fuss, Diana. 1989. *Essentially Speaking: Feminism, Nature, Difference.* New York: Routledge.

Galanaki, Rhea. 1973. "Ελληνικό τοπίο" (Greek landscape). *Continuity* 1 (March): 8.

——. 1975. Πλην εύχαρις (Albeit pleasing). Athens: Olkos.

——. 1979. Τα ορυκτά (Minerals). Athens: Diogenis.

——. 1980. Το κέικ (The cake). Athens: Kedros.

——. 1980–81. "Σχόλια για τη λογοτεχνική παραγωγή" (Notes on literary production) *Chroniko 1981* 12: 101–3.

——. 1981–82. "Η γλώσσα της λογοτεχνίας είναι πάντοτε παράνομη" (The language of literature is always illegal). *Chroniko 1982* 13: 107.

——. 1982a. "Η γυναικεία γραφή και η καταραμένη Πανδώρα" (Women's writing and the cursed Pandora). *Lexi* 15: 364–67.

——. 1982b. Πού ζει ο λύκος (Where does the wolf live)? Athens: Agra.

——. 1982–83. "Πώς βλέπεις τα πράγματα" (How you see things). *Chroniko 1983* 14: 27.

——. 1983a. "Η διαδρομή μιας απάντησης" (The journey of an answer). *Lexi* 23: 405–7.

——. 1983b. Interview. *Diavazo* 69: 21–22.

——. 1984. "Πάτρα: Η αναζήτηση μιας μυθολογίας" (Patra: In search of mythology). *Parathiro* 1: 13–14.

——. 1986a. "Εκατό χρόνια μοναξιάς, του Γκαμπριέλ Γκαρσία Μάρκες. Το σπίτι των πνευμάτων, της Ιζαμπέλ Αλιέντε" (A hundred years of solitude by Gabriel Garcia Marquez. House of the spirits by Isabel Allende). *Lexi* 58: 990–94.

——. 1986b. Ομόκεντρα διηγήματα (Concentric stories). Athens: Agra.

——. 1987. Private interview, Athens, August 5.

——. 1988. Private interview, Patras, July.

——. 1989a. Ο βίος του Ισμαήλ Φερίκ Πασά (The life of Ismail Ferik Pasha). Athens: Agra.

——. 1989b. Private questionnaire, May.

——. 1993. Θα υπογράφω Λούι (I shall sign my name as Louis). Athens: Agra.

——. 1996. *The Life of Ismail Ferik Pasha.* Trans. Kay Cicellis. London: Owen.

——. 1998. *The Cake.* In *The Rehearsal of Misunderstanding: Three Collections by Contemporary Greek Women Poets,* ed. and trans. Karen Van Dyck. Middletown, Conn.: Wesleyan University Press.

Galatariotou, Catia. 1987. "Structural Oppositions in the Grottaferrata *Digenes Akrites.*" *Byzantine and Modern Greek Studies* 11: 29–68.

"Galileo." 1980. *Dictionary of Philosophy and Religion.* Ed. W. C. Reese. Atlantic Highlands, N.J.: Humanities Press, 185–86.

Gallop, Jane. 1985a. "The Father's Seduction." In *The (M)other Tongue: Essays in Feminist Psychoanalytic Interpretation,* ed. Shirley Nelson Garner, Claire Kahane, and Madelon Sprengnether. Ithaca: Cornell University Press.

——. 1985b. *Reading Lacan.* Ithaca: Cornell University Press.

Ganoseli, Irini. 1975. "Η ελληνική γλώσσα στα συντάγματα του ελεύθερου κράτους" (The Greek language in the constitutions of the free state). *Parnassos* 17: 129–33.

Garandoudis, Euripides. 1989. "Πάλι περί λογοτεχνικών γενεών" (Again with regard to literary generations). *Entefktirio* 9 (December): 118–22.

Garner, Shirley Nelson, Claire Kahane, and Madelon Sprengnether, eds. 1985. *The (M)other Tongue: Essays in Feminist Psychoanalytic Interpretation.* Ithaca: Cornell University Press.

Genette, Gérard. 1979. "Valéry and the Poetics of Language." In *Textual Strategies,* ed. Josué V. Harari. Ithaca: Cornell University Press.

——. 1982. *Figures of Literary Discourse.* Trans. Alan Sheridan. New York: Columbia University Press.

Georgiopoulos, Anna. 1991. "Writing after Dictatorship: Identity, Trauma, and History in Rea Galanaki's *Where Does the Wolf Live?*" Senior Project, Yale University.

Germanacos, N. C. 1973a. "Interview with Three Contemporary Greek Writers: Stratis Tsirkas, Thanassis Valtinos, George Ioannou." *Boundary* 2 1: 266–347.

——. 1973b. "Three Young Poets: Jenny Mastoraki, Haris Megalinos, and Lefteris Poulios." *Boundary* 2 1: 507–18.

Ghanas, Michalis. 1983. Interview with Yiorgos Pilichos. *Ta Nea*, May 12.

Giannaris, George. 1979. Review of Το σόι (Kin) by Jenny Mastoraki. *World Literature Today* 53 (4): 726.

Gilbert, Sandra M., and Susan Gubar. 1979. *The Madwoman in the Attic: The Woman Writer, and the Nineteenth-Century Literary Imagination.* New Haven: Yale University Press.

Ginsberg, Allen. 1974. Σύγχρονη ποίηση (Contemporary poetry). Trans. Jenny Mastoraki. Athens: Boukoumanis.

——. 1989. "The Beats at Thirty." Interview with Peter Glassgold. *Columbia University Magazine*, February–March, 25–29.

Gitlin, Todd. 1993. *The Sixties: Years of Hope, Days of Rage.* New York: Bantam.

Gogou, Katerina. 1981. "Five Poems." Trans. Jack Hirschman. *Coffeehouse* 10 (summer): 40–45.

——. 1982. "Katerina Gogou." Trans. Jack Hirschman. *Third Rail* 5: 68–74.

——. 1983. *Three Clicks Left.* Trans. Jack Hirschman. San Francisco: Night Horn Books.

Gotsi, Georgia. 1996. "Narratives in Perambulation: Poe's 'The Man of the Crowd' and Metsakes' 'Αυτόχειρ.' " *Byzantine and Modern Greek Studies* 20: 35–55.

Gourgouris, Stathis. 1988. "Η μυθοπλασία του Καραγκιόζη και το εθνικό ασυνείδητο" (The mythification of Karaghiozis and the national unconscious). *Planodion* 7: 358–66.

——. 1989. "Writing the National Imaginary: The Memory of Makriyannis and the Miracles of Neohellenism." *Emergences* 1 (fall): 95–127.

——. 1996. *Dream Nation: Enlightenment, Colonization, and the Institution of Modern Greece.* Stanford: Stanford University Press.

Gramsci, Antonio. 1985. *Selection from Cultural Writings.* Ed. David Forgacs and Geoffrey Nowell-Smith; trans. William Boelhower. London: Lawrence & Wishart.

The Greek Rule of Law, see Ελληνική νομαρχία.

Grigoriadis, Solonos. 1975. Ιστορία της δικτατορίας (The history of the dictatorship). 3 vols. Athens: Kapopoulos.

Habermas, Jürgen. 1968. "The Movement in Germany: A Critical Analysis." In *Toward a Rational Society: Student Protest, Science, and Politics,* trans. Jeremy J. Shapiro. Boston: Beacon.

Hafner, Katie. 1993. "A Nation of Readers Dumps Its Writers." *New York Times Magazine,* January 10.

Hakkas, Marios. 1988. Τουφεκιοφόρος του εχθρού (The enemy's scabbard). Athens: Kedros.

Hall, Stuart. 1988. "Brave New World." *Marxism Today* 32 (October): 24–29.

Hamilton, Rita, and Janet Perry, trans. 1984. *The Poems of the Cid.* Harmondsworth: Penguin.

Handman, Marie-Élisabeth. 1983. *La violence et la ruse: Hommes et femmes dans un village grec.* La Calade, Aix-en-Provence: Edisud.

Harlow, Barbara. 1987. *Resistance Literature.* London: Methuen.

Harlow, Michael, ed. 1974. *Events: Greece, 1967–1974*. Athens: Anglo-Hellenic Publishing.

Hart, Janet. 1996. *New Voices in the Nation: Women and the Greek Resistance, 1941–1964*. Ithaca: Cornell University Press.

Hartman, Geoffrey H. 1981. *Saving the Text: Literature/Derrida/Philosophy*. Baltimore: Johns Hopkins University Press.

Hartokollis, Petros. 1984. "Η ψυχανάλυση και το πρόβλημα του εγκλιματισμού της στην Ελλάδα" (Psychoanalysis and the problem of its acclimatization in Greece). In Ψυχανάλυση και Ελλάδα: Στοιχεία θέσεις, ερωτήματα (Psychoanalysis and Greece: Facts, positions, questions), ed. Thanasis Tzavaras. Athens: Scholi Moraitis.

Harvey, Denise. 1987. "Poets, Priests, and Politics." *New Statesman*, June 12.

Harvey, John. 1985. *Coup d'Etat*. New York: Atheneum.

Hatzidaki, Natasa. 1976. "Dark Red," "Self-Portrait," and "Continuing Sexual Reports." Trans. Dino Siotis. *Coffeehouse* 2 (spring): 21–23.

——. 1981. "Ultra-Violet." *Lexi* 6: 460–65.

——. 1984. Δυσαρέσκεια (Displeasure). Athens: Plethron.

——. 1985. Ιβίσκοι, Νάρκισσοι (Hibiscuses, narcissus). Athens: Kedros.

Hatziioannou, Elena. 1987. "Δεν ήταν ώρα για βιβλία: Η εκδοτική δραστηριότητα στη δικτατορία" (No time for books: Publishing activity during the dictatorship). *Vima*, April 26, 47.

Hatzilazarou, Matsi. 1979. Έρως μελαχρινός (Dark-skinned Eros). Athens: Ikaros.

——. 1985. Το δίχως άλλο (Without a doubt). Athens: Keimena.

Haug, Frigga, ed. 1987. *Female Sexualization*. London: Verso.

Herzfeld, Michael. 1985. *The Poetics of Manhood: Contest and Identity in a Cretan Mountain Village*. Princeton: Princeton University Press.

——. [1981] 1986. *Ours Once More: Folklore, Ideology, and the Making of Modern Greece*. New York: Pella.

——. 1987. *Anthropology through the Looking-Glass: Critical Ethnography in the Margins of Europe*. Cambridge: Cambridge University Press.

——. 1990. "Silence, Submission, and Subversion: Toward a Poetics of Womanhood." In *Contested Identities: Kinship and Gender in the Anthropology of Greece*, ed. Peter Loizos and Akis Papataxiarchis. Princeton: Princeton University Press.

——. 1995. "Ethnographic Biography." Paper presented at Modern Greek Studies Symposium, November, Harvard University, Cambridge.

——. 1998. *An Ethnographic Biography of Andreas Nenedakis*. Chicago: University of Chicago Press.

Hill, Geoffrey. [1971] 1985. *Mercian Hymns*. In *Collected Poems*. Harmondsworth: Penguin.

Himonas, Yiorgos. 1971. Ο γιατρός Ινεότης (Dr. Ineotis). Athens: Kedros.

——. 1974. Γάμος (Marriage). Athens: Kedros.

——. 1975. Ο αδελφός (The brother). Athens: Kedros.

——. 1979. Οι χτίστες (The builders). Athens: Kedros.

——. 1984a. Έξι μαθήματα για τον λόγο (Six lessons on language). Athens: Ipsilon.

——. 1984b. Τα ταξίδια μου (My journeys). Athens: Kedros.

——. 1985. Ο χρόνος και το σύμβολο (Time and the symbol). Athens: Kedros, Rappas.

——. 1987. Η δύσθυμη αναγέννηση (The low-spirited renaissance). Athens: Ipsilon.

——. 1990. Ο εχθρός του ποιητή (The poet's enemy). Athens: Kedros.

——. 1991. *The Builders*. Trans. Robert Christ. Athens: Kedros.

Hirschkop, Ken. 1986. "Bakhtin, Discourse, and Democracy." *New Left Review* 160: 92–113.

——. 1989. "Introduction: Bakhtin and Cultural Theory." In *Bakhtin and Cultural Theory*, ed. Ken Hirschkop and David Shepherd. Manchester: Manchester University Press.

Hirschon, Renée. 1989. *Heirs of the Greek Catastrophe: The Social Life of Asia Minor Refugees in Piraeus*. Oxford: Clarendon.

Hoffman, Abbie. 1971. *Steal This Book*. Co-conspirator, Izack Haber; accessories after the fact, Tom Forcade and Bert Cohen. New York: Pirate Editions.

Holquist, Michael. 1994. "Corrupt Originals: The Paradox of Censorship." Introduction to *Literature and Censorship*. Spec. issue. *PMLA* 109 (1): 14–23.

Holst, Gail. 1977. "When Greece Is Bad Poetry." *Nation Review* (Sydney) June 24.

——. 1980. *Theodorakis: Myth and Politics in Modern Greek Music*. Amsterdam: Hakkert.

Holst-Warhaft, Gail. 1992. *Dangerous Voices: Women's Laments and Greek Literature*. London: Routledge.

Homans, Margaret. 1980. *Women Writers and Poetic Identity: Dorothy Wordsworth, Emily Bronte, and Emily Dickinson*. Princeton: Princeton University Press.

Huyssen, Andreas. 1986. "The Cultural Politics of Pop." In *After the Great Divide: Modernism, Mass Culture, Postmodernism: Theories of Representation and Difference*. Bloomington: Indiana University Press.

——. 1991. "After the Wall: The Failure of German Intellectuals." *New German Critique* 52: 109–43.

Iatropoulos, Dimitris. 1971. Αντι-ανθολογία (Anti-anthology). Athens.

Inglessi, Chrysi. 1990. Πρόσωπα γυναικών, προσωπεία της συνείδησης: Συγκρότηση της γυναικείας ταυτότητας στην ελληνική κοινωνία (Faces of women, masks of consciousness: The formation of feminine identity in Greek society). Athens: Odisseas.

Ioannou, Yiorgos. 1983. Το δημοτικό τραγούδι: Παραλογές (The demotic folksong: *Paraloges*). Athens: Ermis.

Irigaray, Luce. 1973. *Le langage des dement*. Paris: Minuit.

——. [1975] 1985a. *Speculum of the Other Woman*. Trans. Catherine Porter with Carolyn Burke. Ithaca: Cornell University Press.

——. [1977] 1985b. *This Sex Which Is Not One*. Trans. Gillian C. Gill. Ithaca: Cornell University Press.

——. 1990. *Je, tu, nous: Pour une culture de la différence*. Paris: Grasset & Fasquelle.

Isaïa, Nana. 1969. Ποιήματα (Poems). Athens: Lotos.

——. 1972. *Persona*. Athens: Ermias.

——. 1973. "Poem: Excursion to the Sky." *Omphalos* 1 (3): 16–21.

——. 1975. "Black and White Faces," "The God." Trans. Thanasis Maskaleris. *Coffeehouse* 1 (fall): 34–37.

Isaris, Alexandros. 1992. Οι Τριστάνοι: Ποιήματα, *1966–1992* (The Tristans: Poems). Athens: Nefeli.

Jakobson, Roman. 1971a. "On Linguistic Aspects of Translation." In *Selected Writings II*, vol. 2. The Hague: Mouton.

——. 1971b. "Two Aspects of Language and Two Types of Aphasic Disturbances." In *Selected Writings II*, vol. 2. The Hague: Mouton.

Jameson, Fredric. 1981. *The Political Unconscious: Narrative as a Socially Symbolic Act.* Ithaca: Cornell University Press.

———. 1984. "Postmodernism, or the Cultural Logic of Late Capitalism." *New Left Review* 146: 53–92.

———. 1990. *Late Marxism: Adorno, or the Persistence of the Dialectic.* London: Verso.

Janecek, Gerald. 1984. *The Look of Russian Literature: Avant-Garde Visual Experiments, 1900–1930.* Princeton: Princeton University Press.

Janson, Sue Curry. 1988. *Censorship: The Knot That Binds Power and Knowledge.* Oxford: Oxford University Press.

Joachimides, Christos M. and Norman Rosenthal, eds. 1975. *The Greek Month in London: Aspects of Contemporary Greek Culture.* London: Institute of Contemporary Art.

Johnson, Barbara. 1980. *The Critical Difference: Essays in the Contemporary Rhetoric of Reading.* Baltimore: Johns Hopkins University Press.

———. 1983. "Disfiguring Poetic Language." In *The Prose Poem in France: Theory and Practice,* ed. Mary Ann Caws and Hermine Riffaterre. New York: Columbia University Press.

———. 1989. *A World of Difference.* Baltimore: Johns Hopkins University Press.

Jones, Ann Rosalind. 1986. "Writing the Body toward an Understanding of l'Ecriture Féminine." In *The New Feminist Criticism,* ed. Elaine Schowalter. London: Virago.

Jung, C. G. 1966. *The Spirit in Man, Art, and Literature.* Ed. Sir Herbert Read, Michael Fordham, Gerhard Adler, and William McGuire; trans. R. F. C. Hull. Princeton: Princeton University Press.

Jusdanis, Gregory. 1987. *Cavafy's Poetics.* Princeton: Princeton University Press.

———. 1991. *Belated Modernity and Aesthetic Culture: Inventing National Literature.* Minneapolis: University of Minnesota Press.

Kakaounakis, Nikos. 1976. Μερόνυχτα συνωμοσίας (Days and nights of conspiracy). Vols. 1–2. Athens: Papazissis.

Kakavoulia, Maria. 1985. "Telling, Speaking, Naming in Melpo Axioti's *Would You Like to Dance, Maria?*" In *The Text and Its Margins,* ed. Margaret Alexiou and Vassilis Lambropoulos. New York: Pella.

———. 1992. *Interior Monologue and Its Discursive Formation in Melpo Axioti's* Δύσκολες Νύχτες (Difficult nights). Miscellanea Byzantina Monacensia, 3. Munich: Universität München, Institut für Byzantinistik und Neogriechische Philologie.

Kalokiris, Dimitris, and Eleni Kalokiris, eds. 1988. Spec. issue on Engonopoulous. *Hartis* 5 (November): 25–26.

Kamuf, Peggy. 1980. "Writing Like a Woman." In *Women and Language in Literature and Society,* ed. Sally McConnell-Ginet, Ruth Borker, and Nelly Furman. New York: Praeger.

Kant, Immanuel. 1965. "The Paralogisms of Pure Reason." In *Critique of Pure Reason,* trans. Norman Kemp Smith. New York: St. Martin's.

Kaplan, E. Ann. 1983. "Is the Gaze Male?" In *Powers of Desire: The Politics of Sexuality,* ed. Ann Snitow, Christine Stansell, and Sharon Thompson. New York: Monthly Review Press.

Kappeler, Susanne. 1986. *The Pornography of Representation.* Cambridge, Mass.: Blackwell, Polity.

Kapsalis, Dionysis. 1989. "Ο Χάρολντ Μπλουμ και ο δαίμων του ρομαντισμού" (Harold Bloom and the demon of romanticism). *Proti,* May 6 and 13.

Kapsomenos, Eratosthenis. 1983. "Η σημειολογική προσέγγιση της λογοτεχνίας στην Ελλάδα: Σύντομο διάγραμμα-απολογισμός" (The semiological approach to literature in Greece: A brief outline-report). In Κριτική και ποίηση: Νεώτερα και σύγχρονα ρεύματα (Criticism and poetry: New and contemporary currents), ed. S. L. Skartsis. Πρακτικά δεύτερου συμποσίου ποίησης (Papers from the Second Poetry Symposium), University of Patras. Athens: Gnosis.

Karampetsos, E. D. 1987. "The Poets of the Pinball Generation." *Comparative Literature Studies.* 24 (1): 83–99.

Karapanou, Margarita. 1976. *Kassandra and the Wolf.* Trans. N. C. Germanacos. New York: Harcourt Brace Jovanovich.

———. 1977. Η Κασσάνδρα και ο λύκος (Kassandra and the wolf). Athens: Ermis.

———. 1985. Ο υπνοβάτης (The sleepwalker). Athens: Ermis.

———. 1988. *Le somnabule.* Paris: Gallimard.

———. 1992. *Rien ne va plus.* Athens: Ermis.

Karatzas, Nikos, ed. 1987. Οι ποιητές της Θεσσαλονίκης, *1930–1980* (The poets of Salonika). Salonika: Epiloges.

Karavidas, Yannis. 1987. "Surrealism and the Early Poetry of Nikos Engonopoulos." *Journal of Modern Greek Studies.* 5 (1): 33–46.

Karelli, Zoë. 1957. Αντιθέσεις (Contrasts). Athens: Difros.

———. 1972. "Two Poems." Trans. David Posner. *Charioteer* 14: 16–17.

———. 1973. "Poet." Trans. Kimon Friar. *Literary Review* 16 (3): 388–89.

Karvelis, Takis. 1976. Review of Πλην εύχαρις (Albeit pleasing) by Rhea Galanaki. *Diavazo* 1: 51.

Karyotakis, Kostas G. 1986. Ποιήματα και πεζά (Poetry and prose). Athens: Ermis.

Κατάθεση *73, 74* (Deposition). 1974–75. Athens: Boukoumanis.

Katiforis, Yiorgos. 1975. Η νομοθεσία των βαρβάρων (The legislation of the barbarians). Athens: Themelio.

Katris, Yannis A. 1971. *Eyewitness in Greece: The Colonels Come to Power.* White Plains, N.Y.: New Critics Press.

———. 1974. Η γέννηση του νεοφασισμού στην Ελλάδα (The birth of neofascism in Greece). Athens: Papazissis.

Katsari, Xanthi, ed. 1995. Γυναίκα και λογοτεχνία (Woman and literature). Peripheral Conference, Cultural Center of the Komotini Municipality, November 29–December 1, 1991. Komotini: Dimos Komotinis.

Katsaros, Michalis. 1971. Κατά Σαδδουκαίων (Against the Sadducees). Athens: Keimena.

Kazazis, Kostas. 1983. "Men vs. Women in the Third Wedding." *Journal of Modern Greek Studies* 1 (1): 131–40.

Keats, John. 1959. *Selected Poems and Letters.* Ed. Douglas Bush. Boston: Houghton Mifflin.

Keeley, Edmund. 1982. Συζήτηση με τον Γιώργο Σεφέρη (Conversation with George Seferis). Athens: Agra.

Keeley, Edmund, and Philip Sherrard, trans. and eds. 1981. *Voices of Modern Greece: Selected Poems by C. P. Cavafy, Angelos Sikelianos, George Seferis, Odysseus Elytis, Nikos Gatsos.* Princeton: Princeton University Press.

Kehaiyoglou, Yiorgos. 1976. "Η ποίηση της αντίστασης στην μεταπολεμική Ελλάδα" (Resistance poetry in postwar Greece). *Politis,* July–August, 81–86.

———. 1984. Εις την οδόν των Φιλελλήνων του Ανδρέα Εμπειρίκου (On the road of the Philhellenes by Andreas Embirikos). Athens: Politipo.

Kellner, Douglas, ed. 1989. *Postmodernism/Jameson/Critique*. Washington: Maisonneuve.

Kelly, Mary. 1983. "Woman / Desire / Image." In *ICA Document: Desire*. London: Institute of Contemporary Art.

Κέντρο Μαρξιστικών σπουδών (Center of Marxist Studies). 1986. Η επίδραση των ιδεών του μαρξισμού στη λογοτεχνία μας (The influence of Marxist ideas on our literature). Athens: Kentavros.

Kermode, Frank. 1967. *The Sense of an Ending: Studies in the Theory of Fiction*. Oxford: Oxford University Press.

"Κι οι άντρες γίνονται γυναίκες" (And the men are becoming women). 1969. *Ethnos*, October 4, 7.

Kitromilides, Paschalis M. 1983. "The Enlightenment and Womanhood: Cultural Change and the Politics of Exclusion." *Journal of Modern Greek Studies* 1 (1): 39–61.

Kittler, Friedrich A. 1987. "Film, Grammaphone, Typewriter." Trans. Dorothea E. von Mücke. *October* 41 (summer): 101–18.

Kleist, Heinrich von. 1978. *The Marquise of O, and Other Stories*. Trans. David Luke and Nigel Reeves. Harmondsworth: Penguin.

———. 1986–87. *Penthesilea*. Salonika: State Theatre of Northern Greece.

Kofman, Sarah. 1980. *The Enigma of Woman*. Ithaca: Cornell University Press.

Kolias, Helen. 1988. "Greek Women Poets and the Language of Silence." In *Translation Perspectives IV: Selected Papers, 1986–1987*. Binghamton: National Resource Center for Translation and Interpretation.

Kondos, Yannis. 1975. Τα απρόοπτα (The unforseen). Athens: Kedros.

———. 1978. *Danger in the Streets*. Trans. John Stathatos. London: Oxus.

———. 1979. Φωτοτυπίες (Photocopies). Athens: Kedros.

———. 1982a. Στη διάλεκτο της ερήμου (In the dialect of the desert). Athens: Kedros.

———. 1982b. Τα οστά (The bones). Athens: Kedros.

———. 1982c. *In the Dialect of the Desert: Selected Poems of Yannis Kondos*. Trans. and intro. James Stone. *Journal of the Hellenic Diaspora* 9 (Summer): 105–17.

———. 1983. "Η ποίησή μας είναι από τις πιο δυναμικές στην Ευρώπη" (Our poetry is one of the most dynamic in Europe). Interview with Yiorgos Pilichos. *Ta Nea*, May 4, 8.

———. 1985. *The Bones: Selected Poems, 1972–1982*. Trans. James Stone. Cleveland: Globe Press.

———. 1986. Ανωνύμου μοναχού (By anonymous monk). Athens: Kedros.

———. 1987. Private interview, Athens, July 23.

Kondoyianni, Vasiliki. 1981. "Ξαναδιαβάζοντας την Ελληνική Νομαρχία" (Rereading the Greek rule of law). *Diavazo* 40: 46–50.

Kotzia, Elisavet. 1981. "Ποια είναι η ποιητική γενιά του καιρού μας" (Which is the poetic generation of our time)? *Kathimerini*, January 17–18.

———. 1987. "'Ασκοπη περιπλάνηση" (Purposeless wandering), a review of Η μεγάλη πράσινη (The large green) by Eugenia Fakinou. *Kathimerini*, August 20.

Kotzias, Alexandros. 1979. Αντιποίησις αρχής (Usurpation of authority). Athens: Kedros.

———. 1987. Ιαγουάρος (Jaguar). Athens: Kedros.

———. 1991. *Jaguar*. Trans. H. E. Criton. Athens: Kedros.

Kotzias, Alexandros, and Tasos Vournas. 1984. "Review of *Eleni*, by Nicholas Gage." *Vima*, March 18, 19.

Koumandareas, Menis. 1962. Τα μηχανάκια (The pinball machines). Athens: Fexis.

Kourtovik, Demosthenis. 1990. "Υπάρχει, και λοιπόν" (It exists and so what)? Review of round-table discussion Υπάρχει λοιπόν γυναικεία ποίηση (So does women's poetry exist)? *Eleftherotypia*, February 21.

Koutroulis, G. A. 1971. "Η προχειρότητα της κριτικής ή η κριτική της προχειρότητας: Μια ιστορική και αισθητική ανίχνευση της νέας ποιητικής" (The cursoriness of criticism or the criticism of cursoriness: A historical and aesthetic exploration of new poetry). *Nea Synora* 13 (September–October): 193–202.

Koutsovelou, V., and M. Repousi. 1988. "Φεμινιστικά έντυπα, 1978–1985: Μια πρώτη προσέγγιση" (Feminist printed documents: A first approach). *Diavazo*. 198.

Kranaki, Mimika. 1953–54. "Φαινομενολογία της γενιάς" (Phenomenology of the generation). *Epoches: Angloelliniki Epitheorisi* 6: 3.

Krikos-Davis, Katerina. 1984. "Cats, Snakes, and Poetry: A Study of Seferis's 'The Cats of St. Nicholas.'" *Journal of Modern Greek Studies* 2 (2): 235.

Krippas, G. 1971. Νόμοι τύπου, δημοσιογραφίας, κινηματογράφου, θεάτρου: Ποινικαί διατάξεις περί πνευματικής ιδιοκτησίας μετά νομολογίας και βιβλιογραφίας κατ' άρθρον ως ισχύουν μέχρι Μαΐου 1971 (Press laws for journalism, cinema, theater: Penal provisions regarding intellectual property with case jurisprudence and bibliography in accordance article by article in force until May 1971). Athens: Sakkoulas.

Kristeva, Julia. 1980. *Desire in Language: A Semiotic Approach to Literature and Art*. Ed. Leon S. Roudiez. New York: Columbia University Press.

———. 1984. *Revolution in Poetic Language*. Trans. Leon S. Roudiez. New York: Columbia University Press.

———. 1986. *The Kristeva Reader*. Ed. Toril Moi. Oxford: Blackwell.

Krondiris, Tina, ed. 1992. "Γυναίκα—λογοτεχνία—θεωρία" (Woman—Literature—Theory). Conference Papers, May 14–15. University of Salonika, English Department.

Kuhn, Annette. 1988. *Cinema, Censorship, and Sexuality, 1909–1925*. London: Routledge.

Kundera, Milan. 1984. *The Unbearable Lightness of Being*. Trans. Michael Henry Heim. New York: Harper & Row.

Kyr [Kyriakidou]. 1974. Λυσιστράτη (Lysistrata). Cartoon. *Epikaira*, January 18, pp. 13–14; March 15, pp. 14–15; September 12, p. 57; April 5, p. 15; April 12, p. 14; March 8, p. 14; and September 19, p. 49.

Kyriakidou-Nestoros, Alki. 1988. "Ο χρόνος της προφορικής ιστορίας" (The time of oral history). *Synchrona Themata* 39: 233–38.

Kyrtzaki, Maria. 1992. Σχιστή οδός (Split road). Athens: Ipsilon.

Lacan, Jacques. 1977. *Ecrits: A Selection*. Trans. Alan Sheridan. New York: Norton.

———. 1982. *Feminine Sexuality: Jacques Lacan and the Ecole Freudienne*. Ed. Juliet Mitchell and Jacqueline Rose; trans. Jacqueline Rose. New York: Norton.

———. 1986. *The Four Fundamental Concepts of Psycho-Analysis*. Ed. Jacques-Alain Miller; trans. Alan Sheridan. Harmondsworth: Penguin.

———. 1991. *The Seminar of Jacques Lacan. Book 1, Freud's Papers on Techniques, 1953–1954*. Ed. Jacques-Alain Miller; trans. John Forrester. New York: Norton.

Ladimer, Bethany. 1980. "Madness and the Irrational in the Work of André Breton: A Feminist Perspective." *Feminist Studies* 6 (1): 175–95.

Laina, Maria. 1968. Ενηλικίωση (Coming of age). Athens: Nea Zoi.

———. 1970. Επέκεινα (Beyond). Athens: Kedros.

———. 1975. Αλλαγή τοπίου (Change of scene). Athens: Kedros.

———. 1976. "Indian," "Triumphant," "That Which Comes Before." Trans. Dino Siotis. *Coffeehouse* 3 (fall): 62–64.

———. 1979. Σημεία στίξεως (Punctuation marks). Athens: Kedros.

———. 1983. Interview with Yiorgos Pilichos. *Ta Nea*, May 5.

———. 1984. "Landscapes." Trans. Yannis Goumas. *Prism International* 23 (2): 128–29.

———. 1985a. Δικό της (Hers). Athens: Keimena.

———. 1985b. Ο κλόουν (The clown). Athens: Stigmi.

———. 1985c. "Two Poems." Trans. Yannis Goumas. *Prism International* 24 (1): 60–61.

———. 1986. *Poémes.* Trans. Michel Volkovitch. Montereau Cedex, France: Cahiers du Confluent.

———. 1987. Private interview, Athens, September 18.

———. 1990. Η πραγματικότητα είναι πάντα εδώ (Reality is always here). Athens: Stigmi.

———. 1991. Private interview, Athens, May.

———. 1992. Ρόδινος φόβος (Rose fear). Athens: Stigmi.

———. 1998. Hers. In *The Rehearsal of Misunderstanding: Three Collections by Contemporary Greek Women Poets,* ed. and trans. Karen Van Dyck. Middletown, Conn.: Wesleyan University Press.

Lambropoulos, Vassilis. 1988. *Literature as National Institution: Studies in the Politics of Modern Greek Criticism.* Princeton: Princeton University Press.

LaPlanche, Jean, and J.-B. Pontalis. 1973. *The Language of Psychoanalysis.* Trans. Donald Nicholson-Smith. New York: Norton.

———. 1986. Λεξιλόγιο της ψυχανάλυσης (The language of psychoanalysis). Trans. V. Kapsabelis, L. Chalkousi, A. Skoulika, and P. Aloupis. Athens: Kedros.

Layoun, Mary. 1990. *Travels of a Genre: The Modern Novel and Ideology.* Princeton: Princeton University Press.

Lazou, C. G. 1986. Review of Chronis Missios's Καλά, εσύ σκοτώθηκες νωρίς (Lucky you died young). *Anti*, May 9.

Lemaire, Anika. 1977. *Jacques Lacan.* Trans. David Macey; pref. Jacques Lacan. London: Routledge & Kegan Paul.

Lentricchia, Frank. 1983. *After the New Criticism.* London: Methuen.

Leontis, Artemis. 1987. " 'The Lost Center' and the Promised Land of Greek Criticism." *Journal of Modern Greek Studies* 5 (2): 175–90.

———. 1995a. "Παίζουμε κύρα-Ροδαλίνα" (Can we play, Mrs. Rodalina)? *Eli-trochos* 6 (summer): 21–29.

———. 1995b. *Topographies of Hellenism: Mapping the Homeland.* Ithaca: Cornell University Press.

Leontsini, Mary. 1996. "Gender and Nation or the Gender of Nation: 'The Homesick Wife' of Alexandros Papadiamandis." In *Nationalism and Sexuality: Crises of Identity.* American Studies in Greece, series 2, ed. Yiorgos Kalogeras and Domna Pastourmatzi. Salonika: Hellenic Association of American Studies, Aristotle University.

Lerner, Richard, and Lewis MacAdams. 1985. *What Happened to Kerouac?* 16mm, 96 min. New York: New Yorker Films.

Lernoux, Penny. 1980. *Cry of the People: United States Involvement in the Rise of Fascism, Torture, and Murder and the Persecution of the Catholic Church in Latin America.* New York: Doubleday.

Levi, Peter. 1970. Ο τόνος της φωνής του Σεφέρη (Seferis's tone of voice). Athens: Ikaros.

Levine, Michael G. 1994. *Writing through Repression: Literature, Censorship, Psychoanalysis.* Baltimore: Johns Hopkins University Press.

Lévi-Strauss, Claude. 1981. *Tristes Tropiques.* Trans. John Weightman and Doreen Weightman. New York: Atheneum.

Lexi, Editors of. 1987. Σύγχρονη ερωτική ποίηση (Contemporary erotic poetry). Athens: Kastaniotis.

Liakos, Andonis. 1988. Η εμφάνιση των νεανικών οργανώσεων: Το παράδειγμα της Θεσσαλονίκης (The appearance of youth organizations: The case of Salonika). Athens: Lotos.

Liberaki, Margarita. [1976] 1984. Το μυστήριο (The mystery). Athens: Kedros.

Lodge, David. 1977. *The Modes of Modern Writing: Metaphor, Metonymy, and the Typology of Modern Literature.* London: Edward Arnold.

Loizos, Peter, and Evthymios Papataxiarchis, eds. 1991. *Contested Identities: Gender and Kinship in Modern Greece.* Princeton: Princeton University Press.

Lorde, Audre. 1981. "The Masters' Tools Will Never Dismantle the Master's House." In *This Bridge Called My Back: Writings by Radical Women of Color,* ed. Cherríe Moraga and Gloria Anzaldúa. Latham, N.Y.: Kitchen Table, Women of Color Press.

Lotman, J. M. 1975. "The Discrete Text and the Iconic Text: Remarks on the Structure of Narrative." Trans. Frances Pfotenhauer. *New Literary History* 6: 333–38.

Loukatos, Dimitris S. 1985–86. "Η παροιμία στη σύγχρονη πολιτική γελοιογραφία" (The proverb in the contemporary political cartoon). *Laografia* 34: 143–50.

Lukács, Georg. 1968. *The Theory of the Novel: A Historico-Philosophical Essay on the Forms of Great Epic Literature.* Trans. Anna Bostock. Cambridge: MIT Press.

Lydon, Mary. 1983. "On Censorship: Staying Power." *SubStance* 37/38: 107–17.

Lyotard, Jean-François. 1983. "The Dream-Work Does Not Think." Trans. Mary Lydon. *Oxford Literary Review* 6 (1): 3–34.

———. 1984. *The Postmodern Condition: A Report on Knowledge.* Trans. Geoff Bennington and Brian Massumi. Manchester: Manchester University Press.

Lyotard, Jean-François, and Jean-Loup Thebaud. 1979. *Just Gaming.* Trans. Brian Massumi; intro. Wlad Godzich; afterword Samuel Weber. Cambridge: Cambridge University Press.

MacCannell, Juliet Flower. 1986. *Figuring Lacan: Criticism and the Cultural Unconscious.* London: Croom Helm.

Macherey, Pierre. 1978. *A Theory of Literary Production.* Trans. Geoffrey Wall. London: Routledge & Kegan Paul.

Machiavelli, Niccolò. 1982. *The Prince.* Trans. George Bull. Harmondsworth: Penguin.

Mackridge, Peter. 1985. *The Modern Greek Language: A Descriptive Analysis of Standard Modern Greek.* Oxford: Oxford University Press.

——. 1989. *Dionysios Solomos*. Studies in Modern Greek. New Rochelle, N.Y.: Caratzas.

——. 1990. "Katharevousa, c. 1800–1974: An Obituary for an Official Language." In *Background to Contemporary Greece*, vol. 1, ed. Marion Sarafis and Martin Eve. London: Merlin.

——, ed. 1996. *Ancient Myth in Modern Greek Poetry*. London: Cass.

Mainardi, Pat. 1970. "The Politics of Housework." In *Sisterhood Is Powerful*, ed. Robin Morgan. New York: Random House, Vintage.

Makriyannis, Ioannes. 1965. *The Memoirs of General Makriyannis: 1797–1864*. Ed. and trans. H. A. Lidderdale; foreword by C. M. Woodhouse. London: Oxford University Press.

Mangakis, George. 1984. "Letter to Europeans." In *They Shoot Writers, Don't They?* ed. George Theiner. London: Faber & Faber.

Mansfield, Kathryn. 1981. Μακαριότητα (Bliss). Trans. Maria Laina. Athens: Grammata.

Marceau, Marc. 1967. *La Grèce des colonels*. Paris: Laffont.

Marks, Elaine, and Isabelle de Courtivron, eds. 1981. *New French Feminisms: An Anthology*. Brighton, East Sussex: Harvester.

Maronitis, D. N. 1980. Μίλτος Σαχτούρης: Άνθρωποι—χρώματα—ζώα—μηχανές (Miltos Sachtouris: People—colors—animals—machines). Athens: Gnosis.

——. 1982. Όροι του λυρισμού στον Οδυσσέα Ελύτη (Terms of lyricism in Odysseas Elytis). Athens: Kedros.

——. 1984a. Ανεμόσκαλα, σημαδούρες χωρίς ανεμόσκαλα (Rope ladders, buoys without rope ladders). Athens: Kedros.

——. 1984b. Η ποίηση του Γιώργου Σεφέρη (The poetry of George Seferis). Athens: Ermis.

——. 1984c. Ο Καβάφης και οι νέοι (Cavafy and the young people). Athens: Themelio.

——. 1984d. Ποιητική και πολιτική ηθική (Poetic and political ethics). Athens: Kedros.

——. 1984e. "Τα 18 κείμενα και ο αντιεξουσιαστικός τους χαρακτήρας" (*Eighteen Texts* and its anti-establishment character). *Politis*, May, 24–37.

——. 1985. "Το δικό της δίκιο" (Her own kind of right). Review of Ιστορίες για τα βαθιά (Tales of the deep) and Δικό της (Hers). *Vima*, May 23.

——. 1986a. Η πεζογραφία του Γιώργου Χειμωνά (The prose of Yiorgos Himonas). Athens: Lotos.

——. 1986b. "Excerpts from Poetics and Political Ethics." Trans. Carmen Capri-Karka. *Charioteer* 28: 35–41.

——. 1986c. Πίσω μπρος (Backward forward). Athens: Stigmi.

——. 1986d. "Poetry and Politics: The First Postwar Generation of Greek Poets." *Journal of Hellenic Diaspora* 3 (fall): 91–104.

——. 1987. Μέτρια και μικρά (Medium and short). Athens: Kedros.

——. 1992. Διαλέξεις (Lectures). Athens: Stigmi.

Martinidis, Petros. 1980. "Χωρικές παραστάσεις και χώροι αναφοράς στα κόμικς" (Spatial performances and referential spaces in comics). *Semiotiki kai Koinonia*: 261–73.

Marx, Karl. 1982. Εγκώμιο του εγκλήματος (In praise of crime). Trans. Jenny Mastoraki. Athens: Agra.

Mastoraki, Jenny. 1972. Διόδια (Tolls). Athens: Kedros.

——. 1974. "Τέσσερα ποιήματα" (Four poems). *Deposition 74* 342–45.

——. 1976. "Four Poems." Trans. John Chioles. *Coffeehouse* 2 (spring): 48–51.

——. 1978. Το σόι (Kin). Athens: Kedros.

——. 1979. Review of Οι χτίστες (The builders) by Yiorgos Himonas. *Anti*, May 26.

——. 1982a. Interview. *Diavazo* 50: 64–65.

——. 1982b. "Οι φύλακες" (The guards). *Lexi* 11: 40.

——. 1983a. "Είμαστε ένας λαός ποιητών" (We are a people of poets). Interview with Yiorgos Pilichos. *Ta Nea*, May 3, 8.

——. 1983b. Ιστορίες για τα βαθιά (Tales of the deep). Athens: Kedros.

——. 1985a. "Four Poems." Trans. John Stathatos. *Translation* 14 (spring): 23–25.

——. 1985b. "Three Poems." Trans. Karen Van Dyck. *Translation* 14 (spring): 25–27.

——. 1987. Private interview, Athens, July 28.

——. 1989. Μ' ένα στεφάνι φως (With a crown of light). Athens: Kedros.

——. [1978] 1990. Το σόι (Kin). Athens: Kedros.

——. 1992a. "Απόψε θα πούμε μια ιστορία" (Tonight we'll tell a story). Typescript of memorial speech for Yannis Ritsos.

——. 1992b. Private discussion, Athens, May.

——. 1992c. Letter to author (with comments on Van Dyck 1990b, chap. 5), November 5–17.

——. 1998. *Tales of the Deep*. In *The Rehearsal of Misunderstanding: Three Collections by Contemporary Greek Women Poets*, ed. and trans. Karen Van Dyck. Middletown, Conn.: Wesleyan University Press.

Mauss, Marcel. 1967. *The Gift: Forms and Functions of Exchange in Archaic Societies*. Trans. Ian Cunnison; intro. E. E. Evans-Pritchard. New York: Norton.

Mavilis, Lorenzos. 1990. Τα ποιήματα (Poems). Athens: Kostas and Eleni Ouranis Foundation.

Mayakovsky, Vladimir. 1987. *Plays/Articles/Essays*. Ed. Alexander Ushakov; trans. Victor Chistyakov. Moscow: Raduga.

McClure, Michael. 1982. *Scratching the Beat Surface*. Berkeley, Calif.: North Point.

McDonald, Robert. 1983. *Pillar and Tinderbox: The Greek Press and the Dictatorship*. New York: Boyars.

McLuhan, Marshall. 1964. *Understanding Media: The Extensions of Man*. New York: Signet.

McNally, Dennis. 1979. *Desolate Angel: Jack Kerouac, the Beat Generation, and America*. New York: McGraw-Hill.

McRobbie, Angela. 1985. "Strategies of Vigilance: An Interview with Gayatri Chakravorti Spivak." *Block* 10: 5–9.

Meese, Elizabeth. 1992. *(Sem)erotics: Theorizing Lesbian Writing*. New York: New York University Press.

Melissanthi. 1987. *Hailing the Ascending Morn: Selected Poems*. Trans. and intro. Maria Voelker-Kamarinea. Athens: Prosperos.

Mendrakos, Takis. 1979. "Μια ποιήτρια του σήμερα, Μαρία Λαϊνά: Μια άξια εκπροσώπηση της ποιητικής γενιάς του 70" (A woman poet for today, Maria Laina: A worthy representative of the poetic generation of the 1970s). *Epikaira*, October 25, 86–87.

Merquior, J. G. 1985. *Foucault*. London: Fontana.

Meskos, Markos. 1981. Μαύρο δάσος: Ποιήματα, *1958–1980* (Black forest: Poems). Athens: Ipsilon.

Miller, Jacques-Alain. 1988. *The Seminars of Jacques Lacan.* Bk. 2, *The Ego in Freud's Theory and in the Technique of Psychoanalysis, 1954–1955.* Trans. Sylvana Tomaselli; with notes by John Forrester. New York: Norton.

Miller, Nancy K., ed. 1986. *The Poetics of Gender.* New York: Columbia University Press.

Minucci, Paola Maria, trans. 1992. "Sei poeti greci contemporanei." *Poesia* 5 (50): 34–54.

Mitchell, Juliet. 1982. "Introduction I." In Jacques Lacan, *Feminine Sexuality: Jacques Lacan and the École Freudienne,* ed. Juliet Mitchell and Jacqueline Rose; trans. Jacqueline Rose. New York: Norton.

Mitsakis, Mihail. [1895] 1988. "Αυτόχειρ" (Suicide). In Πεζογραφήματα (Prose writings). Athens: Nefeli.

Moi, Toril. 1985. *Sexual/Textual Politics: Feminist Literary Theory.* London: Methuen, New Accents.

——, ed. 1987. *French Feminist Thought: A Reader.* Oxford: Blackwell.

Montefiore, Jan. 1987. *Feminism and Poetry: Language, Experience, Identity in Women's Writing.* London: Pandora.

Moon, Eric, ed. 1969. *Book Selection and Censorship in the Sixties.* New York: Bowker.

Moullas, Panayiotis. 1992. Ο λόγος της απουσίας: Δοκίμιο για την επιστολογραφία με σαράντα ανέκδοτα γράμματα του Φώτου Πολίτη, *1908–1910* (The discourse of absence: Essay on letter writing with forty unpublished letters of Fotos Politis). Athens: Ethniki Trapeza tis Ellados.

Moutzan-Martinengou, Elisavet. [1881] 1983. "Αυτοβιογραφία" (My story). Athens: Keimena.

——. 1989. *My Story.* Trans. Helen Dendrinou Kolias. Athens: University of Georgia Press.

Mouzelis, Nicos. 1978. *Modern Greece: Facets of Underdevelopment.* London: Macmillan.

Muller, John P., and William J. Richardson, eds. 1988. *The Purloined Poe: Lacan, Derrida, and Psychoanalytic Reading.* Baltimore: Johns Hopkins University Press.

Mulvey, Laura. 1989. *Visual and Other Pleasures.* Bloomington: Indiana University Press.

Νέα κείμενα (New texts). 1971a. Athens: Kedros.

Νέα κείμενα 2 (New texts). 1971b. Athens: Kedros.

Nehamas, Alexander. 1983. "Memory, Pleasure, and Poetry: The Grammar of the Self in the Writing of Cavafy." *Journal of Modern Greek Studies* 1 (2): 295–319.

——. 1987. "Truth and Consequences: How to Understand Jacques Derrida." *New Republic,* October 5, 31–36.

New Texts, see Νέα κείμενα.

New Texts 2, see Νέα κείμενα 2.

Niarchos, Thanasis, ed. 1980. Κιβωτός (Ark). Salonika: Egnatia.

Noutsos, Panayiotis. 1986. Review of Ο φεμινισμός στην Ελλάδα του μεσοπολέμου: Μια ανθολογία (Feminism in Greece in the interwar period: An anthology), ed. Efi Avdela and Angelika Psarra. *Dodoni* 3: 187–201.

Ong, Walter J. 1982. *Orality and Literacy: The Technologizing of the Word.* London: Methuen.

Ortner, Sherry B. 1974. "Is Female to Male as Nature Is to Culture?" In *Women,*

Culture, and Society, ed. M. Z. Rosaldo and L. L. Lamphere. Stanford: Stanford University Press.

Ovid. 1955. *Metamorphoses.* Trans. Ralph Humphries. Bloomington: Indiana University Press.

Pali, see Valaoritis, ed.

Pampoudi, Pavlina. 1971. Σχεδόν χωρίς προοπτική δυστυχήματος (Almost without the prospect of misfortune). Athens: Ikaros.

———. 1974. Τα μωρά των αγγέλων άσπρα και τυφλά (The infants of angels, white and blind). Athens: Ermias.

———. 1977a. "Autobiographical," "The Relationship," "The Alibi," "Wednesday 3." Trans. Kimon Friar. *Coffeehouse* 4 (summer): 19–22.

———. 1977b. Αυτός εγώ (He I). Salonika: Egnatia.

———. 1980. Καρτ ποστάλ (Postcard). Salonika: Egnatia.

———. 1983. Το μάτι της μύγας (The eye of the fly). Athens: Kedros.

———. 1985. Μαύρο του πράσινου (Black of the green). Athens: Nefeli.

———. 1994. Private interview, Athens, July.

Panagoulis, Alexander. 1974. Τα ποιήματα (Poems). Athens: Papazissis.

Panayiotou, G. A., ed. 1979. Γενιά του 70: Ποίηση (The generation of the 1970s: Poetry). Athens: Sisifos.

Panderma, see Christakis.

Panourgia, Neni. 1995. *Fragments of Death, Fables of Identity: An Athenian Anthropography.* Madison: University of Wisconsin Press.

Papadaki, Athena. 1974. Αρχάγγελος από μπετόν (Archangel of concrete). Athens: Mavridis.

———. 1980. Αμνάδα των ατμών (Lamb of steam). Salonika: Egnatia.

———. 1986. Γη και πάλι (The earth once again). Athens: Iakinthos.

Papadakis, Yeorgios, and Manolis Bofiliakis. 1974. Εδώ Πολυτεχνείο! Ένα ηχητικό ντοκουμέντο (Speaking from the Polytechnic! A sound document). Athens: Lyra.

Papadiamantis, Alexandros. 1987. "The Homesick Wife." In *Tales from a Greek Island,* trans. Elizabeth Constantinides. Baltimore: Johns Hopkins University Press.

———. 1989. Η Νοσταλγός και άλλα διηγήματα (The homesick wife and other stories). Athens: Nefeli.

Papadopoulos, Yeorgios. 1967–68. Το πιστεύω μας (Our credo). Vols. 1–2. Athens: Press Office.

Papagaroufalis, Eleni K. 1990. "Greek Women in Politics: Gender Ideology and Practice in Neighborhood Groups and the Family." Ph.D. diss., Columbia University.

Papandreou, Andreas. 1970. *Democracy at Gunpoint. The Greek Front.* New York: Doubleday.

Papandreou, Margaret. 1970. *Nightmare in Athens.* Englewood Cliffs, N.J.: Prentice-Hall.

———. 1983. "Margaret Papandreou: An American Feminist in Greece." Interview, with Andrea Dworkin. *Ms,* February, 88–90.

Papayiorgiou, Kostas. 1989. Η Γενιά του 70 (The generation of the 1970s). Athens: Kedros.

Papayiorgiou, Vasilis. 1979. Κρυπταισθήσεις (Cryptosenses). Salonika: Egnatia.

Paschales, Mathios, see Seferis, George.

Pateman, Carole. 1988. *The Sexual Contract.* Cambridge, Mass.: Blackwell, Polity.

Patilis, Yannis. 1985. Review of Ιστορίες για τα βαθιά (Tales of the deep) by Jenny Mastoraki. *Kritiki kai Keimena* 2 (spring): 149.

——. 1990. Review of Μ' ένα στεφάνι φως (With a crown of light) by Jenny Mastoraki. *Planodion* 12: 439–43.

——. 1993. Ταξίδια στην ίδια πόλη: Ποιήματα, *1970–1990* (Travels to the same city: Poems). Athens: Ipsilon.

——. 1997. "Camel of Darkness: Selected and New Poems." Trans. Stathis Gourgouris. *Quarterly Review of Literature* 36: 3–51.

Patrikios, Titos. 1963. Μαθητεία (Apprenticeship). Athens: Prisma.

——. 1974. Προαιρετική Στάση (Voluntary stance). Athens: Ermis.

——. 1988. Αντικριστοί καθρέφτες (Facing mirrors). Athens: Stigmi.

Patterson, Annabel. 1984. *Censorship and Interpretation: The Conditions of Writing and Reading in Early Modern England*. Madison: University of Wisconsin Press.

——. 1990. "Censorship." In *Encyclopedia of Literature and Criticism*, ed. Martin Coyle, Peter Garside, L. M. Kelsall, and John Peck. London: Routledge.

Peponis, Anastasios. 1970. Προσωπική μαρτυρία (Personal testimony). Athens: Kedros.

——. 1971. "Μαζική ενημέρωση και πολιτικό αποτέλεσμα" (Mass media and political consequences). *Nea Keimena* 168–91.

——. 1974. Η Μεγάλη επικοινωνία (The great communication). Athens: Ikaros.

——. 1987. Private interview, Athens, July 29.

Perloff, Marjorie. 1981. *The Poetics of Indeterminacy*. Princeton: Princeton University Press.

——. 1985. *The Dance of the Intellect: Studies in the Poetry of the Pound Tradition*. Cambridge: Cambridge University Press.

Petridou, Anna, ed. 1982–84. Νέοι λογοτέχνες (New writers). Spec. issues. *Diavazo* 50, 69, 87.

——. 1983. Η γενιά των μπήτνικ (The Beatnik generation). Spec. issue. *Diavazo* 64: 15–42.

——. 1984. Ρολάν Μπαρτ (Roland Barthes). Spec. issue. *Diavazo* 93: 10–44.

Philippides, Dia M. L. 1990. *Checklist of English-Language Sources Useful in the Study (CENSUS) of Modern Greek Literature, 1824–1987*. New Haven, Conn.: Modern Greek Studies Association.

Phocas, Nikos. 1983. "The Poetry of Nikos Phocas: A Selection." Trans. Kimon Friar. *Journal of the Hellenic Diaspora* 10 (fall): 35–57.

Pieris, Michalis. 1988. Ο χώρος και τα χρόνια του Τάκη Σινόπουλου (The space and years of Takis Sinopoulos). Athens: Ermis.

Poe, Edgar Allan. 1975. *The Narrative of Arthur Gordon Pym of Nantucket*. Ed. Harold Beaver; appendices Herman Melville and Jules Verne. Harmondsworth: Penguin.

——. N.d. Ο χρυσοκάραβος (The gold bug). Trans. E. D. Roidis. Athens: I. N. Sideris.

Poetry, see Fostieris, Andonis, and Thanasis Niarchos, eds.

"Poetry Today in Greece," see "Η ποίηση σήμερα στην Ελλάδα."

Poggioli, Renato. 1968. *The Theory of the Avant-Garde*. Trans. Gerald Fitzgerald. Cambridge: Harvard University Press, Belknap.

Politi, Jina. 1976. "Η απώλεια της μούσας" (The loss of the muse). *Kathimerini*, August 22.

——. 1988. "The Tongue and the Pen: A Reading of Karkavitsas' *O Arheologos*." In *The Greek Novel, A.D. 1–1985*, ed. Roderick Beaton. Kent: Croom Helm.

Politis, Linos. [1973] 1975. *A History of Modern Greek Literature.* Trans. Robert Liddell. Oxford: Clarendon. Reprinted with corrections.

———. 1980. Ιστορία της νεοελληνικής λογοτεχνίας (A history of Modern Greek literature). Athens: Ethniki Trapeza tis Ellados.

———, ed. 1981. Ποιητική ανθολογία: Καβάφης, Σικελιανός και η ποίηση ως το *1930* (Poetry anthology: Cavafy, Sikelianos, and poetry up to 1930). Athens: Dodoni.

———. 1982. Ποιητική ανθολογία: Η γενιά του *1930* και ο Σεφέρης (Poetry anthology: The generation of the 1930s and Seferis). Athens: Dodoni.

Pollis, Adamantia. 1965. "Political Implications of the Modern Greek Concept of Self." *British Journal of Sociology* 16 (1): 29–47.

Polychrou, Theodora. 1989. "Ομόκεντρα διηγήματα, Ρέας Γαλανάκη: Μια ανάγνωση" (Concentric stories, Rhea Galanaki: A reading). Master's thesis, Salonika, Aristotle University.

Polydouri, Maria. 1978. "The Poetry of Maria Polydouri: A Selection." Ed. Athan Anagnostopoulos. *Journal of the Hellenic Diaspora* 5 (spring): 41–67.

The Popular Muse, see Η λαϊκή μούσα.

Porter, James I. 1986. "Saussure and Derrida on the Figure of the Voice." *Modern Language Notes* 101: 871–94.

Potamitis, Dimitris. 1970. Ο άλλος Δημήτριος (The other Dimitrios). Athens: Lotos.

Poulantzas, Nicos. 1976. *The Crisis of the Dictatorships.* Trans. David Fernbach. London: New Left Books.

Poulios, Lefteris. 1969. Ποίηση (Poetry). Athens: Kedros.

———. 1973. Ποίηση 2 (Poetry). Athens: Kedros.

———. 1975. "The Box," "At the Trolley Stop," "An American Bar in Athens." Trans. Philip Ramp and Katerina Anghelaki-Rooke. *Coffeehouse* 1 (fall): 54–57.

———. 1977. Ο γυμνός ομιλητής (The naked speaker). Athens: Kedros.

———. 1978. Το αλληγορικό σχολείο (The allegorical school). Athens: Kedros.

———. 1979. "Two Poems." Trans. Kostas Myrsiades. *Grove* 5 (winter): 12–13.

———. 1982. Τα ποιήματα: Επιλογή, *1969–1978* (Selected poems). Athens: Kedros.

———. 1983. Ενάντια (Against). Athens: Kedros.

———. 1988. Τα επουσιώδη (Things of slight importance). Athens: Kedros.

———. 1993a. Αντί της σιωπής (Instead of silence). Drawings by Tasos Mantzavinos. Athens: Kastaniotis.

———. 1993b. "Εννιά ποιήματα" (Nine poems). *Planodion* 19: 179–82.

Pound, Ezra. 1951. *ABC of Reading.* London: Faber & Faber.

Preminger, Alex, ed. 1974. "Epic" and "Lyric." *Princeton Encyclopedia of Poetry and Poetics.* Princeton: Princeton University Press.

Prinzinger, Michaela. 1995. "Μύθοι, μεταφορές και μεταμορφώσεις: Παρωδία και γυναικείος λόγος στην ελληνική λογοτεχνία στις δεκαετίες του '70 και '80" (Myth, metaphors, and metamorphoses: Parody and feminine discourse in Greek literature in the 1970s and 1980s). Ph.D. diss., Freie Universität Berlin.

Προΐας (Proias dictionary). [1933] 1970. 3 vols. Athens: Petros Dimitrakos.

Rafaelidis, Vasilis. 1974. "Η ιστορία του θεσμού της λογοκρισίας και ο κινηματογράφος" (The history of the institution of censorship and cinema). *Deposition '74:* 349–54.

Raftopoulos, Dimitris, ed. 1976. Surrealism. Spec. issue of *Iridanos* (February–March).

Ramp, Philip, Katerina Anghelaki-Rooke, Nana Issaïa, and William V. Spanos. 1973. "Poems by Nikos Karouzos." *Boundary* 2 1: 433–38.

Rappas, Lambis. 1987. Private interview, Athens, July 29.

Richards, I. A. 1936. *The Philosophy of Rhetoric*. Oxford: Oxford University Press.

———. 1960. *Principles of Literary Criticism*. London: Routledge & Kegan Paul.

Ricks, David. 1989. "Eye and Ear: Oral Elements in Twentieth-Century Greek Poetry." Lecture given at Orality and Literacy Colloquium, May, Oxford University. Rev. and pub. as "Secret Political Verses in Twentieth-Century Greek Poetry," *Folia Neohellenica* 8 (1987–89): 65–80.

Ricks, David, and Roderick Beaton, eds. 1993. *Digenes Akrites: New Approaches to Byzantine Heroic Poetry*. Brookfield, Vt.: Ashgate, Variorum.

Riffaterre, Michael. 1978. "The Extended Metaphor in Surrealist Poetry." In *Semiotics of Poetry*. Bloomington: Indiana University Press.

———. 1983a. "The Prose Poem's Formal Features." In *The Prose Poem in France: Theory and Practice*, ed. Mary Ann Caws and Hermine Riffaterre. New York: Columbia University Press.

———. 1983b. *Text Production*. Trans. Terese Lyons. New York: Columbia University Press.

Ritsos, Yannis. 1971. *Gestures and Other Poems, 1968–1970*. Trans. Nikos Stangos. London: Cape, Goliard.

———. 1972. Χειρονομίες (Gestures). Athens: Kedros.

———. 1974. *Selected Poems*. Trans. Nikos Stangos. Harmondsworth: Penguin.

———. 1976a. *Corridor and Stairs*. Trans. N. C. Germanacos. The Curragh, Rep. of Ireland: Goldsmith.

———. 1976b. Ο τοίχος μέσα στον καθρέφτη (The wall in the mirror). Athens: Kedros.

———. 1978. Διάδρομος και σκάλα (Corridor and stairs). Athens: Kedros.

———. 1979. *Ritsos in Parentheses*. Trans. and intro. Edmund Keeley. Princeton: Princeton University Press.

———. 1980. Το μακρινό (The distant). Athens: Kedros.

———. 1985. *Exile and Return: Selected Poems, 1967–1974*. Trans. Edmund Keeley. New York: Ecco.

———. 1991. *Yannis Ritsos: Repetitions, Testimonies, Parentheses*. Trans. Edmund Keeley. Princeton: Princeton University Press.

———, trans. 1964. Μαγιακόβσκη: Ποιήματα (Mayakovsky: Poems). Athens: Kedros.

Robbins, Doren. 1982. "The Furious Outcry of Katerina Gogou." *Third Rail* 5: 65–67.

Robinson, Christopher. 1981. "The Greekness of Modern Greek Surrealism." *Byzantine and Modern Greek Studies* 7: 119–37.

———. 1984. "The Comparison of Greek and French Women Poets: Myrtiotissa, Maria Polydure, Anna de Noailles." *Journal of Modern Greek Studies* 2 (1): 23–38.

———. 1996. " 'Helen or Penelope?' Women Writers, Myth, and the Problem of Gender Roles." In *Ancient Myth in Modern Greek Poetry*, ed. Peter Mackridge. London: Cass.

Robinson, Peter, ed. 1985. *Geoffrey Hill: Essays on His Work*. Milton Keynes, England: Open University Press.

Roidis, Immanuel. 1913. Φιλολογικαί μελέται (Philological studies). Athens: Fexi.

Romanos, Christos. 1985. *Poetics of a Fictional Historian: A Synchronic/Diachronic Approach with a Focus on Alexandros Kotzias in the Context of European Fiction*. New York: Lang.

Roof, Judith. 1991. " 'This Is Not for You': The Sexuality of Mothering." In *A Lure of Knowledge: Lesbian Sexuality and Theory*. New York: Columbia University Press.

Rorty, Richard. 1986a. "The Contingency of Language." *London Review of Books* 9: 3–6.

——. 1986b. "The Contingency of Selfhood." *London Review of Books* 8: 11–15.

Rose, Jacqueline. 1982. "Introduction II." In Jacques Lacan, *Feminine Sexuality: Jacques Lacan and the Ecole Freudienne*, ed. Juliet Mitchell and Jacqueline Rose; trans. Jacqueline Rose. New York: Norton.

——. 1986. *Sexuality in the Field of Vision*. London: Verso.

——. 1989. "Where Does the Misery Come From? Psychoanalysis, Feminism, and the Event." In *Feminism and Psychoanalysis*, ed. Richard Feldstein and Judith Roof. Ithaca: Cornell University Press.

Roufos, Rodis ["The Athenian"]. 1972a. "Culture and the Military." In *Greece under Military Rule*, ed. Richard Clogg and George Yannopoulos. New York: Basic Books.

——. 1972b. *Inside the Colonels' Greece*. London: Chatto & Windus.

Rubin, Gayle. 1975. "The Traffic in Women: Notes on the 'Political Economy' of Sex." In *Towards an Anthropology of Women*, ed. Rayna R. Reiter. New York: Monthly Review Press.

Ryan, Michael. 1982. *Marxism and Deconstructionism: A Critical Articulation*. Baltimore: Johns Hopkins University Press.

Sachtouris, Miltos. 1982a. Χρωμοτραύματα (Colorwounds). Athens: Gnosis.

——. 1982b. *Miltos Sachtouris: Selected Poems*. Trans. and intro. Kimon Friar. Old Chatham, N.Y.: Sachem.

——. 1984a. Ποιήματα, *1945–1971* (Poems). Athens: Kedros.

——. 1984b. *Strange Sunday: Selected Poems, 1952–1971*. Trans. John Stathatos. Frome, Somerset: Bran's Head.

Said, Edward W. 1983. *The World, the Text, the Critic*. Cambridge: Harvard University Press.

Saunier, Guy, ed. 1983. Το δημοτικό τραγούδι της ξενιτιάς (The demotic folksong of *Xenitia*). Athens: Ermis.

Savvidis, George P. 1973a. "Η ποίηση σαν κώδικας ζωής" (Poetry as code of life). *Vima*, May 13.

——. 1973b. Πάνω νερά (At the water's surface). Athens: Ermis.

——. 1982. "Γύρω στην αλληλογραφία της Μαρίας Πολυδούρη" (On the correspondence of Maria Polydouri). In Η προσφορά της γυναίκας στον πολιτισμό (The contribution of woman to culture). Spec. issue. *Nea Estia* 1331 (Christmas): 111–16.

——. 1989. "Το φωτοστέφανο της λέξης" (The halo of the word). Review of Mastoraki's Μ᾽ ενα στεφάνι φως (With a crown of light). *Vima*, November 26.

Savvidis, George P., and Eleni Tsantsanoglou, eds. 1982. "Μικρή ανθολογία ποίησης ελληνίδων" (A small anthology of Greek women's poetry). In Η προσφορά της γυναίκας στον πολιτισμό (The contribution of woman to culture). Spec. issue. *Nea Estia* 1331 (Christmas): 11–41.

Savvopoulos, Dionysis. 1983. Τα λόγια από τα τραγούδια, *1967–1974* (The words to the songs). Athens: Ikaros.

Sayre, Henry M. 1983. *The Visual Text of William Carlos Williams*. Urbana: University of Illinois Press.

Schwab, Peter, and George D. Frangos, eds. 1970. *Greece under the Junta*. New York: Facts on File.

Schwartz, Yevgenny. 1968. Ο δράκος (The dragon). Trans. Katerina Anghelaki-Rooke. Athens: Kalvos.

Seferis, George. 1969. *Three Secret Poems*. Trans. Walter Kaiser. Cambridge: Harvard University Press.

——. 1974. *Days of 1945–1951: A Poet's Journal*. Trans. Athan. Anagnostopoulos. Cambridge: Harvard University Press.

——. 1976. Ποιήματα (Poems). Athens: Ikaros.

——. 1979. Πολιτικό ημερολόγιο, *1935–1944* (Political journal). Ed. Alexandros Xydis. Athens: Ikaros.

——. 1981. *George Seferis: Collected Poems*. Expanded bilingual ed., trans., and intro. Edmund Keeley and Philip Sherrard. Princeton: Princeton University Press.

——. 1984. Μέρες Γ, *1934–1940* (Days III). Athens: Ikaros.

——. 1986a. Η ποίηση στον κινηματογράφο (Poetry in the cinema). Athens: Diatton.

——. 1986b. Χειρόγραφο Οκτ. '68 (Manuscript Oct. '68). Athens: Diatton.

—— [Mathios Paschales, pseud.]. 1989. Τα εντεψίζικα (Rude things). Athens: Lesche.

——. 1995. *George Seferis: Collected Poems*, Rev. ed. Ed., trans., and intro. Edmund Keeley and Philip Sherrard. Princeton: Princeton University Press.

Seferis, George, and Konstantinos Tsatsos. [1938–39] 1975. Γ. Σεφέρης—Κ. Τσάτσος: Ένας διάλογος για την ποίηση (G. Seferis—K. Tsatsos: A dialogue on poetry). Intro. Loukas Kousoulas. Athens: Ermis.

Seferis Evening, see Βραδιά Σεφέρη.

Seremetakis, C. Nadia. 1991. *The Last Word: Women, Death, and Divination in Inner Mani*. Chicago: Chicago University Press.

——. 1994a. Η τελευταία λέξη· Στης Ευρώπης τα άκρα (The last word: Women, death, and divination in inner mani). Athens: Nea Synora.

——. 1994b. "Gender Studies or Women's Studies: Theoretical and Pedagogical Issues, Research Agendas, and Directions." *Australian Feminist Studies* 20 (summer): 107–118.

——, ed. 1993. *Ritual, Power, and the Body: Historical Perspectives on the Representation of Greek Women*. New York: Pella.

Shakespeare, William. 1993. *The Tragedy of King Lear*. Ed. Barbara A. Mowat and Paul Werstine. New Folger Library Shakespeare. New York: Washington Square Press.

Shelley, Mary. 1996. *Frankenstein*. Ed. J. Paul Hunter. New York: Norton.

Showalter, Elaine, ed. 1986. *The New Feminist Criticism: Essays on Women, Literature, and Theory*. London: Virago.

Siaflekis, Z. I. 1984. "Techniques narratives et usage des symboles chez Andréas Embiricos et Jules Verne." *Dodoni* 93: 3–56.

Sideri, Aloi. 1984. Όψεις ονείρου (Facets of a dream). Athens: Agra.

Silverman, Kaja. 1983. *The Subject of Semiotics*. Oxford: Oxford University Press.

——. 1988. *The Acoustic Mirror: The Female Voice in Psychoanalysis and Cinema*. Bloomington: Indiana University Press.

——. 1992. *Male Subjectivity at the Margins*. New York: Routledge.

"Sima acquitted . . . ," see Το εφετείο αθώωσε το 'Σήμα' για το επίμαχο πεζογράφημα κατά τη χθεσινή δίκη με πρόεδρο τον κ. Ντεγιάννη."

Sinopoulos, Takis. 1964. Η ποίηση της ποίησης, *1956–1964* (The poetry of poetry). Athens.

——. 1972. Πέτρες (Stones). Athens: Kedros.

——. 1973. Review of Ποίηση, *1967–1972* (Poetry) by Veroniki Dalakoura. *Continuity* 5: 236–38.

——. 1975. Το χρονικό (The chronicle). Athens: Kedros.

——. 1976. Συλλογή Ι, *1951–1964* (Collection). Athens: Ermis.

——. 1979. *Landscape of Death: The Selected Poems of Takis Sinopoulos.* Trans. Kimon Friar. Columbus: Ohio State University Press.

——. 1981. *Selected Poems.* Intro. and trans. John Stathatos. San Francisco: Wire Press.

——. 1982. Νυχτολόγιο (Nightword). Athens: Kedros.

——. 1986. Τέσσερα μελετήματα για τον Σεφέρη (Four studies on Seferis). Athens: Kedros.

Siotis, Dino, ed. 1982. *Ten Women Poets of Greece.* Intro. Katerina Anghelaki-Rooke. San Francisco: Wire Press.

Siotis, Dinos, and John Chioles, eds. 1979. *Twenty Contemporary Greek Poets.* San Francisco: Wire Press.

Six Poets, see Έξη ποιητές.

Sklaveniti, K. 1988. "Τα γυναικεία έντυπα, *1908–1958*" (Women's printed documents). *Diavazo* 198.

Skouteri-Didaskalou, Nora. 1979. "Η προβληματική του γυναικείου ζητήματος: Ανθρωπολογική προσέγγιση" (The problematic of the women's issue: An anthropological approach). *Synchrona Themata* 5: 75–100.

——. [1984] 1991. Ανθρωπολογικά για το γυναικείο ζήτημα (Anthropological approaches to the women's issue). Rev. ed. Athens: Politis.

Smith, Ole L. 1985. "Marxism in Greece: The Case of the KKE." *Journal of Modern Greek Studies* 3 (1): 45–64.

Soldatos, Yannis. 1991. Ιστορία του ελληνικού κινηματογράφου (History of Greek cinema). Vol. 4, *1967–1975.* Athens: Aigokeros.

Solomos, Dionysios. 1944. Η γυναίκα της Ζάκυνθος (The woman of Zakynthos). Athens: Ikaros.

——. 1985. "The Woman of Zakynthos." Trans. and intro. Peter Colaclides and Michael Green. *Modern Greek Studies Yearbook* 1: 153–71.

Solzhenitsyn, Aleksandr I. 1980. *The Oak and the Calf: Sketches of Literary Life in the Soviet Union.* Trans. Harry Willetts. New York: Harper & Row.

Sontag, Susan. 1967. "On Pornography." *Partisan Review* 2 (spring): 181–212.

——. 1990. *Illness as Metaphor* and *Aids and Its Metaphors.* New York: Doubleday.

Sotiropoulou, Ersi. 1985. "Interview." Trans. Kay Cicellis. *Translation* 14 (spring): 15–22.

Spivak, Gayatri Chakravorty. 1981. "French Feminism in an International Frame." *Yale French Studies* 62: 154–84.

——. 1982. "The Politics of Interpretations." *Critical Inquiry* 6 (1): 259–78.

——. 1983. "Displacement and the Discourse of Woman." In *Displacement: Derrida and After,* ed. Mark Krupnick. Bloomington: Indiana University Press.

——. 1984. "Love Me, Love My Ombre, Elle." *Diacritics* 14 (4): 19–34.

——. 1987. *In Other Worlds: Essays in Cultural Politics.* London: Methuen.

——. 1989. "Feminism and Deconstruction, Again." In *Between Feminism and Psychoanalysis,* ed. Teresa Brennan. London: Methuen.

Stamiris, Eleni. 1986. "The Women's Movement in Greece." *New Left Review* 158: 98–112.

Stanton, Domna C. 1986. "Difference on Trial: A Critique of the Maternal Metaphor in Cixous, Irigaray, and Kristeva." In *Poetics of Gender*, ed. Nancy K. Miller. New York: Columbia University Press.

Starobinski, Jean. 1979. *Words upon Words: The Anagrams of Ferdinand de Sausurre.* Trans. Olivia Emmet. New Haven: Yale University Press.

Stathatos, John, ed. 1975. *Six Modern Greek Poets.* London: Oasis.

Steiner, George. 1976. *Language and Silence: Essays on Language, Literature, and the Inhuman.* New York: Atheneum.

——. 1978. *On Difficulty and Other Essays.* Oxford: Oxford University Press.

Steriadis, Vasilis. 1970a. "Κριτική βιβλίου Ποιήματα, 1963–1969 της Κατερίνας Αγγελάκη-Ρουκ και Ποίηση του Λευτέρη Πούλιου" (Book review of *Poems 1963– 1969* by Katerina Anghelaki-Rooke and *Poetry* by Lefteris Poulios). *Lotos* 9: 47–48.

——. 1970b. Ο κ. Ίβο (Mr. Ivo). Athens: Lotos.

——. 1971. Το ιδιωτικό αεροπλάνο (The private airplane). Athens: Lotos.

——. 1976. Ντικ ο χλωμός (Pale Dick). Athens: Kedros.

——. 1977. Review of Τα λόγια από τα τραγούδια (The words of the songs) by Dionysis Savvopoulos. *Kathimerini*, February 6.

——. 1983. Το χαμένο κολιέ (The lost necklace). Athens: Kedros.

——. 1984. Review of Ιστορίες για τα βαθιά (Tales of the deep) by Jenny Mastoraki. *Kathimerini*, April 12.

——. 1986. "Το γλωσσικό ιδίωμα της γενιάς του '70" (The linguistic idiom of the generation of the 1970s). In Πρακτικά πέμπτου συμποσίου ποίησης (Papers from the Fifth Poetry Symposium), University of Patras. Athens: Gnosis.

——. 1992. Ο προπονητής παίκτης (The player coach). Athens: Kedros.

——. 1994. Letter to author, July 18.

Stevens, Wallace. 1951. *The Necessary Angel: Essays on Reality and the Imagination.* London: Faber & Faber.

——. [1954] 1982. *The Collected Poems of Wallace Stevens.* New York: Random House, Vintage.

Stewart, Charles. 1991. *Demons and the Devil: Moral Imagination in Modern Greek Culture.* Princeton: Princeton University Press.

Stewart, Susan. 1991. *Crimes of Writing.* New York: Oxford University Press.

Stockton, Bayard. 1971. *Phoenix with a Bayonet: A Journalist's Interim Report on the Greek Revolution.* Ann Arbor: Georgetown Publications.

Strauss, Leo. 1952. *Persecution and the Art of Writing.* Glencoe, Ill.: Free Press.

Suleiman, Susan R., ed. 1986. *The Female Body in Western Culture.* Cambridge: Harvard University Press.

Suleiman, Susan R., and Inge Crosman, eds. 1980. *The Reader in the Text: Essays on Audience and Interpretation.* Princeton: Princeton University Press.

Sutton, Susan Buck. 1986. "Family and Work: New Patterns for Village Women in Athens." *Journal of Modern Greek Studies* 4 (1): 33–49.

Συνέχεια (*Continuity*), see Argiriou, Kotzias, and Maronitis.

Tachtsis, Kostas. 1984. "The Modern Greek Novel." Lecture in the Ithaka Program, April 26, Athens.

——. 1986. Interview. *Ichneftis*, November–December, 28–31.

——. 1989. Το φοβερό βήμα (The terrible step). Athens: Exandas.

Tarsoulis, Athena. 1951. Ελληνίδες ποιήτριες, *1857–1940* (Greek women poets). Athens.

Thalassis, Yiorgos. 1991. "Η μεταμοντέρνα παράσταση της ευθείας και του κύκλου. Αφ-ορισμός των στερεοτύπων φύλου, φυλής, εθνικότητας και θρησκείας στο μυθιστόρημα της Ρέας Γαλανάκη Ο βίος του Ισμαήλ Φερίκ Πασά, Spina nel cuore" (The postmodern performance of the straight line and of the circle. Aphorism of the stereotypes of gender, race, ethnicity, and religion in the novel of Rhea Galanaki *The Life of Ismail Ferik Pasha, Spina nel cuore*). *Speira* 3: 99–110.

———. 1992. Η άρνηση του Λόγου στο Ελληνικό μυθιστόρημα μετά το *1974* (The denial of *Logos* in the Greek novel after 1974). Athens: Gnosis.

Theodorakis, Mikis. 1973. *Journals of Resistance*. London: Hart-Davis.

Theotokas, George. 1938. "Some Questions of the Psychology of the Modern Greeks." *The Link: A Review of Medieval and Modern Greek*, 1: 66–70.

Theweleit, Klaus. 1987. *Male Fantasies*. Vol. 1, *Women, Floods, Bodies, History*. Trans. Stephen Conway. Minneapolis: University of Minnesota Press.

Thomson, George. 1975. *Marxism and Poetry*. London: Lawrence & Wishart.

"Those Who Don't Read and the Book," see "Το μη-κοινό και το βιβλίο."

"Το βιβλίο περνάει κρίση" (Book trade in crisis)! 1961. *Epitheorisi Technis* 73–74: 86–101, 75: 234–47.

"Το εφετείο αθώωσε το 'Σήμα' για το επίμαχο πεζογράφημα κατά τη χθεσινή δίκη με πρόεδρο τον κ. Ντεγιάννη" (The court of appeal acquitted Sima for the controversial prose piece during the trial yesterday with President Mr. Deyianni). 1977. *Kathimerini*, June 11.

"Το μη-κοινό και το βιβλίο" (Those who don't read and the book). 1976. *Diavazo* 2: 36–46.

Tram. 1971–76. 5 vols. Ed. Panos Theodoridis and Dimitris Kalokiris. Salonika: Ipsilon.

Tsantsanoglou, Eleni et al. 1979. Σάτιρα και πολιτική στη νεώτερη Ελλάδα από τον Σολωμό ως τον Σεφέρη (Satire and politics in Modern Greece from Solomos to Seferis). Athens: Scholi Moraitis.

Tsaousis, D. G., ed. 1983. Ελληνισμός—Ελληνικότητα: Ιδεολογικοί και βιωματικοί άξονες της Νεοελληνικής κοινωνίας (Hellenism and Greekness: Ideological and lived axes of Modern Greek society). Athens: Estia.

Tsianikas, Michalis. 1987. "Φιλολογική σοβαροφάνεια, κριτική ανεπάρκεια και λογοκρισία" (Philological pomposity, critical insufficiency, and censorship). *Politis*, 65.

Tsirimokou, Lizi. 1988. Λογοτεχνία της πόλης (Literature of the city). Athens: Lotos.

Tsoukalas, Constantine. 1969. *The Greek Tragedy*. Harmondsworth: Penguin.

Tziovas, Dimitris. 1985. "The Organic Discourse of Nationalistic Demoticism: A Tropological Approach." In *The Text and Its Margins*, ed. Margaret Alexiou and Vassilis Lambropoulos. New York: Pella.

———. 1986. *The Nationism of the Demoticists and Its Impact on Their Literary Theory, 1888–1930: An Analysis Based on Their Literary Criticism and Essays*. Amsterdam: Hakkert.

———. 1987a. "Greek Women Novelists." Lecture given in May at King's College, London.

———. 1987b. Μετά την Αισθητική (After aesthetics). Athens: Gnosis.

———. 1989a. Οι μεταμορφώσεις του εθνισμού και το ιδεολόγημα της ελληνικότητας στο μεσοπόλεμο (The metamorphoses of nationism and the ideology of Greekness in the interwar period). Athens: Odisseas.

——. 1989b. "Residual Orality and Belated Textuality in Greek Literature and Culture." *Journal of Modern Greek Studies* 7 (2): 321–35.

——. 1993. "Η θεωρία της διαλογικότητας και η ετερογλωσσία του νεοελληνικού μυθιστορήματος" (The theory of dialogism and the heteroglossia of the Modern Greek novel). In Το παλίμψηστο της ελληνικής αφήγησης: Από την αφηγηματολογία στη διαλογικότητα (The palimpsest of Greek narrative: From narratology to the dialogic). Athens: Odisseas.

Ullman, Leslie. 1979. *Natural Histories.* New Haven: Yale University Press.

Vakalo, Eleni. 1971. Γενεαλογία (Genealogy). Trans. Paul Merchant. Exeter, England: Rougemont.

——. 1978. Του Κόσμου (Of the world). Athens: Kedros.

——. 1981. Πριν από το λυρισμό (Before lyricism). Athens: Symeion.

——. 1982. "Selected Poems." Trans. Kimon Friar. *Journal of the Hellenic Diaspora* 9 (winter): 28–43.

——. 1984. Οι παλαβρές της Κυρα-Ροδαλίνας (The boasting of Mrs. Rodalina). Athens: Ipsilon.

——. 1990. Γεγονότα και ιστορίες της Κυρ-Ροδαλίνας (Facts and stories of Mrs. Rodalina). Athens: Ipsilon.

Valaoritis, Nanos, ed. [1964–66] 1985. Πάλι: 'Ένα τετράδιο αναζητήσεων (Again: A notebook of inquiries) *Pali* 1, 2–3, 4, 5, and 6.

Valetas, G. 1982. "Τα πρώτα φεμινιστικά κηρύγματα στην Ελλάδα" (The first feminist sermons in Greece). In Η προσφορά της γυναίκας στον πολιτισμό (The contribution of woman to culture). Spec. issue *Nea Estia* 1331 (Christmas): 225–29.

Valtinos, Thanasis. 1972. "The Plaster Cast." In *Eighteen Texts,* ed. Willis Barnstone. Cambridge: Harvard University Press.

——. 1973. "The Descent of Nine." Trans. N. C. Germanacos. *Boundary* 2 1: 321–47.

——. 1978. Τρία ελληνικά μονόπρακτα (Three Greek one acts). Athens: Kedros.

——. 1984. Η κάθοδος των εννιά (The descent of nine). Athens: Agra.

——. 1986. Μπλε βαθύ σχεδόν μαύρο (Dark blue almost black). Athens: Stigmi.

——. 1988. "Η λογοτεχνία μας σε κατάσταση οικοτεχνίας" (Our literature as cottage industry). Interview with Yiorgos Pilichos. *Ta Nea* January 4, 18–19.

——. 1989. Στοιχεία για τη δεκαετία του '60 (Facts about the decade of the 1960s). Athens: Stigmi.

Vance, Carole S., ed. 1983. "Diary of a Conference on Sexuality." New York: Faculty Press [Barnard]. Photocopy.

——. 1984. *Pleasure and Danger: Exploring Female Sexuality.* Boston: Routledge & Kegan Paul.

Van Dyck, Karen. 1990a. "Introduction" (as guest ed.) and "The Sexual Politics of Babel." Translation issue of *Journal of Modern Greek Studies* 8 (2): 169–71, 173–82.

——. 1990b. "The Poetics of Censorship: Greek Poetry since 1967." Ph.D. diss., Oxford University.

——. 1994. "Reading between Worlds: Contemporary Greek Women's Writing and Censorship." In *Literature and Censorship.* Spec. issue. *PMLA* 109 (1): 45–60.

——. 1996. "Bruised Necks and Crumpled Petticoats: What's Left of Myth in Contemporary Greek Women's Poetry." In *Ancient Greek Myth and Modern Greek Poetry,* ed. Peter Mackridge. London: Cass.

——. trans. 1998. *The Rehearsal of Misunderstanding: Three Collections by Contemporary Greek Women*. With intro. and notes. Middletown, Conn.: Wesleyan University Press.

Varikas, Eleni. 1987. Η Εξέγερση των Κυριών: Η ανάπτυξη μιας φεμινιστικής συνείδησης στην Ελλάδα, *1833–1907* (The revolt of the ladies: The development of a feminist consciousness in Greece). Athens: Ethniki Trapeza tis Ellados.

——. 1989. "Les longues robes de l'esclavage: Stratégies privées et publiques dans le journal d'une recluse." *Cahiers du CEDREF* 1: 123–34.

——. 1993. "Gender and National Identity in Fin de Siècle Greece." *Gender and History* 5 (summer): 269–83.

Varikas, Vasos. 1970. "Η νέα γενιά μπροστά στο σήμερα" (What the new generation faces today). *Vima*, November 29.

——. 1971. "Ποιητικός αντικομφορμισμός" (Poetic anticomformism). *Vima*, May 16.

Vasilikos, Vasilis. 1976. Εικοσιπενταετία (Twenty-five years). Athens: Papazissis.

——. 1989. Linos Politis Lecture, given October 4, Queen's College Graduate Center, New York City.

Vayenas, Nasos. 1978. *Biography*. Trans. Richard Burns. Cambridge: Lobby.

——. 1979. *Biography and Other Poems*. Trans. John Stathatos. London: Oxus.

——. 1980. Βιογραφία (Biography). Athens: Kedros.

——. 1984. "Three Poems." Trans. Donald Hall. *Amaranth* 8: 41–43.

——. 1986. Ο ποιητής και ο χορευτής (The poet and the dancer). Athens: Kedros.

——. 1987. "Θεωρία ή κριτική" (Theory or criticism)? *Politis*, September, 68–73.

——. 1988. Η εσθήτα της θεάς: Σημειώσεις για την ποίηση και την κριτική (The goddess's gown: Notes on poetry and criticism). Athens: Stigmi.

——. 1989. "Το άγχος του ποιητή: Ο Χάρολντ Μπλουμ και η θεωρία της επίδρασης" (The anxiety of the poet: Harold Bloom and the theory of influence). *Lexi* 87: 803–7.

——. 1991. "Σχόλια για την πρόσληψη του Χάρολντ Μπλουμ στην Ελλάδα" (Remarks on the reception of Harold Bloom in Greece). *Logou Harin* 2 (spring): 147–62.

——. 1994. Η ειρωνική γλώσσα: Κριτικές μελέτες για την νεοελληνική γραμματεία (The ironic language: Critical studies in Modern Greek literature). Athens: Stigmi.

Veis, Yiorgos. 1986. Review of Δικό της (Hers) by Maria Laina. *Diavazo* 140: 65–66.

Veloudis, Yiorgos. 1989. "Ποιητικοί ανταγωνισμοί" (Poetic antagonisms). *Vima*, October 1.

Veltsos, Yiorgos. 1973–74. "Γραφή και ιχνογραφία" (Writing and sketching). *Chroniko 1974* 5: 9–10.

Veremis, Thanos. 1987. "The Military." In *Political Change in Greece: Before and after the Colonels*, ed. Kevin Featherstone and Dimitrios K. Katsoudas. Kent: Croom Helm.

Vernant, Jean-Pierre. 1986. "Feminine Figures of Death in Greece." *Diacritics* 16 (2): 54–64.

Verne, Jules. 1979. Μια μέρα ενός Αμερικανού δημοσιογράφου το *2889* και ο αιώνιος Αδάμ (A day in the life of an American journalist in 2889 and eternal Adam). Intro. Athina Bontzidou. Athens: Ochima.

Vitti, Mario. 1976. "Δύο πρωτοπορίες στην ποίηση της γενιάς του '30" (Two avant-gardes in the poetry of the generation of the 1930s). *Politis*, 72–79.

——. 1987a. Η γενιά του τριάντα: Ιδεολογία και μορφή (The generation of the 1930s: Ideology and form). Athens: Ermis.

——. 1987b. Ιστορία της Νεοελληνικής λογοτεχνίας (The history of Modern Greek literature). Trans. Myrsini Zorba. Athens: Odisseas.

——. 1989. Φθορά και λόγος: Εισαγωγή στην ποίηση του Γιώργου Σεφέρη (Decay and the word: An introduction to the poetry of George Seferis). Athens: Estia.

——. [1974] 1990. Ιδεολογική λειτουργία της ελληνικής ηθογραφίας (Ideological function of Greek ithographia. Athens: Kedros.

Vizyenos, Georgios. 1973. Το αμάρτημα της μητρός μου (My mother's sin). Athens: Estia.

——. 1988. *My Mother's Sin and Other Stories*. Trans. William F. Wyatt, Jr. Hanover, N.H.: University Press of New England.

Vlachos, Helen. 1972. "The Colonels and the Press." In *Greece under Military Rule*, ed. Richard Clogg and George Yannopoulos. New York: Basic Books.

——, ed. 1971. *Free Greek Voices: A Political Anthology*. London: Doric.

Vlachos, Phillipos. 1987. Private interview, Athens, July 24.

Voloshinov, V. N. 1973. *Marxism and the Philosophy of Language*. Trans. Ladislav Matejha and I. R. Tisunik. Cambridge: Harvard University Press.

Vostantzoglou, T. [1962] 1990. Αντιλεξικόν ή ονομαστικόν της νεοελληνικής γλώσσης (Antilexicon or thesaurus of the Modern Greek language). Athens: Vostantzoglou.

Voutieridis, Elias. [1931] 1971. Ο ρυθμικός λόγος στη Νεοελληνική λογοτεχνία (Versification in Modern Greek literature). Athens: Diethnis Epikerotita.

Weigel, Sigrid. 1984a. "Contemporary German Women's Literature." *New German Critique* 31: 53–94.

——. 1984b. "Overcoming Absence: Contemporary German Women's Literature." *New German Critique* 32: 3–22.

White, Hayden. 1973. *Metahistory: The Historical Imagination in Nineteenth-Century Europe*. Baltimore: Johns Hopkins University Press.

——. 1978. *Tropics of Discourse: Essays in Cultural Criticism*. Baltimore: Johns Hopkins University Press.

Whitford, Margaret. 1986. "Luce Irigaray and the Female Imaginary: Speaking as a Woman." *Radical Philosophy* 43 (summer): 3–6.

Wills, Clair. 1993. *Improprieties: Politics and Sexuality in Northern Irish Poetry*. Oxford: Clarendon.

Wimsatt, W. K. Jr., and Monroe C. Beardsley. 1954. "The Intentional Fallacy." In *The Verbal Icon: Studies in the Meaning*, ed. W. K. Wimsatt, Jr. Lexington: University of Kentucky Press.

Winkler, John J. 1990. *The Constraints of Desire: The Anthropology of Sex and Gender in Ancient Greece*. New York: Routledge.

Winnicott, D. W. [1971] 1991. *Playing and Reality*. London: Routledge.

Wittig, Monique. 1976. *The Lesbian Body*. New York: Avon.

——. 1979. *Les guérillères*. Trans. David Le Vay. London: Women's Press.

——. 1980. "The Straight Mind." *Feminist Issues* 1 (1): 103–10.

Wolf, Christa. 1977. *The Reader and the Writer: Essays, Sketches, Memories*. Trans. Joan Becker. New York: International Publishers.

——. 1984. *Cassandra*. Trans. Jan Van Heurck. London: Virago.

——. 1988. *The Fourth Dimension: Interviews with Christa Wolf*. Trans. Hilary Pilkington. London: Verso.

Woodhouse, C. M. 1968. *Modern Greece: A Short History*. London: Faber & Faber.

Wyatt, William F. 1987. "Vizyenos and His Characters." *Journal of Modern Greek Studies* 5 (1): 47–63.

Yakos, Dimitris. 1982. "Ελληνίδες στην λογοτεχνία" (Greek women in literature). In Η Προσφορά της γυναίκας στον πολιτισμό (The contribution of woman to culture). Spec. issue. *Nea Estia* 1331 (Christmas): 180–207.

Yannakaki, Eleni. 1994. "History as Fiction in Rea Galanaki's *The Life of Ismail Ferik Pasha.*" *Kambos* 2: 121–41.

Yannas, Prodromos. 1988. "Containment Discourse and the Making of 'Greece.'" Paper given at the New Wave Conference, October, Ohio State University.

Yannopoulos, George. 1972. "The State of the Opposition Forces since the Military Coup." In *Greece under Military Rule,* ed. Richard Clogg and George Yannopoulos. New York: Basic Books.

Yatromanolakis, Yorgis. 1969. "Ανακάλημα: Ποιήματα" (Recollection: Poems). Typescript. Athens.

——. 1982. Ιστορία (History of a vendetta). Athens: Kedros.

——. 1991. *History of a Vendetta.* Trans. Helen Cavanagh. New York: Hippocrene.

Young-Bruehl, Elisabeth. 1988. *Anna Freud: A Biography.* New York: Summit Books.

——. 1989. "Looking for Anna Freud's Mother." *Psychoanalytic Study of the Child* 44: 391–408.

Zambelios, Spyridon. 1852. Introduction to 'Ασματα δημοτικά της Ελλάδος (Demotic songs of Greece). Corfu.

Zannas, P. A. 1980. Review of Αντιποίησις αρχής (Usurpation of authority) by Alexandros Kotzias. *Politis,* May, 71–80 and June, 78–86.

Zannidaki, Lena. 1974. "Τα μακρυά μαλλιά από τον Αδάμ ως τους Χίππυς" (Long hair from Adam to the hippies). *Epikaira,* October 10, 56–57.

Zatelli, Zirana. 1985. "Birds." Trans. Kay Cicellis. *Translation* 14 (spring): 28–37.

——. 1993. Και με το φως του λύκου επανέρχονται (With the wolf-light of dusk). Athens: Kastaniotis.

Zei, Alki. 1968. *Wildcat under Glass.* Trans. Edward Fenton. New York: Holt, Rinehart & Winston.

——. 1972. *Petros' War.* Trans. Edward Fenton. New York: Dutton.

——. 1979. *The Sound of the Dragon's Feet.* Trans. Edward Fenton. New York: Dutton.

——. 1987. Η αρραβωνιαστικιά του Αχιλλέα (Achilles' fiancée). Athens: Kedros.

——. 1991. *Achilles' Fiancée.* Trans. Gail Holst-Warhaft. Athens: Kedros.

Zervou, Ioanna. 1978. 'Ιχνη (Traces). Athens: Diogenis.

——. 1981. "Το κορμί και ο λόγος" (The body and the word). *Lexi* 3: 200–205.

"Zhdanov, Andrei Alexandrovich." 1986. In *Twentieth-Century Literary Criticism,* vol. 18. Detroit: Gale Research.

"Zhdanov, Andrei Aleksandrovich." 1985. In *Handbook of Russian Literature,* ed. Victor Terrs. New Haven: Yale University Press.

Ziras, Alexis. 1983. "Η τρίτη μεταπολεμική γενιά: 'Ενας πρώτος απολογισμός για την ποίησή της" (The third postwar generation: A preliminary account of its poetry). Typescript.

——. 1989. Γενεαλογικά: Για την ποίηση και τους ποιητές του '70 (Genealogies: On the poetry and poets of the 1970s). Athens: Robtron.

——, ed. 1979. Νεώτερη ελληνική ποίηση, *1965–1980* (Contemporary Greek poetry). Athens: Grafia.

Index

figurative language, 42–44
film, 83–85, 87, 96–98, 104, 140, 143, 173–74, 250n
flag, plastic, 50–55
Fostieris, Andonis, 65
Foucault, Michel, 4–5, 15, 56, 124, 170n, 175n, 222n
Franco, Jean, 122n
Frangopoulos, T. D., 38, 127
Frangoudaki, Anna, 20n
Frantzi, Andia, 69, 124n, 143
Freud, Anna, 4n, 116n
Freud, Sigmund: on detective story, 211–12; on dreams, 4n, 179, 189–92; on femininity, 135, 141; on fort-da game, 117, 157; on masturbation, 116n; on metonymy, 162n; on sorb apple myth, 165; and talking cure, 197n; on unconscious, 121, 124n, 125. See also psychoanalytic theory
Friar, Kimon, 32, 44n, 55, 63n, 235n
Fuss, Diana, 120n

Galanaki, Rhea: biography of, 5–6, 65, 140; and gaze, 219–22; and gender, 147–53; influence on, 127, 140–41, 171; and metonymy, 162–71, 173–74; and mimesis (imitation), 155–56, 160–61; and myth, 171–73; overview of *The Cake*, 147; overview of writing by, 143–46; and repetition, 166–67; techniques of, 128–30, 132, 135–36, 184–85; on women's writing, 7, 161–62
Galileo, 149–50
Gallop, Jane, 135n
gaze, 219–31, 235–37. See also look
GDR. See East Germany
gender, 5–8, 101, 117–21, 130–32, 146–74, 257–58. See also sexuality; woman
generations, poets, 15n, 30, 59, 61–68, 79–80, 95
Genette, Gérard, 39
genre, 28–30, 146–74
gestures, 43–50
Ghanas, Michalis, 61n
Ginsberg, Allen, 59, 71, 73n, 74, 78, 81
Goethe, Johann Wolfgang von, 191–92
Gogou, Katerina, 126
Gramsci, Antonio, 20n
Greek language: demotic versus purist, 14–15, 28, 105n, 205–6; dictionary of, 247; gendered nature of, 130, 146n, 164–65; as private, 259; use of imperfective aspect, 129. See also translation
Greek literature: context of, 3–4, 9n, 37–38, 138, 180; dialogue on, 33–35; genres of, 2, 28–31, 207–8; influence on, 208–9, 214;

and intertextuality, 185–89; and quotation, 137, 186. See also orality; poetry
Greekness, definition of, 33–35
Guillén, Nicolás, 44n

Habermas, Jürgen, 4n, 29, 31
Hakkas, Marios, 13n
Hall, Stuart, 57–58
Handke, Peter, 250n
Hart, Janet, 9n, 122n
Hatzidaki, Natasa, 59–60, 103
Hatzidakis, Manos, 78, 86, 205
Hatzilazarou, Matsi, 156n
Haug, Frigga, 120, 222n, 243n
Haviaras, Stratis, 48
Heine, Heinrich, 113
Helleno-Christian culture, 19n
Heraclitus, 150n
hermeticism, 10, 216, 259. See also ellipsis
Herzfeld, Michael, 3n, 9n, 14n
heterotopia, 170, 258
Hill, Geoffrey, 190n
Himonas, Yiorgos, 176
Hirschkop, Ken, 29n
Hoffman, Abbie, 79
Holquist, Michael, 4n
Holst, Gail, 122n
homeopathy, 51, 171n
homophony, 20–21
homosexuality, 104–6. See also lesbian writing; sexuality
Huyssen, Andreas, 73n

Iatropoulos, Dimitris, 62–63, 77
IDEA (Sacred society of Greek officers), 12
identity, 59, 120n. See also subjectivity
"idionym" law, 13
imitation, 147, 153–61, 163–66. See also mimesis
indeterminacy, 2n, 109, 213, 236–37, 249–50. See also undecidability
Inquisition, 35–36, 175
intertextuality, 179–80, 185–89, 207, 209
Ioannidis, Dimitrios, 106
Irigaray, Luce, 101, 134–38, 155n, 186
irony, 47–48
Isaïa, Nana, 7, 62, 94–95
ithographia, 187–88

Jakobson, Roman, 92
Jameson, Fredric, 29, 88–89, 175n
Johns, Jasper, 89
Johnson, Barbara, xvi, 2n, 132n, 210–11, 214
jokes, 259. See also comic strips
journals / periodicals, 32, 49, 66n, 85–87, 104, 106, 109, 120, 122, 143

Reading Women Writing

A SERIES EDITED BY

Shari Benstock and Celeste Schenck

Autobiographical Voices: Race, Gender, Self-Portraiture
by Françoise Lionnet
Postcolonial Representations: Women, Literature, Identity
by Françoise Lionnet
Woman and Modernity: The (Life)styles of Lou Andreas-Salomé
by Biddy Martin
In the Name of Love: Women, Masochism, and the Gothic
by Michelle A. Massé
Imperialism at Home: Race and Victorian Women's Fiction
by Susan Meyer
*Outside the Pale: Cultural Exclusion, Gender Difference,
and the Victorian Woman Writer*
by Elsie B. Michie
Dwelling in Possibility: Women Poets and Critics on Poetry
edited by Yopie Prins and Maeera Shreiber
Reading Gertrude Stein: Body, Text, Gnosis
by Lisa Ruddick
Conceived by Liberty: Maternal Figures and Nineteenth-Century American Literature
by Stephanie A. Smith
Kassandra and the Censors: Greek Poetry since 1967
by Karen Van Dyck
Beyond Consolation: Death, Sexuality, and the Changing Shapes of Elegy
by Melissa F. Zeiger
Feminist Conversations: Fuller, Emerson, and the Play of Reading
by Christina Zwarg

Karen Van Dyck is Associate Professor of Modern Greek Language and Literature at Columbia University.